Iran

THE BRADT STORY

The first Bradt travel guide was written in 1974 by George and Hilary Bradt on a river barge floating down a tributary of the Amazon. In the 1980s and '90s the focus shifted away from hiking to broader-based guides covering new destinations – usually the first to be published about these places. In the 21st century Bradt continues to publish such ground-breaking guides, as well as others to established holiday destinations, incorporating in-depth information on culture and natural history with the nuts and bolts of where to stay and what to see.

Bradt authors support responsible travel, and provide advice not only on minimum impact but also on how to give something back through local charities. In this way a true synergy is achieved between the traveller and local communities.

*

In 1996 I was invited to visit Iran, which was just starting to open up to tourism. I accepted with some hesitation, having been thoroughly brainwashed by the media's portrayal of a dangerous, restrictive and intolerant country. But I loved the place from the moment I stepped off the plane, dressed in my headscarf and long *ripoush*. Far from being restrictive, it left me feeling freer to explore the markets and other places on my own than almost anywhere else I've been. Since I looked just like the Iranian women around me, there were no stares, and no hassle. And the sights! The great ruins of Persepolis and Bishapur, and the cities of Isfahan and Shiraz, all left an indelible impression. But above all I remember the warmth and hospitality of the Iranian people – oh, and photographing an American member of our group standing under a sign, in large brass letters, 'Down with the USA'.

Patricia Baker uses her insider knowledge to introduce this wonderful country to all people who want to look beyond the newspaper headlines and see a place for what it is. Do go and experience it for yourself – you won't be disappointed.

Hilary Bradt

19 High Street, Chalfont St Peter, Bucks SL9 9QE, England
Tel: 01753 893444   Fax: 01753 892333
info@bradtguides.com   www.bradtguides.com

Iran

THE BRADT TRAVEL GUIDE
Second Edition

Patricia L Baker

Bradt Travel Guides, UK
The Globe Pequot Press Inc, USA

Second edition 2005
First published 2001

Bradt Travel Guides
19 High Street, Chalfont St Peter, Bucks SL9 9QE, England
Published in the USA by The Globe Pequot Press Inc, 246 Goose Lane,
PO Box 480, Guilford, Connecticut 06437-0480

British Library Cataloguing in Publication Data
A catalogue record for this book is available from the British Library

ISBN-10: 1 84162 123 4
ISBN-13: 978 1 84162 123 4

Photographs
Front cover Detail of statue at Persepolis (Hilary Bradt)
Text Patricia L Baker (PB), Paul Bernhardt (PBe), Hilary Bradt (HB)

Illustrations Carole Vincer
Maps Steve Munns

Typeset from the author's disc by Wakewing
Printed and bound in Italy by Legoprint SpA, Trento

Author

Patricia L Baker PhD is an independent lecturer and researcher specialising in Islamic art, with a decade of teaching the history of ceramics and glass to undergraduates. She first visited Iran in 1971 and since then she has been back numerous times. Her interests are primarily Islamic glass and especially Islamic court dress, on which, along with aspects of Zoroastrian costume, she has written for various academic journals; her monograph *Islamic Textiles* was published by the British Museum Press in 1995 and *Islam & the Religious Arts* (Continuum) in 2004. Currently she is a course director escorting special-interest groups to the Middle East for such tour companies as the Association for Cultural Exchange, Cambridge, UK, and is working on another book.

DEDICATION
To
the pessimistic optimist and the optimistic pessimist
'A friend in need is a friend indeed.'

Contents

Acknowledgements

It was a fellow postgraduate student, Manijeh Bayani, who in 1971 introduced me not only to Iran but to the legendary kindness and hospitality of Iranians. It was a fascinating visit and I have fond memories of being taught how to cook rice the Persian way, shell broad beans properly and wear a *chador*, all skills I have since lost. We were both students of Professor Geza Fehevari who managed to instil such a love of and enthusiasm for Islamic art into all his students that even after 30 years and few career openings, most of us have remained 'hooked'. He was also responsible for giving me the opportunity of returning to Iran in the role of guest lecturer on several Swan Hellenic Art Treasure tours, 1975–8. I have never been able to repay the kindness and thoughtfulness of them both, and the hospitality of their families.

In those years one could always identify people with a common interest in Iranian archaeology and architecture by their battered copies of Sylvia Matheson's *Persia: An Archaeological Guide* and although it was last reprinted (excluding pirate copies) in 1976, it still is an invaluable source of information. Even today, Iranian tour guides who were in their infancy during the Islamic Revolution mention her name with great respect and affection although their knowledge of her is purely through this work. I, too, wish to record my debt to her, and also to the authors of two other publications: Lisa Golombek & Donald Wilber (*Timurid Architecture in Iran and Turan*, 1988) and Bernard O'Kane (*Timurid Architecture in Khurasan*, 1987), remembering happy times with him and Amina in Cairo.

These publications were based on research conducted prior to the Islamic Revolution, and of course things have changed. Sylvia Matheson's dirt tracks from one site to another through small villages are no longer there. The 'tracks' are now dual carriageways, the archaeological sites have largely vanished from public view after decades of dust-storms or neglect while many villages have either developed into large townships or been abandoned because a vital water source has been diverted. Most towns now welcome visitors, proclaiming on road signs not their historic heritage but proudly announcing this is where '(Islamic) martyrs are bred'. In more senses than one, Iran is today a different country.

For the first edition of this guide one particular person, Amir Bayat, was extremely generous with his time and help and few of his colleagues, especially Iraj Zowghi, were able to escape involvement. Without the assistance of these two individuals (and their understanding wives), it would have been extremely difficult and taken at least twice as long to find and collect all the necessary information, whether it concerned the whereabouts of historic doors last seen in the late 1970s, the publication of Iranian archaeological reports, or ways of cooking lamb shanks. They listened patiently and then diplomatically suggested other approaches or alerted me to new evidence. However, no-one else should be held responsible for any error or ambiguous phrasing, real or perceived, in the following pages; any fault lies with me. But they *are* directly responsible for me growing to admire and appreciate so much the country and people of Iran; they are two of the best 'unofficial' ambassadors for Iran today. My heartfelt thanks.

I am also most grateful to Nasser Mouradi of Thunder Tours and Travel, Tehran for his assistance and evident concern that all the travel arrangements went smoothly, even if it involved him in a hair-raising motorcycle ride. His staff always describe him as 'a good man'; that I can confirm. A number of local guides have generously given not only their time but also fascinating information about their cities and regions: Jamshid Zarinfer and Aria Gojerati of Shiraz, Hoseyn Nassr and Iraj Jahanbakhsh of Isfahan. For this second edition, Mahmoud Karimi of ITC and his colleague, Mahshid, and especially Jian Bagherpour, formerly of Thunder Tours, have diligently traced information, while Aria in Shiraz, Hoseyn in Isfahan and Iraj Zowghi in Tehran have epitomised that renowned Iranian generosity, despite my endless enquiries. I do most sincerely thank them all, as well as the numerous drivers who have patiently stopped, reversed and skilfully found a way to so many unsignposted places for me.

Yet again the staff of the School of Oriental & African Studies, London University, and of the British Library, London, have uncomplainingly found obscure publications and pamphlets, and reshelved piles of books; I have appreciated their assistance. I must also thank all my travelling companions, whether they suffered me as a group leader enthusing about textiles, ceramics and glass, or as a fellow visitor tramping across fields in search of a carved boulder or column base: to Barbara Brend for her astute comments in eastern Iran and her translation of certain Sa'di couplets used in this text, Alan Forsyth for valuable information and support, John and Val Imber for their witty one-liners in southern Iran and guiding me through certain electronic complexities, to Peter Kelly and another business man, who wishes to remain anonymous, for their useful and inexhaustible supply of insights into Iranian society, culture and politics, to Peg and Dick Foster, and to Gila Salimi for having such confidence in her former teacher writing about her country, the people and the art. The way that Sugra Zaman of Watson, Little took so much pressure off my shoulders yet gently kept my nose to the grindstone has really been appreciated. And I must express gratitude to Bradt Travel Guides for having faith in this project, and to Bradt readers for their comments.

KEY TO STANDARD SYMBOLS

—·—·—	International boundary		⊞	Historic building
·······	District boundary		🏰	Castle, fortress
------	National park boundary		†	Church, cathedral
✈	Airport (international)		ς	Mosque
✈	Airport (other)		🏟	Football stadium
✛	Airstrip		🏟	Stadium
▬▬	Railway		▶	Golf course
··········	Footpath		↳	City wall
⛽	Petrol station or garage		▲	Summit
🅿	Car park		△	Boundary beacon
🚌	Bus station etc		◉	Outpost
⌂	Hotel, inn etc		✕—✕	Border post
🛆	Campsite		◖●◗	Rock shelter
♠	Hut		⎕—⌐	Cable car, funicular
♀	Bar		⌣	Mountain pass
✕	Restaurant, café etc		▭	National park
⊠	Post office		✳	Scenic viewpoint
ℓ	Telephone		❀	Botanical site
ⓔ	Internet café		♧	Specific woodland feature
⊞	Hospital, clinic etc		⚱	Lighthouse
⚱	Museum		≁	Marsh
🐘	Zoo		�㇙	TV antenna
ⓘ	Tourist information			
$	Bank			
⚱	Statue, monument			
∴	Archaeological or historic site			

Bradt

Other map symbols are sometimes shown in separate key boxes with individual explanations for their meanings.

Introduction

Mention to relatives and friends that you are going to Iran, and the chances are that they will stare, pause, swallow and hesitantly if not increduously ask 'Iran? Are you sure?' You may well feel they have a point after your first contact with Iranian Consulate staff as it seems that officialdom (but not necessarily any official) is conspiring against you visiting Iran and learning first-hand something about the country, its history and its culture, past and present. Why cannot the pre-recorded telephone messages give correct and accurate information about the visa procedure succinctly? Why is it so difficult to penetrate this electronic barrier? Is it really impossible to devise an up-to-date information sheet which lists all those little important details which will save everyone concerned time, energy and good humour. Why, for example, don't they warn female visitors to the consulate offices to wear a headscarf to gain entry, or that applications will be received for consideration only when the (unstated) procedure is in its final stages? The list continues... but persevere and the rewards will be worth all the angst and anxiety.

Iran is one of those countries, like others in the Middle East and elsewhere, where issues concerning religion and the modern world confront you at all turns and compel you to consider your own stance. It is impossible to return from even a short visit and not feel that, while seeing magnificent historic architecture and evidence of ancient civilisations, you have also been witnessing history in the making. Yet some people will say that, having travelled and stayed in Iran before the Islamic Revolution, they have no wish to return to see it now. I cannot agree. The experience is invaluable, and one comes back with a better-informed opinion – perhaps changed, perhaps confirmed, but at least based on evidence seen at firsthand.

Of course, there have been changes since the early days of the Revolution when officialdom frowned on all music save for martial tunes and religious songs; as of August 2000, Western instruments such as pianos may now be purchased, and Iranian 'rap' is broadcast on the airwaves. But not all changes are occasioned by official policy. Over the last two years I have been aware of women wearing more black *chadors* and black or dark blue *manteaux* on the streets of Tehran, instead of the pastel coats I had seen earlier. I assumed this was responding to a new government directive until friends pointed out that more women were working for the government (where black is the standard uniform), and that Tehran's increasing pollution was persuading many to wear darker colours to reduce washing and dry-cleaning bills.

And this pollution is a growing problem. I am told that passengers on flights coming from Dubai and Bahrain are visibly shocked as the plane approaches Tehran Airport: 'Suddenly there is this yellow custard instead of glorious blue sky' was one comment. The appalling, senseless driving of many private car-owners is another problem. On the other hand, foreign visitors to Iran are pleasantly surprised at the general cleanliness of the streets, and the care and upkeep of the central reservations and the roundabouts. I am always amused at the positioning of park benches, tea houses, children's swings, etc on the roundabouts as if they are rewards for risking life and limb against oncoming cars. Often, surprise is expressed that the mosques are usually so empty of people (once my group witnessed a Muslim equivalent of the Salvation Army on one huge city roundabout, trying to persuade people to join them in prayer), while the shrines are so full of women. For Iranian women there are comparatively few opportunities to meet others and relax. Access to sport and leisure facilities is limited for them, adult education is in its infancy, and as for Iranian TV – you need to be a sports fanatic! A coach trip to a shrine some kilometres away offers a welcome chance to get away from the house, meet new (female) friends and talk about things that matter.

However, I think that every foreign visitor, without exception, is struck by the friendliness and warmth of Iranians throughout this enormous country. In other countries it is sometimes difficult for individuals within a tour group to talk with anyone other than the guide, the driver, or the hotel and shop staff, and some argue that to experience fully a country and a people, one must be an independent traveller. In Iran this is not the case. Indeed, it could be argued that in Iran (as with China until recently), forces conspire against the independent traveller, especially those who don't know the language; the country is just not geared up to this kind of tourism. Everything takes so much longer to sort out, and indeed the visitor is so dependent on Iranians helping that the term 'independent traveller' is almost a misnomer. Group travel in Iran can and does open doors in more senses than one – it cuts down endless queuing and waiting for buses and the like. No Iranian is deterred by numbers; guides and lecturers are often interrupted in their 'spiel' by a crowd asking if the group is American or German, how long are they staying, will they come for tea, do they know David Beckham, how many children do they have, do they like Iran, etc.

What else can I say? Of course there are downsides to Iran, as to everywhere, but go now, while it is possible to wander around a world-famous site like Persepolis and not meet another foreigner other than your companions.

Part One

General Information

IRAN AT A GLANCE

Location Asia; borders with Iraq, Caucasian and Central Asian republics, Afghanistan and Pakistan

Area 1,650,000 km², three times the size of France

Climate Most regions: long, hot summers; short sharp winters. Marked contrasts in northwest, east and central desert regions.

Population Over 70 million; more than 60% living in cities and towns

Government A theocracy with a Supreme Leader, an Assembly of (Theological) Experts, a Council of Guardians and elected Parliament and President

Capital Tehran, population 16 million, including outskirts

Other major towns Ahvaz and Mashhad (population 2 million each), Shiraz and Isfahan (1.5 million each), Hamadan and Tabriz (1 million each)

Language Farsi (an Indo-Aryan language) alongside dialects of Turkish, Arabic, Kurdish

Alphabet Based on the Arabic script, reading from right to left

Religion Predominantly Shi'i Muslims, with some Sunnis; also Zoroastrians, Christians and Jews

Currency Rials (10 rials = 1 tuman)

Exchange rate £1 = 16,656, US$1 = 8,850, €1 = 11,474 (February 2005)

International telephone code +98

Time GMT +3½

Weights and measures Metric

Electricity 220 volts, 50 Hz

National flag Three horizontal stripes of green, white and red with repeated legend 'Allah Akbar' ('God is great')

National anthems Sourud-i Jumhuri Islami Iran ('Song of the Islamic Republic of Iran'); Sourud -I Iran ('Song of Iran')

Public holidays Fixed holidays: February 11, March 20 and the week following (Nou Rouz), April 1, June 4 and 5. Also numerous Muslim holidays dated to the lunar calendar, which means these fall approximately ten days earlier each year.

Background Information

GEOGRAPHY AND CLIMATE

It is difficult to convey the reality of a land mass of 1,650,000km², but Iran is three times the size of France, or the size of the United Kingdom, France, Spain, Italy and Switzerland all combined. The Zagros Mountains in the west form a natural barrier with Iraq, and to the north are the Caucasian republics and those of Central Asia, all formerly within the Soviet Union. To the east are Afghanistan and Pakistan, while the Gulf and the Sea of Oman mark Iran's southern limits. It is a land of great contrasts, physically and climatically, as mountain ranges surround virtually the entire country while a huge desert sits in the centre. Apart from the Zagros chain in the west, there are the Alborz range in the north, the Makran Mountains in the south and the foothills of the Hindu Kush in the east.

This means that towns on the same latitude but on either side of the mountains have sharply different rainfall: Dezful (western Zagros, 143m altitude) receives approximately 358mm a year whereas Isfahan (eastern Zagros, 1,570m altitude) gets a mere 108mm. Much less rain falls in the Great Desert basin where some areas are considered unable to support any life. Generally speaking, regions south of latitude 34° north get rain mainly during January, while those north of this receive most rainfall during the spring, especially April. An exception is the Caspian region, where the heaviest month for rain is October.

No-one readily associates snow (*barf*) with Iran yet about two-thirds of the republic usually have winter snowfalls (January–February) because of the average high altitude throughout the country. Tabriz (1,349m) in the northwest has about 30 days of snow a year, about ten days more than Arak (1,753m) to the east, whereas Isfahan, at a higher altitude, gets about seven days and Yazd (1,230m) about half this. Of course, areas of very high altitude such as Mount Demavend, especially its northeast face, Takht-i Soleyman in Alborz range and Sabalan (4,500m) in Iranian Azerbaijan have perennial snow as well as glaciers (see page 58).

There are three if not four distinct climates in Iran: most regions have the continental climate of long, hot summers and short, sharp winters. In the northwest, the Iranian province of Azerbaijan shares a similar climate to that of Switzerland and further east, along the south shore of the Caspian, it is as humid as in the south but without those much higher temperatures. In the central desert region it is dry and blisteringly hot.

NATURAL HISTORY AND CONSERVATION
Birds and animals

Most recent records, dating from June 2000, indicate that Iran has 86 protected wildlife reserves but in practice there is little supervision of hunting, and the severe drought of that summer caused great damage; the government ministry concerned is massively underfunded and understaffed. Nevertheless over 490 species of **birdlife** have been recorded in Iran. The desert regions south and southeast of Tehran are home to the bustard, courser, sandgrouse and ground jay, while in the steppes the long-legged buzzard, Eurasian kestrel, roller and various bee-eaters can usually be seen. As one would expect, birds preferring colder temperatures such as the golden eagle, bearded vulture, alpine swift, wallcreeper and snow finch frequent the mountain ranges, while in the forests and woodlands of, for instance, Iranian Azerbaijan there are wood pigeons, green woodpeckers, shrikers, nightingales, thrushes etc. Lake Orumiyeh in this region was made a bird reserve in 1967 and a breeding colony of over 20,000 pairs of wintering

PLANT LIFE FROM MOUNTAINS TO COAST
David Sayers

The flora of Iran is complex and, contrary to what is often thought, far from just desert plants with seasonal flowers. The more than 7,500 species are made up of elements in varying importance from the floras of the several surrounding plant geographic regions. Several genera are represented by many species while, in direct contrast, some are relict species, survivors from floras that long ago had a wide distribution. The varied climate, particularly rainfall, and the varied topography interact and provide numerous different habitats to support the diverse flora, from desert to temperate forest. However, inevitably man has impoverished the environment by taking timber and fuelwood, as well as using the land for grazing and cultivation, so that the little true natural vegetation remaining may be seen only in the remotest places.

Very simply, a narrow band of humid forest runs along the coastal plain of the Caspian Sea and up to 2,500m elevation on the northern slopes of the Alborz Mountain range. It is not continuous, but runs from the Azerbaijan border in the west to the Golestan National Park in the east. Varying with altitude, hornbeam, elm, ash, lime are common, while others include the oriental beech and relict species from the once widespread forests of the Tertiary period such as *Pterocarya fraxinifolia*, *Gleditsia caspica*, *Parrotia persica*. In the east, the forest becomes drier with some changes in the species composition. The semi-humid forest of the Zagros Montains, which has a relatively high spring rain but a dry summer, runs along the western margins of the Iranian plateau from the Turkish border, through Kurdestan and Luristan into Fars, and is characterised by an open canopy of low, round-topped deciduous oaks, greater flamingos has been recorded in the past. A little further south, the seasonal marsh of Talab-i Aqgul, some 90km south of Hamadan, 20km south of Malayer, is a favourite migration stage for Siberian and Scandinavian wetland birds for some four or five months. The lush wetlands of the south Caspian shore are wintering grounds for pelicans, Siberian cranes, herons, gulls, spoonbills and cormorants. Caspian seals and otters may also be found there. As temperatures drop, so the herons and pelicans, along with plovers, ospreys and oystercatchers, make their way south towards the Gulf, where the mangroves and palm forests are home to oriental Afro-tropical birds such as the palm dove and Indian roller.

As for **fauna**, the mountains and forests of the north have many types of deer, such as red, roe and fallow deer, as well as the Mesopotamian deer, and predators like wolves and foxes, but hunting (totally unlicensed) is taking a heavy toll. Wild sheep and goats were once common in the northeast Alborz and north of Shiraz, with wild boars further east, and the Pazan ibexes in the Bisitun area, but few survive. It seems that snow leopards, which once

mostly *Quercus brantii*. Between these two forested areas lies open steppe, which gradually tapers towards the deserts of the central Iranian depression with occasional evidence of former dry forests – either of juniper with some shrubs and trees such as hawthorn, or dominated by pistachio. The highlands here offer dwarf scrub and thorn-cushion formations. The cushion plants are especially intriguing – individuals of *Gypsophila aretioides* are thought to live a thousand years. Semi-desert shrublands characterise the vegetation of the Persian Gulf and in the deserts are dwarf scrub formations or salt-adapted plants.

To see trees, the best areas are undoubtedly along the Caspian coast, from time to time taking excursions inland into the Alborz Mountains, especially along the Azerbaijan border, and also in the Golestan National Park east of the Caspian Sea. And then there are the Zagros Mountains. Late April/early May is a beautiful time to visit, when trees are in full leaf on the Caspian coast. As you ascend, you pass through all the stages of spring from tender, newly expanded leaves to bud burst and dormancy, while herbaceous plants and ground orchids blossom beneath. This can also be a good time to visit the middle and upper elevations of the drier mountains to see the large number of endemic Persian species of *Astragalus, Cousinia, Acantholimon, Silene, Onobrychis, Nepeta, Onosma, Euphorbia, Salvia,* and more; the richest in southwest Asia. Iran is probably best known for its flowering bulbs, plants well adapted to summer drought and cold winters; they flower early to catch the best spring-growing conditions. The broad alpine belts of the Alborz and Zagros mountains and the mountain triangle between Kirman, Bam and Sirjan can be the best places to see *Galanthus, Crocus, Erythronium, Fritillaria, Iris, Tulipa, Allium,* all very familiar to gardeners.

inhabited the area east of Mashhad, and the Mazandaran tigers are now extinct, as is the lion, last seen in 1942; there are no details about cheetahs, officially estimated at less than 50 in number in 1991. The hotter central and southern Iran are home to jackals, cheetahs and mongooses, date and palm squirrels, gerbils and jerboas. Also in these regions are camels, usually dromedary rather than the shaggy twin-humped Bactrians of eastern Central Asia. Several areas are known for bat caves: Shapur's cave near Bishapur for *Rhinolophus euryale* and *Miniopterus schreibersi*; the village of Ahmad Mahmudi, southwest of Shiraz, for *R. hardwickei* and *Rousettus aegyptiacus*, and the northern shores of Lake Parishan (formerly Famur) nearby for *Pipistrellus kuhli.*

The pollution of the Caspian Sea during the dying years of the Soviet Union and current illegal netting have had a severe effect on the Iranian **fisheries** but the sturgeon is still breeding – just. Buying caviar, though, is best left for your departure, from the duty-free shops at the international airports, eg: Tehran. Salmon trout, chub and carp are found in mountain streams, while warm-water sea fish abound off the southern coast of Iran.

Flora

The best time to see the natural flora of Iran, some 6,000 recorded species, is around April and early May when the mountains and steppes are once more carpeted with new grass, fruit-tree blossom and masses of wild flowers, now that the high price of imported artificial fertilisers and pesticides has limited extensive use. Wild irises and poppies can be seen almost everywhere, but the *Iris barnumae* is found only in the Azerbaijan region and *Iris spurgia* in the Caspian wetlands. Of the 80 species of tulip, 12 are recorded in Iran, the most widespread being *Tulipa biflora*. Especially striking is the *Tulipa clusiana* with its red and white petals and the yellow *Tulipa urmiensis,* found, as its name suggests, north of Lake Orumiyeh. The saffron crocus (*crocus sativus*), one of the eight Iranian species, is mainly found in eastern Iran and the so-called 'autumn crocus', although it has six stamens rather than the three of crocuses, is well represented, including the *Colchicum persicum* of central Iran which flowers March to April. The city of Shiraz is justly proud of its sweet-smelling roses used in the local production of rose jam, syrup, and rose-water perfume. And of course most people know of the Shiraz grape. Most of Iran's vineyards were ripped up during the early years of the Islamic Revolution (see page 49) but there has been extensive replanting in the last five years. For further details, see box, pages 4–5.

Water

Water has always been a perennial concern in Iran, especially after 13th-century Mongol conquests destroyed dams and irrigation channels. The ingenious engineering of *qanat* (underground water channels), whereby water was tapped from the aquifer level on the mountainsides and guided down to the cultivated fields, has largely fallen into complete disuse now that new irrigation systems are being installed. However, the lines of *qanat* inspection holes, looking like disintegrating termite hills, still mark the landscape, especially in Yazd region. A feature of Iranian towns are the roadside water channels (*jub*) which are permanently or daily flooded with water. These serve to lower the temperature as well as move rubbish, but also tend to trap unwary car drivers attempting to squeeze into restricted parking spaces.

HISTORY

A note on dates As in India and China, official circles in the Iranian Republic prefer the designation BCE (Before Common Era) and CE (Common Era) rather than the Western/Christian abbreviations, BC and AD; this will be the system used here. Where the Muslim lunar year (as recorded in a building inscription) falls between two solar years (eg: the Muslim Hijra year 1347 ran July 20 1928 – July 8 1929), I have noted only the latter year.

Archaeological excavations have shown that the Neolithic period in the Iranian context dated from around 7000BCE. Evidence of copper smelting, pottery making and textile production has been found, along with proof that the potter's wheel was introduced around 3500BCE. The sites of Tell-i Iblis and Tepe Yahya, east of Kirman, have provided artefacts and clear signs of settlement dating from the so-called Proto-Elamite period, 3200–2800BCE and a recently published survey of archaeological investigation carried out in the 1970s reveals that the region between Susa and Malyan is rich in surface finds from the 4th millennium BCE. Trading contacts with the Sumerians of Mesopotamia (now Iraq) increased as the Elamite centres of Susa and Haft Tepe were established. For today's visitor, the most important and visual evidence of the Elamite civilisation is at Choga Zanbil, the remains of a stepped-pyramid temple in a huge complex. Political interference by the Mesopotamians into Elamite territory led to armed confrontation, and in c2006BCE the Elamite army captured the last king of Ur, exiling him to Anshan (modern Malyan, southeast of Izeh). They never, however, controlled all of Iran. In the northwest of the country below the Caucasus, archaeological finds from Haftavan and Dinkh Tepe, near Lake Orumiyeh, reveal the settlements here also traded with Mesopotamia. Here, too, there was technical innovation, with fine zoomorphic pottery vessels such as those found in the Hasanlu excavations, dating from c1350BCE. The extensive military campaigns of the Assyrian king, Ashurbanipal, in 639BCE spelt the end of most if not all of these settlements east of the Zagros Mountains.

Little is known of eastern Iran during this time, but with the decline of the Assyrian Empire control of western Iran was assumed by two (tribal?) families, the Medes (from the region of Media) and the Persians (from *Pars*, the region around Shiraz), linked tentatively by marriage. However, instead of accepting Median rule, the Pars commander, known in western sources as Cyrus II (the Great), defeated the Median ruler – his maternal grandfather – at Pasagarda, and extended his territorial control to include Elamite settlements in the south. This was the start of the Achaemenid dynasty.

The Achaemenids (550–330BCE)

From Iran, the Achaemenid Empire stretched west into the Balkans and eastwards perhaps as far as the Tian Shan Mountains, today's Chinese frontier, all controlled from the northern summer capital of Hamadan (Ekbatana of Alexander the Great), the winter capital of Susa in the south, Pasagarda and later Persepolis.

Cyrus brought Lydian Anatolia into his lands in 547BCE and then took Babylon and Syria in 539BCE, earning a reputation for justice and religious tolerance by allowing the Jews to return from Babylonian exile and reinstalling the Babylonian divine images to their shrines. Central Asia was the next goal but there Cyrus met his end, in c529BCE, followed by the death of his son Cambyses four years later. Not everyone concurred with the selection of Darius, one of Cambyses's relatives, as successor, and his victory over these enemies is recorded at Bisitun. Campaigns extended Achaemenid control into Ethiopia from Egypt, Afghanistan and India, and west into Europe along the Danube and into Greece, while Darius I the Great (d486BCE) also undertook a massive road- and canal-building programme (including the precursor to the Suez Canal), and the construction of great palace complexes such as Persepolis. His numerous subject peoples were not required to accept Zoroastrianism and his rule was associated with tolerance and prosperity. A banking system, a uniform weights and measures standard and a merchant navy were established.

The military momentum continued but as supply lines stretched to breaking point the vassal lands gradually slipped from Darius's control. Alexander the Great (the Macedonian) timed his invasion well. Although he survived only seven years after taking Persepolis in 330BCE, Alexander has passed into Iranian history as a great man, responsible for building a wall (see page 142) to protect civilised people (Iranians) from Barbarians in the north and east.

Archaeological interest in the 1960–70s concentrated on sites associated with Achaemenid history, even more so when the late shah (see page 15) proclaimed that his reign was a direct extension of 'uninterrupted Iranian rule' established by Cyrus (he even introduced a short-lived dating system to embody this idea, eg: March 21 1976 was re-dated as New Year's Day 2535). Massive restoration projects and new excavations were undertaken in Persepolis, Pasagarda, Susa, Naqsh-i Rustam and Bisitun in time for the 2,500th anniversary celebrations of this rule in 1971.

The Seleucids (323–c240BCE)

Alexander's sudden death stunned his men; he had seemed so invincible. His military generals and governors strove to retain control over the conquered territories, with Seleucid I taking charge of the Iranian lands, ruling from Ctesiphon (south of today's Baghdad). Greek settlements and temples were established – but from around 310BCE the remnants of Alexander's army slowly withdrew from the eastern provinces in order to defend the Seleucid regime west of the Euphrates. The frontier between the west and the east came to be located very definitely west, not east, of the Zagros Mountains. The Seleucids finally succumbed to Rome after the Battle of Magnesia in 180BCE.

The Parthians (c238BCE–224CE)

The early history of this family (also known as the Arsacids) and its founder Arsaces is shrouded in mystery, but we know that as the Seleucids withdrew the power vacuum was filled by the Parni, a tribe moving down from the Central Asian steppes in c238BCE. Preoccupied with defending Syria, the Seleucids failed to challenge Arsaces of Parni, and in 210BCE he was recognised as a powerful vassal ruler in Parthia in the northeast and the southern Caspian regions; the southwest provinces remained largely under the control of the Elymais (c147BCE–c225CE) who paid annual tribute to the Parthian shahs. This regional power group is known from its coinage and a few inscriptions, and was probably the last remnants of earlier Elamite authority.

The Parthian shah Mithridates I (c171–139BCE) campaigned against the Seleucids, winning control of Media by 148BCE, but in the east the Scythian tribes were causing serious problems, a threat implicitly recognised in the location of the first Parthian capital, Nisa (now in Turkmenistan). As internal security was established, so trade on the Silk Road flourished, carrying Chinese silk westwards in payment for glass, jade and the 'blood-sweating' horses of Ferghana, Central Asia. By 113BCE Mithridates II (c124–87BCE) had moved into eastern Syria and the Caucasus against Rome, but family squabbles after his death stopped further advance. Rome moved into action, only to have half its forces slain and a further 25% captured. Nevertheless, continuing family feuds prevented the Parthian command from taking advantage. An uneasy truce dramatically ended with the invasion of Mesopotamia by the Roman Emperor Trajan in 114. His death three years later, as foretold by the oracle at Baalbek, Lebanon, prompted Hadrian to accept the Euphrates as the frontier, but peace was in name only. Major campaigning recommenced in 195, with the Parthians losing most of Mesopotamia but inflicting a massive defeat on the Roman army in 217. However, there was another challenger, the emerging Iranian family of Sasan and, in April 224, at the Battle of Golpaygan, Parthian rule was brought to an end by the Sasanids.

The Parthian dynasty lasted 474 years but remarkably little of its civilisation and culture is visible to the visitor in Iran; one has to journey to Hatra in Iraq and Palmyra in Syria. Apart from the striking bronze Shami statue (see page 76) there are only a few eroded low-reliefs and fragmentary archaeological finds. Later occupation of the major Parthian settlements of Damghan, Rayy, Hamadan, and Ctesiphon destroyed the architecture, and until recently officialdom had other archaeological priorities. However, its military skill has been recorded throughout Europe and the east, with depictions of the famed Parthian shot, in which the warrior on horseback turns back in the saddle, drawing his bow. Renowned also were the Parthian trousers, dismissed by the Roman military as 'effeminate' garb, but carefully portrayed in all their finery by 2nd- and 3rd-century sculptors of Palmyra (Syria) and Hatra (Iraq). As with the Achaemenids, the Parthians were Zoroastrian and established a firm association between the priesthood and kingship by constructing 'coronation' fire temples, and developing the cult or temple fire.

The Sasanids (224–658CE)

Tradition holds that Sasan, who gave his name to the dynasty, was the high priest at the Zoroastrian shrine of Anahita, at Istakhr near Persepolis. Claiming family ties with the Achaemenids, one of Sasan's descendants, Ardashir (d255), then in control of Shiraz and Kirman regions, defeated the last Parthian ruler, Artabanus V (see page 9), and established a dynasty which ruled Iran for over 400 years. The main Sasanid sites of Bishapur, Firouzabad and Taq-i Bustan reveal little of the efficient adminstration, which included town planning, irrigation systems and a system of schools, colleges and hospitals. But the kings' exploits are recorded in the Persian poem, the *Shah-nameh* (see page 253) which later inspired many Iranian artists. The regime was responsible for gathering together what remained of the Zoroastrian scriptures after Alexander the Great's destruction of the royal archives, but this formalisation of the faith was accompanied by persecution of the existing Jewish, Manichaean and Christian communities in Iran; such intolerance sowed the seeds of its own destruction.

The political and military rivalry with Rome, and later Byzantium, continued. The Sasanid army, from their capital, Ctesiphon, headed west, almost reaching the walls of Constantinople (Istanbul) and temporarily occupying Syria and Egypt. Its victories over Rome were recorded in huge rock carvings as at Bishapur but the campaigns exhausted both empires which levied ever-increasing taxes to finance the wars.

Islam and the Arab conquests

The Western perception of the spread of Islam is largely based on 19th-century opinion: fanatical Muslims eager to attain paradise by dying in battles against the 'infidel'. However, this fails to explain the staggering speed of the territorial conquests after the death of the Prophet Mohammed in 632 in Arabia: averaging 16–19km a day, Syria was taken in 636, Egypt in 641, Mesopotamia in 648. The answer is to be found in centuries of religious intolerance pursued by both the Byzantine and Sasanid regimes, and the heavy taxes levied on their subject peoples. By contrast, the Muslims offered freedom of religious practice to the 'People of the Book' (ie: Jews and Christians) and lower taxes.

The Sasanid army was defeated in 637 in Iraq, with the last Sasanid shah finally tracked down and killed in 651, but it was some 350 years before the Persian Pahlavi script was totally abandoned for the Arabic script and language. The administration of the Islamic Empire, which in its heyday stretched from Spain/Portugal and North Africa in the west to the Great Wall of China in the east, was run first from Syria, and later from Iraq (Baghdad) under the Abbasid Caliphate (749–1258). Islamic history is tortuously complicated with territorial boundaries changing almost every campaign season; today's borders were fixed only during the mid-20th century. When the opportunity arose, warlords throughout the empire took advantage of weak caliphs paying only lip-service to Baghdad, so from 800CE various families were in virtual control of certain parts of Iran, the most important in this context being the Seljuk house (see below). Despite such fragmentation, this early medieval period (750–1200) was a time of flourishing trade and commerce with Europe and the east, and of great scientific and technological advance in most fields. By contrast Europe was in the Dark Ages.

The Seljuks (1038–c1220)

From around 800, numerous Turkic-speaking tribes spread into the Islamic regions from Central Asia, most to act as mercenaries; one of these was the Seljuk family (also spelt Saljuq) which entered the service of the Khwarizm (today Turkmenistan) ruler in the 1020s. Quickly tiring of taking orders, the family turned the tables and by 1043 had firm control of Nishapur and the eastern provinces. Its authority spread south and westwards, with control of the regions shared among the family. The Seljuk sultans gained a reputation for being firm but just rulers of Sunni Islam, and great patrons of the arts and sciences, constructing mosques (see *Isfahan*) and tomb towers, colleges and *caravanserais*. Exciting artistic and technological developments in architecture, ceramics, metalwork and textiles took place, influencing work for centuries after. Trade and commerce also flourished; it looked as if peace, territorial unity and continuity had finally arrived. The invading roughnecks of the 12th century, the Crusaders, were a mere irritation in the Seljuks' western provinces. More problematic were the so-called Assassins (see page 90) of the Ismaili Shi'is assassinating political and military leaders, and, even more dangerous, the advancing Mongol armies.

The Mongols (c1220–c1340)

The first Mongol invasion in 1218 virtually destroyed Seljuk authority. Although modern Mongolian commentators promote Genghis Khan as a statesman and military hero, all the 13th-century Persian and Arabic chroniclers portrayed him and his men as a totally destructive force. Even if their accounts were exaggerated, many historic cities were definitely razed to the ground and the country's water irrigation system destroyed, with only southern Iran escaping unscathed. The second invasion of 1250s under Genghis Khan's grandson, Hulagu, finished Abbasid authority in Baghdad and eradicated the Assassin threat. In time, the Mongols – who came to be known as the Il-Khanids in Iran – were converted to Islam and an exquisite monument survives as evidence of their patronage: the Mausoleum of Oljeitu at Sultaniyeh. Commerce and trade recovered too, as noted by Marco Polo, though the other Mongol legacy, the black death, endured for centuries.

However, Iran experienced political fragmentation: a commander in the Mongol army seized control over central Iran (Isfahan, Yazd and later Kirman and Iraq). His Muzaffarid dynasty was short-lived (1314–93), but a small Sunni *madrasa* in Isfahan shows artistic quality and craftsmanship. In northern Iraq and Azerbaijan, a Mongol tribe, the Jalayrids, took control (1336) but yielded authority to the house of Timur Leng in the closing years of the 14th century.

The Timurids (1375–c1415 in western Iran; until c1500 in eastern Iran)

Today's Uzbekistan Republic is also promoting a tireless warrior with blood-stained hands as a national hero: Amir Temur or Timur Leng (Tamerlaine). Claiming direct descent from Genghis Khan, this Turkic chief dreamt of re-establishing the Mongol Empire. Ruling from Samarkand, he led annual campaigns into Syria, Anatolia, India (sacking Delhi in 1399), Russia (up to the gates of Moscow), and even China, before his death in 1405. Family squabbles resulted in territorial fragmentation but by 1420 his son Shah Rukh (d1447) controlled most of the Iranian provinces from his Herat capital, and it is in eastern Iran, around Mashhad, where much Timurid architecture, with its distinctive ceramic-tiled exteriors and 'ribbed' vaulting, still survives.

In western Iran power had passed in the late 14th century to two Shiʿi tribal confederations, the Aq Qoyunlu and the Qara Qoyunlu (White and Black Sheep, respectively). The heartland of Aq Qoyunlu authority was in today's eastern Turkey, and by 1470 it had taken control of Qara Qoyunlu's Azerbaijan and Iraqi territory. Expansion continued into southern Iran and eastwards, which explains the Aq Qoyunlu buildings in Isfahan. A resounding defeat in 1473, however, against the Ottomans, meant that it was only a matter of time before the new political force, the Safavid family, took centre stage.

The Safavids (1501–1736)

Safavid court historians were so successful in manufacturing ancestral links for this dynasty that little is certain about the family's actual origins. The story goes that a famous Sufi shaikh, Safi al-Din (d1334), was a popular Sunni mystic and teacher at Ardabil, on the western Caspian shores, and as the two Qoyunlu confederations battled for supremacy and the Ottomans attacked, people looked to this Turkish-speaking 'guru' for spiritual and political leadership. During the 15th century his followers became known for their commitment to Shiʿi Islam (see pages 23) and so the lines of future dynastic rivalry were drawn: the Sunni Ottoman sultanate and the emerging Shiʿi Safavid dynasty. The Muslim pilgrimage centres of Mecca and Medina passed into Ottoman authority, so in their place the Safavid shahs promoted the Shiʿi shrines of Kerbela, Mashhad and Ardabil, after proclaiming *Ithna ʿAshari* Shiʿism as the state religion. Sultan and shah fought constantly for control of the Zagros Mountain regions and their populations, while the Uzbek tribes carried out damaging raids in the northeast, and the Afghans attacked from the east.

Despite such troubled times, the European traders in Iran were aware only of the magnificence and wealth of the Safavid court. They marvelled – as do today's visitors – at the turquoise domes of Isfahan, the soaring tiled portals first seen in Timurid constructions, while its fine textiles and carpets attracted hundreds of merchant adventurers vying for trading privileges awarded by the shah.

The Afsharids (1736–c1750)

The Sunni population of Afghanistan increasingly questioned Safavid authority and found a leader in Mir Ways, the former Safavid governor. Attacks began in earnest in 1722, with many Iranian towns falling to the Afghani rebels until Nadir Khan, a Safavid general from eastern Iran, took control. By 1727 Nadir Khan had recaptured territory seized by the Afghans and been rewarded with governorships that amounted to the complete control of all of Iran except Azerbaijan, Isfahan and the southwest. Three years later he forced the Ottoman army out of Hamadan, Azerbaijan and the Caucasus. Tired of installing Safavid puppet rulers, he took the crown and title with the dynastic name of Afshari in 1736, and proclaimed Sunni Islam as the state religion from his Mashhad capital. The campaigning continued even into India, exhausting the Iranian people and an economy already disrupted by Afghan incursions, famine and plague. He was assassinated in 1747, and once again Iran's territorial unity was divided among various regional warlords.

The Zand family (1750–94)

Eagle-eyed readers have spotted the word 'family' in this heading. The Zand rulers, especially its founder Karim Khan Zand (d1779), never assumed the title 'shah', stating that they were acting as regent (*vakil*) for the Safavids. An army officer of the last Safavid shah, Karim Khan assumed control of southern Iran in the chaotic years following Nadir Shah's assassination and reintroduced Shi'ism. After his death the usual family disputes broke out which, despite the reassertion of authority by the able Lutf Ali Khan Zand, enabled the Qajar family powerful in the northern provinces to extend southwards. Agha Mohammed Qajar captured Lutf Ali Khan in Bam and executed him in 1794. It was the end of Zand rule – noted then and now for its justice and moderation, especially in Shiraz, the former Zand capital, which retains charming examples of Zand architecture.

The Qajar Dynasty (c1757–1924)

The Turkoman Qajar family of the Caspian region had fought for the Safavid dynasty on the battlefield so, as that regime disintegrated, the Qajar family seized authority in Azerbaijan, took Isfahan from the Zands and moved into the eastern Iranian provinces, re-establishing Shi'i Islam. The man in charge was Agha Mohammed, whose brutality was attributed to his forced castration by an Afsharid shah. His sadism proved too much even for his courtiers, who contrived his murder in 1797. Establishing Tehran as the capital, his nephew and successor, Fath Ali Shah (d1834), proved politically astute, surviving the interventionist policies and expansionist ambitions of Napoleonic France, Victorian England in India, and Tsarist Russia, while fighting off Ottoman campaigns in the Zagros range and Afghan incursions in the east. It was no easy task; the Treaty of Turkomanchay (1828) alone resulted in Iran losing its Caucasian lands to Russia and paying a massive war indemnity, bankrupting the state.

As with the Ottoman sultans, the Qajars saw reorganisation of the army and administration as a solution to their problems. To the shahs, these reforms presupposed centralisation of power in royal hands, but others argued they should lead to democratic constitutional rule, free from foreign interference. The argument raged throughout the final years of the 19th century, culminating in the 1906 Constitutional Revolution. Shortly before his death in 1907, Shah Muzaffar al-Din was forced (when the Shi'i theologians withdrew support) to agree to a constitution on Belgian lines, but his successor was hostile. Nationalist forces seized Isfahan and then Tehran, deposing the new shah in favour of his son, a minor. Fortunately the Great Powers were too occupied by World War I and the Bolshevik Revolution to take advantage of the political turmoil. In Iran Reza Khan, a brigade commander, quickly rose in authority becoming prime minister in 1923. Two years later the National Assembly declared the end of Qajar rule. Calls for a republic on the lines of newly established Kemalist Turkey gathered strength and, worried that this would inevitably mean increased secularism, Iranian theologians pressed Reza Khan to become shah.

The Pahlavi Dynasty (1926–79)

Reza Khan adopted 'Pahlavi' as the dynastic name, we are told, because it was a popular title for an unbeatable warrior, a champion wrestler (see page 116), and recalled the pre-Islamic language and script of Iran. Whatever one's personal views of Reza Shah's rule – his tomb in Rayy was quickly destroyed in the early days of the Islamic Revolution – like Kemal Ataturk in Turkey, he managed to save the country from being totally absorbed by one or other of the Great Powers; other leaders were not so successful. Much of his reform programme was aimed at welding Iran into one nation (compulsory school teaching in Farsi, dress reform, etc) while establishing a national system of schools and hospitals, and constructing roads and railways (in the 1910s only two all-weather roads existed in Iran). When he was ousted in 1941 by Britain and the Soviet Union – because of his pro-German leanings – in favour of his son, Mohammed Reza, Iran was very different from when he assumed control. His personal finances had also undergone a great change, increasing from one million rials in 1930 to 680 million (then £7 million sterling) in 1941.

After the war, British influence at court paled as the USA increasingly exerted its authority, while Soviet military withdrawal from the Tabriz region after World War II meant pressure from that quarter lessened. However, within Iran xenophobia remained. After Prime Minister Mossadegh nationalised Iran's oil and petroleum industry in the early 1950s, the young shah was forced into exile, but the CIA soon engineered his return and the fall of Mossadegh. Various reform programmes were introduced including the so-called White Revolution, designed to reassign land ownership to the peasantry. Lauded then by many Western commentators, recent appraisals argue that it was disastrous, increasing the hardship for farmers while safeguarding the wealthy.

Mohammed Reza (crowned in 1967) became increasingly autocratic and remote. Political parties were banned, save for the one which he controlled, and the parliament (*majlis*) merely rubber-stamped all royal decisions. Leading theologians including a certain Hajji Sayyid Khomeini were deported or jailed, and anyone with left-wing leanings left the country or risked imprisonment. The press, radio and TV were heavily censored and even in book publishing, all texts had to be approved or shown to have pre-publication orders for 3,000 copies. The reputation of his secret police, the SAVAK, was fearsome. Meanwhile revenue from oil and petroleum was pouring into the country, only to flow out to pay for a massive armaments programme. The gap between rich and poor yawned, while middle-class dissatisfaction at soaring inflation and extensive corruption increased, but the West, apprehensive of Soviet territorial ambitions, continued unquestioning support. The ultimate folly was the costly celebrations marking the so-called 2,500th anniversary of 'uninterrupted Persian rule' in 1971. By 1976 there was little public support for the shahs; I witnessed soldiers being bussed in, dressed as construction workers in spotless white overalls, to provide 'spontaneous' cheering for a royal motorcade. The following year government funding for religious institutions and the 'clergy' was substantially cut. As serious unrest grew, those who could left or sent their children abroad. Martial law was imposed in the autumn of 1978 but public demonstrations continued, despite hundreds being killed in a hail of bullets. Mohammed Reza flew out of Iran on January 16 1979, dying in exile in 1980.

The Islamic Republic
In the closing years of Mohammed Reza's rule, Muslim theologians throughout Iran had refused to hold the Friday service, as a sign of their disapproval of the regime on religious grounds. Instead, smuggled tape cassettes of the speeches of Ayatollah Khomeini and other banned theologians passed from hand to hand. Now the shah was gone, Khomeini returned from his French exile to ecstatic popular acclaim in February 1979 and set about establishing an administration based on Shi'i Islamic law. The first general election was held in May 1980 and, presumably thinking he had full American support, Saddam Hussein of Iraq invaded four months later, claiming the oil-rich region of southwest Iran. Iranian forces quickly regained lost territory but the war continued, with enormous losses on both sides. A ceasefire was finally agreed in 1988, though an official peace agreement remained unsigned; by then many young Iranian men had been killed (perhaps as many as one million) and without a fully developed welfare system in place, their wives and families suffered further distress.

During this difficult time, a full reorganisation of the legal system, the administration and taxes was undertaken; Iran was to become a theocracy. Just as the shah had brooked no opposition in his last years, so the new regime was determined to forestall any restoration of the monarchy. Theologians and officials moved to eradicate every element of 'Westoxification' (*gharbzadigi*) from Iran (see page 55).

The prolonged detention of American Embassy staff in Tehran from October 1979 for 444 days, and the Western conviction that the Islamic Revolutionary government was deeply involved in the training and funding of certain hard-line politico-military organisations elsewhere, resulted in a total breakdown of diplomatic relations between Iran and the West, exacerbated by the Salman Rushdie (*Satanic Verses*) issue, and the shooting down of an IranAir passenger jet, killing 250, by the US cruiser, *Vincennes*. The official US D'Amato trade embargo (see pages 43–4) and consequent economic sanctions are still in existence, although modified, at the time of writing. Diplomatic relations with the United States have not improved and if anything have increasingly soured since 9/11.

Ayatollah Khomeini died in June 1989, and since then there have been changes, some with official blessing, some merely tolerated. For the visitor, perhaps this is most apparent in the changed appearance of Khomeini in paintings. In the first years of the revolution he was shown as a glowering, prophetic figure with black beard, furrowed brow and heavy eyebrows, but increasingly now a benign, avuncular image with soft white beard and a slight smile is portrayed.

POLITICS AND ECONOMY
The supreme leader and the president

Under the current constitution, Iran is governed by a *faqih* or supreme (spiritual) leader until the re-emergence of the 12th Imam (see page 23). This Supreme Leader is chosen for life by the Assembly of (Theological) Experts, whose members have been elected for a seven-year term once their candidacy has been approved by the Leader and the Council of Guardians of the Constitution. Ayatollah Khomeini (d1989), it was widely acknowledged, clearly had been the person to fill this office as being the most just, pious and able theologian, but such unanimity was not immediately accorded to his successor, Ayatollah Ali Khameini. The important Council of Guardians is headed by the Supreme Leader who selects six voting members, while a similar number is selected by the Supreme Judicial Council and approved by Parliament (*Majlis*). As Iran is a theocracy, all are from the *ulama* ('clergy', theologians-cum-jurists) and under current legal interpretation no woman can 'join' the *ulama*. This Council undertakes to safeguard and uphold the Islamic state, the constitution, and approve all parliamentary dealings, decisions and resolutions. An Expediency Council of 25 members has been established to 'negotiate' between the *Majlis* and the Council of Guardians consisting of the Guardians, the president, the head of the judiciary and the parliamentary speaker.

The president of the republic is directly elected by all resident Iranians over the age of 16 for a four-year term, but stands for office only with the approval of the Council of Guardians; after two successive terms in office he cannot offer himself for a third term. On election, the president may appoint 24 cabinet ministers who have to be confirmed in office by the *Majlis*; following constitutional amendments during Rafsanjani's presidency, the office of prime minister has been abandoned. The current president, Ayatollah Mohammed

RISE OF KHOMEINI: TOWARDS THE REVOLUTION

1902 Birth of Ruh-Allah Khomeini. By 1944 he was a Qom madrasa teacher, proposing active 'Muslim' involvement in politics, and supported *vilayet-i faqih* (government control by Islamic law), later the cornerstone concept behind the Islamic Revolution.

1962 Khomeini opposed new government ruling revoking requirement of swearing-in on the Koran, by any newly-elected local and provincial officials, arguing this would allow Bahais open participation in politics.

Jan 1963 Joined with other theologians against the shah's White Revolution, saying it increased the shah's power and American influence in Iran.

Mar 1963 Paratroopers attacked Khomeini's college in Qom, causing fatalities.

Jun 1963 (Ashura) Khomeini described the Shah's government as 'fundamentally opposed to Iran'. His arrest was followed by demonstrations during which many protestors were killed (the 15th Khordad).

Aug 1963 Released; re-arrested Oct 1963–May 1964.

Oct 1964 Khomeini condemned as 'high treason' the new legal status protecting American personnel in Iran. Arrested and exiled first to Turkey, and then to Najaf, Iraq, for 13 years. His lectures, publicly criticising the shah, were published in 1970.

Dec 1970 Demonstrations were held in Khomeini's name by Tehran University students, and by Qom students in 1975.

Oct 1977 Sudden death of Khomeini's eldest son led to Tehran demonstrations, accusing SAVAK of involvement.

Jan 1978 Mass protest in Qom following scurrilous Tehran press attack on Khomeini; many killed. Forty days later (customary funeral commemoration) a demonstration in Tabriz was held, and 40 days later there were similar protests in 55 cities across Iran.

Sep 8–9 1978 At least 4,000 protesters killed by shah's forces in Tehran: 'Bloody Friday'.

Oct 1978 Khomeini moved to France, after shah demanded Najaf expulsion. Crippling strikes by Iranian oil workers began.

Dec 1978 (Moharram) Iranian theologians and students demonstrated against curfew. On the ninth day, a million demonstrators collected in Shahyad/Azadi Square, near airport; next day (Ashur) two million protesters demanded abolition of monarchy.

Jan 16 1979 Shah left Iran.

Khatami, was elected in 1997 and 2001 by landslide margins. He will not be eligible to stand in 2005.

The *Majlis* currently has 290 directly elected members serving a four-year term, and for the last few parliaments there have been several women MPs. The Zoroastrian community is represented by one MP, as is the Jewish sector, but as Iranian Christians number about 100,000, they have two seats in parliament. There are no well-defined, established political parties as in the West, but candidates are known for their individual leanings. The speaker of the *Majlis* has an important and influential position, and following the 2004 elections, Mr Haddad Adel was confirmed in office with the approval of the Council of Guardians.

Immediately prior to the parliamentary elections of February 2004, the Council of Guardians disqualified some 2,000 reformist candidates from standing for election, an action widely criticised in the Western media; this has resulted in a much altered political balance in parliament.

Western perceptions of revolutionary Iran

Anyone visiting Iran for the first time should remember that in the 1970s the Western media was largely uncritical of the shah's regime. The praise lavished on the shah and his immediate family in publications was occasioned more by official stipulation than reasoned investigation. The wide-spread notion, still found today in the West, that the late shah had established an active Western-style democracy in Iran before he was ousted, is unfounded; his rule was autocratic.

Many new visitors to Iran presume that all Iranian theologians speak with one voice, but since the 1980s there have been many outspoken declarations among the *ulama*, not always finding favour with the authorities. Some feel that having established an Islamic state to its satisfaction, the *ulama* should withdraw from active political life and resume its former pastoral responsibilities; presently the official view is that active involvement in politics should continue. The evolving relationship between Islam, Iran and the modern world is avidly discussed and the passion these debates arouse should not be underestimated, as demonstrated by public interest in the court hearings of clerics Abdullah Nouri and Mohsen Kadivar.

Parliamentary debates are just as highly charged. There are essentially two main positions: the 'conservative' wing who hold that the quickest route to achieve a (spiritual) well-being nationally is by a uniform path; that a woman's role is primarily associated with the family and the home; and that the fortunes of the poor will be improved by spiritual care and government subsidies, the awarding of franchise allocation in the market. Support for this view is generally found among the rural communities and *bazaris* (merchants). The 'liberal' wing prefers another vision of society, one relating the spiritual ideal to the individual and the material world, arguing for the individual to progress along the spiritual path at his/her own pace; recognising the importance of investments in major projects to revitalise the economy and to create new jobs for the ever-increasing population; and working towards reintroducing Iran to the international community and creating greater opportunities for women (even within the *ulama*). Such ideas largely find favour among urban voters of Tehran, Shiraz, Isfahan, among women and among the young educated groups, as seen in student demonstrations in Tehran in 1999, which were met by a swift reaction from police and militia.

Western women often feel hostility towards the Iranian regime, and in particular to its treatment of women. This is largely based on a (mis)understanding of the situation in pre-revolutionary Iran – and a personal reaction to the official stipulation requiring headcoverings for all women in Iran. Over half of the Iranian population is female, and the government cannot afford to ignore them. In the 1970s, opportunities for Iranian women were in fact virtually confined to the upper social circles, and indeed 'grass-roots' women's groups played an important role in bringing about the Islamic Revolution, as they often remind the authorities. Generally speaking, women across the social classes have a more strident public voice and greater participation now. Since 1980 there has been positive discrimination in education and certain professions, eg: doctors, dentists, and teachers, because Islamic social convention prefers that women should 'deal' with women. Some 50% of university students and at least 33% of faculty members are women. Their political involvement has amended laws on employment, divorce, maternity leave and child custody.

Nor can Iranian youth be ignored. Over 70% of the population is under 30 years old; while young they require education and training and later employment to the tune of 800,000 new jobs every year. In the late 1970s under 50% of those aged between six and 24 were literate; today, despite a doubling of population, it is said 93% can read and write, and university student numbers have increased ten-fold.

The economy

For centuries Iran's economy and trade were based on textiles and carpets, in processed or raw yarn, dyes and mordants, but by the end of the 18th century foreign mass-produced fabrics were flooding the home market. The economy collapsed. Under foreign pressure, the Qajar administration sold off trading concessions in tobacco, sugar, railway construction and telegraph installation to non-Iranians; even carpet production was largely foreign owned. By the early 20th century the exploration and exploitation of Iran's oil and petroleum reserves were in foreign hands, prompting nationalisation in the 1950s and a political crisis. Heady prices for petroleum products in the 1970s brought great wealth into the country, but rampant inflation too. Huge sums went into importing arms and weapons, which then sat rusting in military stores, and into sending students abroad to further their education. Little was done to revitalise or restructure the economy outside the oil industry; then as now, the average manufacturing workshop had fewer than ten employees. The shah's White Revolution of 1961–3 (reassigning agricultural land rights) resulted in more power passing to the shah and tens of thousands of peasants barely able to survive.

Unrest in the late 1970s saw vast numbers leaving Iran, and few of those already abroad returned. With the establishment of the Islamic Republic all foreign and private industries were nationalised, and work on international projects (like the Tehran Metro) was abandoned as foreign consortia withdrew. The new administration faced a brain drain, while heavy losses in the Iran–Iraq war resulted in a further scarcity in skills and expertise. The three-year closure of universities and colleges during Iran's 'Cultural Revolution' meant fewer still were qualified to fill the vacuum.

The US trade embargo and other economic sanctions, a drop in world oil prices, production difficulties and a steep decline in tourist numbers (far below the half million visitors per annum in the mid-1970s) have created additional problems. Fearing yet more assets leaving the country, the government even banned the export of Iranian carpets for some years (see page 44). The Rafsanjani two-term presidency was marked by a massive surge in imports, very lucrative business for the right-wing 'bazaari' classes, and little else. Few of his large-scale projects, which numbered in the tens of thousands, were ever completed, other than a massive programme of road upgrading. There is little sign of large-scale planning and investment in the economy, and unfortunately two major projects regarding health facilities and sewage provision, supported by Britain and other EU members, were turned down by the World Bank, yielding to American pressure. Presently, according to official sources, inflation is running below 20% per annum but is probably higher.

A number of Free Trade Zones are now operating, eg: the Gulf islands of Kish and Qeshm, and the port of Chabahar, along with a few Special Economic Zones which function in a similar fashion. These zones permit unlimited foreign involvement, including bank operations, a free market exchange, removal of import restrictions and 20 years of tax exemption. In 1992 some restrictions concerning foreign shareholding in Iranian-based companies were lifted, but a certain official ambivalence remains; rather than amending or revoking laws, it is more usual to turn a blind eye to circumvention. Increasingly, Iranian companies are establishing offices in Dubai in attempts to bypass bureaucratic difficulties; in 2004, over 26,000.

Agriculture struggles on with a lack of machinery, limited irrigation systems and a poor infrastructure of cold-storage units and refrigerated trucks. Things are slowly improving: the replanting of Iran's famous vines, ripped up in early revolutionary zeal, for instance. Visitors to Isfahan's central Maydan (square) will now see most of the shops occupied and trading, in great contrast to four years ago, although poor earnings and high unemployment still affect the bazaars of Yazd and Kirman. The major employer, as in the 1960s and 1970s, continues to be the government, despite a revolutionary pledge to reduce such staffing drastically. The ongoing habit of moving staff every six months or so obviously hampers project continuity and supervision.

Diplomatic relations

If certain circles see the need for foreign investment (see page 18), the Council of Guardians and other influential bodies do not necessarily concur. And headline diplomatic confrontation hasn't helped. Aside from the Salman

Rushdie issue, the detention of a German businessman in the late 1990s caused a stand-off in Irano-German relations. The state visits of President Khatami to Europe and the East did raise the national profile, and led to more considered and informed reporting in the foreign media. But then the speeches of the Bush administration leading up to and during the Coalition action in Iraq, describing Iran as part of the 'axis of evil', were less than helpful. On the other hand, the Iranian government's detached stance regarding its earlier promises to the UN's atomic watchdog (IAEA) to allow tougher inspection of its nuclear facilities is incurring much criticism. At the time of writing, Irano-Canadian diplomatic relations are at an all time low after the death in custody of a female Canadian Iranian-born photo-journalist arrested for photographing the Tehran Evin jail, and the acquittal of her police interrogator in June 2004.

Future months will reveal if the Bush administration will realise the full extent of the change in the political balance it has introduced into the Middle East by its Iraqi intervention. The Iraqi Shiʿis, formerly totally politically isolated under Saddam Hussein's regime, are now free to formulate a policy with like-minded Shiʿis in Lebanon, Syria, Eastern Turkey and Iran. If the new Bush administration refuses to actively support an equitable agreement of the Israel-Palestine issue, this could have very serious repercussions.

PEOPLE AND LANGUAGE

Caught in a Tehran traffic jam, inevitably one's thoughts turn to Iran's population. The 1992 census determined it totalled just under 60 million, with a density of 35 people per square kilometre. Six years later, official figures suggested the population had risen to over 70 million, predicting that by 2015 it would be around 110 million. Currently, just under 60% live in the major cities: Tehran, the capital, with at least seven million (1992) in the centre, Ahvaz and Mashhad almost two million, Shiraz and Isfahan 1.5 million, Tabriz and Hamadan perhaps slightly less, with more people each year moving from rural areas to find work. During Rafsanjani's presidency (1989–97), 400,000 jobs were created in one year; now 800,000 new jobs are needed each year just to keep pace.

Much has been made of Iran's nomads. Apart from anthropological studies, most publications could be classed as romantic fiction, extolling the 'freedom' of seasonal wanderings (which are actually finely orchestrated migrations). For decades official concern over epidemics, child education, drug and arms smuggling, national security and taxation led to village-settlement programmes, while the 1960s White Revolution caused serious problems over grazing and water rights for the nomads. It has meant that from being 25% of the population in 1900, nomad-pastoralists fell to 6% in 1970s. However, if travelling in say the Shiraz region in late April or mid/late October, you may still see one or more extended family groups, perhaps numbering as high as 75, accompanied by hundreds of sheep and goats, moving to fresh pastures.

Language

Only about 50% of Iranians speak Farsi (Persian), the official language of Iran, as their mother tongue, though most can understand it and read it. In the south, Arabic is mostly spoken while Turkish is common in the north and northwest; Armenian is present in the Caucasian foothills and in the Isfahani enclave; Kurdish-Persian is spoken in the western Zagros while Bakhtiari or Baluchi dialects are used in the southeast. The recent influx of Afghan refugees has seen an increase in Pushto. In the 1930s Reza Shah Pahlavi tried to 'purify' Farsi of Turkish and Arabic words on the lines of the Académie Française, but the Islamic Revolution has of course led to an increased emphasis on Arabic, the language of the Koran.

Farsi is an Indo-Aryan language so there are some similarities in words (eg: *mader* or mother) and grammar with certain European languages. After the 7th-century Arab Muslim conquests, the Pahlavi script for Farsi was abandoned and the one now used is based on Arabic (reading from right to left), with additional letter forms for specific Farsi consonants, eg: *p, g* and *ch*, so the alphabet consists of 32 letter forms not including short vowel markings. Each letter has three written shapes, depending on its location within the word, just as certain European hand-written lower and upper letters (eg: *o, e*) have when joined to other letters. Unfortunately, there is no one accepted transliteration system to render Farsi into the Roman (eg: English) alphabet, so the city of Isfahan may be shown as Espahan, Esfahan, Ispahan etc and Qom as Qomm, Qom or even Ghom. Major road signs are usually given both in Farsi and in the Roman alphabet; mileage is also shown in both numeral forms, both reading left to right. In this book, the most common or simplest rendering is given, eg: Mecca instead of the correct Makka, Koran rather than Qur'an, Mohammed for Muhammad, but at times the transliteration found in publications or on maps will also be included. Following usual transliteration convention, the glottal stop in Farsi is indicated by the symbol ᶜ (e.g. Shiᶜis).

Other than Arabic (for Koranic studies), the other foreign language taught in schools is English, but older city dwellers may know some French or German. That said, travelling independently around Iran without a modicum of Farsi is extremely difficult and presumes on the good nature of Iranians. It is all too easy to miss an important notice or a spoken warning, and reap the consequences. Apart from road signs and the occasional tourist menu, *very* little information is given in any language other than Farsi.

RELIGION

The state religion of Iran is the Shiᶜi *Ithna ᶜAshari* branch of Islam, though a number of Sunnis still reside in the country. According to 1986 official statistics, 99.38% of the population were Muslim, 0.36% were Christian and 0.05% were Jewish (though this number has decreased with emigration), 0.02% were Zoroastrian, 0.17% Hindu and there were a few Sikhs. No Bahais nor atheists were recorded.

Article 13 of the constitution protects the rights of all religious minorities in Iran with the exception of the Bahais.

Islam

According to Muslim belief, Allah, the one uncreated God, has revealed the message of salvation three times. The first time, believers mistakenly assumed the revelation was meant only for them, the chosen people (ie: the Jewish community), so it was revealed again through the Prophet Isa (Jesus) but his followers (Christians) erred in believing Isa was the son of the Creator God, an impossibility given that there is but one God. So it was revealed a third and final time as the Koran through the Prophet Mohammed (d632CE). Thus there are references in the Koran to several biblical episodes, as well as shared beliefs, such as the Day of Judgement, the concept of paradise and hell, free will, the continuing battle between good and evil, and the messianic promise.

There are two main branches of Islam, Sunnism and Shi'ism, the latter being further subdivided. The Shi'is (from *Shi'at Ali* or Party of Ali) do not recognise the three caliphs (*khalifa*: deputy) who assumed control 632–56 after Mohammed's death, believing that the Prophet had transferred all spiritual and temporal authority to his cousin and son-in-law, Ali, and his descendants through his wife Fatima, Mohammed's daughter. To the Shi'is (for obvious reasons the 19th-century English term 'Shi'ites' is now discouraged) the prophetic tradition has continued with and through these divinely guided leaders (*Imams*) who hold the key to the hidden meaning of the Koran – continued that is, according to one section of the Shi'i community, until the seventh generation when Imam Ismail went into concealment; in time he will reappear to prepare the community for the Day of Judgement. His followers are known as the Ismailis, with today's temporal leader, the Aga Khan. But other Shi'is (later known as the *Ithna 'Ashari*, which means literally 'Twelvers') believe that another descendant was chosen as the 7th Imam and that this line continued for another five generations before the (12th) Imam disappeared in 940, to reappear in due time. This is the branch of Shi'ism found in Iran. In the 1980s some Iranians wondered if Ayatollah Khomeini was indeed the reappeared 12th Imam; the overthrow of the Pahlavi regime and founding of the Islamic state seemed nothing short of miraculous.

The Sunnis, in contrast, believe that the prophetic mission ended with Mohammed's death and so reject the idea that Ali and his family were divinely guided. Accordingly, they accept the validity of the first three caliphs and other rulers who followed, holding that they are acting in accordance with the *sunna* (example) of the Prophet.

Zoroastrianism

This is held to be the earliest formulated religious philosophy in the world to have survived to the present day. Recent linguistic analysis of the Avesta scriptures and Gatha hymns indicate that Zoroastra (Zarathustra) was preaching in the Irano-Central Asia region in c1400BCE, if not earlier, although traditionally it was thought he lived 258 years before Alexander the Great destroyed Persepolis in 330BCE. His message, predating Judaism, Christianity and Islam, also centred on the uncreated God, Ahura Mazda, creator of all things, as well as ideas on paradise and hell, on free will, on a messianic promise, and the struggle between good and evil in which good would ultimately triumph. To assist in the battle against evil, Ahura Mazda created evocations of Himself as divine manifestations, such as Mithra, the Lord of Contract, Justice (see page 99). The Achaemenids were perhaps the first rulers in Iran to establish Zoroastrianism as the state religion (see page 188), and it remained dominant until the spread of Islam in the mid-7th century CE. The status of this community in Islamic law was not as clearly defined as for the Jews and Christians, and in the 9th and late 17th/18th centuries persecution caused many Zoroastrian families to flee to northern India, where they became known as the Parsi (from Fars province, Persia).

In 19th-century Qajar Iran their situation improved due to British and Indian diplomatic involvement, and in 1979 the community quickly announced its support of the Islamic Revolution. Today there are some 100,000 Zoroastrians living in Iran, with parliamentary representation, mainly residing in Tehran and Yazd. There are thriving communities in England, the USA, Canada and Australia as well as India (particularly Bombay).

Judaism

The religious tolerance shown by Cyrus the Great, the Achaemenid ruler (d529BCE) to the Jewish people, is remembered on two counts: first, after conquering Assyrian Mesopotamia he permitted the Jews to return to Jerusalem, and, secondly, he actively assisted in the rebuilding of the Temple there. There were at least two Jewish consorts of Iranian kings: the biblical Esther whose story is depicted in the 3rd-century CE synagogue murals from Dura Europos (National Museum, Damascus) and who is said to be buried in Hamadan; or the tomb that they found there could be that of the second Jewish consort, of the Sasanid shah Yazdigird I (d420CE). Later Sasanid rule saw persecution of both the Jews and Christians, but generally speaking the community was protected in early Islam because of its legal status and trading connections. Life became much harder later, especially during the Safavid and Qajar regimes, although there was some respite under Nadir Shah Afshar. Pogroms, especially in Mashhad in 1839, led the community to ask for British protection and many fled to Herat (Afghanistan), only to be forcibly repatriated in 1856. When opportunities arose, many travelled northwards into Central Asia and west into Ottoman lands.

The 1966 census showed some 60,000 Jews still residing in Iran, mainly in Tehran, Isfahan and Hamadan, but since the establishment of the Iranian Republic perhaps less than half remain; in Hamadan for instance only 47 Jews were recorded in the 1996 census. It is assumed that many have strong Zionist sympathies, and there have been arrests under suspicion or charges of espionage. In the last few years foreign visitors have been advised by their own governments not to visit Jewish sites, cemeteries or synagogues but, although feeling disturbed by the neglect and damage, I have never encountered any problem from the local people or authorities.

Christianity

A certain John of Persis attended the 325 Council of Nicaea when numerous Christian communities in Mesopotamia, the Caucasus and elsewhere were under Sasanid authority. The reign of Shapur II (d397) brought severe persecution during which perhaps 35,000 Christians were killed, but in 424 the Iranian Church was still recognised as largely independent. The official break from Byzantium and the Orthodox Church came in 431, when Patriarch Nestor, a Persian by birth, was accused of denying the concept of Christ born Incarnate, thereby rejecting the title of *Theotokos* ('Mother of God') for Mary. His followers, later known as the Nestorian Church (now the Assyrian Church), fled for safety into Sasanid lands, only to find that unrest in the Caucasus had provoked Shah Yazdigird II (439–57) to order the forced conversion of Armenian Christians (Gregorian Church) to Zoroastrianism. Despite such persecution few Christians assisted the Byzantine war effort against the Sasanid regime because Byzantium rejected the validity of these Eastern churches, forbidding their rituals and liturgies. So when the Muslim Arabs entered Iran in the late 7th century and offered religious freedom and lower taxes, they were welcomed and indeed those promises were kept for many years. However, later waves of persecution, especially under Timurid rule, dramatically reduced the Christian community. Matters improved under the Safavid regime (1502–1735) as the shahs were mindful of European trade and of Armenian Christian and Jewish expertise in silk trading. The great influence wielded by the French, British and Russian ambassadors at the 19th-century Qajar court also ensured a measure of protection, and in 1898 a large section of the Nestorians in the Orumiyeh region was received into the Russian Orthodox Church.

Today there are perhaps 100,000 Christians in Iran, mainly of the Armenian church, recognising the Yerevan Patriarch and generally living in Tehran, Isfahan and Shiraz. As a legacy of 19th-century foreign missionary work, there are Presbyterian, Anglican, Lutheran and Catholic congregations, especially in the capital. Immediately following the Islamic Revolution, the then Iranian Anglican bishop and his wife (but not their son) survived assassination but Anglican schools and hospitals were closed. Later the Persian Bible Society, Tehran, was closed and all files confiscated. Other than in Isfahan, where the churches are often open to visitors, and Tehran, it is difficult to get access to churches without prior arrangement.

Bahaism

Iran will always be connected with the Bahai movement, recently estimated to have six million followers worldwide, but for many, the term 'persecution' is too gentle a word to describe the situation in Iran. Officially there are no longer any Bahais residing in the Islamic Republic of Iran, although it has been suggested that some 330,000 still live there. The faith affirms the ultimate unity of all the great religious leaders (Zoroastra, Jesus, Mohammed, the Judaic prophets, Gautama Buddha, Krishna) as historic manifestations of The Word, saying 'the earth is but one country and humanity its citizens'.

Their story begins in the 1840s when a charismatic theologian Sayyid Ali Mohammed Shirazi won over many followers by his piety, saying that he was the gate (*bab*) opening the way for the imminent return of the Hidden (12th) Imam. His later proclamation in 1848 that he himself was the Imam led to his execution in Tabriz, after some 3,000 of his followers were killed. Further persecution followed after a Bahai assassination attempt on the Qajar shah failed, and to escape the following pogrom many fled to Iraq and Syria and so into South America, and Turkey and Europe. The headquarters of Babaism, renamed as Bahaism in the 1860s, was established in Akka, which to many Muslims smacked of strong Zionist involvement. In the mid-1950s the Bahai's Tehran offices were severely damaged and the shah was implicated. In 1979 the Bab's house in Shiraz was destroyed, Bahai cemeteries desecrated, and all endowments, properties and personal records confiscated.

EDUCATION

Schooling for both boys and girls is compulsory from the age of seven years to 15, but only in nursery schools are both sexes taught in the same class. Literacy rates, so woefully low in the 1970s, have dramatically improved and a much greater part of the curriculum is now given to Arabic/Koranic studies, with a few hours per week assigned to English teaching in most secondary schools. With a high youth population and few job opportunities there is a tremendous demand for university education, but many places remain reserved for children of Iran-Iraqi veterans ('Families of the Martyrs'), whatever their pass-marks in the national examinations. The number of universities has mushroomed though few teachers have had research or teaching opportunities outside Iran. Attempts to introduce segregated instruction at this level were not successful, but students sit according to gender.

Iran perhaps leads the world in the field of theological studies at university level, with student numbers increasing over 500% since the 1970s. The main centres are Qom, and Mashhad where the basic seven-year course (ie: secondary level) includes Arabic grammar, rhetoric and literature, plus studies of the Koran, the *Hadith* (sayings of the Prophet Mohammed) and Islamic law. Students can then follow another eight years' study and qualify as a *mojtahid* (interpreter of theological law). The teaching method is by convention, instruction and rhetoric, rather than being discursive, hypothetical and analytical.

Practical Information

WHEN TO VISIT

Visits to the south coast of Iran (eg: Bandar-i Abbas) are best made in the winter months when humidity and heat levels are at their lowest, while spring and autumn are the best times to travel around central and northern Iran. The summer months of June through to early September are best avoided as the temperature can be in the high 40°C, although it is a dry heat except on the south coast.

Take the numerous public holidays into account if your visit is connected with business and/or your time is limited. Try to avoid *Ramadan*, the first ten days of *Moharram*, and the first week of the *Nou Rouz* celebrations, for instance, when staffing in offices and government departments will be minimal and all forms of long-distance transport and hotels will be extremely busy (especially during *Nou Rouz*).

SUGGESTED ITINERARIES

The following itineraries presuppose all arrangements have been made in advance, or that a taxi or car will be used. If local bus transport is used, extra time will be needed to organise tickets and journey times will be longer.

Eight to ten days

One day sightseeing in Tehran; flight to Shiraz for three nights including city sightseeing, a full day in and around Persepolis, and another day in Bishapur or Firouzabad; flight or drive to Isfahan for at least three or four nights in Isfahan, with two full days city sightseeing; return to Tehran for museum visits.

Ten to 15 days

Alternative 1 As above with the addition of two nights in Yazd and two nights in Kirman (or one in Kirman, the other exploring Mahan and surrounds), and if possible overnighting in Kashan.

Alternative 2 Before visiting Isfahan and Shiraz, travel to Ardabil from Tehran, overnighting in Bandar-i Anzali (or conversely fly from Tehran to Tabriz); three nights in Tabriz for city sightseeing and a day trip to Maku (Black Church); return south to stay in Qazvin or Zanjan; then to Hamadan for overnight or to Tehran for Isfahan; then Shiraz.

The shrines of Qom, south of Tehran, and of Mashhad in the northeast will be important visits for any Muslim but access to these religious complexes is strictly limited for non-Muslims. There are splendid historic buildings in the vicinity of Mashhad, but these are not located in 'clusters' as in Isfahan and Shiraz. Iranians enjoy visiting the coast and forests of the southern Caspian shores, as well as shopping opportunities on certain Gulf islands (especially Kish and Qeshm islands).

TOURIST INFORMATION

Theoretically every major city in Iran has a tourist office but these are rarely located centrally and are poorly signposted if at all. The inexpensive, official **road map** (6,000 rials, about US$0.75) published by Ershad Geographic Organisation, is available from well-stocked street kiosks, at airports, hotel bookshops, etc, and from Stanfords (12–14 Long Acre, London WC2E 9LP; tel: 020 7836 1321; fax: 020 7836 0189; www.stanfords.co.uk). An invaluable resource, it identifies the approximate locations of filling stations, tourist inns (*mehmansaray*, with a restaurant and simple accommodation) as well as incorporating new roads.

The British Foreign & Commonwealth Office issues travel advice on BBC2 Ceefax page 470 (www.fco.gov.uk). However, this is not fully revised regularly and so outdated information is sometimes retained.

TOUR OPERATORS
General
UK
Note If telephoning or faxing the UK from overseas, omit the first 0.

Coromandel (Andrew Brock Travel Ltd) 29a Main St, Lyddington, Oakham, Rutland LE15 9LR; tel: 01572 821330; fax: 01572 821072; email: ABROCK3650@aol.com; www.coromandelabt.com. Offers two tours, including a 17-day car tour.
Magic Carpet 1 Field Close House, Ascot, Berks SL5 9LT; tel: 01344 622832; fax: 01344 626940; email: info@magiccarpettravel.co.uk; www.magic-carpet-travel.com. Offers several escorted group tours each year, as well as tailor-made itineraries. It will also deal with the visa procedure for independent travellers for approximately £85 (see pages 31–3).
Silk Road and Beyond 371 Kensington High St, London W14 8QZ, tel: 020 7371 3131; fax: 020 7602 9715; email: sales@silkroadandbeyond.co.uk; www.silkroadandbeyond.co.uk. Currently offers personal tours for two or more people with three itineraries, with other extension trips possible; also a tour combining Uzbekistan and Turkmenistan with Iran.

There are two new operators:

Adventure Overland 9 Ridge Rd, Mitcham, Surrey CR4 2ET; tel: 020 8640 8105; email: simons@adventureoverland.com; www.adventureland.com
Persian Voyages 12d Rothes Rd, Dorking, Surrey RH4 1JN; tel: 01306 885894; email: info@persianvoyages.com; www.persian voyages.com

Iran
Note If telephoning or faxing from outside Iran, omit the first 0 from the regional code. Despite relatively new regional and city codes, there are no 'official' published telephone directories for Iran, not even for Tehran, and certainly no equivalent of *Yellow Pages*.

Iran Silk Tour and Travel Company (Harir Safar) Unit 4, No 34/20th Alley, Vali-I Asr Av, Tehran; tel: 021 8721155, 8725818; fax: 021 8723904; email: ir_silk@dpimail.net
Iran Tourist Co (Bonyad), 257 Motahari Av, Tehran 15875-6315; tel: 021 8733050, 8739819; fax: 021 8736158; email: info@ irantouristco.com; www.itto.org. Offers two basic itineraries accompanied by a national guide, but willing to customise for groups.
Pasargad Tours 146 Africa Av, Tehran 19156; tel: 021 20588334455; fax: 021 2058866, 2050790; email: info@pasargad-tours.com; www.pasargad-tour.com. All tours are accompanied by a national guide.
Thunder Tour & Travel 488 North Jamalzadeh, Dr Fatemi Av, Tehran 14196; tel: 021 6433677-8; fax: 021 6936526; email: info@thundertour.com; www.thundertour.com. Offers five itineraries including trekking and boating tours; and can also arrange hotel/air/train reservation facilities as well as customise their package for individual travellers, and arrange 'letter of invitation' (see page 31) at nominal cost (waivered if other services supplied). All tours are accompanied by a national guide if required.

Special interest
Association for Cultural Exchange Study Tours Babraham, Cambridge CB2 4AP; tel: 01223 835055; fax: 01223 837394; email: ace@study-tours.org; www.study-tours.org. Currently offers one tour a year with a specialist lecturer/leader.
Martin Randall Travel Voysey House, Barley Mow Passage, London W4 4GF; tel: 020 8742 3355; fax: 020 8742 7766; email: info@martinrandall.co.uk; www.martinrandall.com. Runs one tour a year to Iran with a specialist lecturer/leader.
The Traveller (formerly British Museum Traveller) 92–93 Great Russell St, London WCIB 3PS; tel: 020 7436 9343; fax: 020 7436 7475; email: info@thetraveller2004.com; www.thetraveller2004.com. Offers one or two tours a year to Iran with specialist lecturer and tour manager.

For 'adventure' trips, see below.

Horseriding and trekking
UK
In The Saddle Tel: 01299 272 997; email: rides@inthesaddle.com; www.inthesaddle.com. Deals with Louise Firouz in Iran, who was responsible for establishing studs of Caspian and also Turkoman horses there.

If you wish to combine such a break with a tour, both can be organised through Magic Carpet or Thunder Tour & Travel (see above).

In Iran
The Kassa Company 9 Naghdi Alley, Shariati St, Tehran 15637; tel: 021 7510463; fax: 021 7510464; email: info@kassaco.com; www.mountainzone.ir. Runs field trips

RIDING IN TURKOMAN COUNTRY

Past Gonbad (north-east Iran) and its pencil-shaped tomb-tower of 1006CE, we turn off on to a minor road between flat stubble fields to the ranch: a vision of lean and shining horses of various colours, gently swishing their tails as they take their evening meal in the late afternoon sun. The owner, Louise Firouz, has long experience of Iran, and yet longer of horses. A first night is spent in the cool, secure darkness of the framed felt tent known as an *alajiq* (approximately 'mobile home') with sleeping bag and a layer of padding on a floor-spread of felt. Turkoman horses, for which Louise claims an ancestry as distinguished as that of the Arabians, have been developed into the Akhal Tekke. Those that we meet are eager but well-mannered; they are very willing to get into the smooth trot, which must once have been of great use for raiding parties. However, we begin in walk. I have been allocated Kongur, who has large, kind eyes, a coat of stubble stalks, and a long dark mane. 'Shall we trot?', suggests Kongur. No, we shall not, not yet.

We cross a dusty river bed, and a very small village. There is an introductory canter. Then the path rises by improbably steep fields, some terraced since Parthian times. There are brambles, hawthorns and wild pomegranates. Lunch is nose-bags for our friends and an extended picnic, brought by the support team, under oak trees – too much of this ancient woodland is being sold off to be pulped for paper. We reach a high and partly inhabited summer village. The support lorry has arrived before us and pitched two-person tents with zipped fronts, a communal tent for meals, and at a little distance a latrine-tent discreetly turns its back on the camp but gives on to a superb view. The smiling cook creates a hearty meal on a primus and heats water in metal jugs in the ashes of a fire. We recline on the communal felt, drinking non-alcoholic beer. Then retire to individual tents past picketed and rugged horses. Other days bring canters on open paths, a camp in the green-wood at the source of the Gorgan River, a high prairie scattered with flowers, a Scythian ruin, hills like the Sussex Downs writ-large. We become very much at ease with our individual horses. We also appreciate the kindness of the Turkoman support staff and, round the veil of language, we catch glimpses of their wit.

Comfortable riding clothing is needed with long sleeves and, so far as I am concerned, also a lightweight riding hat. A large cotton-scarf can be draped round the hat to provide some shade or it can do head-scarf duty when necessary. The saddles are substantial and comfortable, but for persons who do not normally ride five hours a day, an extra sheepskin might not come amiss. A switch can be picked from a tree. A torch is useful in the tent, but the starlight is preferable outside.

for the Mountaineering Federation in Tehran, and will organise hill-walking and trekking for foreign visitors (preferably, a minimum of 4 persons). The best time would be in the spring for the wild flowers. The office can arrange bike rental for mountain-biking. Men can wear shorts for this, either knee- or mid-thigh length, but for all trips (except skiing) women must wear full-length trousers (or skirt) and long-sleeved, knee-length shirt or tunic, with, of course, the obligatory scarf. Skiing can also be organised. The office will deal with the visa paperwork for the visit, and reserve any hotel accommodation in Tehran etc. Certainly the managing director answers email enquiries promptly, and Tehran friends recommend the office.

TIME DIFFERENCE

GMT + three hours 30 minutes (ie: 12 noon GMT is 15.30 in Iran). On March 21 until September 21, an hour is 'added' for Iranian summertime, so on some days in September and October, 12 noon GST is 14.30 in Iran. One time zone operates throughout the country. To catch VOA or BBC World Radio news, tune in on the half-hour.

RED TAPE
Visas

The visa procedure has eased considerably over the last five years; now about three weeks are needed for the formalities and, once the all-important reference number has been received by the consulate from Tehran, visas can be issued in 36 hours, perhaps less (in one incredible instance, one hour), *providing* there is no holiday closure (see pages 51–3).

All nationalities except Israelis are allowed to apply for a visa. Anyone domiciled in the USA should approach the Iranian Interests Section of the Pakistani Embassy, Washington DC (or the nearest Pakistani consulate), or the Iranian Mission at the United Nations, New York. Those resident elsewhere, however, including US passport-holders, should contact the Iranian embassy or consulate in their country of residence for information, visa forms etc. Unfortunately, the current information issued both in London and Washington is imprecise, inaccurate and incomplete. Before making a long journey to the office, do request exact opening times/day for the particular service you require, and clarify the methods of payment, and how the documents are to be returned to you. Although the procedure for British and US passport-holders is complex, other nationalities, including those from Germany, the Netherlands, Scandinavia and Italy, have fewer problems in this respect.

Although it is not made clear in the visa information distributed by the Iranian Embassy in London and the office in Washington DC, *note that the Iranian consulate will not permit entry into the building unless lady visitors wear headscarves and, more importantly, will not receive or consider visa applications, whether for tourism or business, until the Tehran Ministry of Foreign Affairs has approved a formal 'invitation' from an Iranian national, company or institution, and issued a reference number to the relevant Iranian consulate.* This invitation has to include certain passport details and other information including the name of the applicant's father.

The most efficient way of getting a **tourist visa** is to contact a travel agent in Iran (see pages 29–30), who will effectively issue an 'invitation' into the country. Either you or your domestic tour operator will need to fax over a copy of the relevant pages of your passport, together with all other travel details, and these documents are then taken by the travel agent to the Foreign Ministry on your behalf. Approval for a visa is usually granted by the Foreign Ministry in Iran within one to two weeks, when a reference number is issued. At this point, the Iranian travel agent will notify you or your tour operator of the approval. On receipt of this notification, you should take your passport to the local consulate, and fill out the application form; a visa is usually issued within a day or so. Payment for the travel agent's service varies, but is usually around US$30–50, and is made to the travel agent on arrival in Iran.

For **business travellers** wishing to stay in Iran for more than 72 hours, their Iranian business contact needs to make an application to the Ministry of Foreign Affairs in Tehran, which will then issue the essential reference number to the Iranian embassy in the country concerned, after which the visa procedure outlined below will kick in. For stays of less than 72 hours, the Iranian business contact still has to apply to the ministry for approval and a reference number, but the traveller then picks up the relevant 72-hour visa on arrival at Mehrabad Airport, Tehran, immediately to the left of the passport hall; at the time of writing, the visa fee for 72-hour British business travellers is the US$ equivalent of £40 sterling, payable at the adjacent bank counter. Remember to take a photocopy of the relevant visa notification for the airline check-in desk, to prove that your entry has been approved.

Only when the reference number has been received will the embassy staff accept the visa application form, photographs and passport. It sounds horrendously complicated but it isn't (unless you hit a cluster of national and religious holidays), though a few extra grey hairs are guaranteed. With other Iranian consulates, this system is not necessarily in operation. In Holland, for example, applicants may write to the consulate requesting a visa without an 'invitation', though apparently less than 50% of such unsupported applications are successful.

For the actual visa application, a completed visa form with two photographs, the passport (valid for six months from date of departure, with at least two blank pages and containing no evidence of visiting Israel) and fee (UK citizens from £40; US citizens applying in USA, from US$50 non-returnable but may be waived if resident abroad) need to be sent in to your nearest Iranian consulate. Female applicants should wear a headscarf for their visa photographs. Visas are valid for one month's duration after entry. A request for a multiple-entry visa has to be submitted by the sponsor in the 'invitation', not by the applicant at the consulate.

For the duration of your stay in Iran, you remain the 'invited guest' of the person, company, or institution who/which initiated the procedure. In other words, that sponsor bears total responsibility for your well-being and good behaviour and will bear the brunt of any repercussion.

For a visa extension or amendment, go to the relevant local government office (in Tehran this is the Ministry of Foreign Affairs; outside Tehran go to the local police headquarters) with at least one photograph (bescarved for women). For another extension, reapply to that same office as the relevant files will still be there. Be warned that any dealing with officialdom will take at least three times longer than you could imagine (see pages 51–3 and 59).

There is a visa waiver system in operation for Kish Island (see pages 215–16) but it is valid only for Kish with no opportunity to extend or alter the visa for travel on the mainland.

Be warned: Westerners turning up at an Iranian border cannot expect to be issued with a visa (even a five-day transit) over the counter. Stories of successful individual travellers should be rigorously investigated, rather than accepted at face value. In one publicised case, a Dutch tourist travelled to Turkey believing that she could obtain an Iranian visa there quickly and cheaply. In Istanbul she was directed to Erzerum 1,220km away, where she was correctly informed that the Iranian Embassy in Ankara (877km, back-tracking) had sole issuing authorisation in Turkey; there she was told processing would take more than four weeks after the surrender of her passport.

Note: Any woman, whatever her nationality, will be refused actual entry into Iran if her dress does not conform to acceptable standards (see *Dress* for details, page 63). This 'suitable' dress and a headscarf must be donned before approaching the border or disembarking from a flight and retained until leaving Iran. If travelling by an IranAir international flight to Iran, ladies check in wearing or showing a headscarf, which can then be removed until entering the boarding lounge; in other words, the IranAir flight is considered as Iranian territory.

Iranian representation overseas

Embassy of Islamic Republic of Iran, UK 50 Kensington Court, London W8 5DB; tel: 020 7937 5225; fax: 020 7938 1615; www.itto.org/. Not a user-friendly system, it is well-nigh impossible to get past the telephone automated answer response.

Iranian Mission, USA United Nations Building, New York, NY; tel: 212 687 2020 or 2209 Wisconsin Avenue NW, Washington DC 20007; tel: 202 965 4990; fax: 202 965 1073.

GETTING THERE AND AWAY

On arrival, an **immigration form** must be completed (you retain the pink carbon copy until leaving Iran), and a simple customs declaration form which is surrendered to customs officers. The main international airport in Iran is currently Mehrabad Airport, Tehran, but foreigners with valid visas can also enter/exit Iran by way of various Arab Gulf states eg: Abu Dhabi and Bahrain to Shiraz, Bahrain to Mashhad, Dubai to Ahvaz and Bandar-i Abbas airports. Sometimes the exit guards check your baggage check-in tag with that on your luggage. (For transport from Tehran Mehrabad Airport into the centre, see *Taxis*, page 70.) The same procedure is followed at the land frontiers.

By air

Direct and indirect flights operate from the UK, but there are presently no direct flights from or to any American or Canadian airports. Remember to reconfirm your flight 72 hours before departure.

IranAir Most of the aircraft used on domestic IranAir flights are nearing the end of their serviceable life, especially those purchased from ex-Soviet republics whose service history cannot be guaranteed. The last major crash was in February 2004, when a Kish Airflight came down, killing everyone on board. Think twice about using any non-Boeing, non-McDonnell Douglas or non-Fokker plane for internal flights. Note that no alcohol is permitted on board, and that women should dress suitably (see page 33). The airline's website, www.iranair.com, is not particularly helpful.

British Airways (www.ba.com) Currently five flights a week (Mon, Tue, Thu, Fri, Sat) direct from London Heathrow to Tehran

KLM (www.klm.com) via Amsterdam, with Air UK flights from various British airports to Amsterdam

Gulf Air (www.gulfairco.com) London Heathrow – Bahrain – Tehran

Turkish Airlines (www.turkishairlines.com) London Heathrow – Istanbul – Tehran

Air France (www.airfrance.com/uk) London (various airports) – Paris – Tehran

Emirates (www.emirates.com) London Heathrow – Dubai – Tehran

In 2005, a new company, Mahan Airlines (tel: 0121 554 1555; www.mahan-airlines.com) commenced flights to Tehran out of Birmingham International, UK.

By road

There are border-crossing points from Turkey (via Dogubayezit); from the Republic of Azerbaijan (via Baku/Astara); from Turkmenistan (via Ashkhabad, or Sarakhs); and from Pakistan, though the latter is not advisable at present. You can get only a five-day transit visa at the border; a tourist visa must be obtained in advance. For documentation required, see pages 31–3 and 45.

By train

From Pakistan; reportedly also from Moscow. Current details have proved impossible to obtain. Despite reports to the contrary it is not viable to cross by train from Turkey – cross the border by car or taxi to Tabriz, then take a train from there. In 2001 the Syrian press reported that a weekly rail service from Damascus to Tehran, via Mosul and Tabriz, had been re-established, but given the present security situation in northern Iraq, and the Iranian government's attitude towards the American presence in Iraq, this form of transport cannot be guaranteed hassle-free for foreigners.

There are rumours that a measure of privatisation of Iranian railways will be soon allowed but this could result in even less control over the haulage of hazardous materials; in February 2004 a train derailment and explosion near Nishapur left almost 300 people dead and a 50m-deep crater.

By sea
From Dubai, with boats docking at Bandar-i Abbas. There are no published schedules, so prospective travellers need to ask around once in Dubai.

HEALTH
with Dr Felicity Nicholson
Before you go
It is advisable to be immunised against typhoid, meningitis, polio, tetanus, diphtheria and hepatitis A; two doses of hepatitis A vaccine given 6–12 months apart lasts for 20 years. For a long stay consider vaccinations against tuberculosis. Visit your doctor or a recognised travel clinic (see below) around eight weeks before you leave.

As on any trip a small medical kit is useful. Do include some oral rehydration powders (eg: Electrolade) in case of diarrhoea, which is a common complaint among hot and tired travellers. Imodium and Lomotil are recognised standbys and the smallness of codeine phosphate tablets is advantageous if you also suffer vomiting. If symptoms persist and/or you have a fever and/or blood in the stool, do seek medical advice. Although the temptation is to keep fluid intake down to a minimum, especially if you have a lengthy bus journey ahead, this can quickly lead to dehydration. Hot tea, the local cola drink, yoghurt and plain rice – and don't neglect salt – will help to replace the missing elements.

If travelling in the Caspian region and southern Iran, consider taking anti-malaria tablets. Consult a doctor for the best advice as to which tablet to take. To minimise the risk of nausea, try taking the tablets in the evening with food. Insect repellents and cover-up clothing can help ward off voracious mosquitoes. Maria O'Shea, author of *Culture Shock – Iran*, suggests lavender oil or citronella oil as excellent and safe insect repellents for children and pregnant women, or for people with sensitive skin who cannot tolerate DEET-based products (eg: Repel). Mosquito coils and the like can be purchased everywhere. Regarding other insects, avoid flea-pit hotels and very cheap local buses; saving a few dollars can result in great discomfort.

As in western Europe there is a danger of rabies. Few dogs in Iran are kept as pets, so they are not domesticated in the same way as in Europe or North America. In particular, avoid sheepdogs as they are trained to see off unwelcome guests. Stand still and if necessary make as if you are throwing a stone in their direction, shouting angrily. If you intend to spend a long time travelling or are staying in rural areas, consider having a course of rabies shots before departure. Ideally three doses of vaccine should be given over four weeks, so careful planning before your trip is required. If you are bitten, regardless of whether you have been vaccinated or not, wash the wound in soap and water, apply antiseptic and seek medical help as soon as possible.

Travel clinics and health information
A full list of current travel clinic websites worldwide is available on www.istm.org/. For other journey preparation information, consult www.tripprep.com. Information about various medications may be found on www.emedicine.com.

UK

Berkeley Travel Clinic 32 Berkeley St, London W1J 8EL (near Green Park tube station); tel: 020 7629 6233

British Airways Travel Clinic and Immunisation Service There are two BA clinics in London, both on tel: 0845 600 2236; www.ba.com/travelclinics. Appointments only (Mon–Fri 9.00–16.30) at 101 Cheapside, London EC2V 6DT; or walk-in service Mon–Fri 09.30–17.30, Sat 10.00–16.00 at 213 Piccadilly, London W1J 9HQ. Apart from providing inoculations and malaria prevention, they sell a variety of health-related goods.

Edinburgh Travel Clinic Regional Infectious Diseases Unit, Ward 41 OPD, Western General Hospital, Crewe Rd South, Edinburgh EH4 2UX; tel: 0131 537 2822; www.link.med.ed.ac.uk/ridu. Travel helpline (0906 589 0380) open 09.00–12.00 weekdays. Provides inoculations and anti-malarial prophylaxis and advises on travel-related health risks.

Fleet Street Travel Clinic 29 Fleet St, London EC4Y 1AA; tel: 020 7353 5678; www.fleetstreetclinic.com. Vaccinations, travel products and latest advice.

Hospital for Tropical Diseases Travel Clinic Mortimer Market Building, Capper St (off Tottenham Ct Rd), London WC1E 6AU; tel: 020 7388 9600; www.thehtd.org. Offers consultations and advice, and is able to provide all necessary drugs and vaccines for travellers. Runs a healthline (09061 337733) for country-specific information and health hazards. Also stocks nets, water purification equipment and personal protection measures.

LONG-HAUL FLIGHTS
Dr Felicity Nicholson

There is growing evidence, albeit circumstantial, that long-haul air travel increases the risk of developing deep vein thrombosis. This condition is potentially life threatening, but it should be stressed that the danger to the average traveller is slight.

Certain risk factors specific to air travel have been identified. These include immobility, compression of the veins at the back of the knee by the edge of the seat, the decreased air pressure and slightly reduced oxygen in the cabin, and dehydration. Consuming alcohol may exacerbate the situation by increasing fluid loss and encouraging immobility.

In theory everyone is at risk, but those at highest risk are shown below:

- Passengers on journeys of longer than eight hours duration
- People over 40
- People with heart disease
- People with cancer
- People with clotting disorders
- People who have had recent surgery, especially on the legs
- Women on the pill or other oestrogen therapy
- Women who are pregnant
- People who are very tall (over 6ft/1.8m) or short (under 5ft/1.5m)

A deep vein thrombosis (DVT) is a clot of blood that forms in the leg veins. Symptoms include swelling and pain in the calf or thigh. The skin may feel

Interhealth Worldwide Partnership House, 157 Waterloo Rd, London SE1 8US; tel: 020 7902 9000; www.interhealth.org.uk. Competitively priced, one-stop travel health service. All profits go to their affiliated company, InterHealth, which provides health care for overseas workers on Christian projects.

MASTA (Medical Advisory Service for Travellers Abroad) London School of Hygiene and Tropical Medicine, Keppel St, London WC1 7HT; tel: 09065 501402; www.masta.org. Individually tailored health briefs available for a fee, with up-to-date information on how to stay healthy, inoculations and what to bring. There are currently 30 MASTA pre-travel clinics in Britain. Call 0870 241 6843 or check online for the nearest. Clinics also sell malaria prophylaxis memory cards, treatment kits, bednets, etc.

NHS travel website, www.fitfortravel.scot.nhs.uk, provides country-by-country advice on immunisation and malaria, plus details of recent developments, and a list of relevant health organisations.

Nomad Travel Store/Clinic 3–4 Wellington Terrace, Turnpike Lane, London N8 0PX; tel: 020 8889 7014; travel-health line (office hours only) 09068 633414; email: sales@nomadtravel.co.uk; www.nomadtravel.co.uk. Also at 40 Bernard St, London WC1N 1LJ; tel: 020 7833 4114; 52 Grosvenor Gardens, London SW1W 0AG; 020 7823 5823; and 43 Queens Rd, Bristol BS8 1QH; tel: 0117 922 6567. For health advice, equipment such as mosquito nets and other anti-bug devices, and an excellent range of adventure travel gear.

---

hot to touch and becomes discoloured (light blue-red). A DVT is not dangerous in itself, but if a clot breaks down then it may travel to the lungs (pulmonary embolus). Symptoms of a pulmonary embolus (PE) include chest pain, shortness of breath and coughing up small amounts of blood.

Symptoms of a DVT rarely occur during the flight, and typically occur within three days of arrival, although symptoms of a DVT or PE have been reported up to two weeks later.

Anyone who suspects that they have these symptoms should see a doctor immediately as anticoagulation (blood-thinning) treatment can be given.

Prevention of DVT
General measures to reduce the risk of thrombosis are shown below. This advice also applies to long train or bus journeys.

• Whilst waiting to board the plane, try to walk around rather than sit.
• During the flight drink plenty of water (at least two small glasses every hour).
• Avoid excessive tea, coffee and alcohol.
• Perform leg-stretching exercises, such as pointing the toes up and down.
• Move around the cabin when practicable.

If you fit into the high-risk category (see above) ask your doctor if it is safe to travel. Additional protective measures such as graded compression stockings, aspirin or low molecular weight heparin can be given. No matter how tall you are, where possible request a seat with extra legroom.

Trailfinders Travel Clinic 194 Kensington High St, London W8 7RG; tel: 020 7938 3999; www.trailfinders.com/clinic.htm
Cambridge Travel Clinic 48a Mill Rd, Cambridge CB1 2AS; tel: 01223 367362; email: enquiries@cambridgetravelclinic.co.uk; www.cambridgetravelclinic.co.uk. Open 12.00–19.00 Tue–Fri, 10.00–16.00 Sat.
Travelpharm The Travelpharm website, www.travelpharm.com, offers up-to-date guidance on travel-related health and has a range of medications available through their online mini-pharmacy.

Irish Republic
Tropical Medical Bureau Grafton Street Medical Centre, Grafton Buildings, 34 Grafton St, Dublin 2; tel: 1 671 9200; www.tmb.ie. A useful website specific to tropical destinations. Also check website for other bureaux locations throughout Ireland.

USA
Centers for Disease Control 1600 Clifton Rd, Atlanta, GA 30333; tel: 800 311 3435; travellers' health hotline 888 232 3299; www.cdc.gov/travel. The central source of travel information in the USA. The invaluable Health Information for International Travel, published annually, is available from the Division of Quarantine at this address.
Connaught Laboratories PO Box 187, Swiftwater, PA 18370; tel: 800 822 2463. They will send a free list of specialist tropical-medicine physicians in your state.
IAMAT (International Association for Medical Assistance to Travelers) 1623 Military Rd, 279, Niagara Falls, NY14304-1745; tel: 716 754 4883; email: info@iamat.org; www.iamat.org. A non-profit organisation that provides lists of English-speaking doctors abroad.
International Medicine Center 920 Frostwood Drive, Suite 670, Houston, TX 77024; tel: 713 550 2000; www.traveldoc.com.

Canada
IAMAT Suite 1, 1287 St Clair Av W, Toronto, Ontario M6E 1B8; tel: 416 652 0137; www.iamat.org
TMVC (Travel Doctors Group) Sulphur Springs Rd, Ancaster, Ontario; tel: 905 648 1112; www.tmvc-group.com/ancaster.hotml.

Australia, New Zealand, Singapore
TMVC Tel: 1300 65 88 44; www.tmvc.com.au. Twenty-three clinics in Australia, New Zealand and Singapore including:
Auckland Canterbury Arcade, 170 Queen St, Auckland; tel: 9 373 3531
Brisbane 6th floor, 247 Adelaide St, Brisbane, QLD 4000; tel: 7 3221 9066
Melbourne 393 Little Bourke St, 2nd floor, Melbourne, VIC 3000; tel: 3 9602 5788
Sydney Dymocks Building, 7th Floor, 428 George St, Sydney, NSW 2000; tel: 2 9221 7133
IAMAT PO Box 5049, Christchurch 5, New Zealand; www.iamat.org

South Africa
SAA-Netcare Travel Clinics Private Bag X34, Benmore 2010; www.travelclinic.co.za. Clinics throughout South Africa.

TMVC 113 DF Malan Drive, Roosevelt Park, Johannesburg; tel: 011 888 7488; www.tmvc.com.au. Consult the website for details of eight other clinics in South Africa.

Switzerland
IAMAT 57 Chemin des Voirets, 1212 Grand Lancy, Geneva; www.iamat.org

In Iran
In the major cities, the **water** is safe for cleaning teeth but as it is heavily chlorinated (neighbouring Tajikistan and Afghanistan suffer cholera outbreaks) you will probably prefer to drink bottled water.

Opportunities to strip off and sunbathe are obviously severely limited in the Islamic Republic, but the force of the Iranian sun is powerful and there is comparatively little shade so avoid excessive exertion during midday hours and wear a sunhat. Women should wear theirs over a scarf. Clothing in natural fibres is most comfortable for the hotter months but evening temperatures can drop suddenly, especially in the hills, so take a light sweater too.

Take usual precautions when walking across rough and stony ground, and through shrubbery and vegetation, against snakes, scorpions etc. It can happen to you. If you are entering a ruined building from broad sunlight, make a noise so that any snakes retreat.

Medical facilities
Every major hotel in the main Iranian cities has doctors or paramedics on call; otherwise, any business contact or friend, or your embassy, will recommend a doctor or dentist. Note that few dentists operate during the 28 days of Ramadan. The hospitals are good, as I can attest, but somewhat basic by Western standards and few medical staff have had any opportunity to study in the West. The Iranian authorities give international 24-hour medical emergency services every assistance, but American citizens should be aware that the current US embargo could be problematic for credit-card payments.

Even small towns have well-stocked pharmacies as Iranians vie with the Lebanese as the world's worst hypochondriacs. That said, take adequate supplies of any prescribed drug you need, or at least full details, so the best equivalent can be traced, because most Western brands are not available.

SAFETY
Crime
Any crime carries severe penalties in the Islamic Republic. It is likely that the greatest danger you face (other than crossing the road – see below) is having your wallet, purse or camera snatched, especially in Isfahan. Keep photocopies of the most important pages (including the visa if possible) of your passport and air ticket, and spare passport photos separately, and don't flash money or expensive camera equipment ostentatiously. The British Foreign and Commonwealth Office has warned that bogus policemen had approached

A BUSINESSMAN'S VIEW
'Fluvius'

One of the perks of being a businessman involved in overseas work is that glowing feeling that someone else is paying for the travel and accommodation. Even better when the destination is unusual and redolent of the mysteries of far-away lands. Iran will not disappoint the sentient traveller: it has a rich history and cultural traditions. Above all, it is very different from Europe and America. Scratch beneath the surface of modernism and you will find a world of cultural nuance, literary allusion and a history to match any, involving the sweeps of empire and transition.

There are several issues of business culture in Iran to rapidly absorb. In general, overseas business travellers may talk of prevarication as an artform in the Middle East but it will mostly come down to doing the homework about what the client requires and whether there are funds in hand. Business in Iran is booming and contracts are being placed all the time so somewhere the prevarication is replaced by action. The savvy will be able to spot the drift of an opportunity by asking firm questions and getting their Iranian counterparts to follow agendas and sign minutes of meetings. Politeness and warm greetings are no substitute for serious and contested negotiations. As a measure of development of the business, the strength of the discussions, as opposed to mere civility, will tell the businessman he is on the right track.

Iranians are practised negotiators from birth. Children will be seen haggling over prices in the corner grocery store. Negotiation is a national sport that most Iranians love. It is a highly entertaining form of conversational jousting with (often) considerable humour. Just listening to two Iranians twist and turn to gain the upper hand in settling a price is a house of delight and they love it themselves. So the overseas businessman brought up on fixed prices and glacial or bored stares from shop assistants is an innocent waiting to arrive.

some visiting foreigners, advising that in such circumstances you should insist on seeing an identity card and inform the restaurant, shop or hotel of the incident. Remember that no Iranian policeman has the right to take or retain your passport unless you are in a police station.

Iran is very safe for women travellers. Harassment is now minimal, especially if you wear the *manteau*, as it is assumed you are Iranian and/or Muslim. But be aware that it is very unusual for a single woman to walk unescorted in public at night.

Road safety

You are more likely to be in danger if you insist on importing your car. There were 19,000 road deaths and over 70,000 injuries reported in Iran in 1999.

The overseas businessman must prepare for this sport. Practise a sour or disappointed look at the first mention of a discount. Work at this in front of the mirror. Until tears roll down your cheeks looking at your reflection, you still have not practised enough. Even with this new skill you will need resilience, patience and determination.

The business traveller should be aware that the Iranian authorities take a dim view of foreign travellers wandering off to remote and possible sensitive spots such as border regions. Stick to the beaten path of tourism; it is not overly patronised, contains plenty of interest and means you avoid coming under suspicion.

Other helpful hints (purely on the basis of serendipity) would be:

- Always look both ways before crossing a one-way street.
- Do not believe zebra crossings are there for the pedestrian to cross unharmed.
- Do not blow your nose in public.
- However inappropriate for the weather, wear a collar and tie as far as possible, because it fits the Iranian idea of a foreign male businessman.
- Men should not try to shake the hand of a woman in public.
- Catch up on some good reading.
- Be careful where you take photographs.

Most of all I would recommend that the businessman should expect to be surprised. We all get jaded travelling around the world from one concrete and glass bunker to another but Iran will definitely not be like that. Try the local food (apart from the delicious kebabs) and fruit juices, and revel in the difference. Think of The Priory but without obnoxious and preening celebrities, and with the added bonus of being cheaper.

This guide outlines so many fascinating places to see around Iran and hopefully the business traveller can be encouraged to experience some of them.

Leaving aside the nightmare of Tehran traffic, which guarantees road rage and ulcers, be aware that Iranian lorry and coach drivers work very long hours, few private vehicles have reflectors or working lights and their drivers disregard every rule in the book. Traffic does not necessarily stop at a red light, nor wait until green before setting off. Regard zebra crossings as merely road surface decorations. Pedestrians take their life into their own hands crossing the road and the sight of their terror-stricken faces forms the chief entertainment for motorists. If a driver flashes his/her lights it does *not* mean it is safe to cross; your presence is being acknowledged, but not necessarily your continued existence on this Earth. On the other hand, having started to cross, do not turn tail or break into a run; both actions constitute a personal challenge to the driver to continue the pursuit.

Personal conduct

Be aware that it is easy to break an important social convention without realising it and this can affect your safety (see *Travelling around*, and *Cultural dos & don'ts* below). Did you know, for instance that in summer 2004, the smoking of 'hubble-bubble' water pipes in public was banned on the grounds that it promoted 'licentious behaviour'?

If you are confronted with officialdom, do not lose your temper, do not shout, do not threaten. Be polite, apologetic if not abject. Ladies, forget all feminist scruples and cry. Always insist on seeing someone who speaks English (any other Western language will be difficult).

WHAT TO TAKE (see also page 63)

As the authorities identify backpacks with amoral behaviour, drug taking and the like, it is advisable to use a **case** or **bag** to avoid misunderstanding. Luggage has to be securely locked for intercity bus trips and internal flights, and padlocks are readily available. A **torch** is useful for exploring ruined buildings etc, and because street lighting is erratic. The water is heavily chlorinated and very hard; a **moisturising cream** may sound effeminate but is a godsend, as is **lipsalve**. As Muslim law stipulates washing under running water, bath and basin **plugs** are not usually provided. For the same reason, **toilet paper** is usually found only in the better hotels and restaurants (to be deposited in waste-paper bins, as Iranian soil pipes have small diameters); you may not fancy using the toilet's cold-water douche. Feminine **sanitary products** are expensive and difficult to obtain outside urban centres. Take an electrical **plug adaptor**; the voltage is usually 220 and the plug is the two-pin rounded variety as found in France (though at least one Tehran hotel has been refurbished with three-pin square plugs). **Camera** batteries and slide (*diapositive*) films are difficult to find (see pages 60–1). Don't forget **sunglasses** and extra supplies of **prescribed medication** (see page 35 on).

Where possible, in Part Two of this guide I have given Koranic references for building inscriptions (I like knowing what the calligraphy says), so if you share this interest pack a **translation of the Koran**; paperback versions with chapter/verse notation are in print.

Lastly, because you will meet friendliness and kindness throughout Iran, why not take some local **postcards** from home to give as small mementos? They give pleasure to adults and children alike.

WEIGHTS AND MEASURES

Visitors need only to use the metric system.

MONEY AND BANKING

Currently it is forbidden to import and/or export Iranian rials. A single fixed exchange rate is in operation; around 8,850 rials to US$1 and 11,500 rials to €1 in February 2005. Notes are printed in denominations of 20,000, 10,000, 5,000, 2,000, 1,000, 500 and 200, and coins 250, 100, 50 and 10. Although the rial is the stated currency, Iranians frequently refer to tuman (ie: 10 rials) thus something priced as 100 rials is generally spoken of as costing 10 tumans, so *do clarify* before agreeing to purchase. Having a calculator to hand is useful so price negotiations between you and the vendor can quickly and easily be communicated. For small purchases such as fruit, nuts and so on a basic recognition of Farsi numeral symbols is useful (page 265).

Presently no currency declaration form is required from foreign visitors (but official rules and regulations change constantly), but independent and business travellers need to show a bank currency exchange receipt for payment of all hotel charges, flight ticket payments etc which are calculated in US dollars. A dual pricing system operates in major hotels whereby Iranian nationals (whose salaries are very low by Western standards) pay less than foreigners who pay in US$. At the time of writing, an IranAir international flight ticket purchased abroad in hard currency entitles the purchaser to one free internal flight booked at the same time. Officially the exchange regulations are identical for each hotel, but until recently there have been differences in how the official exchange rate is calculated.

Euros, Japanese yen and occasionally UK sterling are accepted, but generally only in the bank branches located in the best hotels in the largest cities; US dollars, on the other hand, are welcome everywhere. **Travellers' cheques** (but not those of American banks; remember the embargo!) can in theory be exchanged, but generally only at the largest hotel banks in the main centres, where a 4% commission is levied. Neither travellers' cheques nor credit cards are now directly accepted by hotels for payment of accommodation, meals etc; the payment must be in cash (changing the travellers' cheques at the hotel bank, for instance) or on account with an Iranian company. Short-stay visitors will find it much easier to take quantities of US dollars in cash, in small denominations. Memories of the large-scale forgery of dollar bills in ex-Soviet territories in the early 1990s still linger, so new bills are preferred. **Credit cards** such as Mastercard (excluding American Express and Visa because of the US embargo) can be used for major purchases such as carpets, but billing may be processed through Dubai, Switzerland or Germany. There are no ATM machines available for transactions involving foreign bank accounts.

Changing money at Tehran Airport on arrival in the baggage hall is possible if the bank is open and the queue minimal. However, it is better to use a hotel bank as the staff are well versed in dealing with visitors and use the minimum of paperwork. Bank working hours are generally 08.00 to 16.00 (closed Thursday afternoon and all day Friday), but are erratic during **public holidays**; banks in hotels have more limited opening times. If a lengthy holiday is approaching, get enough rials to see you through.

Using the free-market exchange (black market) is not advisable for foreign visitors and currently there is no great difference in rates (eg: US$1 = 8,850 rials official rate, to 8,950 unofficial). Don't accept offers to change money from strangers on the street. Money transfers from abroad to an Iranian bank can be arranged, but friends or traders might be able to recommend someone who can organise a transfer more efficiently.

BUDGETING

The following is a rough approximation of a daily budget for a single independent traveller, who has not prepaid for any domestic travel and hotel/meal arrrangements, intending to visit one important and a minor tourist site each day. Note that stays, meals and visits in tourist centres such as Tehran, Isfahan and Shiraz will be more expensive than in other less-visited towns.

As of July 2004, site/museum charges were slashed for foreigners who were previously charged much more than domestic visitors; for instance in 2003, entry to the Carpet Museum in Tehran was 30,000 rials but is now 3,000 rials. It is unclear how long this directive will remain in force and at the time of writing, certain sites not under the authority of the ICHO (Iranian Cultural and Heritage Organisation) are retaining the former charges.

Hotel overnight	US$40
plus 15% service and 2% tax	US$7
Three meals, including 15% tax and 5% gratuity	US$18
Transport (eg: intercity bus, or half-day taxi)	US$12
Site/museum charges	US$1
Other (eg: soft drinks, tips to mosque guardians, laundry)	US$4
Total	US$82

OTHER EXPORT AND IMPORT RESTRICTIONS

Apart from currency restrictions, the export of **gold** over 150gm in weight, antiques (interpreted as items over 50 years old) and certain electrical goods is technically forbidden. Some export restrictions remain on **carpets** and rugs, largely relating to the place of production, size (totalling a maximum of 12m^2) and value. If you are with a travel company, the Iranian guide will advise; otherwise it is best to have a friend or colleague accompany you to the airport so that, if the customs officials object, you can hand the offending article to your friend and try another time. The duty-free section on departure from Tehran's Mehrabad Airport was enlarged as of Spring 2000; good buys are art or history books published in Iran, cassettes, Iranian caviar, and American cigarettes; all purchases are priced in US$ and in *rials*. As of March 2000, the US government modified its **D'Amato sanctions** so that the US importation of Iranian caviar, carpets and nuts, including pistachios, is now permitted.

Concerning imports into Iran, the usual restrictions on narcotics, weapons and pornographic material such as videos, tapes and books etc apply, but the customs officer's definition of pornography can be at Louisa Allcott's *Little Women* level if you prove irritating. Leave any lurid dustjackets at home. In 1999 camcorders and/or video cameras had to be declared at point of entry/exit, and although the custom officers are totally disinterested, be aware this ruling is theoretically still in force. No alcohol may be imported into the Islamic Republic of Iran, even for private use; if supplies are found in your baggage you, your companions and your sponsor will suffer.

If importing your **car** temporarily, you will need a current international driving licence, a *carnet de passage*, car registration, third party insurance (valid for Iran), a nationality badge, a red warning triangle and spare parts. As second-hand cars change hands in Iran for almost the same price as a new car, Iranian customs officials will not believe any story of theft or vehicle write-off unless you have proof. They will assume you have sold it and fine you accordingly.

GETTING AROUND

On all forms of public transport except planes and the Tehran Metro men will probably be asked to change their seats to avoid sitting by female strangers. Note that costs given are approximate.

City transport

Tickets (200 rials for single direct journey) for **public buses** are purchased before boarding, at kiosks and/or shops nearby. Sometimes more than one ticket is required for one journey. This should be given to the driver, which is easy for men who get on by the driver, but impossible for women who enter by the back door as they must avoid brushing past male passengers. If travelling with a companion of the opposite sex, agree beforehand on a meeting place as you may well get separated in the crush. A Tehran trolleybus service operates between Imam Hoseyn Maydan and the eastern bus terminal. *Taxi khatteh,* the equivalent of the Turkish *dolmus* (shared taxi or minibus), operates on agreed routes within towns, and also in the outskirts; you pay the assistant. The Tehran Metro is at last operating with cheap, clean double-decker Chinese trains between Karaj and Azadi Square; and the underground Metro between Azadi Square and Sade Ghiyeh near the bazaar opened a few years ago (see page 70).

Private **taxis** are hailed from the roadside, and it's best to use the locally registered ones (eg: white and green taxis in Shiraz). As the driver swerves towards you, yell out your destination; if he brakes, he's willing to go that way. Before the journey, ask colleagues or hotel staff the approximate cost of the journey and get written or verbal directions, unless the ride is to a notable landmark; taxi drivers do not undergo the same rigorous tests as, say, London cabbies. Outside Tehran do consider hiring a taxi for a day or half-day, especially in Ahvaz, Isfahan, Mashhad or Shiraz, as it is the cheapest, most convenient form of transport offering freedom of routes and stops.

A private taxi from Mehrabad Airport into the centre should cost approximately 25,000 rials (US$3) but there are 'shared' taxis at 5,000 rials per person, prepaid at the taxi kiosk. Do *not* accept lifts in 'unofficial' taxis.

By intercity road transport

There are usually two types of bus service, first and second class. The price difference is neglible but the level of comfort isn't; treat yourself. The 895km drive from Shiraz to Tehran by 'deluxe' Volvo costs 66,000 rials (US$7.50). Seats are numbered and assigned according to gender or family groups, with smokers at the back. Tickets are purchased up to a week in advance from the bus station or bus company's city office, with three or four departures an hour on the busiest routes, although there are no timetables in circulation. During *Ramadan* and *Nou Rouz*, reservations must be made well in advance. The bus terminal (with toilets located near the *namaz-khaneh* or prayer room) is generally located on the outskirts of town but large cities such as Tehran have more than one, so check from which terminal the bus departs. Short stops are made every five or six hours (ensure you know the departure time) but it's best to take some food/drink with you. As in pre-revolutionary times, all public vehicles have to register at the police control points entering and leaving city limits, so carry your passport in hand-luggage in case it is required. All luggage going into the baggage holds should be padlocked.

By rail

There are three main (overnight) services: Tehran–Mashhad, Tehran–Tabriz and Tehran–Isfahan–Kirman. As with intercity buses the price difference between first and second class is minimal but the standard of comfort isn't. A single ticket from Tehran to Mashhad costs approximately 35,000 to 150,000 rials (US$4 to US$17.50), depending on the service; and Tehran to Tabriz, which costs approximately 60,000 rials (US$7); a train ticket from Isfahan to Mashhad will set you back 85,000 rials (US$10). The service isn't fast and the timings of arrival/departure are often inconvenient. Tickets are sold from the main-line station up to two weeks in advance, and queuing to buy a ticket is a supreme test of patience and physical endurance, so think of approaching a travel agent to organise this.

It is unclear whether the weekly rail link to/from Damascus, Syria, via Mosul and Tabriz (see page 34) is available for foreign passenger use, given the security situation in northern Iraq.

By air

As a result of the continuing D'Amato trade embargo, there has been a problem obtaining spares and replacement parts. Much of the domestic air fleet is reaching the end of its serviceable life and while the Boeing and Fokker planes are well maintained, those craft purchased from ex-Soviet territories often possess a less reliable service history.

Currently, if you use IranAir for your international flight to Iran, one free internal flight is allowed. This sounds generous but a one-way ticket from Shiraz to Tehran costs approx US$26, and from Yazd to Tehran US$22. To purchase a domestic flight ticket in Iran, you will need to book some time in advance, taking your passport and payment in *rials* along with a bank exchange receipt. Organising this takes time and patience so, unless you have time to waste, consider booking in advance (eg: through Magic Carpet Travel) or using an agent such as Thunder Tour (see page 29) who will keep the booking active. Otherwise, remember to confirm and reconfirm your ticket at the local IranAir office. Allow plenty of time to get to the airport (particularly in Tehran where traffic is frequently gridlocked) and to check in. On entry to any airport terminal building there is a security check: men with all their baggage go through one door, and 'sisters' with theirs through another. At the check-in desk abandon any idea of polite queuing; block all-comers and use elbows forcibly. You may be required to show your passport on passing to the next security check – again arranged according to gender – leading to the departure lounge.

An airport porter will expect at least 2,500 rials per case to/from the baggage hall and car or taxi, and more if he is required to 'negotiate' with the authorities on your behalf.

By private car

At present there is no car rental system available in Iran, but a driver and car can be hired for a day or longer (see pages 116–17 and 248) through a travel agent or a good hotel. Even with experience of Beirut, I would not choose to drive in Iranian cities, especially Tehran. That said, the roads are well engineered with very few potholes, but road signs (in both Farsi and the Roman alphabets) are few and far between, as are petrol stations. Motor spares, especially for foreign-made cars, are difficult to find (the US embargo again) even in the main urban centres. Petrol station toilets are usually poor; more preferable are *namaz-khaneh* (road-side prayer room) washrooms.

It is compulsory to wear seat belts, although many drivers and front-seat passengers don't. Speed limits are in operation, at least in theory: 110km/h on motorways, and 80km/h at night; some roads have speed cameras in operation. Some towns operate commercial vehicle and/or bus drive zones, and police seem to operate on a fine-incentive system; in 1999 the Isfahani traffic police happily booked every tourist bus picking up/setting down passengers by the Abbasi Hotel. Driving at night is extremely hazardous (see pages 40–1). If you break down, display the red warning triangle some distance behind the car, and ask passing vehicles to summon police, garage assistance or both. As the driver, do not even think of leaving the scene of any accident before police agree to you departing. Any incident involving a person will probably mean imprisonment until the matter is investigated, especially if it resulted in a fatality; financial compensation of up to US$50,000 will have to be deposited for possible payment to the victim's family *before* any release can be contemplated. If your car is badly damaged, obtain an official report (especially necessary for the frontier customs if you have imported it; see page 45).

The emergency police number is 110. Traffic police have white caps, and their cars are white with a blue stripe.

ACCOMMODATION

In 2003 there was a 35% hike in hotel prices and every autumn the hotels are officially instructed of the new room rates for foreigners. For the first time, in 2004 some prices were reduced in some cities and it is rumoured that hotels will soon be allowed a measure of independence in their pricing. Look under individual towns for recommended hotels but please note that the prices relate to autumn 2004, and not all include the 17.5% tax, nor breakfast. As noted above, two room-pricing systems operate: Iranian nationals pay in rials, and foreign visitors in US$. In important business centres (eg: Tehran and Ahvaz) there may be no discount for single occupancy of a room. If you are with a companion of a different gender who is not your spouse, do not expect to share a room together; the manager knows that local police and *Pasdaran* will not turn a blind eye. If the passport of your spouse carries a different family name, take the precaution of having a photocopy of your marriage certificate with you.

Essentially there are three types of places to stay. The **mosafirkhanehs** (literally 'traveller's place') catering for Iranian nationals are sometimes willing to take foreign budget travellers but may refuse, especially independent women travellers, knowing local police will object. If this is what you're after, ask a taxi driver to take you to the nearest place – expect to pay US$6–12 per night. Check the room and think whether saving a few dollars is really worth it (though you could always have a scrub-down next day in the local *hamam* or bathhouse – see page 234 – a real cultural experience). Good value and generally much cleaner are the official (Bonyad) Tourist Inns or **Mehmansarays**, which offer basic but adequate accommodation (generally under ten rooms), usually with private facilities of a sort. Then there are **hotels**. Most 'two-star' (*very* basic) hotels will have rooms with private (often unspeakable) facilities. Be prepared for poor maintenance even in so-called five-star hotels. Prices are fixed according to demand rather than a regulated system linked with hotel 'star' rating.

In the rooms there will be a symbol (an arrow, a picture of the Ka'ba in Mecca etc) indicating the *qibla* direction for prayer, a prayer mat, a small clay tablet (for Shi'i prayer prostrations) and a Koran; no Gideon's Bibles here. Until recently, some bathrooms in a certain Isfahani five-star hotel bore evidence of a theological directive requiring toilet pedestals to be relocated to avoid the occupant facing towards or against the *qibla* direction during usage. If plastic mules or sandals are provided in the room, these should be used for the bathroom and left by its door.

No youth hostels are available in Iran, and camping or staying in a stationary vehicle overnight will arouse great suspicion. If you are caught without accommodation in a rural area, ask for help from local police, who will assist (either by putting you up in a family home or in police grounds).

EATING AND DRINKING

If accepting an invitation to visit a family home, it is usual to take a small present; see page 62.

In local restaurants and cafés, the portions are geared to the pockets of the locals while, in luxury hotels, the portions are usually very generous and some Western dishes will be on the menu. Although many Iranian families will not have meat every day, restaurant vegetarian food is extremely difficult to find because eating outside the home is equated with eating meat or fish. All the meat served is *halal* (slaughtered according to Muslim law); pork products are not available except to Armenian Christian families resident in Isfahan, so all sausages, salami or mortedella are made from beef or lamb. Forks and spoons, but not knives, form the usual table cutlery and, as in other Muslim countries, the right hand is used for taking bread etc.

In town and village restaurants, ladies or mixed company will be directed to the 'family' area, whereas men without female companions will sit in a male-only section. Whether in a café or family house, men and women tend to sit according to gender rather than relationship. In a private house in villages, you may eat at floor level rather than at a table, so prepare for aching leg muscles. The kitchen is considered as the women's domain so men should not enter unless invited.

Managing to pay for a restaurant meal with Iranian friends is a major problem. The habit of 'going Dutch' is simply not an Iranian convention, and if you are a woman, the problem is compounded. It may sound like a freeloader's paradise but of course it is not. One possible answer is to talk to a sympathetic waiter to ensure that you get the bill, and have extra cash in case other friends or relatives join your table.

There are enormous difficulties finding a café or restaurant open during the daylight hours of *Ramadan* (see page 52), when it is *very* important not to be seen in public smoking, drinking or eating.

Drinks

All alcohol is banned although the Christian communities, as in Isfahan, are allowed wine strictly for communion use. Happily, Iran's famous vineyards are now being recultivated after most were uprooted in revolutionary zeal; the grapes are for eating, and the production of grape juice, syrups and vinegar. Iranian (non-alcoholic) beer is terrible, though Delster is just about palatable if well chilled. A very passable non-alcoholic 'lager' is *Bavaria*, now imported from Dubai. It's available only in large centres at about 4,000 rials from local shops (US$0.50) but more in restaurants and hotels – just slightly more than the Iranian bottled beer but worth every rial. Local carbonated soft drinks tend to sweetness, and the fruit juices, either freshly pressed or in cartons, are more thirst quenching, such as pomegranate juice, *talebi* (cantaloupe melon) juice, and carrot juice with a scoop of ice-cream from fruit-juice shops. The refreshing, pressed-lime sodas of pre-revolutionary Iran are unfortunately no longer available (presumably because the soda isn't) but another refreshing drink, *doogh* (yoghurt and water, like Turkish *ayran* or Indian *lassi*) is available.

Food

Iranian cuisine is one of the world's finest, an intriguing mixture of sweet and sour that owes nothing to the Chinese version. Iranian *khoresht*, dishes of meat and fruit, may sound uninspiring but wait until you've tried duck or chicken in pomegranate and walnut sauce (*fasinjan*), lamb in morello cherries or apricots, beef or lamb with spinach and prunes (*aloo*) and chicken and *zereshk* barberries etc. Delicious. Also try *abgoosht* (literally water-meat) which is served in a jug-like container with a pestle; this is a concoction of slowly simmered pulses, meat and vegetables. Drink the liquid and then (after removing any bones) crush the vegetables, beans and meat into a gooey mess, then eat with bread like a meat paste; definitely comfort food.

SOME PRICES OF INTEREST

Single local bus ride without changing	200 rials
'Bavaria' beer	4,000 rials
4 AA batteries	4,000 rials
Fuji film ASA 100	12,000 rials
Recorded cassette (original, not pirated version)	10,000 rials or less
Cinema ticket (depending on town and film)	5,000–10,000 rials
'Pizza' Iranian style	about 20,000 rials
Double hamburger	about 10,000 rials
Carton of Winston cigarettes	10,000 rials
Cup of 'Nescafe'	4,000–10, 000 (more in five-star hotels)
A litre of petrol (car)	8,000 rials (increasing 20% each year)

White rice and bread are the staple food. A delicious change is rice with butter slowly steamed until a crunchy, caramelised layer is formed. Fresh fish such as trout from the many farms, prawns and shrimps from the south coast, and sturgeon from the Caspian Sea are flown in daily to the major cities. As for world-famous Iranian caviar, it is easiest to find and purchase at airport duty-free shops on departure: the best and most expensive is Beluga, with *asetra* and *sevruga* (also called *darakul*) less expensive.

The Iranian equivalent of British fish and chips, or American hamburger and French fries, is *chello-kebab*, a skewer of grilled lamb, served with plain rice, with or without a raw egg on top.

And of course there's the special delight of *falludeh* ice, a sorbet with wispy 'noodle'-like strands, eaten with lime juice.

Meals

Breakfast is usually bread, a white *feta*-like cheese with green herbs, *mast* yoghurt (which in Shiraz has a smoky flavour), and tea taken without milk. Coffee, also taken without milk, is imported and thus is not widely available outside luxury hotels, where a wider breakfast menu is also served. There are four main types of bread: *lavash* is a thin, flat white bread, best when very fresh as otherwise it looks and tastes like a bathmat; *sangak* is made from brown flour, and is thicker and oval in shape (but check for any stones that have become embedded during the baking process); *taftun* is crispy and round; and lastly, there's *barbari*, a deep oval white loaf with a crispy crust. A rough price for breakfast in a four-star hotel would be the equivalent of US$4–6 plus tax, or half this in a two- or three-star hotel.

Lunch, taken around midday, is generally a rice and meat dish, often *chello-kebab* served with a dish of either green herbs, or cucumber, spring onions and tomatoes and usually served with a sweetened yoghurt dressing, often luridly coloured like some American bottled dressings. In a good tourist restaurant, the main dish as at dinner will cost around 40,000 rials plus service; fish is more expensive.

Dinner, eaten after 20.00, is generally at least three courses, consisting of thick barley or lentil soup, perhaps an appetiser, then a meat or fish dish with rice and a side salad, before finishing with seasonal fruit (70,000-90,000 rials plus service). Iranian ice-cream is very good but the traditional version, made with gum-mastic, is an acquired taste with its distinctive flavour and 'chewy' consistency. Few Iranians will take hot tea after eating chilled melon, and for most foreign visitors drinking iced or chilled water just after eating watermelon is a guaranteed stomach-churning combination. Thick black coffee akin to Turkish or Arab coffee, served in a small cup and always without milk, is occasionally available. As sugar is added during its making, specify the amount of sugar required as you order: *sa'adeh* (without sugar) or *kam shekar* (with more sugar). Instant coffee (known as 'Nescafe' or 'American coffee') is usually available only in luxury hotels and restaurants, but milk will not generally be included unless requested.

PUBLIC HOLIDAYS

Organising travel, accommodation and any business appointments during lengthy holidays such as *Nou Rouz* will require much planning and repeated confirmation to keep the bookings active. During *Nou Rouz* and *Ramadan* many offices, especially government departments, will be minimally staffed and keep erratic and shorter hours. It will be difficult during daylight hours of the 28 days of *Ramadan* to find restaurants and tea houses open except in four- and five-star hotels, and few dentists will accept patients (to avoid giving mouth-washes). Fasting inevitably means tempers are shorter, and little work is achieved. Try to avoid such times.

There are two main types of holidays, those in the **solar calendar** and those relating to the **lunar calendar** (ten days or so less than the solar year, and linked to the sighting of the new moon). Those marked with ★ mean that behaviour of foreign visitors must be low-key and extremely decorous.

Solar

These are National Days, falling on the same day each year. The main ones are:

February 11 Khomeini assumed control in 1979
March 20 Mossadegh's nationalisation of oil and petroleum companies
April 1 Establishment of the Islamic Republic in 1979
June 4★ Death of Khomeini in 1989; and
June 5★ Khomeini's arrest in 1963 and consequent anti-Shah
demonstrations

There is also the **three-week** *Nou Rouz* (Iranian New Year) beginning on the night of March 20, the spring equinox. Originally a Zoroastrian festival, though now an established part of Iranian life, it is a time for wearing new

THE TRAGEDY OF KERBELA

Hoseyn, the younger son of Ali and Fatima, was born in Medina (in today's Saudi Arabia) in 626CE. On the death of the (Umayyad) Caliph Muawiya in 680, recognised as the leader of all Muslims by the Sunni community, Hoseyn was 'invited' by the Medina governor to take an oath of allegiance to his successor, Yazid. Aware of imminent danger, Hoseyn, advised by its citizens to avoid taking this oath, left the city for Mecca and then Kufa in Iraq. Pursued by the Umayyad army, he told his supporters, numbering 72 excluding women and children, to leave him to his fate but they refused to desert him. The Umayyad forces poisoned the waterholes en route and Hoseyn's relative, Abbas Abu'l Fazl, volunteered to find drinkable water, losing both hands in the process. The small force reached Kerbela on the second day of *Moharram* and again Hoseyn ordered his men to flee. They refused and battle commenced. Hoseyn, the third imam, and all 72 supporters were killed on 10 *Moharram* 61AH (680CE).

clothes and giving gifts, so if visiting or staying with friends it would be wise to get a supply of new banknotes for the children of friends, janitors, cleaning staff etc. The first week is usually observed with family visits following a strict, unstated protocol. There is a total close-down of services on the first day, and thereafter reduced services which slowly improve as the days go by. Most businesses close for two weeks, and all schools and universities close for the whole three weeks.

Conversely, the winter solstice on the night of December 21 is considered an inauspicious time, so many people stay at home or pass the time with friends.

Lunar

All of these are Muslim holy days; the shorter lunar calendar means the holiday date advances approximately ten days each year. Under the Pahlavi regime, most of these were officially banned or ignored but they have now been reinstated; some are specifically Shi'i in character.

Ramadan★ 28 days from October 5 2005 (on sighting of the new moon), and from September 26 2006. During this time, all Muslims with very few exceptions must refrain from drinking, eating and smoking during daylight hours, and even non-Muslims must not be seen in public doing any of these, otherwise the consequences will be very serious. No weddings are held in this month.

Id-i Fitr November 4 2005, October 26 2006. Important three-day feast marking the end of Ramadan with gifts given to staff. Full-day closure on first day.

Moharram★ 28 days commemorating the tragic death of 3rd Imam, Hoseyn. Radio and TV programmes will be subdued during the first ten days, and women wear more sombre-coloured clothing.

Tassu-i and ʿAshura★ 9th and 10th day of Moharram February 21–22 2005, February 11–12 2006, marking the eve and actual day of Hoseyn's death with performances of the 'mystery-play' retelling the Kerbela story (see above). On the 9th day, processions of athletic young men carrying the giant wooden *nakhla* (a large structure shaped like a palm leaf said to resemble Hoseyn's coffin) are avidly watched by girls. Attend either *only* if invited and accompanied by friends and leave your camera behind.

Id-i Qorban January 22 2005, January 12 2006 feast marks the end of pilgrimage season; sheep sacrificed.

Ruz-i Qatl-i Ali November 1 2005, October 22 2006

Imam Sadeq's martyrdom December 13 2005, December 3 2006

Arba'in-i Hoseyni★ April 4 2005, March 25 2006 40th day after Hoseyn's death.

Imam Hassan's Martyrdom & Prophet Mohammed's death April 13 2005, April 3 2006.

In addition, government offices and institutions, and some shops will also be closed on the following days:

Birthday of the 12th Imam September 24 2005, September 14 2006

Imam Reza's birthday January 5 2005, December 26 2006. The city of Mashhad is especially busy.

Id-i Qadir-i Khom February 3 2005, January 24 2006 (Prophet Mohammed appointed Ali as his successor)

Imam Sadeq and Prophet Mohammed's birthday May 3 2005, April 23 2006; note that Sunnis celebrate the Prophet's birthday on a different date.

Such holidays can mean office (including Iranian consulates abroad), bank and shop closures for over a week. In June 2000, for example, the national holidays of June 4 and 5 were augmented by that marking Prophet Mohammed's death (June 2), a Friday, and an extra day of mourning announced by the government.

SHOPPING

Shopping hours are generally 09.00 to 13.00, and from 16.00 to 20.00 (later in the summer), closed Friday. During *Nou Rouz*, *Ramadan* and *Moharram*, expect shorter opening hours, especially in the bazaars.

For daily supplies, small corner shops sell everything, but check the expiry date. In the large cities there are a few supermarkets, such as Rifah in Tehran, which stock household items and furniture. Prices, especially of luxury and electrical goods, can range widely depending on whether the supplier is a small-scale importer or a franchise-operator for a government-registered charity (see pages 65–6); certain cheaper items (eg: motor-car spares) may be counterfeit.

The **bazaars** of Iran have well-earned reputations both as rabbit warrens and for haggling. Very few (eg: Tabriz, Zanjan) are located within a defined block; most (eg: Isfahan) have developed over the centuries to no pre-determined plan. The medieval system which facilitated market inspection for weights and measures, pricing and quality, by gathering like trades in sectors (eg: coppersmiths in one quarter, goldsmiths in another, booksellers elsewhere) has been largely retained, so it is a matter of finding the correct section. Never presume you will easily find it or the shop again, so take the trader's business card and next time ask directions; usually another trader will assign a small boy (who will expect a small tip) to take you there. Almost all traders have electronic calculators which facilitate bargaining for foreigners. Check whether rials or tumans are being quoted (see pages 43–4).

If you loathe haggling then the **Iranian Handicrafts Organisation** shops are strongly recommended. There, prices are fixed in rials/tumans, but do check what exchange rate is being used, as it can be extremely disadvantageous if the local manager is ignorant of current rates. A visit to an IHO at least gives an idea of local prices, and Iranians often frequent these centres too.

With expensive purchases such as **carpets** (see *Export restrictions* on page 44), avoid going into a carpet shop with a group to buy and don't be hassled into deciding within 30 minutes. It is safe to get rugs sent home (probably routed through Italy or Germany), and if you pay by credit card the billing will probably travel the same route (the US embargo again), and you'll have the cover of the card guarantee.

The **gold** (18 carat unless specified otherwise) and silver prices are published in newspapers everyday, so the jeweller will weigh the piece and add something for the workmanship. The gold is of a high quality but often set with paste and semi-precious stones. It is unlikely that one can find a bargain without active participation by an Iranian friend, as gold is the established hedge against inflation and Iran has no gold mines of its own.

I cannot stress enough how useful, comfortable and cheap ladies' *manteaux* are (see page 63). I'm told the oversized shoulder pads (as featured in 1980s US TV soap operas) are going out of fashion, but I'm not convinced. There is a universal size, though the length may need adjusting. The price, as of 2004, was from about US$15 upwards depending on quality of fabric, colour, trimmings etc.

Carpets, miniature paintings, printed cottons, marquetry work (eg: picture and mirror frames, pen and cigarette boxes) and leather goods are popular purchases, but consider too a pair of cotton *giveh* slippers, pistachio nuts and dried apricots or limes, spices like saffron or *sumak*, or pomegranate juice to make *fasinjan* at home. As will be noted in the relevant sections, some towns are famous for certain products, for instance the rose-water of Shiraz and the sweetmeats of Yazd. Isfahan is known for its block-printed cottons, the price range reflecting the fabric quality, the number of blocks and dye/mordant baths involved; salted cool water is recommended for the first washing. Good quality Kirman embroideries (on scarlet wool fabric) and Resht patchwork are now difficult to find; look and compare. Miniature paintings are produced by college-trained artists in traditional styles; the finer the detail, the higher the price. Painting on 'bone' is always more expensive as tourists seem to prefer such work. Forget about acquiring an antique example of classical Persian painting. Firstly, export authorisation will be needed, and secondly there is a lively market in buying antique paper, washing it and painting on top.

As for handmade **carpets**, as distinct from machine-made, there are essentially two types and two pattern compositions. In both, look for secure fringes, good firm weft-edges and selvages or cords (clumsy over-sewing can hide cut edges). **Kelims** are plain weaves without any pile knotting, involving less yarn and production time and cost less. The quality can range from the very fine (used as throws, drapes) to thick and hard-wearing. Complex and fine pattern detail means extra weaving time which will be reflected in the price. Kelims with long weave-slits in the pattern are more prone to future wear and tear. The second type incorporates pile-knots over the whole or part of the surface, which involves more work and yarn, so these carpet prices are higher than kelims. The official ban on exporting pile carpets was lifted a few years ago, but on your departure custom officials may ask to see your carpet, and the receipt (see *Export restrictions*).

There are two essential pattern compositions: one based on classical 'court' designs characterised by curvilinear motifs carried on arabesque scrollwork, and the other on 'tribal' patterns which have a more angular, geometrical appearance. The variations in patterns are infinite, as are their prices, quality and indeed the number of books about carpets. Always remember that so-called vegetable dyes and countless hours of work cannot transform a bad design into a work of art. You are more likely to get a bargain (though not necessarily 'authentic' Persian production) at home rather than from Isfahan, whose carpet dealers are notorious among Iranians.

CULTURE AND ENTERTAINMENT

Social life in Iran is firmly family orientated; 'friends' are usually members of the family.

In the first years of the Islamic Revolution, most of the theatres, the Tehran Opera House, cinemas and of course discos and nighclubs were closed, as it was considered that such entertainment was morally reprehensible, tainted by 'Westoxification' (page 15). But in recent years Iranian theatre, and especially film, with directors like Kiarostami, Ibrahimifar, Mehrjui, Bahmalbar et al, have blossomed. Films like *Children of Heaven*, *The White Balloon* and *Taste of Cherry* have all been nominated for or won prizes abroad. Subjects range from women in Islamic society, modern life and religious devotion, to Iran–Iraqi war themes and child abuse. The Iranian International Film Festival takes place annually in Tehran, usually in late February.

During the Pahlavi regime (1926–79) the traditional annual *taziyeh* or 'passion play' performed in *Moharram* (see page 53) was officially banned. Today most towns organise a performance which retells the tragedy of Ali's son, Hoseyn, and his family in their final hours at Kerbela. Casual foreign visitors are not appreciated on these occasions, so attend only if specifically invited by a close Iranian friend. This advice also applies to the *Moharram* processions.

In the early years of the revolution only martial music, recitations or chanting of religious works were allowed but shortly before Ayatollah Khomeini's death it was announced that the sale and purchase of musical instruments were permitted. Musical performances now take place (with certain provisos) and since August 1999 the import of 'Western' instruments, such as pianos, has been allowed. In 2000, *The Phantom of the Opera* could be heard on the tannoy system in an Isfahani five-star hotel and music with a Latin-American beat was being transmitted on radio/TV. However, official disapproval of American and Western rock, reggae etc remains. Clandestine cassette tapes of favourite émigré Iranian singers and musicans, along with upbeat Indian pop, can be bought on the black market, and there is a growing home industry promoting young singers who sound like the émigré stars. In the mid-1990s it was not permitted for men to listen to female singers (passions would be inflamed) so it was usual practice, while driving, to change cassettes as one drove up to and departed from road checkpoints.

TV and radio

Iranian TV has six channels in Tehran with lots of good children's cartoons, mainly dubbed, and at least one wildlife programme transmitted each evening. Live sports coverage, often football or basketball, is frequently shown with the camera tactfully avoiding any close-up of lycra wear during athletic meetings. The TV news coverage of home and international events was wide-ranging with extensive live footage, but since the February 2000 electoral swing towards 'liberal' candidates there has been a noticeable change. The English-language news is at 23.00 on Channel 4, or 12 midnight on Channel 5, depending on your location. Until recently, Iranian TV films were increasingly based on historical themes, or recalled the heroic sufferings of the Iraqi conflict. The pace was never more than slow and there was always an unambiguous moral to the plot. The mid-1990s' 45-minute 'God slot' every sunset now lasts for about 15 minutes except on holy days. The virtual absence of young girls in TV commercials, children's gameshows, sports etc is immediately noticeable. Satellite dishes were banned in 1995 as the authorities feared unsuitable programmes were being received (reportedly the American *BayWatch* series, with its silicone-endowed females, was very popular); now watching satellite TV is permitted only to those with government permits, such as the guardians of public morals. But depending on one's geographic location in Iran, Turkish or Arab TV channels can be received. Video cassettes can be obtained; for instance that of Princess Diana's funeral was available within days of the event. Regarding radio, tune into BBC Radio World Service/VOA on the half hour for the hourly broadcasts.

Newspapers and books

Four newspapers are printed in English: *Kayhan International*, *Tehran Times*, *Iran Daily* and *Iran News*. Of the national papers in Farsi, one of the most widely read was *Hamshahri*, because of its numerous classified advertisements; however, recently it was ordered to confine its publishing and sales to Tehran. Since then another, *Jame Jam*, published by Radio TV Iran, has taken its place because it is on sale nationally, is cheap and also has a good classified section.

It is possible to read the English language newspapers *Iran Daily* on the internet: www.iran-daily.com, and the *Tehran Times*: www.tehrantimes.com. Both are published and printed in Tehran. There has been a marked change in contents and criticism since the elections in February 2000, when there was full coverage of the notorious vote-counting muddle, offering a wide diversity of views. A crackdown in press coverage followed and another in 2004, following public disquiet over the disqualification of some 2,000 parliamentary candidates from standing for election. Over 20 newspapers and magazines have been closed by the Council of Guardians and the standard of reporting now verges on the innocuous. Parliamentary requests for an official investigation into press closures have been rejected by the Supreme Leader as being against Islamic law.

Other than TEFL and computer manuals, few English-language publications are available except pirated, ex-copyright versions of pre-1979 Western works on Persian art, history and archaeology. The Iranian-published English translations of such important Persian poets as Omar Khayyam, Hafiz and Sa'di are generally extremely poor and unfortunately no literate version of the Iranian epic, *Shah-nameh*, is still in print, although recitations from it (in Farsi) can now be heard again in *chay-khanehs*. Modern novelists – all established writers before 1979 – include Sadeq Hedayat (who wrote the classic *The Blind Owl*), Simin Daneshvar and Dawlat Abadi.

Museums and tourist sites

As of July 2004, the offices of the Iranian Cultural Heritage Organisation (ICHO) and the Iranian Touring & Tourism Organisation (ITTO) were brought under one umbrella and immediately it was announced that entry charges for foreigners to all the ICHO monuments would be reduced to the same level as those for nationals. This represents a huge saving for the foreign visitor: a ticket for Persepolis was 60,000 rials (US$7) now costs 6,000 rials (US$0.70). Few people think this order will remain in force for long, so be prepared for its disappearance, but rejoice if you find it still operating. Presently, entry charges for sites (eg: the All Saviours Cathedral in Isfahan) not administered by the ICHO remain unchanged at the former (high) levels.

Sports

Sports in Iran are strictly gender-segregated so public attendance is limited to male spectators, except where segregated seating (rarely found) has been installed. Indeed, medical concern is being voiced over women's health, and ex-President Rafsanjani's daughter, Faizeh, was a prominent campaigner in the late 1990s for greater access to facilities for women. There are two large sports centres, exclusively for women members, in Tehran at Hejab St 1 & 2 and there is active female participation in hill-walking, volleyball, karate, and even five-a-side football. A major problem is the absence of a 'proper' sports dress design which is acceptable in all quarters, which would allow the televising of women's team events and full participation in international events abroad; the Iranian lady archer who took part in the 2000 Olympic Games wore a manteau and headscarf. This is being worked on at present. Meanwhile as can be seen in Iranian TV 'breakfast-time' workouts, the men in track suits attack the usual warm-up exercises, while exercises for women (featured separately) in *manteau* and headscarf solely comprise arms outstretched, turning the wrists through 180 degrees.

Iranian men are sports mad, especially for football – as seen in the 1998 World Cup – volleyball and baseball. Interest has revived in wrestling, and the 1998 visit of a US team marked the beginning of a new diplomatic interchange, soon dropped, between the two administrations. If you have the opportunity, visit a local *zur-khaneh* (see pages 87 and 116) to see the rigorous calisthenic routines the wrestlers perform. Many *zurhaneh*s were closed by the late shah to curb the spread of anti-royalist propaganda, but have now re-opened; even the most intellectual Iranian males know all the vocal audience responses for the sessions.

Camel-riding has its supporters, especially in the south, while in the north and west **shooting** and **riding** are popular, with one Iranian woman taking part in the 1996 and 2000 Olympics archery competition. Once a year in early June there is a women's horse race near Khorramabad. Tehran has a **tennis** club and 18-hole **golf** course. **Skiing** is popular in Tehran, Hamadan, and Tabriz from January to the end of March, especially during *Nou Rouz* (see page 51), and at weekends, ie: Thursday and Friday. The main ski resorts are Darbansar (for beginners), Shemshak, Ab-Ali and Dizin (fashionable) at Shaleh; the equipment is cheap. The slopes, with the exception of Mount Towchal which has chair-lifts, are gender-segregated.

I am told **mountain climbing**, north of Tehran, Hamadan and in the Azerbaijan region, is both exciting and popular. The usual safety rules apply: wear suitable clothing for any unexpected weather conditions and always tell people of your route, estimated arrival and return times. It is wise to obtain official permits, and the tour company Kassa (see pages 29–30), which organises trips for the Mountain Federation of Iran, is very helpful; email: info@kassaco.com. Useful information is on its website: www.mountainzone.ir/News/newsarchive3.htm. Perhaps more popular among young Iranians (as it offers rare 'boy-meeting-girl' opportunities) is *kuh navardari* or **hill walking** in the mountains, especially along the paths of Darband, Velenjak and Kolok Charl, north of Tehran, which are dotted with rudimentary tea houses ideal for short breaks. Again **Kassa** can assist with routes and maps.

As for **swimming**, there are certain segregated pools or designated times/days for male or female use. In the sea, women sit on the shore in a certain area and enter the water fully clothed, including the headscarf; foreign ladies can swim in costumes (not bikinis) providing they cover themselves to the water's edge. Bathing shorts, but not thongs, are permitted for men on male-only beaches, but not elsewhere. **Scuba diving** (men only) is possible off Kish Island, where there is a good beach open to tourists, with showers, toilets and bar (dry!) – swimsuits are permitted, but take your passport. There are **sailing** and **waterskiing** facilities on the Caspian and at Amir Kabir Dam (north of Karaj, Tehran).

Hamams

Particularly if you are staying in very modest hotels, think of visiting a *hamam* (public bath); there are separate times/days for men and for women (see page 234). Always go before, not after, eating a meal. You will emerge squeaky clean and scoured to one surviving millimetre of skin. The desk person will organise your session after you decide whether to have a massage or shampoo as well as the 'bath' (somewhat of a misnomer because hot and cold water are sloshed *over you*). 'Plunge pools' are available only if the *hamam* is in a special spa area. Your clothing and valuables can be secured under lock and key, but never undress to the point of nudity. Towels, bath wraps, soap and shampoo can be provided at a small extra charge, as can tea and coffee.

Games

All gambling, such as cards, dice-playing and backgammon, is prohibited under Islamic law; in summer 1999 a car driver was reportedly jailed for having two large soft fabric 'dice' cubes dangling from his rear-view mirror. The revolutionary proscription on the sale and purchase of chess sets was lifted in 1989, and now chess competitions take place.

OFFICE LIFE

The working week is theoretically around 40 hours per week, with annual leave of about 30 days per annum. Most government offices are open 08.00–14.00 Saturday to Thursday (though the Ministry of Foreign Affairs closes Thursday and Friday), with other offices, workshops, bazaars, etc generally having longer working days.

There is a confusing multiplicity of **public holidays** (see pages 52–3) when offices, government departments and bazaars are shut. If visiting Iran for business, do allow at least three times the number of days you think necessary to see people – even if appointments have been confirmed. To cope with inflation and low wages, most Iranians have more than one job which usually involves crossing town and meeting the inevitable traffic jam, so appointments are often subject to long delays or last-minute cancellations.

CULTURAL DOS AND DON'TS

Just to repeat: no eating, drinking or smoking in public during daylight hours of the 28 days of *Ramadan* (see page 52). The repercussions otherwise will be very serious for you and your sponsor.

Apart from close family relatives (eg: husband/wife, parent/children, brother/sister) it is not done for a Muslim to touch the opposite sex except in an emergency or danger. Thus if an Iranian ignores an outstretched hand, this is not rudeness: strictly speaking, handshaking between the sexes is not acceptable. Remember that a German businessman was detained for years on the grounds of 'having knowledge' (British F&CO biblical coyness!) of an unrelated, unmarried Iranian woman (see page 21). If asked out by a member of the opposite sex, you should enquire who else (eg: another friend or relative) will be coming.

PHOTOGRAPHY

Print film is available in major cities from photography and/or camera shops, which can also arrange developing and printing, or from shops in four- and five-star hotels. However, the lack of other processing facilities and low sales demand mean slide film (transparencies or diapositive) is not often found. The US embargo means that Kodak film is difficult to find in any quantity (check for expiry date) and the latest brand products are unlikely to be available, so do take adequate supplies; the site of Persepolis, for instance, will eat film. The sunlight is very 'white', so ASA/ISO film speeds of 64 or 100 should form the bulk of your film and remember to pack a lens hood. That said, a few films of 200 or 400 will be useful for interior shots where flash is not allowed (eg: shrines, museums). Fuji films have a good reputation for capturing 'true' green values but I have yet to find a film able to convey the depth of blue in 17th-century tile work (eg: Isfahan), other than in close-up shots. A UV lens filter should 'cut through' the air pollution of Tehran and Isfahan, and a 'tobacco' filter always gives sunsets that added quality. The deep contrast of light and shade on architectural brick and plaster carving is most dramatically caught by black and white film, and indeed much of Iran's landscape does not possess great colour constrast.

Bright sunlight and excessive heat can quickly drain camera batteries, so you are strongly urged to take a spare, *especially if a lithium or special high-tech type is needed.* These will not be available in Iran, but familiar everyday batteries (eg: AA), can be bought in the major centres.

If possible, take a telephoto lens which will be useful for such sites as Naqsh-i Rustam and Bisitun, for any passing tribespeople and the occasional sneaky close-up portraits. A macro-lens will assist in photographing architectural, sculptural and ceramic details in such places at Persepolis, Pir-i Bakran etc.

Entry into a 'working' religious building or into a private home entails removing shoes at the edge of the carpet, rug or floor covering to prevent street filth being brought in. Feet (especially women's) should be covered with socks or nylons which should be put on discreetly beforehand – it has been argued that ladies' bare toes drive men to thoughts of sexual fantasy. Shoes are removed just at the transition of pavement or earth to floor covering. *Not* before. *Not* after. By all means untie or slacken shoes before, but remove shoes/sandals *only* at the transition point and likewise on leaving, when you slip on your shoes; they can be fastened up later at leisure. Ignoring this convention causes great disquiet and disgust, perhaps akin in Western society to excavating one's nasal passages in public and examining the contents minutely before consumption.

If visiting a family house (removing your shoes in the entrance hall) and using the bathroom or toilet, slip on the sandals placed near the bathroom door and return them when re-emerging. Such footwear is not worn elsewhere in

Flash (and sometimes photography itself) is not generally permitted in museums and popular shrines, so a small flexible tripod can be useful. The glorious dome interiors in Isfahan cry out for photography and very successful results can be obtained by setting a very slow speed at f.8, and placing the camera on the ground pointing up; a single flash will not give the same effect.

Pack the handbook and don't bring a new camera without giving it a test run beforehand. Currently, any video camera or camcorder should in theory be declared to Iranian customs on entry and exit, but the forms are in short supply and in Farsi. Regarding Iranian airport security X-ray machines, these are generally film-safe, especially for low-speed films, but for films ASA/ISO 400 and over use a lead bag or keep in a separate bag for hand inspection.

There are the usual restrictions on filming/photographing military installations, equipment and personnel; this includes civil airfields so *do not take photographs on the tarmac*. This warning must be taken seriously. A Canadian woman photo-journalist was arrested recently while photographing a Tehran prison, and died after 'falling on concrete' while in custody. The minimum penalty will be confiscation of the film, possibly the camera itself and, if you get stroppy, the confiscation of all cameras, film and equipment of others in your party and possibly much, much worse. Iranian social convention is disturbed by foreign men wishing to take 'posed' photographs of women but, generally speaking, women (especially with children) are relaxed with foreign women photographers, even more so if prints are sent. Get the address written down (in Farsi) and, for despatch, simply paste this on to the envelope, adding the name of the town and IRAN, and you will have done your bit for international friendship.

the house. The toilet won't necessarily have toilet paper, but if you take some with you, this and any other used sanitary paper product should be jettisoned into the waste-paper bin as the small waste pipes become easily blocked.

In taxis, long-distance buses and so on passengers sit according to gender or family. On city buses, men go to the front, ladies to the back section, and ne'er the twain shall meet, so if travelling with a companion agree where to meet before you are separated!

If in need of help or assistance, it is best to approach a person of the same gender.

As noted above, it is deemed highly unusual for a single woman to walk unescorted in public at night; it will be assumed she is a prostitute.

All forms of pornography are banned, and of course the definition of 'pornography' never lies with the owner. All publications by Salman Rushdie are banned, along with all alcohol (see pages 44–5) and drugs. The authorities are very determined to stamp down on the growing drug problem, so lorries, intercity buses, etc are often searched; penalties are severe. As in China, homosexuality 'does not occur' in Iran and such behaviour is forbidden and illegal, carrying harsh penalties. Men often hold hands and embrace each other, but this has no sexual connotations.

POLICE

In the past year or so, all the various 'police' units are being brought under a central control – a welcome move. The traffic or road police now wear white caps and have white cars with a blue stripe while the security police have bright green uniforms with a dark green cap, and white cars with a dark green stripe; some security police wear 'combat fatigues'. The ranks is shown by the stars or pips on the shoulder (officers), and by stripes on the sleeve (non-commissioned officers). At present, because there are so few tourists in Iran, the scheme of Tourist Police is in abeyance.

The emergency telephone number is 110.

INTERACTING WITH PEOPLE

Visiting Iranian friends or a family, it is customary to take flowers, sweetmeats or chocolates etc and, if possible, wrap them. To show you are more important than any gift, your host will probably place it unopened to one side but the gesture has been really appreciated. By all means praise the house, the food and hospitality offered but never a household item (eg: dish, glass) unless you are sure it is nailed to the floor or otherwise permanently fixed, or you could be deeply embarrassed having to accept it as a gift (and having therefore to part with a prized possession when the visit is reciprocated).

At a family meal, even your third refusal to eat or drink more will not be accepted, but persevere.

As in visiting any Muslim household, foreign ladies should expect to be closeted with the women, although they may be treated as 'honorary men' for the visit. Similarly, foreign men might not see the ladies of the household during their stay.

For any appointment, arrive on time but with little expectation that others will do the same; often business appointments or meetings will be cancelled with little or no notice.

Iranians are intensely proud of their country, its history and cultural heritage, and rightly so. They often make very amusing and critical jokes about themselves, their society and public personalities, but can be quickly hurt or insulted by any jokes or denigration expressed by a foreigner. Just be an appreciative audience, not a commentator.

Even the sweetest-tempered Iranians tend to be irritable and ratty during *Ramadan* (see page 52). And during the first ten days of *Moharram*, women tend to wear more sombre-coloured *manteaux* and headscarves.

If you wish to compliment someone on a child, a new baby, a new possession, etc, it will really be appreciated if you precede or supplement your compliment with the phrase *ma'shallah* which asks for Allah's blessing, so thwarting evil.

DRESS
Men

Before 1997 full-length shirt sleeves were required but now elbow-length are deemed acceptable. Garish colours and vivid Hawaian shirts should be avoided. Shorts, even knee length, are not acceptable, except for mountain biking. Ties are not widely worn by Iranian men; during the first years of the Islamic Revolution some believed that the *kravat* was a hallmark of anti-revolution intellectuals, similar to how the Red Guard in 1970s China viewed spectacles. However, in May 2004 at least one North Tehran clothing store has put ties in its window display. Designer stubble is still 'in' (formerly the mark of a revolutionary), but most Iranian men visit a barber every other day; it is cheap (about US$3 including tip in Isfahan) and very relaxing, I am told.

Women

Western media appear to delight in spreading scare stories. The dress code is simple and inexpensive, but to ignore or flout it is guaranteed to upset people, even if this is not expressed in words, and Iranian women clearly and warmly appreciate foreign ladies making the effort. The scarf, to be worn all the time except in the privacy of the hotel bedroom, should be at least $1m^2$ so that the nape of neck and ears are concealed. A nun-like coif is not needed; Iranian women will soon warn if too much hair is showing.

As for the actual dress, the essential requirement is to conceal distracting feminine bumps and curves and any bare skin save hands and face. Forget the semi-circular *chador* which takes years of practice to wear successfully, especially when carrying bags, cameras and packages. (It is however required in some shrines, eg: Shah Cheragh in Shiraz, and the Qom and Mashhad precincts, but may be hired or borrowed.) Instead, wear the loose-fitting *manteau* (or *ripoush*), a full-length, long-sleeved 'coat' made of lightweight cotton, poplin etc for summer, and thicker fabrics for winter. These can be purchased easily from US$15 upwards; many visitors buy several to use as theatre- or evening-coats back home. But if you are saving every penny, a knee- or lower-thigh length, long-sleeved tunic is acceptable, but only if worn with ankle-length skirt or loose trousers underneath. The *manteau*, however, is so much cooler and comfortable in high temperatures. The fabric should be opaque, of course, and plain or discreetly patterned; 'Jackie Collins'-styled padded shoulders are still fashionable. Other than during *Moharram* (see pages 52–3) when more muted colours are generally worn, pastel colours such as rose pink, powder blue, beige and old gold are popular. White (a mourning colour), and emerald green (recognised as the Prophet's colour) are best avoided.

TIPPING

Hotel porters will be satisfied with 1,000 rials for each bag or case, while airport porters will expect 2,500 and more if you want help through customs. For toilet attendants, perhaps 100 rials is sufficient and petrol attendants are usually given something, usually about 500–1,000 rials. A service charge is generally added to a restaurant bill, but add another 5% as a personal gratuity. Mosque and tomb

LIVING IN IRAN
Robyn Lyons

Of course I was nervous about going to live in Iran; politics cannot be ignored, and neither can the *chador*. But life in the Islamic republic for an accompanying spouse has turned out to be a surprisingly exciting and stimulating experience. As in any country, the expatriate life is whatever you choose to make of it. But Iran is in many ways exceptional, and is rapidly rising to the top of our list of favourite countries to live in.

In a short visit the tourist can get a little taste of what the country has to offer; extraordinary landscapes, a long and rich history, beautiful Islamic architecture, romance, the nightingale and the rose ... now imagine living with this on you doorstep month in, month out. A delight. And while on the subject of getting little tastes, one of the great advantages of living in Iran – as opposed to simply visiting – is the chance to buy and try all the delicious, seasonal (and cheap) products available in the bazaar. None of the ubiquitious chelo kebab for us, but a rich variety of delicate and delicious dishes.

Appreciation of the changing seasons, and the stately progress of the Iranian calendar (not the same as the Muslim Hijra one), beginning with the long Nou Rouz (New Year) holiday and punctuated by frequent and inexplicable public holidays, is another bonus. In fact time takes on quite a strange dimension. Which year are we in anyway? 2005? 1384? Which month, which day? Iranians have their weekend on Thursday and Friday, expatriates have theirs on Friday and Saturday, and most of our friends and relations in other countries have theirs on Saturday and Sunday... no wonder we sometimes feel strangely lost.

One of my fellow accompanying spouses spends half his time skiing on accessible, cheap and virtually empty ski slopes ... others study Farsi, or

guardians unlocking doors etc should be given upwards of 2,000 rials, depending on their help. As for taxi drivers, if you have negotiated the price already (eg: a half-day trip), he will hope this does not include a tip; if he has been extra helpful, why not add 10% extra. For an Iranian tour guide, so much depends on the time, effort, and work he or she puts into the job, but think of at least US$1 a day from each person if it's a large group, or US$5–7 a day each if travelling by yourself or with one or two friends; the driver is about one-third less, but again much depends on whether he has been particularly helpful.

Remember that wages are low and inflation high, and the benefit system for the mentally ill, disabled and elderly is not as sophisticated and generous in Iran as it is in the West.

GIVING SOMETHING BACK

The concept of 'charity' differs in each culture, and both Iranian officials and individuals will be affronted by any action they see as patronising and learn about carpets, or hike in the mountains, or trawl the bazaar for treasures…

After winter skiing comes the glorious surprise of spring, followed by the heavy heat of summer when most of Tehran migrates to the Caspian coast, and then the welcome relief of autumn when families picnic in parks, besides major roads, on busy roundabouts late into the night. Is this safe? Of course, although it has to be said that the greatest danger to anyone in Tehran is getting run over. The tourist hardly has time to learn how to cross the road, but the lucky resident has plenty of time to hone his/her skills.

Indeed Iran is one of the safest places I have lived in, and the wearing of a baggy manteau and a 1950s home counties headscarf makes one feel very secure. Not once have I been bothered or harassed. And when the disguise has been penetrated, and it has been discovered that I am British, there are no recriminations, only inevitable cries of 'MANCHESTER UNITED! DAVID BECKHAM!' This man must be one of the greatest ambassadors of peace today.

Inevitably, there are frustrations for the resident: the smiling electrician who claims that the power is low because it is Ramadan; the inability of vendors to serve people in any sense of order, the petrol pump attendant who lets you fill up with diesel before asking if this is what you really wanted. Even the initial charm of *tarof* ('politeness') can wear off. But all is forgotten when a stranger invites you for tea and cakes, or the electrician suddenly discovers, after several cups of tea, that there is after all a solution – an inexplicable one, but a solution nevertheless. And a dozen grinning men jump out of the Mercedes Benz strapped to a vehicle transporter to help push your immobilised vehicle to a garage. So don't waste time worrying about problems; there is always a solution and it is inevitably found with style.

interventionist. On all streets, there are metal charity-box stands, often decorated with a rose or tulip symbol, placed by the kerb. If you wished, you could contribute money. These boxes are usually for the **Emdad** organisation for orphans and the poor; its administrators are responsible to the Supreme Leader. An important charity is **Bonyad** (the common shortened term for the Organisation for the Oppressed and Disabled of the Islamic Revolution), which administers most of the Iranian property and holdings of the late shah's Pahlavi Foundation charity, and of former high-ranking courtiers. (Thus a number of tourist hotels are run by Bonyad.) Said to be the francise holder of Mercedes, BMW, Volkswagen and Toyota, the full scale and financial value of the Bonyad assets are not known as there is no legal requirement to make its annual accounts public; its head is responsible only to the Supreme Leader and over 40,000 people are in its direct employment.

There is also the *Vaqf*, or religious endowment, for mosques and other religious buildings. Since early Islamic times, individuals and businesses have assigned property and/or rents over to a building to pay for its upkeep, repairs and equipment. Thus a popular monument might be awash with funds but another falling into terminal decline. For instance, the person heading the *Vaqf* administration for the Shrine of Imam Reza, Mashhad, is responsible for donations and also for investment in all associated economic activities such as manufacturing, farming, housing projects and food-processing plants. It is one of the most influential and wealthy institutions and, as with the Bonyad, its head reports to the Supreme Leader and there is no legal requirement for the publication of annual accounts.

From talking to people in Iran and asking them about 'giving something back', the reaction is always the same: tell your friends and family how much you enjoyed your visit to Iran. So the greatest gift to them will be in disseminating accurate information rather than hyperbole about the current situation in Iran, arguing for and promoting a better understanding. And, of course, redistributing some of your hard-earned money in the bazaars of Iran will improve the lot of everyone.

Part Two

The Guide

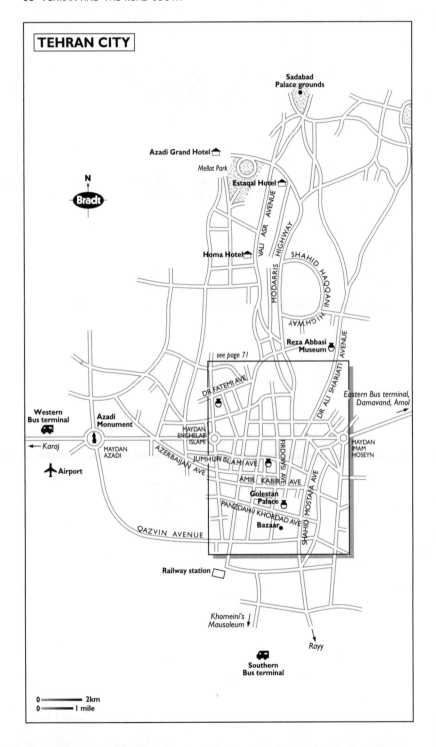

TEHRAN CITY

Sadabad
Palace grounds

Azadi Grand Hotel

Mellat Park

Estaqal Hotel

VALI ASR AVENUE

MODARRIS HIGHWAY

SHAHID HAQQANI

Homa Hotel

N
Bradt

HIGHWAY

Reza Abbasi
Museum

DR ALI SHARIATI AVENUE

see page 71

DR FATEMI AVE

Eastern Bus terminal,
Damavand, Amol

Western
Bus terminal

Azadi
Monument

MAYDAN
ENGHELAB
ISLAMI

MAYDAN
IMAM
HOSEYN

← *Karaj*

MAYDAN
AZADI

AZERBAIJAN AVE

JUMHURI ISLAMI AVE

FIRDOWSI AVE

✈ Airport

AMIR KABIR AVE

SHAHID MOSTAFA AVE

Golestan
Palace

PANZDAH-I KHORDAD AVE

Bazaar ●

QAZVIN AVENUE

Railway station ☐

Khomeini's
Mausoleum ↓

Rayy ↘

Southern
Bus terminal

0 ▬▬ 2km
0 ▬▬ 1 mile

Tehran and the Road South

Looking at the sprawl of modern Tehran spreading up into the Alborz foothills, it is difficult to believe that before 1795 when it became the Qajar capital it was an insignificant village 'possess[ing] nothing, not even a single building, worthy of notice' (Thomas Herbert, 1627). Then there were unimpeded views of Mount Demavend (5,670m) and the Alborz. Today, with the number of private cars almost doubling since 1985, low-lying smog usually hides the mountains two hours after sunrise. No wonder the citizens of Tehran escape when they can to the hills and the Caspian region to breathe fresher air.

By 1850 the city's population had escalated to around 90,000, more than a four-fold rise in 50 years, to enjoy its improved water supply, extended bazaars and newly built *caravanserais*. In late 1867, inspired by the urban planning in St Petersburg and the work of Haussmann in Paris, Shah Nasir al-Din ordered the French military engineer General Buhler to tear down the city walls, in-fill the defensive ditch to form thoroughfares wide enough for European-styled carriages, and extend the walls of the Arg (citadel) and double the number of gates to 12 (of which all have since been destroyed). By 1920, the population was estimated at 210,000, and it then quadrupled again by 1946. Since then the figures have soared: a conservative estimate in 1992 was over 6.5 million in the immediate centre with half again in the outlying suburbs, and forecasts for 2010 currently estimate 15–27 million residents.

With such expansion, what historic buildings Tehran has are constantly under threat. Less than 50 buildings are listed, yet it has been estimated that the Bazaar and Udlayan district alone have over 5,000 buildings of architectural merit.

GETTING THERE

Mehrabad airport is currently the only airport serving the capital, at the time of writing. The new Imam Khomeini Airport, a joint venture with Austrian and Turkish companies, located further to the west, is now finished at a cost of £260 million, but shortly after the airport's opening in 2004, it was forced to close by a section of the Iranian army, concerned about such an important national symbol being under a foreign 'authority'. It was also reported in the

Western media that a Korean consignment of uranium had been damaged during unloading. A new deal has brought IranAir into the airport venture and once it reopens, this airport will deal with all international flights and Mehrabad will in time be used exclusively for internal flights, currently serving 20 Iranian centres (see under individual cities). A taxi from the airport into the centre will cost about 20,000 rials, or 5,000 in a shared taxi (prepayment at airport kiosk). Do not take an unofficial 'taxi' as there is a risk of mugging. There are numerous intercity buses operating to and from three terminals: the East (tel: 021 7864010), South (tel: 021 5060047-8) and West (tel: 021 4656870). During rush hours (07.00–09.30 and 15.00–20.00) especially, any road journey will take *at least* twice the time as massive gridlocks occur all over the city.

The railway station is near the military garrison Qalah Morgh; ask the taxi-driver for Maydan Rah Ahan. The ticket office is not in the station but in a building to the left. Allow at least 60 minutes before train departure time. This is not an area to wander around in.

The first line of the Tehran underground, built with Chinese signalling and carriages, opened in February 2000 and runs from Sade Ghiyeh (near Maydan Imam Khomeini) to Azadi Square, where it joins with the overground section extending to Karaj. It is proposed to construct another three lines at least. A single ticket from Sade Ghiyeh to Azadi Square is 650 rials. Rush hours, best avoided, are from 06.00 to 09.00, and 14.00 to 17.00 hours.

ACCOMMODATION

The Tehran International Fair, usually held in the last week of September or the first week of October, means all hotels in Tehran are busy and often room charges are increased during this period.

As of 2003, no travellers' cheques nor credit cards are accepted for payment of bills (eg: rooms, meals) by hotels. Individual travellers making their own arrangements must take enough cash (preferably US dollars) with them or use the reservation facilities of an Iranian or foreign travel firm (see pages 28–30) which will then organise payment.

Top end
Laleh (formerly the Intercontinental) (378 rooms) Dr Fatemi Av; tel: 021 8965021–9, 8966021–9, 8967021–9; fax: +8965517, 8965599; email: info@lalehhotel.com; www.lalehhotel.com. On the main approach road to/from Mehrabad Airport, this is the most central five-star hotel (and a favourite with Western correspondents reporting the early days of the Islamic Revolution in the late 1970s). Coffee shop, three restaurants, shops, bank. Refurbished in 1998 with UK three-point plugs. Close to Lalehi park, shops, the Carpet Museum, and Museum of Contemporary Art. Strongly recommended. US$152 double, US$129 single; tax included; breakfast extra US$6.
Azadi Grand Hotel (formerly the Hyatt; Bonyad) (640 rooms) Chamran Highway near the National Exhibition Centre and the Evin prison; tel: 021 2073021–9; fax: 021 2073038; email: info@azadigrandhotel.com; www.parisianhotels.com. A total refurbishment of this hotel started in late autumn 2004, and is scheduled to last 12

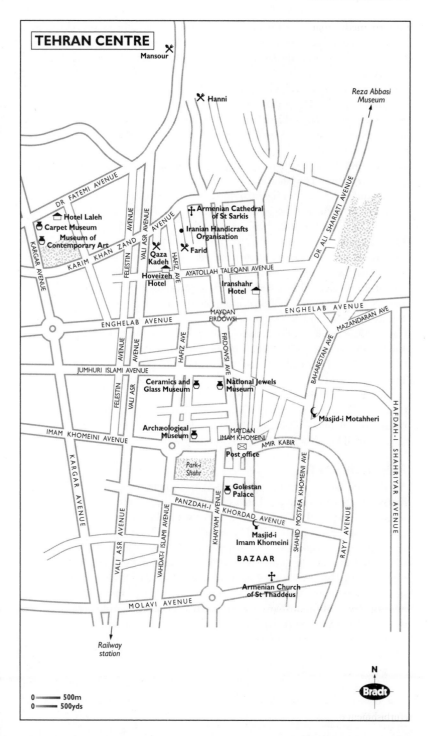

TEHRAN CENTRE

Mansour

Hanni

Reza Abbasi Museum

DR FATEMI AVENUE

Hotel Laleh

Carpet Museum

Museum of Contemporary Art

KARIM KHAN ZAND

KARGAR AVENUE

FELESTIN AVENUE

VALI ASR AVENUE

HAFIZ AVENUE

Armenian Cathedral of St Sarkis

Iranian Handicrafts Organisation

Qaza Kadeh

Farid

Hoveizeh Hotel

AYATOLLAH TALEQANI AVENUE

Iranshahr Hotel

DR ALI SHARIATI AVENUE

ENGHELAB AVENUE

MAYDAN FIRDOWSI

ENGHELAB AVENUE

MAZANDARAN AVE

AVENUE

AVENUE

HAFIZ AVE

FIRDOWSI AVE

BAHARESTAN AVE

JUMHURI ISLAMI AVENUE

FELESTIN AVENUE

VALI ASR

Ceramics and Glass Museum

National Jewels Museum

HAFDAH-I SHAHRIYAR AVENUE

Masjid-i Motahheri

IMAM KHOMEINI AVENUE

KARGAR AVENUE

Archæological Museum

MAYDAN IMAM KHOMEINI

Post office

AMIR KABIR

Park-i Shahr

VALI ASR AVENUE

VAHDATI ISLAMI AVENUE

KHAYYAM AVENUE

PANZDAH-I KHORDAD AVENUE

Golestan Palace

SHAHID MOSTAFA KHOMEINI AVE

RAYY AVENUE

Masjid-i Imam Khomeini

BAZAAR

Armenian Church of St Thaddeus

MOLAVI AVENUE

Railway station

0 ——— 500m
0 ——— 500yds

N

Bradt

months; during this time 'clients are being accommodated in the Estaqlal Hotel'. In the northern outskirts so drive into/out of the centre can be horrendous during rush-hours. No shops outside the hotel nor other attractions, other than the NEC and Luna Park in the immediate neighbourhood. Currently US$155 double, US$130 single; tax included; breakfast extra US$8.

Esteghlal (formerly Hilton) (542 rooms) Tel: 021 +2040011–15; fax: 021 2047041; email: sales@esteghlalhotel.com; www.esteghlalhotel.com. Another four-star hotel in a neighbouring location. US$155–194 double, US$130–155 single; tax included; breakfast extra US$8.

Homa Hotel (IranAir) (172 rooms) close to Vanak Square; tel: 021 8793021–39; fax: 021 8797179; email: Homahotel@yahoo.com; www.homahotelgroup.com/english.html. Central location. Bank, shops, IranAir office. US$120 double or single; excluding tax; breakfast included.

Three star

Ferdowsi Grand (182 rooms) Junction of Ferdowsi Av and Forughi St; tel: 021 6727026–31; fax: 021 6711449; email: info@ferdossigrandhotel.com; www.ferdossigrandhotel.com. Restaurant, breakfast room, coffee area, pâtisserie shop (own ice-cream sundaes!). A highly recommended hotel in the centre. Within walking distance of the National Archaeological Museum, the Golestan Palace, the Ministry of Foreign Affairs and the British Embassy (a complicated one-way system means a longer drive). US$75 double, US$60; tax and breakfast included.

Hoveizeh Hotel (formerly Takht-i Jamshid and Villa) (178 rooms) Corner of Taleghani and Ostad Nejatollahi St; tel: 021 8804344–58; fax: 021 8904823. Approximately US$70 single.

Iranshahr Hotel Corner of Karim Khan Zand Av and Iranshahr St; tel/fax: 021 8846450; email: info@hotel-iranshahr.com. Centrally placed. US$52 double; US$35 single; tax and breakfast included.

RESTAURANTS

All Tehran's five-star hotels have good-value restaurants, especially the French **Rotisserie** restaurant at the Laleh Hotel. Also highly recommended are two restaurants that both lie in the area just east of Maydan Vali Asr, on avenues Enghelab and Jumhuri Islami. The subterranean **Qaza Kadeh** (tel: 8903842) sometimes has a *Shah-nameh* recitation. Main courses cost around 60,000 rials; soup/dessert both approximately 20,000 rials, including service and tax but not a personal tip. Near by is the **Farid** (tel. 8904104), which serves a speciality of steamed 'blue fish'. Main courses here are 80,000 rials, including service/tax, but not a tip. All menus are 'international', including the ubiquitous kebabs, but rarely any *khoresht* (fish) dishes. For more exotic cuisines, check out the English-language newspapers.

Alternative options are the cheaper **Mansour** opposite Saiee Park on Vali Asr Avenue (tel: 8723790/2), which has a full lunch or dinner for 45,000 rials, including service/tax but not tip. Close by, but double the price (90,000 rials, plus soup/dessert at approximately 35,000 rials each) is **Nayeb Restaurant** (tel. 8713474).

Two traditional Iranian food restaurants are **Hanni**, on the corner of Mottahari Street at Vali Asr Avenue (tel: 8906982), charging around 60,000 rials for a meal on the same basis as above, while **Azari Rah** on Ahan Square, Vali Asr Avenue (tel: 5373665) is slightly cheaper at 50,000 rials. There are no *khoresht* restaurants (like British fish restaurants); one just asks the waiter if a *khoresht* dish is 'on special' that day/evening. It may be, though it usually isn't.

THINGS TO SEE AND DO

Tehran is not a pedestrian-friendly city. There are few signposts and road names displayed, so the following information is arranged more or less according to the location and/or cluster of buildings in certain neighbourhoods.

The **Azadi Monument** (literally 'Freedom') standing 45m high on a huge roundabout on the western approach road to Tehran, is usually the first building noticed by foreign visitors after arriving at Mehrabad Airport. It was designed by an Iranian architect and built by a British construction team as part of the late shah's '2,500th' extravaganza in 1971. The influence of 14th-century Timurid architecture is evident in the intersecting rib network, while the turquoise-coloured glaze brick emphasis on the white Hamadan granite is derived from late 12th-century Seljuk decoration. In the 1970s there were two museums in the building, a permanent display upstairs with visitors standing on a travelator, and temporary displays in the basement galleries; only the latter is generally open to the public (09.00–12.00, 14.30–17.30). However, reaching the monument calls for rock-steady nerves as pedestrians have to cross six moving lines of traffic – not for the faint-hearted.

The **Carpet Musem** (*Karegar-i Shamali*, north of Lalehi Park) is within short walking distance of Laleh Hotel. About 100 carpets and rugs are usually on show in this museum opened in 1977 (entry 3,000 rials; *open 09.00–17.00; closed Mon*). The ground floor display is arranged more or less in chronological sequence, working in an anticlockwise direction, beginning with a replica of the Pazyryck rug (c5th century BCE, the oldest known knotted carpet found in Siberia in the 1940s, now held in St Petersburg). It includes superb examples of 16th–17th-century Safavid rugs including the so-called Polonaises which caused a sensation at the 1867 Paris Universal Exposition. But you may prefer decoding the 18th-century 'garden' carpets with their stylised irrigation channels (including fish) and *chenar* plane trees (see page 173). The impact of European art and taste on 19th-century Persian carpet design grows more marked as you walk around, whether it is the reproduction of a Watteau oil painting or a large 'family-tree' of American presidents with a 1904–05 date presumably made for the 1904 Louisiana Purchase Exposition, St Louis. The upstairs gallery serves as a temporary exhibition space, but generally includes more 'tribal' work. It is worthwhile investigating the small shop in the main entrance hall as a number of the Farsi publications have English summaries, but the postcards on sale surprisingly do not illustrate any of the museum pieces. A small cafeteria is opposite but be warned: the attendant professes never to have change and you should check his prices against the display notice.

A few minutes' walk away to the south is the **Museum of Contemporary Art** (*Honar-i Moíaser*); entry 3,000 rials, *open 09.00–19.00, Fri 09.00–14.00*. This gallery is always full of young people eager to hear your reactions to the paintings displayed both in the main galleries and in the temporary exhibition section in the basement, the latter housing shows organised by foreign cultural associations. Art students in Iran can major in either 'traditional' or in the 'modern' schools or styles, though instruction and practice in both are encouraged. As Islamic Art historically favoured two-dimensional work (some theologians argued against the relevance and legality of three-dimensional work outside architecture), it is not surprising to find the emphasis here is on oil painting rather than sculpture, but there is a wide diversity of approaches from the figural to the 'soft' abstract (ie: action painting is out but op art is in).

Continue walking south along Kargar Avenue, across Azadi Avenue and down to Jumhuri Avenue, from where an easterly walk will lead eventually to another cluster of museums near the Ferdowsi Grand Hotel. The **National Jewels Museum** (formerly Crown Jewels Museum) in a section of the Bank Melli (central office), off Ferdowsi Square (entry 30,000 rials; *open 14.00–16.30; closed Wed–Fri*). The labelling in English and Farsi is minimal, but the glitter and colour of the pieces set against a crimson red fabric are eye-catching. Perhaps the most interesting pieces are the crowns, as one works out the historical artistic antecedents of the Kiani crown worn by Fath Ali Shah (d1834) with its 1,800 pearls (see page 75), and the one made for Reza Shah's coronation in 1925 with their clear allusions to Sasanid diadems (3rd–7th century CE). To me, the world's largest pink diamond (182 carats), the *Darya-i Nur* (Sea of Light), sister to the *Kuh-i Nur* in the British crown jewels is – well, just large; both were part of the booty plundered by Nadir Shah Afshar during his 1739 Indian campaign (see page 254).

Surely the ugliest and most preposterous bejewelled object is the Globe of Jewels made for Qajar Shah, Nasir al-Din in 1869 or 1875. The wooden stand and frame are covered with gold sheet and smothered in jewels, while the globe itself has the land masses picked out in diamonds and rubies, the oceans in emeralds; altogether there are over 51,000 gemstones totalling 18,200 carats.

Just to the west is the **Ceramics and Glass Museum** (*Abgineh*) at the junction of Jomhuri and Vahdat Islami streets. Finally opened in 1980, it is housed in the 1915 mansion of a former prime minister in Reza Shah's government, and from 1953–60 it functioned as the Egyptian Embassy, so the building itself has architectural merit (entry 3,000 rials; *open 09.00–17.00, closed Mon*). There are two floors of displays: the upper floor includes the dramatic 'Nishapur' slip-painted ceramics of the early medieval period, some of the 12th–13th-century lustreware from the Gurgan and other excavations, 14th-century pottery from Takht-i Soleyman and some later Safavid and Qajar ceramics. The majority of the glass, some 260 pieces, is exhibited on the ground floor. It's well lit, but labels, whether in Farsi or English, are conspicious by their absence.

Also in this area is the **(National) Archaeological Museum**, the main archaeological museum of Iran (formerly Iran Bastan Museum) in Imam

Khomeini Avenue, but check first whether this section is still open because it is rumoured that the authorities are planning a major revamping which will entail complete closure for some years; however, the Islamic Museum next-door will be kept open, and the Reza Abbasi Museum (see pages 78–9) with its more modern display layout includes some exquisite archaeological pieces from the Achaemenid and Sasanid periods. As from July 2000, the combined entry charge for both buildings was 60,000 rials but as of July 2004, when most museum charges were dramatically reduced, the charge is 6,000 rials *(open 09.00–17.00, closed Mon)*. This museum was the brainchild of Andre Godard (d1965), the French archaeologist and architect who was its first director. (He also established the first school of architecture in Tehran, based on the French system, and designed a number of 'national' tomb monuments in Shiraz, Firdowsi etc.) The vaulted brick entrance was designed to recall the famous Sasanid audience hall at Ctesiphon, Iraq. After its completion in 1936, the Pre-Islamic collection of artefacts was displayed on the ground floor, with Islamic art exhibited on the first, but today the Islamic collection is now housed in a new building to the right of the entrance. The displays in both buildings are designed to be visited in an anticlockwise direction and, as the English labelling of objects in both

BLAZING MAJESTY OF A QAJAR SHAH
Fath Ali Shah (d1834) was

> ...one blaze of jewels, which literally dazzled the sight on first looking at him... A lofty tiara of three elevations was on his head, which shape appears to have been long peculiar to the crown of the Great King. It was entirely composed of thickly set diamonds, pearls, rubies and emeralds, so exquisitely disposed, as to form a mixture of the most beautiful colours, in the brilliant light reflected from its surface... His vesture was of gold tissue, nearly covered with a similar disposition of jewellery; and crossing the shoulders were two strings of pearls, probably the largest in the world... But for the splendour, nothing could exceed the broad bracelets round his arms and the belt which encircled his waist; they actually blazed like fire, when the rays of the sun met them... [There was the throne] platform of pure white marble, an apt emblem of peace, raised a few steps from the ground, and carpeted with shawls and cloth of gold, on which the King sat in the fashion of his country, while his back was supported by a large cushion encased in a net-work of pearls.

R Ker Porter *Travels in Georgia, Persia, Armenia* ... 1821, vol I, pp 325–6, describing the Nou Rouz royal audience, Golestan Palace, in 1818 museums is brief to the point of terseness, it is useful to have a rough chronology/listing of major archaeological sites to hand.

In the 1936 building, the first cabinets display ceramics dating from the 4th millennium BCE, but visitors are always attracted by the superb unglazed zoomorphic vessels from the 1000BCE Marlik settlement on the Caspian. Remember to look out for the polished reliefs, capitals and statues of the Achaemenid period (6th–4th centuries BCE); this gleaming, rich brown colour is how the real Persepolis stone quality should look (see page 186), not today's grey, pitted surface. In the bay before it stands the lower half of the famous Darius the Great statue found at Susa (see page 205) in 1972, recording his victorious campaigns in Egypt and declaring 'This is the stone statue which Darius ordered to be made in Egypt so that in the future, he who looked on it would know that the Persian Man held Egypt'. On the side walls there are two panels of glazed, moulded brick from Achaemenid times, reminding visitors that their palaces had richly decorated tiled and painted walls. Further on is a feat of 1st and 2nd-century CE bronze casting, the moustached and bearded Parthian warrior (1.94m high), found at Shami (see pages 9 and 210). A new cabinet shows the remains of a 3th–4th-century CE man found in a salt mine near Zanjan, north Iran, probably from the Parthian era. In the current arrangement the Sasanid period is poorly represented; the gold and silver gilt platters decorated with scenes of hunting and courtly entertainment displayed in the 1970s have been removed and all that are shown are examples of carved and moulded plaster of Paris, stone capitals and some mosaics from Bishapur. At the time of writing, access to the upper floor was still closed.

The museum shop here is virtually non-existent; you will have better luck in the new Islamic Museum next door, where the visit should start on the uppermost floor. Here the displays (organised anticlockwise) are shown in an approximate chronological order, whereas the floor below emphasises development of various media in separate sections (eg: Korans in the central well, with other manuscripts showing calligraphic styles; paintings in surrounding cases; one sideroom houses textiles, another ceramics, and so on). Again labelling is minimal. The shop on the first floor is a treasure trove of posters (good value), packets of postcards, books etc, with a very helpful manager.

Also in the area, further south, is the **Golestan Palace** (Rose Garden) off Maydan Khordad. All traces of mid-18th-century construction by the Zand regime were almost totally obliterated by the early Qajar shahs and, rubbing salt into the wound, Agha Mohammed ordered the bones of Karim Khan Zand to be exhumed from his Shiraz grave and placed under the main threshold to be trodden on by all. The palace pavilions then built by Fath Ali Shah were in turn largely torn down during the extensive and lengthy construction programme (1867–92) of Nasir al-Din Shah, although two main sections were saved: the *Talar Divan Khaneh* or Audience Chamber of the Marble Throne (*Takht-i Marmar*) and the *Imaret-i Badgir* (Wind Tower) in the south. But the work of that shah too suffered. The huge *Taziyeh* hall, used for Moharram performance and inspired by the Royal Albert Hall in London (as seen by the shah during his 1876 state visit), was destroyed in 1946, and his 1891 *Kakh-i Abyas* (White Palace) was razed to make way for offices of the Ministry of Finance, the Bank Melli, and the Ministry of Roads. Also inspired by the shah's 1873 visit to Europe, which included Versailles with its famous mirrored gallery, is the Hall of Mirrors within the Golestan complex which served as the coronation room for both Reza Shah and his son; it remains intact.

Entry into the complex, with separate tickets for individual museum sections from the ticket office cost approximately 5,000 rials each (*open 09.00–17.00; closed Sun, Thurs*). With this ticketing arrangement, you must decide at the ticket office which sections you wish to visit. Unless one has special interests (labels and other information are virtually non-existent except in the ethnographic museum), visitors will probably be satisfied with the **Ethnographic Museum**, with its series of miniature regional displays with small wax figures, and the **Marble Throne veranda** (thus two separate tickets) followed by a walk in the courtyard to look at the various tiled panels, all extremely decorative with the distinct Qajar palette of yellows, pinks, and blues. There is a good but expensive giftshop next door to the Ethnographic Museum. Straight across the courtyard from the main gate is the Marble Throne veranda decorated with mirrors and other goodies seized by Agha Mohammed from the Zand palace buildings. The throne-couch itself, not the most beautiful artefact made by man, was carved by Isfahani craftsmen in 1807 or 1841 (depending upon whom you read) and was where the shah sat during public audiences; Reza Shah Pahlavi was the last ruler to receive from his courtiers birthday and *Nou Rouz* greetings on this throne. On the veranda a door leads into a small portrait chamber decorated with oil paintings of rulers, historic and mythical, a bevy of European ladies and garden scenes; Fath Ali Shah's portrait is over the chimney. Next door is the main **Painting Gallery**, and then the **1875 Hall of Mirrors**, and the **European Art Gallery**. The twin-tower pavilion is the **Shams al-Emerah** built by Nasir al-Din, which now houses a small collection of calligraphy (no labels in English) in a splendour of mirrors and plasterwork. This was the first five-storey building to be constructed in Tehran, which Lord Curzon described in 1892 as 'a very creditable specimen of the fanciful ingenuity that still lingers in modern Persian art'. Continuing around this gaily tiled courtyard you come across the **Photography Gallery and Archive**, the **Tent House**, now used for conferences, the so-called **Diamond Room**, a tea house and toilets.

East of this cluster, on the south side of Maydan Baharestan (northeast of Maydan Imam Khomeini) is one of the most photogenic historic mosques in Tehran. Constructed mainly in the Qajar period, this is the **Masjid-i Motahhari** (formerly Masjid-i Sepahsalar, Commander in Chief) and its adjacent *madrasa*. The official policy promoted by Reza Shah Pahlavi in the 1930s led to most of Tehran's mosques closing down along with the *madrasa*s; it has been estimated that by 1942 only 24 mosques were open and operating in the capital. That is certainly not the case today. I understand the complex is closed to foreigners as it is now a fully functioning theological college again.

Built by two high-ranking officials in the court of Nasir al-Din Shah in 1879–81, when its location was just inside the city walls, for many years it was one of the largest four-ivan mosques in Tehran. Two massive minarets flank the recessed entrance which leads into a courtyard surrounded by twin-storeyed arcades of college rooms; in all there are some 60 chambers. Tiles with full-blown floral motifs in typically flamboyant Qajar style decorate the courtyard, while a tile inscription band gives details of the original endowment. The prayer hall dome, 37m in height, is supported by 44 columns.

South of Maydan Baharestan in the main Bazaar area is the **Masjid-i Imam** (formerly Masjid-i Shah) built according to inscriptions in the *qibla* ivan in 1808–13 on the orders of Fath Ali Shah (d1834); at that time it faced the main citadel. Much of the mosque, its central courtyard with the four-ivan layout and the *muqarnas* vaulting in the ivans recalls the royal buildings of 17th-century Isfahan, but the tile decoration is in the gloriously flamboyant Qajar style. It was repaired by his grandson Nasir al-Din Shah some 60 years later.

The **bazaar** is located within the block edged by Khayyam Avenue (in the west), Panzandah Khordad Avenue (north), and Shadid Mostafa Khomeyni (east). Traffic around this area is horrendous so don't expect a taxi to wait for you. An Armenian church of **St Thaddeus** (*Hazrat-i Talavus*), one of the handful in the capital, is located to the southeast section, off the Shadid Mostafa Khomeyni, on Shahid Mostavi running west. The 19th-century **Armenian Cathedral of St Sergius** (*Hazrat-i Sarkis*) is at the north end of Shahid Ostad Nejatollah, just south of Karim Khan Zand Avenue (*open every day except Sun*). Just south of the Armenian Cathedral is one of Tehran's **Iranian Handicrafts Organisation** shops on Ostad Nejattollah, well worth a visit if haggling in the bazaar calls for too much stamina.

There are numerous other museums: the **Decorative Arts** in Karim Khan Zand Avenue, the **Post Museum** with its extensive philately collection on Maydan Imam Khomeini, and the **13th Aban Museum** in the northwest corner of that square which commemorates the figural sculpture of Sayyid Ali Akbar San'ati and the heroes of the Revolution and the Iran–Iraq war.

Do make every attempt to visit the **Reza Abbasi Museum**, 927 Dr Shari'ati Avenue (northeast Maydan Ferdowsi) recently reopened after its 1998 renovation (entry 3,000 rials – about US$0.50; *open 09.00–12.00, 13.00–16.00, closed Mon*). This is *the* place to see some of the masterpieces of classical Persian book-painting from the 14th century and other eye-catching archaeological treasures. If it was not for the polished Persepolis statuary and reliefs in the Archaeological Museum, I would put this as top of the museum list. There are five galleries with the top floor displaying some of the most important archaeological finds in gold and silver. Vessels from Ziwiye and Marlik dating from the 1st millennium BCE, as well as treasures from other Achaemenid sites, feature alongside the silver-gilt 'hunting' platters of the Sasanid dynasty. The displays on the second floor concentrate on Islamic ceramics and metalwork up to and including the Qajar period. The Painting Gallery is located on the first floor and manuscript illustrations range from the separate leaves from early *shah-namehs* to the album studies of the late Safavid period. Each is labelled in Farsi and English but information is usually confined to the name of the work and a date. There is even less information in the adjacent Calligraphy Gallery, although this too displays work of renowned artists. The ground floor is where temporary exhibitions are shown. The gift-cum-book shop is disappointingly small with a tiny selection of publications and mementos.

An enjoyable, unrushed half-day can be spent exploring **Sa'dabad Palace**, constructed to house the Pahlavi family and officials in 410ha of grounds (enter at main gate, with separate tickets for each 'house' purchased from this main ticket office, from 2,000 to 3,000 rials for each 'house'; *open 08.00 until sunset*). If you don't feel like walking up, a small minibus shuttle operates around the complex about every 15 minutes. If nothing else, such a visit reminds one how the late Mohammed Reza Shah (d1980) removed himself from the everyday life of Tehran. Today, of course, residential housing has spread onto this previously isolated hillside. Some of the palace-mansions now function as headquarters for various municipal services (eg: water), others house art collections and a few are occasionally used to accommodate visiting VIPs, so entry into the Mellat Palace (formerly White Palace) in particular cannot be guaranteed; the presence of an armed guard on any drive up to a mansion will warn you. Photography is allowed in the grounds but not inside any building. I suggest two visits to the Mellat Palace and to the Green Palace, but there is also the Museum of Fine Arts (the former Court ministry), the small Reversions and Admonition Museum (the Queen Mother's house), the Military Museum and the Natural History Museum among others. The Bihzad Museum refers not to the famous 16th-century Persian painter but a 20th-century artist and his work.

The **Mellat Palace** (entry 3,000 rials) is introduced by a pair of giant bronze boots, all that remains of a huge statue of Reza Shah (d1941) standing by the side of the staircase. If nothing else, they remind visitors that to enter, shoes have to be removed (to protect the stone floors); cameras too must be left. Labelling is virtually non-existent in any language and the wardens are monosyllabic. Slabs of green onyx and ormolu ornaments are everywhere, and the house has a desolate feel; the large, finely worked carpets do nothing to raise the spirits. It was said that army life so conditioned Reza Shah that he preferred sleeping on the floor rather than in a bed, and certainly this house does not feel lived in.

Further up the hill from Mellat Palace is the 1925 **Green Palace** (entry 3,000 rials) so called because it is faced with a distinctive special greenish/yellow marble, which reminded one visitor of 1950s Fablon plastic coverings. Reza Shah was responsible for ordering this construction and certainly his small office has a more personal ambience than the Mellat. Elsewhere the excess of mirror work, blue brocade silk curtains with silver metal thread fringes, tassels in the bedrooms and the crimson silk dining rooms speak more of the excesses of his son, Mohammed Reza. It's wonderfully hideous and in the best of worst possible tastes.

A similarly large complex, but a world apart, is the **Mausoleum of Ayatollah Khomeini**, located in the southwest of Tehran not far from Mehrabad Airport and on the road to Qom, off the Besat Highway. The complex is situated adjacent to the huge cemetery, Behest-i Zahra, named after an epithet of Fatima, the Prophet's daughter and wife to Ali, the first Imam. In the late 1970s, this cemetery became closely associated with the revolutionary movement against the Pahlavi regime as many of those killed in the 1978 demonstrations were buried here; after the September 8 1978 demonstration over 4,290 burial certificates were issued for this site. No wonder this was the place selected by Ayatollah Khomeini for his first public speech six months later. Many of the soldiers killed during the Iran–Iraq war were also buried here and photographs of the central fountain which once ran with blood-red coloured water (symbolising the Martyrs' sacrifice) featured on the front page of many Western newspapers.

Today the Mausoleum of Khomeini may be only half-finished but it already dominates the landscape, particularly at night when the central golden-domed tomb and the surrounding buildings on each corner of an enormous 'terrace' are illuminated. (Entry is free; shoes, bags etc to be deposited at the mausoleum entrance. Ladies enter to the left, gentlemen to the right; a cafeteria and toilets are located in the car park near the main entrance.) Only half of the floor area of the actual tomb building has been completed but already this section is equivalent in size to London Heathrow Terminal 4 check-in area, and has similar revealed rather than concealed pipes and structural girders. Acres of green onyx slabs cover the vast floor while a glass drum adorned with giant, fat, blood-red tulip motifs (blood of the martyrs) sits uneasily over the cenotaph grille. This marriage of expenditure, materials, scale and concept is not sublime.

SOUTH OF TEHRAN
Rayy
Before the 19th-century, biblical Rhages was a more important town than Tehran; it lies 10km south of the capital but Tehran has now engulfed it. Said to be the twelfth city of the world to be created by Ahura Mazda, and the place where Tobias and the angel stopped after the wedding in Hamadan (see pages 91–2), the town was rebuilt and renamed as Europos by Seleucus Nikator (c300BCE), the same person responsible for Apamea and Dura Europos in Syria. There were important Parthian and Sasanid settlements here and Harun al-Rashid, the famous Abbasid caliph whose son was later to be involved in the sudden death of Imam Reza (see page 251), was born here in 763CE. It became an important administrative centre under the Seljuk sultanate when it became known as 'the most beautiful city of the East', second only to the Abbasid centre of the Islamic Empire, Baghdad. Very little of that remains as Rayy was almost totally obliterated by the Mongol armies in the 1220s.

To many Iranians, the most important monument in Rayy is the **Shrine of (Shah) Abd al-Azim** which houses the graves of the descendants of the 2nd and 4th Imams, and Hamzeh, a brother of the 8th Imam. Even during the late shah's time, non-Muslims were not permitted to enter but could catch glimpses into the first courtyard from the 1950 concrete memorial-tomb of Reza Shah, who had died during his South African exile, its monumental proportions reminiscent of certain Lodi tombs in Delhi; it was one of the first Pahlavi monuments to be destroyed in 1979. The shrine itself was lovingly repaired and decorated during the Safavid period, with additions including the mirror-work in the 19th century. It was here, on leaving the shrine, that Nasir al-Din Shah was assassinated in 1896.

To the north of the shrine are the heavily restored remains of a Seljuk tomb tower locally known as **Tughril Beg** after the sultan (d1063), although it was built over 60 years later. It stands about 20m high, with a diameter, about 16.5m but it has lost its original conical dome. The exterior is broken with 22 flanges, so there is a passing resemblance to the famous tomb tower of Gonbad-i Qabus in northeastern Iran. In the hills behind is a **Qajar rock-cut relief** depicting the unfortunate Qajar shah, Nasir al-Din, with his ten sons, and another earlier panel showing Fath Ali Shah (d1834) with some members of his enormous family (he was said to have fathered 189 children). This is **Chesme Ali** (Spring Water of Ali) whose pure soft water ensured its reputation as a carpet-washing centre over the last two centuries.

It was near here that, during the 1920–30s, American archaeological teams excavated the site of **Nagareh Khaneh** and found, among other items, remnants of woven silk fabrics, thought to date around 900–1220CE. The textile world was astounded by the discoveries and when further pieces came on to the open market during and after World War II, they were eagerly snapped up by the major museums in the West; in the late 1970s scientific analyses revealed that many of the newly acquired 'Buyid' pieces were in fact clever forgeries. This is also the location of the **Shrine of Bibi Shahrbanu**. The story of this shrine is closely linked to that of a Zoroastranian shrine outside Yazd, in southeastern Iran (see page 225), and similar to that of St Tikla of Maaloula, outside Damascus. It is said that a daughter of the last Sasanid shah, Yazdigird III, married to the 3rd Imam, Hoseyn, grandson of the Prophet Mohammed, fled here to escape the overtures of an Umayyad general. At her behest, the mountain opened and then closed around her, saving her from a fate worse than death. Probably this was originally a shrine to Anahita, the Zoroastrian divinity. Evidence of 10th-century building work has largely disappeared under continuous rebuilding from the 15th century onwards.

Continuing south some 10km will bring you to the remains of a huge brick complex, **Tepe Mil**, dating from Sasanid times. It is thought this was an important fire temple with royal audience halls and associate buildings. Little was readily identifiable in the mid-1970s and today it is more of a monument to modern reconstruction skills.

It is about 20km further on to **Varamin** which is home to the heavily restored tomb tower of Ala al-Din (c1289), whose exterior is decorated with 32 angled flanges, and an early 14th-century **Masjid-i Jami**, built on the four-ivan plan. It is thought that the Il-Khanid ruler, Oljeitu, paid for this mosque, which was then completed by his successor in 1322. Almost a century later it needed repairs as two panels in the prayer chamber refer to the Timurid ruler, Shah Rukh (page 247). A great deal of restoration and rebuilding work was undertaken in the 1970s when it was constantly hidden under a mass of scaffolding but at last this has largely finished. Enough of the strap-brickwork decoration in turquoise and cobalt blue and the carved plasterwork remain to allow the imagination to picture the original scheme of decoration and the clean proportions. There are the remains of two other Il-Khanid structures in Varamin. One is just a portal to the **Masjid-i Sharif** of 1307, not far from the Masjid-i Jami, and the other is the **Imamzade Yahya**, whose splendid tile-*mihrab*, now in the Hermitage Museum, St Petersburg, gives a late 13th-century date for the buildings itself.

Qom

One hundred and fifty-four kilometres southwest from Tehran, this city is the second most sacred place in Iran, because it was here that Fatima, the sister of the 8th Imam, Imam Reza (and not Fatima, the Prophet's daughter and wife of Ali) fell ill in Saveh on her way to Mashhad and died in 816. The city has grown extensively since 1971, my first visit, with a road and traffic system designed to cope with a daily influx of pilgrims and visitors; indeed, unlike many Iranian cities and towns, the road-direction signs are clear and numerous.

When the town was established is unclear, for its water supply has always been poor and brackish so there was little logic for a settlement. Perhaps it was founded by the Arab Muslims after conquering the region in 644 but possibly there was a sizeable settlement in existence then, for we know Zoroastrianism remained influential here until 901. By then Qom was also known for its Shi'i theologians although there was no sign of a special tomb to commemorate Fatima. It was rumoured this was the birthplace of that powerful political figure of Hassan al-Sabah, leader of the Ismaili sect, the Assassins (see page 90). Perhaps that was why the Mongols exacted such a fierce revenge on the small town, as it was then, massacring most of the population in 1221. In the 14th century it was best known for its hunting, and many Iranian rulers wintered here; a shrine for Fatima was in existence, but by all accounts it was a modest complex. All that changed with the Safavid regime (1501–1735). As champions of *Ithna 'Ashari* Shi'ism, the Safavid shahs undertook a programme of construction and repairs to the Qom shrine, as they would do with those of Kerbela, Ardabil and Mashhad, perhaps hoping to persuade Iranians and other Shi'is to forego the Hajj to Mecca and Medina. The rebel Afghans exacted their revenge and even with royal Qajar patronage, Qom's population in 1872 was a mere 4,000.

Today it stands at approximately one million, owing much of its reputation as a theological teaching centre to the charismatic theologian, Ayatollah Haeri-Yazdi (d1935), one of Ayatollah Khomeini's teachers. As for the town's water, new reservoirs were constructed soon after the revolution.

Getting there

Its proximity to the capital means that intercity buses are the quickest, easiest and cheapest form of transport. Because access to the shrine complex, even into the first courtyard, is forbidden to non-Muslims, most foreign visitors do not stay overnight.

The golden dome and twin minarets of Fatima's shrine, **Hazrat-i Ma'sumeh**, dominate the skyline. It is, as Lord Curzon said, the 'Westminster Abbey of many of her kings', for the shrine houses the remains of four Safavid shahs (Safi I, Abbas II, Soleyman I, and Sultan-Hoseyn) and two Qajar rulers, Fath Ali Shah (with two of his sons) and Mohammed Shah along with countless high officials of the Qajar court. In recent years a large *maydan* has been paved surrounded by a bazaar, souvenir shops and sweetshops selling the local delicacy, *sohan,* a thin butter 'brittle' with pistachios. Just before the main entrance to the first courtyard, the tiled doorway on the right marks the entrance into the *madrasa* where Ayatollah Khomeini studied. The city has been, and still is, witness to some of the liveliest and most thought-provoking theological debates, discussing the role of the *ulama* (clergy) in revolutionary Iran, whether Shi'i law precludes women from fully participating in the *ulama*, and asking if a temporary marriage contract during engagement will offer a solution to the ever-increasing divorce rate for newly married young couples.

A short description of the complex follows but note that it is based on information and maps published in the late 1970s; no account of any repairs or construction appears to have been published since then. An earlier arrangement of four courtyards in the complex was revised in Safavid times, when the *Madrasa Faydiyeh* was built over two of the courts, with a small hospital (*Dar al-Shifa*) behind. In the late 19th century a huge courtyard, *Sahn-i Jadid,* was constructed to cope with pilgrims. Several *madrasas,* including that of *Jani Khan*, were extensively repaired at this time, and the dome and drum over Fatima's cenotaph was gilded and the chamber extensively clad in mirrorwork. Such funding dried up as the Qajar regime faltered. Increasingly, during the first half of the 20th century, theological studies and the colleges involved in their teaching received markedly less royal patronage and funding. However, with increasing secularism in Ottoman and then Kemalist Turkey, Shi'i theologians returned to Iran, and particularly to Mashhad and Qom. Disused *madrasa*s in the sacred precinct were repaired and reopened, and with the installation of Ayatollah Haeri-Yazdi from Arak and his numerous students, the rejuvenation of Qom as a teaching centre and a pilgrimage place really began.

As of 1975, the main entrance opens immediately into the *Sahn-i Jadid*, renamed *Nou Atabaki*, where the festival prayers are held. Directly opposite on the far side is the passageway which leads to the Old Treasury. To the left is the tomb of Shah Safi (d1642) and behind that of Abbas II (d1666) along with the entrance into the Masjid-i Bala Sar, which formerly housed the museum. To the right a passage leads into the *Sahn-i Kuhneh*, where Fath Ali Shah is interred at the far end. Behind this courtyard are the *Madrasa Faydiyeh* and the *Dar al-Shifa*.

There are three old historic monuments in Qom, two of them in the **Bagh-i Sabz**. One is the **Imamzadeh Ali ibn Abi-Ma'ali ibn Ali Safi** at the south end. It was built in 1360 for a local amir and his family by a craftsman who went on to erect three other mausoleums. Its 12-sided exterior (but octagonal interior) once supported a double dome, hemispherical inside but tent-like on the outside, but today they have been replaced. The carved plasterwork on the exterior was originally colourfully painted. The second tomb tower, **Imamzadeh Khvaja Imad al-Din**, is 30 years later in date and housed the mortal remains of three brothers, as recorded in an inscription inside. Also with a 12-sided exterior, the tent-dome rests on a 16-sided drum. When last seen it was in good condition with an elaborate portal, decorative brick-ends and 'probably best preserved example of an entire polychromed interior that has survived in Iran' though it has since been repaired; the inscription is Koranic (K43). In the eastern part of the city is the **Imamzadeh Shah Ismail** of 1374, similarly richly decorated with a double dome, but with an octagonal exterior and square interior.

From Qom, it is about 100km south to Kashan (see page 106). When looking at a road map I am always intrigued by the Iranian village given as Nufel Le Chato on some early 1990s maps (the spelling on later maps is often 'Neufle'). This settlement wished to honour Ayatollah Khomeini, and so redesignated itself after the French town outside Paris where the Ayatollah lived in exile, Neauphlé le Château.

Southwest of Qom is **Saveh**, associated with a type of lustre and enamel-painted ceramics which was thought to have been made here in the 13th century, and more importantly for its double-spiral staircased minaret, considered to be the earliest still standing in Iran, linked to the *Masjid-i Maydan* of 1062 in the centre of town. Further down the same road is another early minaret with splendid brickwork patterning, this time belonging to the *Masjid-i Jami* of 1111. The prayer hall of this second mosque was probably constructed at the same time but much restoration and rebuilding was carried out in both the Mongol and later Safavid periods.

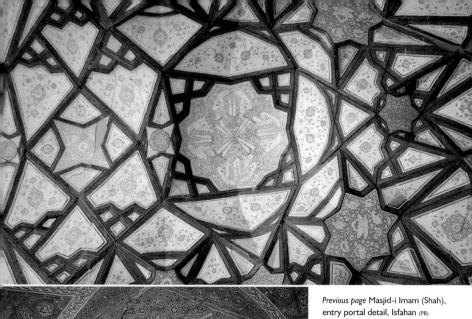

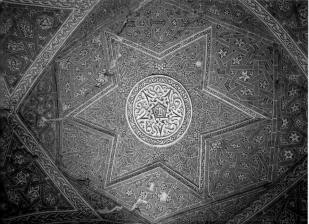

Previous page Masjid-i Imam (Shah), entry portal detail, Isfahan (PB)

Above Detail of plasterwork of the Safavid house, Na'in (PB)

Left Detail of 14th-century plasterwork, Oljeitu's mausoleum, Sultaniyeh (PB)

Below Masjid-i Jami, Natanz (PB)

West of Tehran: Qazvin and Hamadan

QAZVIN

About 150km west of Tehran lies Qazvin, founded by the Sasanid Shah Shapur I (d272) on the great central plain criss-crossed by caravan routes to the Zagros Mountains and Mesopotamia (Iraq), the Caucasus and the Caspian. The town quickly fell to the Arab Muslim armies in 644 and prospered as the trade routes were made secure, with members of the Abbasid caliphate visiting the town en route for eastern Iran. In the 12th century the regional administration became destabilised as the Assassins established strongholds around Alamut to the north. Order was restored by the Seljuk sultanate, but then the city suffered at the hands of the Mongol armies in 1220 and 1256. The political rivalry between the Ottoman and Safavid empires in the early 16th century was translated into military confrontation and Tabriz, the first Safavid capital, proved too close to the battlefield. The court moved down to Qazvin in 1555 until the Ottoman threat forced it to relocate to Isfahan in 1597, leaving behind the royal gardens, pavilions and offices. Even so, in 1628 foreign visitors reported that the city extended over 11km, with a population of about 150,000. By 1700 Ottoman incursions and earthquakes had left Qazvin in ruins, with few defences to withstand Afghan attacks against Safavid authority. Prosperity returned to a degree with Qajar rule, but again the city's location made it strategically important to Russian and then Soviet occupying forces during both world wars.

Getting there

By road from Tehran, the intercity buses take over two hours. Once you are there, as the town map indicates, most of the sights are within walking distance of each other.

Accommodation and eating out

There is really only one good hotel, the three-star **Hotel Marmar** on the main Tehran–Qazvin road before the police station (tel: 0281 2555771–5; fax: 0281 2555774). It is possible and indeed preferable to drive to and visit Alamut from here but it will necessitate a two-night stay, leaving very early in the morning and returning late evening to Qazvin. A good restaurant is **Yas** in a small blind alley off Taleqani Avenue.

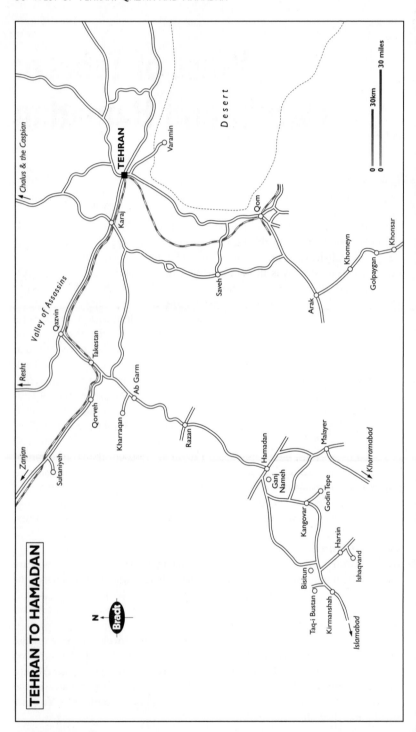

TEHRAN TO HAMADAN

Things to see and do

Very little remains of the pre-20th-century walled town of Qazvin except for the **Tehran Gate**, decked out in its 19th-century yellow, blue and black tiling, looking rather lost and forlorn standing alone. Most visitors make their way immediately to the **Imamzade Hoseyn**, which enshrines the remains of Hoseyn, a son of the 8th Imam (passing at the top of the road, a *zur-khaneh* or wrestling gymnasium – see page 116 – identified by the external tiled cornice of wrestlers and 'Indian clubs' – the caretaker happily shows people around). The main entrance vestibule into the Imamzade is also decorated with 19th-century Qajar tiles in pastel shades depicting full-blown roses and other flowers. This brings the visitor into a huge octagonal courtyard (representing the four quarters of the world overset with the four gardens of Paradise). In the centre stands the shrine with its mirrored glass veranda. Unless earlier foreign tourists have been improperly dressed or noisy, there should be no problem about entering through the shrine's massive silver doors, women using the left-hand door and men the right, leaving shoes at the attendants' desks (no photography is allowed inside). The shrine was clearly active during Safavid times because an inscription records that a daughter of Shah Tahmasp paid for restoration work in 1630, but most decoration is much later. On Fridays and holy days many families come here on pilgrimage, having lunch as they sit in the courtyard alcoves. As you walk round the exterior of the building, look at the paving stones, especially those to the left of the main veranda. Some of these are gravestones bearing emblems denoting the gender and profession of those commemorated.

A short walk from here is the **Masjid-i Jami** (about 500m from Ali Qapu), slightly set back from the main road. Head down the passageway and into the courtyard of this four-portal mosque. The inner arcades of the courtyard, with the characteristic Qajar pink and yellow tiles on their façades, have been extensively restored in the last decade, and there has also been 19th-century 'prettification' following on from extensive late-17th-century repairs to two of the four ivans. The real reason for visiting is the main prayer hall to the left. It is thought to have been built over a ruined Zoroastrian fire temple, but for the last four years repairs and a forest of scaffolding have prevented access to this chamber. But in case the restoration is completed soon, it might be useful to include a brief description of this early 12th-century chamber ($15.25m^2$). It is dominated by a huge, 19m, hemispherical dome supported on four large squinches. A monumental, floriated, Kufic brick inscription around the dome-base states that the Seljuk governor of Qazvin, Khumartash (d1136) ordered its construction in 1106, finishing nine years later. Given that the Seljuks were staunch Sunni Muslims, it is intriguing that there is also an unusual reference to Ali, the son-in-law of the Prophet Mohammed. Slowly the eye adjusts to the understated decoration of subtly coloured brickwork and carved plaster, once colourfully painted. A lengthy inscription band (K3:133; 27:40; 16:34) snakes over three walls in a series of giant trilobed meanders, while other inscriptions record the list of endowments to the mosque from shop rents, villages taxes and so on.

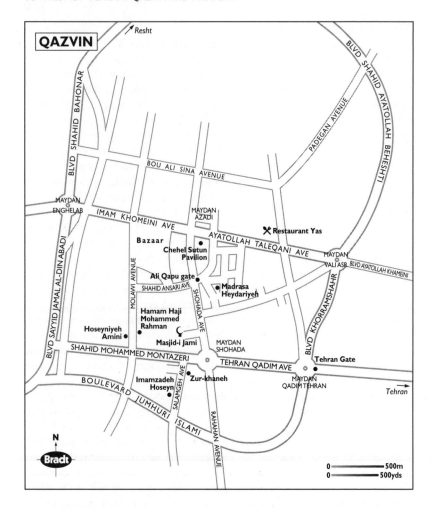

If on-site, the architect in charge of works welcomes visitors into his office in the far-left corner of the courtyard. Speaking a fluent mixture of French, German and English, he delights in showing photographs (some pre-1960), drawings and maquettes of the mosque and other local monuments. Try not to disturb the male students working in the library directly opposite. The 19th-century winter hall downstairs has pleasing proportions but this has now been converted into a library for female students, who are happy to let foreign ladies (but not men) invade their space.

Behind the mosque are the **Hamam Haji Mohammed Rahim**, and a little further on to the left, **Hoseyniyeh Aminiha**. Both were built during the 19th century, the first being, as the name suggests, a public bath (men only) and the other used to house the Moharram 'mystery play' that retells the story of Hoseyn's tragic death at Kerbela and is performed every year. Turning north along Molawi takes one towards the bazaar and the 19th-century

Masjid-i Nabi, and further east to the main square of Maydan Azadi. On its south side, almost concealed by bus shelters, is hidden a small Safavid garden pavilion, the **Chehel Sutun**, constructed around 1545 possibly by or for Shah Tahmasp (r1524–76) along with two other pavilions that haven't survived it. This intimate building, originally open on four sides (now glassed in), and a chamber on the ground floor, served as the 'coronation' hall of Shah Ismail II in 1576, and of Shah Abbas I twelve years later. In the 19th century, the local Qajar governor repaired the upper floor structure covering the exterior arches with exuberant tiling, but during the 1970s restoration, when the present garden was also laid out, some original Safavid decoration was found. The upstairs hall now serves as a small local museum with a display of mainly Qajar pottery, lacquer, metalwork and textiles, with minimal labelling in Farsi and English. Sets of postcards and publications are usually on sale, often much cheaper than in the main tourist centres.

Close by is the only other Safavid building surviving in Qazvin, the 17th-century **Ali Qapu** or monumental entrance into the former palace complex. For over 40 years it has been the police headquarters, so neither access nor photography is permitted. About 250m southeast and not far from the *Masjid-i Jami*, geographically and chronologically speaking, are the remains of a two-ivan **Madrasa Heydariyeh** located in a school yard; the guardian may seem reticent, but only because foreign visitors create intense excitement among the schoolboys. Modern buttresses and a dome support the prayer hall, built c1115, probably just after the *Masjid-i Jami*, while a 'new' basement successfully combats rising damp (many restoration programmes have involved a generous use of concrete which has resulted in serious damp problems). Much remains of the early 12th-century brickwork with its subtly fired colouring, touches of turquoise and cobalt glazed brick inserts, together with a fine plaster *mihrab* decorated with florid motifs and floriated Kufic.

As the crow flies it is a mere 35km northeast to **Alamut** via Shahrestan, and for the most part the road is good. But the journey will still take time. Until five years ago it still required a four-wheeled vehicle and a night under canvas, a great improvement on Freya Stark's two-day journey by mule. Today, Alamut itself is not in a good state of repair, but Shamran in the valley and another fortress at Soru, 100km east of Tehran, still retain something of their multiple defence walls and round towers.

If you are interested in patterned brickwork, there is a cluster of fine medieval examples near to Qazvin. The first is in the outskirts of **Takestan**, southwest of Qazvin on the road to Hamadan. This is the **Imamzadeh Pir**, built c1100 in what is a rather unattractive location. The plan is square both inside and out, with engaged columns flanking the single entrance and a single dome on squinches. Clearly the ground level around the Pir has risen by over one metre because you have to walk down to see the north-facing frontage, grimy but still original. The interior, now firmly padlocked, should be covered with plaster decorated in strap-work designs, with details similar to those found in Qurveh's *Masjid-i Jami*, some 35km away, but I could make out only rows of bricks in the gloom. The second example is **Imamzadeh Abdullah**, a 15th-century tomb in

THE ISMAILI ASSASSINS

As the Fatimid regime of Egypt and Syria began to crack and fragment in the 1060s, the Ismaili community (see page 23) in Iran began to dig in, securing strongholds to defend their villages and land. This valley of the River Alamut soon gained an international reputation as the 'Valley of the Assassins', with its chain of impregnable fortresses dominating the trade routes, and its team of highly trained men willing to sacrifice their own lives to safeguard the leaders of the Ismaili community, such as Hassan al-Sabbah in Iran and Rashid al-Din Sinan in Syria (the 'Old Man of the Mountains' as described by the Crusader chronicler, Joinville). These were the highly trained young men whose clandestine activities spread terror among the Crusaders and Muslim military leaders as they infiltrated inner court circles to 'remove' those who threatened their own community – leaders like the Seljuk sultan and champion of Sunni Islam, Malik Shah (r1072–94), his vizier Nizam al-Mulk (assassinated 1092; see page 125) and Richard Coeur de Lion. As recorded by Marco Polo, rumours spread that Hassan al-Sabbah could instil such loyalty and single-mindedness only by drugging his followers (known as Hashashiyya, from which comes 'assassin') and promising them the delights of paradise. The reality was that this was a tight-knit community with a rigid hierarchy under a charismatic leader, renowned for his scholarship and library. His death in 1125 resulted in serious disquiet within the community, and without the protection of the strongholds such as Alamut, perhaps its very survival would have been threatened. Later successors followed more pragmatic policies, establishing links with neighbouring political powers, but the Mongol invasions changed all this. Circumstances allowed Hulagu, the Mongol commander, to seize and imprison the leader of the Iranian Ismaili community in Qazvin, 1256, heralding a massacre in which the fortresses were surrendered.

The community scattered throughout Iran but in the 1770s it was in control of Kirman and Bam, with the blessing of the Zand family. The leader of the Ismailis was honoured with the title of Agha Khan by Fath Ali Shah (d1834), but by 1840 the religious atmosphere had so changed that the community left for India.

the village of **Farsajin**, just before Qurveh. Its octagonal exterior is echoed on the inside, and it has a double dome, hemispherical over the interior and an external tent or pyramidic form. At some point an entrance portal and vestibule were added. In **Qurveh** itself, ask for the **Masjid-i Jami**, to the northwest on the old Sultaniyeh–Zanjan road. A faded, painted inscription beneath its prayer dome dates this chamber and the two barrel-vaulted siderooms to 1023, perhaps re-using material from an earlier Sasanian fire temple judging from some very large bricks in the lower dome area. The *mihrab* probably also dates from the early 11th century, though alterations were made about two or three centuries later when repairs were made to the dome. Remains of painted plaster decoration in the drum and squinches supporting the dome probably relate to another inscription dated 1179. Like many early Islamic buildings in Iran, the visual impact is not immediate but its charms slowly reveal themselves.

But the real delight is on the horizon. Returning to the main Qazvin–Takestan–Hamadan road, drive about 35km towards Hamadan, turning west just before **Ab-i Garm** to **Hisar-i Armani** for **Kharraqan** (125km northeast of Hamadan). After about 30km on this recently upgraded asphalt road, two splendid Seljuk **Kharraqan** tomb towers located in a small cemetery come into view. Both were badly damaged in the 2002 earthquake but prompt action by the local gendarmarie using available timber saved them from complete collapse. Just look at their superb brick-work patterning. First recorded only in 1963, the tower to the east was constructed in 1068 while its companion, also octagonal inside and out, is thought to be slightly later in date. A staircase in the buttress to the left of the door went from the crypt to the roofspace between the two domes (approximately 7m in diameter) presumably for later repair work. Little remains now of the original painted plaster on the interior, which depicted hanging mosque lamps, a stylised tree with a bird stiffly sitting on each branch, and an inscription reading 'Blessings on its owner' but it is the external brick decoration that is such a joy. There are over 30 patterns in recessed and relief brick, including a Koranic inscription (K59:21–4) and its date makes this one of the earliest (securely) dated double-dome constructions in Iran. The second tower, with even more glorious brick decoration and with each blind niche divided into three zones, was built in 1094. The Koranic quotations here are K59:21–4 under the exterior dome, and K23:115 on the door frame: 'What, did you think that We created you only for sport, and that you would not be returned to Us?'. Again double-domed, it too has a staircase going up into the roofspace concealed in a buttress. There is nothing to identify who was interred in either tomb but because of visual similarities with that 10th-century masterpiece of brickwork, the tomb of Ismail Samanid in Bukhara, Uzbekistan, scholars think the Kharraqan towers were constructed for a local military commander, perhaps originating from Central Asia, by a local Zanjani mason.

Back to the main road, another 65km towards Hamadan takes you through **Razan**, which possesses two more (so-called Darazin) tomb towers, the Gonbad-i Hud thought to be Seljuk and the Azhar about 3km further east, possibly Mongol/Il-Khanid construction. Continuing towards Hamadan, you might note the signs for Ali Sadr and Lalejin. The caves of **Ali Sadr** were 'discovered' in the 1970s, although they were used in Safavid times to house refugees (perhaps fleeing from Ottoman incursions), and one hires a pedalo to view the magnificent natural beauty of stalagmites and stalactites. You could also enjoy a visit to the local potteries of **Lalejin**, whose production was very well regarded in pre-revolutionary Tehran.

HAMADAN

It is best to overnight in Hamadan (altitude 1,645m) formerly the ancient 7th-century BCE Median stronghold and then the Achaemenid summer capital,

Hagmatana, in the foothills of the Zagros Mountains linking Iran with Iraq (Mesopotamia). Its location near Mount Alvand (3,575m) and the pass across the Zagros always gave it a mercantile and strategic importance. In 550BCE the Achaemenid Cyrus the Great defeated the Medes and took control of the region and this city which, according to Herodotus, was defended by seven walls, the last two being of silver and gold (a clear allusion to great commercial prosperity). Alexander the Great was its next conqueror in 331BCE but he paid heavily with the death of his friend, Hephaestion. The city flourished under the Parthian regime as an important cultural centre but then was neglected in Sasanid times. By 645CE, the Arab army had swept through bringing Islam; at first the town profited from the new political order but the 10th century brought a series of disasters: in 931 large numbers of the inhabitants were massacred by a local warlord, 25 years later a serious earthquake caused great damage, and during religious riots in 962 many lost their lives. Peace and prosperity were restored under Seljuk rule in 1100, but then the Mongol armies sacked the city in 1221 and again in 1224. Hamadan was later embroiled again in political and military conflict, first suffering under Timur Leng (d1405), then from the rivalry between the Aq- and Qara Qoyunlu tribal confederations, and the Safavid–Ottoman conflict. From 1724 the region was incorporated within the Ottoman Empire until Nadir Shah Afshar retook it finally in 1732. Despite the English traveller Buckingham describing the city as 'a pile of ruins' in 1816, the population of Hamadan four years later stood at 40,000. This had halved by 1889. Today it stands at about one million, with a city plan largely laid out in 1928 by a German architect.

Its high altitude means heavy snowfalls from November until mid-March. As a medieval Arab poet commented:

> Even the heat of the fire becomes frozen in Hamadan
> And the cold there is a chronic evil.

Getting there and around

By road, take an intercity bus from Tehran, Qazvin, etc. Within the city, it will be quicker and easier to take a local taxi to visit the various places.

Accommodation

There are two top-of-the-range hotels. The three-star **Bou Ali** (Bonyad) is on Bou Ali Street up from the Avicenna tomb roundabout (tel: 0811 8252788; fax: 0811 8252824; 45 rooms; US$79 double & single). Rooms in the main building and the annex are clean but with 1970s' furnishings, although the public rooms have been totally renewed. The recently opened, privately owned three-star **Hotel Baba Tahir** is on Maydan Baba Tahir (tel: 0811 4227181–4; fax: 0811 425098; US$91 double & single).

Things to see and do

Frankly, with one exception, Hamadan has more historic interest for the visitor than aesthetic architectural delights, but the surrounding area has much

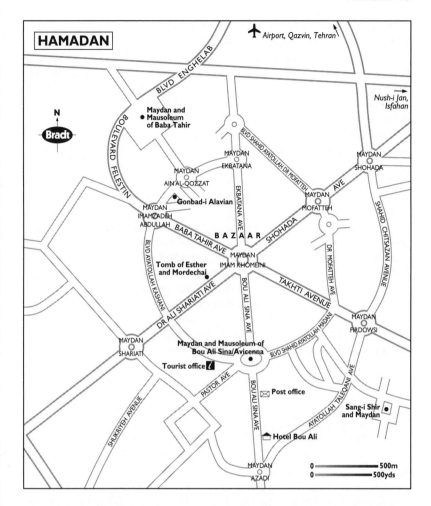

to offer, whether you are keen on history, archaeology or crafts (Hamadan is a known carpet centre). The **Tomb of Avicenna** (Ibn al-Sina or Ibn Sina), on the roundabout down from the Hotel Bou Ali, is a good example. This 10th-century Muslim scientist, who originated from Central Asia, was mentioned in Chaucer's *Canterbury Tales* but the monument itself dates from 1952 and was clearly inspired by the early 11th-century Gonbad-i Qabus monument in northeastern Iran (see page 143). The museum on the ground floor is a splendid example of how dull and uninformative a museum display can be, with umpteen printed versions of Avicenna's great works in various languages, and minimalistic Farsi labelling. But there is a good view of Mount Alvand from the upper platform outside, and the gardens are pleasant, although one dices with death crossing to and from the roundabout. Avicenna (born c980) fled from his enemies at court in Bukhara (Uzbekistan), arriving in Hamadan in about 1015 to practise as a doctor for some nine years. He then moved to

Rayy and Isfahan, returning to Hamadan to die of colic in 1037. Most of his 130 or so books have been lost but fragments remain to show he wrote knowledgeably on economics, poetry, philosophy (influencing St Thomas Aquinas) and music as well as physics, mathematics and astronomy. His *Book of Healing* and *Canon of Medicine* became the standard medical textbooks in Europe until the mid-17th century; it is from such Muslim scientists that we get such words as algebra, alchemy, alcohol and alkaline.

Another modern tomb (1951, repaired 1970) set in another pleasant garden commemorates **Baba Tahir**, author of metaphysical works but more renowned for his passionate mystical poetic quatrains which, it was said, could melt the snows of Alvand. No-one is sure when he lived or died other than it was between 900 and 1300 but his Sufi love poetry remains a favourite and is still often set to music.

One tomb of historic rather than architectural interest is that of **Esther and Mordechai**, off the Maydan Imam Khomeini roundabout, set back behind a green fence whose gate is usually firmly padlocked. However, the guardian, an Iranian Uriah Heep, is generally on duty on Fridays. This small brick tomb is probably medieval in date with a (modern) devotional area below street level, but local tradition says it is much older, housing the graves of Esther and her uncle Mordechai of the Old Testament (despite the fact that an inscription was found naming the deceased as Elias and Samuel, sons of a certain Ismail Karlan). Another theory is that it was the tomb of Susan, the Jewish queen of the Sasanian shah Yazdigird 1 (399–420). Entry into the tomb itself is through an old stone doorway (leaving shoes outside) which leads into various small prayer rooms and the main chamber with the two cenotaphs. The one to the right is said to be that of Esther, the Jewish consort of either Xerxes 486–65BCE or his successor Artaxerxes (d424BCE), but actually both are replicas of the 13th- or 14th-century cenotaphs destroyed by fire from pilgrims' candles; the actual graves are in the crypt below. You remember the biblical story: at Susa in southern Iran a newly appointed Achaemenid court chamberlain, Haman, envious of the influence of Esther and her uncle, spread rumours that the Jewish community was conspiring against the emperor and argued for their extermination. Warned by Mordechai, Esther arranged a sumptuous royal banquet during which Haman was tricked into suggesting great rewards for Mordechai, thinking these were intended for himself. At a second banquet he was denounced by Esther who then won royal permission for all the Jews to return from exile. Every Purim in the Jewish calendar, delicious pastries called 'Haman's ears' are still happily munched.

Before you leave Hamadan, visit the **Gonbad-i Alavian**, a glorious if dusty tomb located in the playground of a girls'-school yard, off Maydan Ain al-Qozzat. Take a torch as the interior is very dark. The keyholder lives in the small house immediately to the left after the school gate. It is thought this was the mausoleum for members of the Alavian family, who controlled Hamadan for two centuries, but when it was built exactly is unclear. To some scholars its elaborately carved plaster of leaf and flower motifs resemble Seljuk decoration as found at Divrigi and elsewhere in Turkey – as well as on the

1148 Mausoleum Gonbad-i Surkh in Maragha (see page 163) – but others argue the almost three-dimensional, lace-like 'baroque' quality of its motifs is early 14th-century Il-Khanid work. The original roof has gone and much of the brick and plaster strapwork exterior has been restored but don't be put off by the present monochrome colour, dust and gloom; let the plasterwork speak to you. The Koranic inscriptions inside (K53:1–35), on the *mihrab* (K36:1–9), outside (K76:1–9) and over the entrance (K5:55–6) refer to rewards and punishments, death and paradise, the importance of prayer and charity-giving – all very apposite for a mausoleum and possibly the plaster leaf- and plant-forms symbolise the gardens of Paradise.

I am less enthusiastic about the so-called **Lion of Hamadan** (*Sang-i Shir*), located in a public area in the southeast. The passage of time together with the local tradition of kissing and greasing its nose to find a husband, mean much imagination is needed to identify this battered stone sculpture as a lion, but it is agreed that this could well be a Hellenistic memorial lion to Hephaestion, the beloved general and close companion of Alexander the Great, dating to the late 4th century BCE. Nothing else of Herodotus's Ekbatana is visible to the visitor, although archaelogical excavations in the 1920s uncovered two tablets naming Darius the Great (d485BCE), and Artaxerxes II. In the 1970s 25 hectares were acquired for archaeological excavations and remains of a 9m thick defensive wall were uncovered, which was originally protected with regularly placed towers. In 1974, 15 slipper coffins, probably 1st century BCE or CE, were uncovered in a Parthian cemetery, and since 1983 two stretches of the ancient city wall, along with houses and alleys, have been located.

AROUND HAMADAN

The real reason for staying in Hamadan is its proximity to other towns and attractions in the area, aside from the Ali Sadr Caves and the Lalejin potteries.

About 10km west of Hamadan is **Ganj Nameh** (literally Book of Treasures). High up on the rock face, looking north, are two large panels carrying Achaemenid trilingual inscriptions recording the victories and lineage of Darius the Great and his son, Xerxes (d465BCE), and giving thanks to the Zoroastrian deity Ahura Mazda. The road branches south for Kirmanshah (on some early post-revolutionary maps, marked as Bakhtaran) passing some interesting sights. The first is **Kangovar**, some 95km from Hamadan and set back on the right (north) of the main road. This was the ancient Concobar of the first century CE, known for its temple to Artemis (the Greek version of the Zoroastrian Anahita) and later for the palace of the Sasanid shah Khosrau. By medieval times its reputation among travelling merchants had sunk to being that of a place full of muggers and thieves. Many 19th-century European visitors suggested archaeological investigation around the standing columns and the immense stone platform, but extensive excavation was only undertaken from 1968 until 1977, with the final report published (in Farsi) in 1996 (unfortunately unavailable to me). From brief reports of the 1970s, the first excavations revealed a plan similar to Persepolis, with double staircases up to the main terrace where a columned temple once stood; everything seemed to suggest an Achaemenid construction. However, as work progressed, the finds pointed instead to the late Seleucid/early Parthian times, or even to Sasanid occupation with later Islamic buildings and workshops.

Today the site is largely overgrown, and there are no signs nor a site-map at the ticket office (though they do have good postcards of other sites in the area). The path from the ticket office leads to the remains of the double staircases fronted by some re-erected column shafts. Scrabbling up the mound and looking back, you might make out the fired-brick walls of the Islamic workshops below. A little further up, to the extreme left, is a good view down on to more recent excavations which uncovered yet more columns and bases, while high up by the road fence a mosque rests on the original stone platform.

If archaeological sites are of interest, **Godin Tepe** lies about 13km south east of Kangovar (coming from Hamadan turn south just before Kangovar to the signposted township of Godin, which is located just south of the Tepe) and as remains of certain mud-brick buildings (level V) have been consolidated, visitors can get a better understanding of the site. Canadian excavation work from 1965 onwards revealed buildings dating 2600–1600BCE, which included an eight-columned hall largely destroyed by earthquakes, and a later Median citadel (level II) with a 30-columned audience hall, towers and magazines. Most of the residences had a raised square hearth in the main room with an elevated seat and footstool for the owner at one end and seating for guests along the side walls. Remnants of staircases showed houses had at least one upper floor, but for an idea of their external appearance, perhaps the Assyrian reliefs at the British Museum hold the key. The last season, in 1973, produced even more sensational dating evidence, pushing occupation of the site back to c4500BCE (level X), with striking artefacts uncovered from level V (3200–3000BCE).

From Kangovar, the road from Hamadan leads towards Bisitun and Taq-i Bustan; if you have them, keep a telephoto lens or binoculars to hand. All this countryside is associated in Persian legend and in late medieval book illustrations with the two star-crossed royal lovers, Khosrau and Shirin.

Among archaeologists, the region is famous for the exquisite (but frequently forged) Luristan bronzes, some of which are displayed in the Archaeological Museum and the Reza Abbasi Museum, Tehran. Used to embellish horse equipment, as standard finials etc, these cast bronzes with their powerful stylised animal forms were manufactured in this region from the 1st millennium until c600BCE, and some perhaps even date from the 3rd millennium BCE.

As you come towards **Bisitun**, the immense rockface recording the victories of Darius the Great dominates the skyline. Just before the town, there is a Safavid bridge on the right, but drive on to the large lay-by on the left. At (modern) road level on your right there is a small reclining statue concealed under a rusting canopy. Although recently emasculated, he is now provided with a new head. On close inspection you can just make out a club in the background and the lionskin under the figure: this is Herakles (Hercules) complete with a Greek inscription stating it was carved for Hyakin in 148BCE

KHOSRAU AND SHIRIN

Hearing of the great beauty of Shirin, the Armenian princess, a young Sasanid prince (later Khosrau II) sent his own portrait with an artist on his own wondrous horse, Shabdiz, to try to bring her to the Sasanid court. Falling in love with the picture, Shirin secretly stole away on Shabdiz, unaware that Khosrau was riding towards Armenia having quarrelled with his father. Their paths crossed (Khosrau even caught sight of Shirin bathing in a pool) but, neither recognising each other, they returned to their homes: Khosrau to succeed to the throne, and Shirin with her unrequited love. A rebellion then caused Khosrau to flee to Armenia where the two finally met and fell passionately in love. But the course of true love never runs smooth. Determined to regain his throne, Khosrau asked for help from the Byzantine emperor, cementing the agreement by marrying a Byzantine princess. Restored to power, he then begged Shirin to join him despite his recent marriage.

But Shirin, now queen in her own right and angry at his duplicity, sent a message of rejection from her palace, Qasr-i Shirin. Dejected and depressed, she yearned for fresh milk from her mountain pastures and commissioned a young engineer and mason, Ferhad, who had the strength of two elephants, to carve a channel through the mountains. Head-over-heels in love with her, Ferhad achieved this feat in weeks, but jealous Khosrau schemed to prevent any further liaison and to profit from Ferhad's skills. Persuading Ferhad to excavate a pass between the mountains at Bisitun, and carve a sculpture of Khosrau on Shabdiz at Taq-i Bustan, he promised Shirin would be Ferhad's once these impossible tasks were achieved. Hearing this, Shirin visited Ferhad who became so reinvigorated in his work that the king feared he would have to keep his promise; he lied to the engineer announcing that Shirin had suddenly died. Ferhad killed himself and a shocked Shirin was at last persuaded to visit Khosrau's palace to hear his explanation. After many recriminations, the two lovers were reunited but only briefly. Khosrau, the story goes, was stabbed to death by a stepson maddened by the beauty and devotion of Queen Shirin and she, rejecting his advances, killed herself over Khosrau's body.

in honour of a local governor. But the most important set of inscriptions are about 10m to the left and very high up. If the scaffolding which has been happily rusting for over eight years (without a workman in sight) is still in place, the best view of Darius's proclamation is across the road, standing on the cover over the concrete conduit.

The modern road is on a much higher level than the original Royal Achaemenid road that ran from western Turkey across the Zagros Mountains to Hamadan and then south to Susa. Alexander the Great must have passed this way and presumably the significance of this enormous 18x7m carved panel was explained to him. However, later travellers variously described the panel as showing Shalmenezer and the ten captive tribes of Israel, Esther leading her community away, Jesus and his 12 disciples, a Sufi mystic with his followers, or a schoolmaster reprimanding his pupils. It actually depicts the Achaemenid emperor Darius the Great with his generals behind, standing victorious on the rebel Gaumata who refused to accept the succession of Darius. Above, a winged figure, generally identified as Ahura Mazda of Zoroastrian belief, witnesses the submission of eight provincial governors who supported Gaumata's claim to the Achaemenid throne; the ninth figure of a Scythian chief with its inscription was added a few years after the main section was begun in 521BCE (see page 192).

The panel inscriptions were first copied by Henry Rawlinson in 1836, then adviser to the local governor, using ropes and ladders ('the interest of the occupation entirely did away with any sense of danger') and like the Rosetta Stone, now in the British Museum, their decipherment was fundamentally important to our understanding of the ancient languages of Babylonian, Old Persian and Elamite. Recording that Gaumata was killed near here at the Battle of Kundurush on September 29 522BCE, Darius had carved: 'This is what I did by the favour of Ahura Mazda in one and the same year after that I became king [521BCE]. Nineteen battles I fought, by the favour of Ahura Mazda I smote them and took prisoner nine kings. One was Gaumata by name a Magian; he lied thus he said "I am Smerdis the son of Cyrus"; he made Persia rebellious.' Darius's right to rule was emphasised: 'Eight of my family were kings before me. I am the ninth. We inherit kingship on both sides,' promising: 'The man who co-operated with my house, him I rewarded well; who so did injury, him I punished well.' Its purpose is obvious but where did the idea of carving such a relief come from? Archaeologists point to Urartian rock carvings in Turkey and further east, but the nearest source of inspiration is the rock-relief at Sar-i Pol-i Zuhab, 150km west (see page 101).

Later rulers left their mark below Darius's proclamation but to see these, you have to get closer, remembering this is a busy main road; just above the first set of steps is a worn low relief depicting the Parthian shah, Mithridates II, receiving the homage of four provincial governors while on the right his descendant, Shah Gotarzes II (c38–50CE), on his battle-horse is lancing an enemy as a Roman-styled Nike (Victory) flies overhead. Both have been damaged by a 17th-century panel inscription describing the endowment of a nearby *caravanserai*.

Further on from Bisitun is the Sasanid *paradeisos* of **Taq-i Bustan** (entry 3,000 rials). As one passes a huge military base on the left of the main road, on the opposite hillside is a huge (undecorated) rock-cut surface that marks the remains of an immense platform. Legend has it that near here was an enormous reception area where the Sasanid rulers received envoys from the Chinese and Roman empires in great splendour.

A right turn leads to the two small 'grottoes' of Taq-i Bustan. This is a popular lunch spot for local families and for pilgrims making the road journey to Kerbela in Iraq. The entrance to the site is past the *chello-kebab* cafés, at the far end of the pool; from here, it's a short walk to the first 'grotto', among elaborately carved column capitals, some showing a Sasanid shah holding the diadem or Ring of Authority, brought here from the Bisitun locale. The word 'grotto' is inaccurate although there is an air of fantasy about this place. The exact function of these two man-made caves is unclear but the hunting scenes depicted on the two side walls suggest this was part of a favourite Sasanid royal hunting park or *paradeisos*. A stylised Tree of Life, perhaps symbolising the Zoroastrian Tree of All Seeds, from which all known plants germinate, is carved either side of the main 'grotto' with Rubenesque victory angels above. At the back of the cave a huge, almost free-standing figure of rider and horse has been carved from the rock, while above stands (left to right) the Zoroastrian goddess, Anahita, pouring a libation, a kingly figure in the centre and Ahura Mazda. But which Sasanid shah is depicted here and below as the warrior-hero? The particular crown suggests it is Firoz (r459–84) but this shah had a disastrous military career, culminating in his capture and ransom in Central Asia after ordering a cavalry charge right into a concealed staked ditch. Scarcely a record one would wish to have commemorated. The most likely candidate is Khosrau II (r590–628) with his legendary horse Shabdiz, who brought Byzantine Syria and Egypt under Sasanid control before his murder (see page 97). It is said he went hunting with 300 horses, 1,160 slaves with javelins, 1,040 slaves with swords and staves, 700 falconers, 300 riders with hunting-panthers, 70 leopards, 700 hounds and 200 minstrels, and such scenes are beautifully depicted on both side walls. The recently installed chain infuriatingly restricts viewing, although a longer chain along each wall would simply and effectively solve this; one sometimes despairs of officialdom. High up on the far left is a low relief of Mohammed Ali Mirza, son of Fath Ali Shah, recording his governorship of the region, dating from 1822.

The next 'grotto' contains the figure of Shapur III (r383–8) with his grandfather Shapur II (d378) on the right. The inscription just visible is in the Pahlavi script, largely abandoned after the Arab conquest in the 7th century. A little further along is a low relief of the investiture of Ardashir II (r379–83) with Ahura Mazda on the right, while Mithra, the Zoroastrian 'Lord of Contract' or 'Justice' stands on a lotus dais, carrying a *barsom* of twigs for the sacred fire (see page 165). In Zoroastrian belief this manifestation of Ahura Mazda crossed the heavens daily in his sun-chariot (thus, his halo of sunrays) to check that all were keeping their word, but when he was adopted as a deity in his own right by Roman soldiery, his rituals were followed in secrecy in underground or windowless temples. Under the feet of Ardashir II lies a defeated enemy, probably a Roman emperor. It has been suggested that his beard identifies him as Julian the Apostate (who reintroduced temple worship in the place of Christianity across the empire) who invaded Sasanid territory as far as Ctesiphon before being defeated and dying in 363. But this was 16 years before Ardashir came to the throne; furthermore Ardashir II led no campaigns against Rome during his reign, so the bearded figure's identity remains a mystery. Just to the right of this panel is the natural spring that probably made this spot so appealing to the Sasanid shahs and explains the depiction of Anahita in the first 'grotto'.

Returning to the main road, a drive back to Bisitun and then south in the direction of Khorromabad will take you to Nurabad through lovely countryside; it is possible to make a round trip back to Hamadan via Malayer and Nush-i Jan. Or you could take the road into Kirmanshah and drive towards Qasr-i Shirin. **Kirmanshah** (some early 1990s maps may show Bakhtaran), originally founded by the Sasanids in the 4th century CE, has little of historic or architectural interest, especially after constant Iraqi bombardment during the 1980s. There is, however, the early 20th-century Takiyeh of Muavin al-Mulk with interesting tiled panels in the three performance areas. Those of the first courtyard reveal the function of the small complex with a large panel, to the right just after the entry, depicting a preacher reciting one of the Ashur eulogies about Hoseyn while veiled ladies sit at his feet, and men dressed in white flagellate themselves in the commemorative parades along the bottom section. In the main covered hall each panel shows an episode of the Kerbela story (see box, page 52); look for the one depicting Zaynab, Hoseyn's sister, berating the Umayyad ruler in Damascus after the battle; close by the throne, as if they were actively involved in 7th-century Umayyad politics, are European envoys in 19th-century dress, a reflection of Iranian europhobia a century ago. The final open courtyard has a large panel showing a Sufi mystic with the ritual vessels and dress elements, while the back of the 'stage' is covered with moulded tiles alluding to Iranian archaeological monuments and historic or legendary figures. A visual delight for tired eyes. But a little to the southeast are the villages of **Deh-i Nau** and **Ishaqvand** (sometimes spelt as Sakavand). On the cliffs above the two settlements are three rock-cut tombs (another is near Sorka-deh village) associated locally with legendary Ferhad, the engineer who loved Queen Shirin (see page 97). Judging by the low-relief depicting a priest with uplifted hands in prayer, these Zoroastrian tombs, about 2m wide and 1.75m deep, date from the 4th or 3rd century BCE.

Rather than travelling north from Kirmanshah to Sanadaj and then Takht-i Soleyman (see page 163), one could continue westwards to Islamabad (70km) and Qasr-i Shirin, the centre of old Luristan. If taking this road, don't pack away the binoculars or telephoto lens, but remember the proximity of the Iraqi border. A number of archaeological teams worked on various sites in this region down towards Ilam (Chavar, Tepe Var Kabud and Bani Surmah) where remains of ancient palaces and extensive cemeteries were discovered, mostly dating from the 3rd millennium BCE. Three kinds of burials were uncovered: individual interment under the family house (as often found in Anatolia), mass interment in pits just outside the settlement, and thirdly, burial in large stone vaults constructed from beautifully dressed stone with luxurious grave goods to match.

Another 50km or so brings you to Qaleh-i Yazdigird, badly damaged in the Iran–Iraq war, but before this there is **Dukkan-i Da'ud**, investigated by Sir Henry Rawlinson in 1836. The locals then said this tomb chamber carved high up out of the living rock housed the remains of a Jewish blacksmith who became a local ruler, but today archaeologists argue it is Median or early Achaemenid in date, while others associate it with the Seleucid low-relief (1.5x0.9m) carved below the tomb, depicting a Zoroastrian priest holding a *barsom*. The tomb itself has two sections: the first functioned as a columned antechamber, 9.6m wide, with a door leading into the narrower tomb chamber with a small ossuary pit dug out of the rock floor.

Less than 5km away is another rock carving of great interest to archaeologists and which probably inspired the Achaemenid stonemasons working for Darius the Great at Bisitun. Slightly to the east of the village of **Sar-i Pol-i Zuhab** is the famous relief, possibly carved c2200–1900BCE. A local ruler, probably King Anubanini of Lullubi, is shown standing on a platform supported by captives, with his foot firmly on the chest of a fallen enemy. Facing him is the goddess Ishtar or Ianna, identified by her starred totem, presenting him with a ring or diadem while holding two roped prisoners. The similarity to the later Bisitun relief is striking. (There are four other Bisitun reliefs relating to Lullubi rulers nearby but much more inaccessible.) Below the main relief you can just make out a Parthian carving commemorating the victory of Shah Vologazes (II or III) over his rival Shah Mithdrates IV, c147CE.

The extensive site of **Qaleh-i Yazdigird** was excavated by the Royal Ontario Museum, Toronto, in 1975–8. The citadel's square towers were clearly 3rd-century Parthian in date but occupation of this hill citadel continued for another thousand years. Remains of fine wall-plaster decoration, carved, moulded and colourfully painted, were found. Some were patterned with stylised floral motifs, while other schemes contained scantily clad men and women, possibly entertainers, and cupid forms.

About 30km way is **Qasr-i Shirin** 'Castle of Shirin' (see page 97) and just before the city centre, by the Tourist Inn, mounds of earth concealed the remains of a large Sasanid complex just visible before the 1981–9 Iran–Iraq war. Opinions were divided as to its form and function, some identifying it as an enormous, domed fire temple over 16m² set in gardens, while others argued it was a massive audience hall for Khosrau II. Nearby, another Sasanid complex known as Imaret–i Khosrau ('Refectory') was entered by a double staircase at the eastern end, and stables, store rooms and ten courtyards were identified mainly from drawings made in the 1930s; recently these drawings, and therefore these conclusions, have been questioned. What is clear is that the complex and the town of Qasr-i Shirin were severely damaged by the Byzantine emperor, Heraclius, in 628CE, and then Arab armies some ten years later.

The drive south from Bisitun is through lovely countryside. At Nurabad ask directions for the village of Morabad and **Tepe Baba Jan**, excavated by a British team in 1966–69. You pass Harsin, and in this area at **Ganj Dareh** Canadian archaeologists found evidence of early Neolithic occupation with a suggested carbon-14 dating of c8450BCE. A severe fire around 7300BCE actually helped conserve certain artefacts and the mud-brick architecture, vitrifying the clay. The pottery was crude with no signs of imported trade goods but the walls, sometimes surviving up to 2m high, were carefully plastered. Some 30km further on, the main mound **Tepe Baba Jan** revealed settlement from the 4th millennium BCE but the most important finds emerged from later levels, especially those from c900–700BCE. The groundplan and architectural details (such as blind niches, the arrow slit forms) of these later buildings were similar to those found at Nush-i Jan to the east and Hasanlu further north, incorporating defences to safeguard both the property and the inhabitants. The large columned hall had side rooms and a portico under which a horse skeleton with harness and vessels was found. This burial probably dated from a destructive fire which swept the site, perhaps caused by invading Scythian tribesmen in the 7th century BCE. On the eastern tepe nearby another fortified building with a central chamber, 10.4x12.5m, was excavated. A spiral ramp led to a second storey, but what was striking was the rich painted plaster decorating the walls of the central chamber, and sherds of painted ceiling tiles, decorated with squares or diamond forms. After the fire the site was not abandoned as there was some evidence of Achaemenid occupation, but for some reason everyone left before the Seleucids took control of the region.

The site of **Nush-i Jan** lies almost due east of Tepe Baba Jan but is best approached from the Hamadan–Malayer road, about 10km south from the Jowkar crossroads, approximately 10km north of Malayer itself. British archaeologists worked on this small Median site, about one-sixth of the main Apadana platform at Persepolis, from 1967–74. Four principal buildings were found on this outcrop: two temples, a fort and a columned hall with an enclosing wall. The central temple, probably constructed before 700BCE, had a narrow entrance leading into an antechamber possessing a stepped 'Maltese cross' ground plan and a spiral ramp (like Tepe Baba Jan) to an upper level. It then led to a sanctuary with a triangular cella and large blind windows with 'toothed' lintels decorating the walls. A brick fire-altar (85cm high) with four steps was screened from the entrance and, perhaps to protect its sanctity from later squatters, the temple was filled with shale to a depth of 6m and carefully bricked in. This was a tremendously important find: perhaps the earliest temple with fire-altar in situ found in western Iran. The second temple, located just to the west, had similar rooms and a spiral ramp but with a different orientation and an assymetrical ground plan. The fort measured 25x22m, approximately the size of the Gate of All Lands at Persepolis (page 188), with four long magazines and a guardroom with another spiral ramp for access to at least one other floor, while the hall with a slightly irregular ground plan was somewhat smaller with twelve columns supporting a flat roof. Very little stone was used in construction throughout the site but the bricks (especially in the vaults) were often carefully shaped. For some reason the site was then left largely unoccupied until the Parthian period (c1st century CE).

The road south takes you to **Borujerd**, an important military town in the 19th century when the Qajars struggled to keep control over the local tribes. More recently it was the home of the famous theologian Ayatollah Hoseyn

Tabataba'i Borujerdi (d1962). Its Masjid-i Jami still retains its Seljuk domed prayer chamber among extensive 19th-century restoration work in the courtyard. In the late 1990s the guardian here was very suspicious of foreign visitors 'dropping in' and unless you have a spare hour to kill while he telephones for permission, it is advisable to withdraw gracefully if he objects to your presence. In the same area is the Imamzadeh Ja'far with a distinctive 'sugar-loaf' dome, similar to those found in south Iran, which looks very out of place this far north. The tombstone is dated 1108 but some scholars believe the tomb building is later. About 110km to the southwest is **Khorramabad**, known for the massive Sasanid bridge spanning the river Kashkan, and the remains of its citadel in the centre of town. There is also a free-standing Seljuk minaret. Just south of here an annual horse race for women riders only is held.

The town of **Arak** is known today for its aluminium smelter works and a huge petrochemical factory (the brainchild of Rafsanjani), but in the 19th century its fame rested on carpet production. This was Sultanabad, where an enormous complex, 'The Qalah' (Fort), of carpet workshops was established in 1877 by the Ziegler company of Manchester UK; it was possibly their representatives who brought the famous twin 16th-century 'Ardabil' carpets, now in London's Victoria and Albert Museum and in Los Angeles County Museum of Art, to London in the late 1880s. Readers with links to the Ismaili community (see *Religion*) might make a short detour to **Anjedan**, 37km east of Arak. This village has long historical associations with Ismaili Shi'ism; even when the Assassins were thrown out of Alamut and lost any regional control, there was an active community here until the early 18th century. In the late 1970s it possessed two recorded historical monuments, both recently heavily restored: the 1480 tomb of Ismaili Shah Qalandar and the tomb of Ismaili Shah Garib, built eight years later.

Some 100km southeast towards Isfahan, passing the small town of **Khomeyn** (60km from Arak), so closely associated with Ayatollah Khomeini ('of Khomeyn'), is the town of **Golpaygan**, perhaps established by the Sasanids after the famous victory over the Parthians here in 224CE. Its Masjid-i Jami has a fine domed prayer hall dating from 1105–18, constructed on the order of the son of the Seljuk Sultan, Malik Shah. The rest of the courtyard buildings are 19th-century additions, paid for by one of Fath Ali Shah's wives when her son was governor here. The brickwork inside this chamber is admittedly not the finest, nor are the proportions of the chamber, especially the narrow 'squeezed' corner squinches and the heavy piers, which led one writer to comment that it was 'a masterpiece of pessimism' but it is definitely well worth a few minutes' investigation. Leaving the chamber and the mosque by the right-hand portal, walk down (southeast) into the small friendly bazaar by the main road. Almost directly opposite is a fine minaret, dated 1100, whose balconies were reached by two separate spiral staircases. At its base stand two later stone lions; the heads of their victims protrude from their mouths.

Back on the road again, the next pleasant stop is on the far southern outskirts of **Khonsar**. I always wish I had more time to walk in the shady streets of Khonsar, edged with magnificent chenar trees, but instead I content myself with looking at the early-20th-century house across the stream, before leaving the town towards Isfahan. It has seen better days and presently is occupied by a number of families struggling to make ends meet, but it is still splendid with a clock (not working) over the main entrance, low reliefs of lions and also Qajar soldiers, and slowly disintegrating balconies. The tiled spandrels give details of its 1910 construction and original owner, a local wealthy merchant who had made the pilgrimage to Mecca. If you can gain entry, the servants' quarters, storerooms and cistern are off the main vestibule. Steep steps lead into the courtyard with a fine Qajar pool in the centre; today this court is occasionally used for the local *Moharram* ceremonies. The owner's quarters were located on the upper veranda level, as the remains of stained glass in intricate patterning over the doorways suggest.

From Kashan to Isfahan

KASHAN

Kashan (260km from Tehran, 210km from Isfahan) will always be associated in Islamic art for its high-quality ceramics (*kashi*) production which dates from the 12th century, even enduring the Mongol campaigns. It is also renowned for its manufacture of costly silks and carpets for the Safavid court. The 17th-century English merchant, Thomas Herbert, estimated there were then 4,000 families in the town mainly involved in textiles, which would mean that the community was then 'in compass not less than York or Norwich... The houses are fairly built, many of which are pargeted and painted; the mosques and *hamams* are in their cupolas curiously ceruleated with a feigned turquoise...' Undoubtedly he would also have heard that Kashan was the place from where the Three Wise Men set out for Bethlehem. Almost 250 years later, other English travellers reported that Kashan boasted 24 *caravanserais*, 35 hotels for foreign merchants, 34 *hamams*, 18 large mosques, and 90 small shrines but in such a bad state that Lord Curzon commented, 'A more funereal place I had not yet seen.' Matters were made no better by its reputation for poisonous scorpions.

Getting there

The easiest way to reach Kashan is by intercity bus, although the Tehran–Isfahan/Yazd–Kirman train service stops in the town. There is a new multi-lane toll road (not used by intercity buses) which passes behind the Bagh-i Fin gardens, from Tehran and on to Yazd. Be warned: petrol stations are few and far between.

Accommodation

Two or three days could happily be spent exploring Kashan and the locale, but the accommodation available may deter you. For years the town's hotels have banked money rather than spend it on room improvements. However, **Hotel Amir Kabir**, situated near to the Bagh-i Fin, 7km from the centre (tel: 0361 30091–5; fax: 0361 30338; US$57 double, US$37 single), now has new management and already two of its six floors have been refurbished to a basic three-star standard. Otherwise, only the **Saiieh Hotel** on Darvazi Dawlat

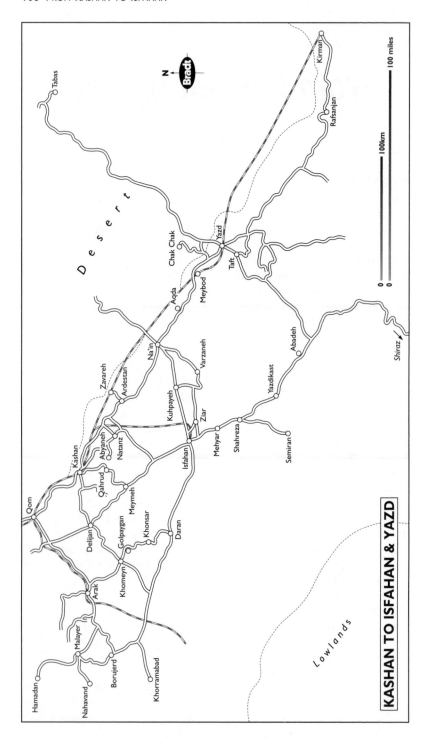

KASHAN TO ISFAHAN & YAZD

Abazar Street near Maydan Shohad Motahheri (tel: 0361 444535–6; 45 rooms; US$31 double, US$23 single) offers a reasonable alternative.

Things to see and do

The Safavid family obviously had a soft spot for Kashan, as Shah Abbas I requested that he should be buried here in preference to Ardabil, Qom or Mashhad. His body lies in the 13th-century tomb of **Habib ibn Musa**, understood to be a descendant of 7th Imam Musa ibn Qasem; the tomb is now incorporated into a large mosque complex decorated in 19th-century Qajar times. His cenotaph is the black marble one to the right as you enter the crypt; women have to hire *chadors* at the entrance. It is a short walk west from here into the extensive bazaar complex, which contains a number of interesting historic *hamams*, mosques and *khans*. As for the shops, it seems that one in ten is somehow connected with carpet-making, whether selling woollen yarn, renting design cartoons, selling swifts or dealing in carpets. The **Mosque of Mir Emad**, built in 1461 for Jahanshah, the leader of the Qara Qoyunlu tribal confederation, and justly famous for its multi-layered plaster *muqarnas* decoration, is mostly 19th century in date, when the local Qajar governor undertook large-scale restoration-work. On the same side of the street, with a 19th-century tiled entrance, is the **Hamam Khan** which, despite the mess, is still in use so women may be refused entry at certain times. It retains the basic original plan although there are some careless repairs and alterations. A short

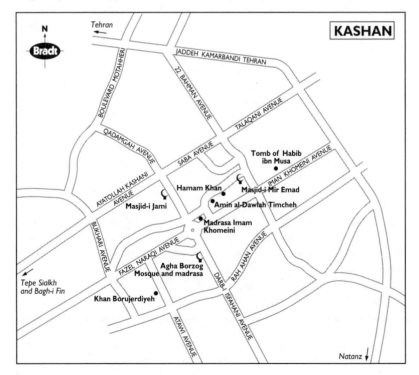

amble on the same side is the 19th-century **Khan Amin al-Dawlah Timcheh** with its soaring dome painted with original decoration, and further on the **Madrasa Imam Khomeini** (formerly Sultan), built with 52 student cells during the reign of Fath Ali Shah. A few Seljuk monuments remain in the city. Continue walking through the bazaar until the main road is reached and turn right for the **Masjid-i Jami**, extensively repaired in the 18th century, but still with its 1073 minaret; and, about 500m southeast, the 12th-century **Manar Zayn al-Din**. By retracing steps to the bazaar entrance, this main road leads to the **Masjid and Madrasa of Agha Bozorg**, named after a famous theologian and jurist who was born in a neighbouring village and who was also known as Mehdi Naraqi (d1829). This 19th-century complex incorporates a deep sunken courtyard with a central ablution pool. The basement under the prayer hall acts as a winter assembly hall. Two wind towers, cunningly disguised as minarets, flank the main prayer ivan, dramatically accentuating the dome. Close to the bazaar is the four-ivan **Masjid-i Maydan-i Sang** (also known as Maydan-i Fayd), essentially a Timurid construction of 1462–4, which possesses one of the five surviving tiled *minbars* in Iran; this example, the work of Haydar 'the tile cutter', has two pattern compositions, one on each side. Its superb tiled *mihrab*, dating to 1226, is now in the Berlin museum, Germany.

Three 19th-century residences are nearby: the Khaneh Borujerdiyeh, Khaneh Tabatabiyeh and the recently opened Khaneh Abbasian (separate entry fees; *open from 08.30 every day*). The **Borujerdiyeh** (entry fee: 2,000 rials), formerly the house of a Kashani tea dealer, is perhaps the best known as its distinctive dome over the main audience *talar* appears on postcards and posters. The **Tabatabiyeh** house (entry fee: 20,000 rials), to the left as you exit, is somewhat larger, with a clear division between the private family *anderun* apartments by the main entrance, the servants' quarters (extreme right) and the public *birun* rooms across the main court. The ornate plaster decoration is bichrome grey and white augmented with lively landscape paintings in the two side chambers of the *talar*. But the real delight is the newly opened **Khaneh Abbasian** (entry fee: 20,000 rials), down the street opposite the Borujerdiyeh. This enormous complex, built on several levels, is so extensive with numerous staircases, *talars*, courtyards and chambers that one can become quickly disorientated. The richly carved plaster decoration is in high relief on a Wedgewood blue or pale terracotta ground, often complemented with coloured window glass set in highly patterned pierced screens. Deliciously over the top. All three residences bring home to the visitor how rich and influential late-19th-century merchants were, so if you are thinking of buying a modern Kashan carpet, just remember that the Abbasian family made their fortune in carpet dealing.

About 8km southwest of the centre, and well worth a visit, are the gardens established by the Safavid shahs to break their occasional royal progresses, the **Bagh-i Fin**. Halfway along this road, the tiled pyramidic dome to the south side marks the tomb of Abu Lulu, honoured here in Iran for 'liquidating' Caliph Umar (d644), selected as caliph in preference to the Prophet's son-in-

AMIR KABIR (1807–52)

This 'Grand Commander' had lowly beginnings: his father was a cook in the Royal palace while he started as a stable groom to the court. However, his abilities were quickly recognised and he was soon appointed as a finance minister to the military in Iranian Azerbaijan. Aged 22, he joined the diplomatic team sent to St Petersburg and the Russian Caucasus, during which time he visited schools, factories, chambers of commerce and theatres. Only a handful of court officials had been sent abroad and these visits evidently had a lasting impact on him. He returned to the Caucasus in 1837, and spent four years in Erzincan (eastern Turkey) as an official negotiator, drawing up the Iranian–Ottoman frontier. These were the heady years of the Tanzimat period in Ottoman Turkey when the sultanate was yielding to constititutional demands, and undertaking reorganisation programmes affecting every aspect of economic and social life. On his return to Tehran in 1847 Amir Kabir was quickly promoted to tutor to the Crown Prince, then promoted again to Chief Army Minister, and finally Chief Minister in 1848.

Iran was teetering on the edge of bankruptcy after paying a huge war indemnity to Russia (Treaty of Turkomanchay, 1828), and he moved immediately to fill the state coffers by cutting civil service pay and pensions and ordering tax to be paid direct to Tehran instead of through court tax agents; palace officials were not amused. But the public loved him as he ordered investigations into government corruption and bribery and gave the go-ahead for the construction of bazaars, canals and factories, sending craftsmen to Russia and Ottoman Turkey for training. To stem the flood of imports, customs duties were increased while domestic manufacture and agriculture production were assisted. He was involved in everything, even actively sponsoring private citizens for small-scale contracts, instituting national prizes for art and design, and establishing the first state college organised on Western lines. But, with each project, the anger of his enemies at court intensified. On November 16 1851 he was dismissed and exiled to Kashan, but that was not enough for his enemies, who engineered his assassination in January 1852. With his removal, the reorganisation programme came to a shuddering halt for many decades.

law, Ali, an insult to all Shiʻis. As the tilework shows, it was extensively repaired in Safavid and then Qajar times. A little further, on the opposite side behind some houses, two mounds are visible, the larger being **Tepe Sialkh**, excavated by the French 1933–7. In the Tehran Archaeological Museum the elegant long-spouted pottery vessels, shaped like stylised sandpiper birds, were found here during archaeological work. The earliest level (Sialkh I), which revealed stained-red human remains buried underneath houses, has been dated to the 5th millennium BCE, perhaps earlier. The pottery finds from level

II, c4000BCE, showed indisputable use of the potter's wheel, but for some unknown reason the residents then abandoned this site for the smaller mound. This second settlement was probably destroyed by fire around 3000BCE, and there was a gap of about 2,000 years before both sites were reinhabited. The new residents had other customs, employing stone foundations for their mud and wood buildings and burying their dead away from the town with the distinctive 'sandpiper' vessels as grave goods, along with trade items from the Gulf. During the 9th and 8th centuries BCE, a military attack caused the residents to flee, never to return. All the archaeological finds have been removed from the site, but the outlines of buildings are just visible.

The **Bagh-i Fin** (entry fee 2,500 rials; museum entry 1,000 rials) is at the end of the avenue (the toll road runs immediately behind) and still retains much of its Safavid layout, with a central pavilion placed over the artesian water channels, though repair and rebuilding work was carried out by Karim Khan Zand of Shiraz, then by Fath Ali Shah of the Qajar dynasty and again in early 2000. A number of 19th-century foreign dignitaries, including the English envoy, Sir John Malcolm, broke their journeys here en route from Bushir to the Tehran court. But there was a darker side to its history: in 1852 the forward-looking Iranian Chief Minister 'Amir Kabir' (see page 109) was assassinated here in the small *hamam* to the left. Banished from the Tehran court, he was told the shah planned to restore him to favour and, in preparing for the ceremony, he visited this *hamam*, ignorant that it was a royal plot to kill him. There is a small museum, which has some of the finds from Sialk.

ON THE ROAD

On the old caravan road south to Isfahan is **Qahrud**, about 45km away on the Meymeh road, with its Masjid-i Jami (formerly Masjid-i Ali). It will be locked when you visit as its lovely 1307 Kashan tiles were stolen in the 1960s, even though they were subsequently recovered and reset in the *mihrab*. It also possesses a fine carved door dedicated to 'The Crown of the Community and Religion … the Seal of the Age', the work of an Isfahani woodworker. If time and petrol supplies allow (see page 105) consider a detour to **Abyaneh** (altitude 2,500m) in the hills, some 70km east of Kashan, close to Natanz. A small 13th-century fortress safeguarded this picturesque Zoroastrian village until Safavid sectarian intolerance drove many of the community to India; even today the official tourist pamphlet omits any reference to Zoroastrianism. A ruined but extensive fire temple built in three stages, perhaps dating from the 3rd century CE, lies in the centre of town, and nearby is the *Masjid-i Jami* with a Safavid entry portal and vestibule, with a Seljuk *minbar* and a 14th-century *mihrab* inside the prayer hall. However, the real joy is the vernacular architecture of mud-brick houses with wooden balconies and decorated doors, in narrow alleyways.

Or you could travel to Isfahan, taking the new Kashan–Yazd road southeast and turning west at Na'in; this route allows you to see some beautiful monuments en route. A short diversion west on this road at Bad leads to **Natanz**, nestling in the foothills in a beautiful setting, with the remains of the pre-Islamic castle Qaleh-i Vashaq just to the north. A beautiful portal, decorated with turquoise and cobalt glazed inserts, dated 1317, is the first thing one sees at the Masjid-i Jami complex, which dates mainly from post-Mongol times; this led into the *khanaqeh* here to accommodate visiting sufis. A much smaller, insignificant doorway takes visitors into the four-ivan mosque, built 12 years before, incorporating an earlier Seljuk octagonal structure. The Mausoleum of Shaikh Abd al-Samad al-Isfahani with its tiled tent dome was constructed some two years after. The *muqarnas* vaulting inside is beautiful as is the plasterwork throughout in the complex. Not far away in the northwest is the **Masjid-i Koucheh Mir**, which reportedly still retains a splendid carved plaster *mihrab* (K11:114–5) dating to the 11–12th centuries.

ARDESTAN

The next interesting towns on the Kashan–Yazd road are Ardestan and, slightly to the east, **Zavareh** (branching off in the centre of Ardestan). Zavareh was an important centre on the trade routes from Sasanid times until the late 11th century, which explains the number of important monuments here. The way to the **Masjid-i Jami** is through the covered bazaar. Scholars consider this to be one of the earliest known mosques in Iran, built on the four-ivan courtyard plan in 1135, according to the Kufic inscription (K9:18) running unusually around the court façade; such detail is generally placed inside the prayer chamber. Unfortunately, its gentle slide into decline noted in the late 1970s has accelerated steeply. It had a beautifully carved plaster *mihrab* with Koranic verses (K7:52) in the angular Kufic script, and in cursive Naskhi (K9:18), while the dome, supported by trilobed squinches, was decorated with another inscription (K3:187–8). Slightly to the southeast is the **Masjid-i Pa Minar** of 1069, according to the minaret inscription; this makes it one of the earliest firmly dated monuments to survive in Iran, although most of the mosque's plasterwork is 300 years later.

Ardestan was once a strongly fortified town in the 10th century. Its **Masjid-i Imam Hasan** was founded during Seljuk times as a *madrasa*, perhaps the first in Iran built with a portal flanked by two minarets, although only one minaret has survived. But the purpose of the visit is the **Masjid-i Jami** whose domed prayer chamber was built possibly on top of a fire temple during the reign of Malik Shah (d1092; see page 124) with comfortably generous, trilobed squinches. Its main brick inscription concerns further building in 1158, and another in the prayer ivan of 1160 perhaps denotes the year when the present four-ivan layout was established. The plasterwork here is some of the best surviving in Iran, whether you look at the remains of the delicate trefoil and split palmettes once covering the prayer ivan, the deeply cut elegant inscription of the arch-soffits, or the richly carved *mihrab*. In the courtyard, pavement grilles now prevent access down two staircases leading to the winter prayer hall below.

NA'IN

You must find time for Na'in, some 95km southeast of Ardestan (145km from Isfahan); the **Na'in (Tourist) Inn** (tel: 0323 2253081; fax: 0322 2253665;

US$39 double/single) has eight simple but attractive rooms with private facilities and a good restaurant.

Most books on Islamic architecture refer to the **Masjid-i Jami** (1,500 rials) here, because something of its original 10th-century 'Arab' plan remains. This 'Arab' concept of positioning arcades running parallel to the enclosing walls quickly fell out of favour as more patrons plumped for an open court dominated by two or four tall ivans, and a domed prayer chamber. As well as the (much- restored) brick patterning of the courtyard piers, some lovely mid-10th-century plasterwork remains in the prayer chamber, but unfortunately a high wooden railing really limits access and viewing. In the arch soffits and spandrels large rosettes separated by cartouches have been carved deeply, while some pillars are covered with plaster strapwork framing clusters of small mulberry-like fruits. If only one could get closer. Here and there a few 14th-century tiles enliven the brickwork. To the extreme left as you exit is the **Hoseyniyeh** with a real stage for the performance of the *Moharram* play, and from its far doorway the remains of the town's citadel are visible.

Just across the small square is the local **Ethnographic Museum** (entry only 1,000 rials, amazing value). Mention an ethnographic display and I usually experience a sinking feeling, but this is housed in a superb Safavid house of 1560. One enters to find a central sunken courtyard with rooms on both levels. Do persuade the knowledgeable curator, who speaks very good English, to take you round; his wife is a noted carpet maker in the locale. He has persuaded the townspeople to lend him interesting archival material, such as marriage contracts, as well as metalwork and ceramic objects. One display contains the *shalvar ve qamis* (trousers and tunic) as worn by Zoroastrian women in the 19th century, which are comparable in quality to items in the Victoria and Albert Museum, London; those tiny motifs are not printed but hand-embroidered. The best is yet to come: the rooms on the right of entry are stunning with their mid-16th-century plaster decoration intact. The depictions on the *talar* walls and ceiling tell of the Prophet Yusuf (biblical Joseph) whose beauty was such that the pharaoh's female slaves cut their hands in amazement, and the Egyptian queen, Zulaykha, resorted to covering her bedroom walls with erotic paintings in an attempt to seduce him. Yusuf took to his heels and lived to tell the tale. The small sitting-room next door is just as beautifully decorated. There is a striking correlation between this work and designs and compositions on famous Safavid court carpets in major Western museums, and of course Persian paintings of the same date.

Some 3km away in a northeasterly direction is **Mohammediyeh**, now virtually absorbed into Na'in. It is known for its wind towers (*badgir*s), some of which serve to ventilate small weaving shops producing camel-hair and pure woollen fabrics, exported to Syria and Lebanon; listen for the click-clack of the looms and gently push the doors open. The whole suburb seems to be actively engaged in some form of textile manufacture. In a visit lasting less than an hour, I saw warp threads being stretched, the threading of a loom reed and pit looms in operation. I also walked to the **Masjid-i Sar-i Kucha** (ask directions), although unfortunately there wasn't enough time to explore the citadel ruins and the *Masjid-i Jami*. The Sar-i Kucha is (now) a small building looking like a shrine for it has no courtyard, which is unusual for Iran. Both it and the alleyway may date from the 10th–11th century, because entry is through a side chamber into a tiny prayer room, with another side chamber on the other side. Its real claim to fame is the fine Kufic inscription painted along the interior walls and the base of the dome. Some of it, especially around the *mihrab*, has now disappeared, but it has a specifically Sunni rather than Shi'i emphasis; that supports a late 11th-century dating, given that the Seljuks, the champions of Sunni Islam, were then in control. The inscription may look battered, but closer inspection reveals beautifully proportioned letters with elegantly curved 'swan-neck' hypostyles.

WEST FROM NA'IN

The road from Na'in to Isfahan passes **Kuhpayeh**, where the *Masjid-i Jami* has one of the handful of tiled *minbars* still surviving, probably made in 1528 when the tiling scheme in the prayer chamber was installed (although some scholars consider the tiling to be c1335). From here one could continue south for approximately 33km, and then 25km east to visit **Varzaneh** (100km east of Isfahan) whose *Masjid-i Jami* and 20m-high minaret were built c1100 – although the mosque was largely rebuilt in the Timurid 15th century. The tilework (incorporating the name of Shah Rukh, see page 247, the son of Timur Leng) of the ivan leading to the prayer chamber on the *minbar* and the *mihrab* is splendid. It is on the *mihrab* that the date 1444 is recorded, after the Koranic inscription (K3:38–9). The different appearance of the north ivan results from 17th-century Safavid repairs.

There are three other Seljuk minarets closer to Isfahan which may be approached from Varzaneh travelling west or from Kuhpayeh for 45km in the direction of Isfahan, turning south to see those at Barsiyan, Ziar and, a few kilometres before Isfahan, Gar (also spelt Jar). The one at **Barsiyan**, about 45km southeast of Isfahan on the old caravan road to Yazd, was built in 1097, probably then a little taller than its present 35m. Its cylindrical base has a diameter of 5.75m but it tapers to 4.2m at the top, where there is a brick inscription (K22:76–7). The mosque below dates largely from the first half of the 12th century, so something clearly must have happened to the earlier structure. The dome had to be rebuilt in 1421 and then its courtyard was revised during the reign of Shah Tahmasp (1524–76). Across the river is **Ziar**, whose Safavid *caravanserai* was repaired in Qajar times; the amazing minaret here has provoked much discussion. Two very different dates, 1155 or 1289, have been given for this highly decorated shaft, some 50m high with its balcony intact, rising from a square plinth. Turquoise-glazed brick elements were used to pick out the Koranic inscription (41:33); these favour the later date. A similar wide dating has been given to another minaret, the *Manar-i Saraban* in Isfahan (see page 128) similarly decorated and with an identical Koranic verse. Here the names of the four caliphs after the death of the Prophet Mohammed are included, so this must be a Sunni, not Shi'i, monument which strongly suggests it was built during the Seljuk period (that

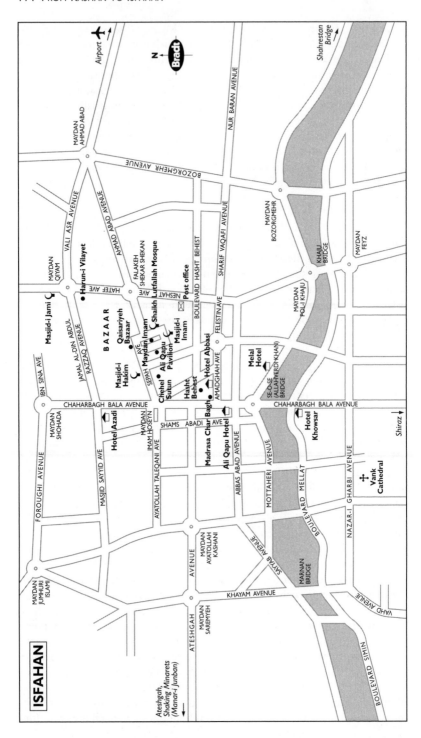

is around 1155) and this Ziar minaret is now thought to be mid-to-late 12th century. To round off this collection, the **Gar** minaret on its octagonal base was built in 1122, according to its inscription, to serve the mosque endowed by Sayyid Reza Abu'l Qasem.

About 65km southeast of Na'in (towards Yazd) is **Aqda** (also spelt Aghda), once known as a strong Zoroastrian centre. There are no magnificent historic buildings here, but the village is well worth walking around. Its Masjid-i Jami is thought to date from the 14th century, but only the winter prayer chamber retains an echo of those Timurid proportions, while outside is a large Hoseyniyeh (1875) for the *Moharram* ceremonies. A number of Aqda's other monuments have either been extensively rebuilt (eg: 1679 *Masjid-i Shams*) or closed (1645 *hamam* and 1618 cistern). The police have at last vacated the 1846 *caravanserai* built by the merchant Hajji Abul Qasim Rashti, but no-one knows what will happen to the building now. Despite this, the village has a pleasing atmosphere and the locals are very happy but curious that visitors want to walk around exploring the narrow alleys, the houses, the city gate and so on.

ISFAHAN

The proverb 'Isfahan is half the world' could be taken to imply (accurately in this case) that this city is home to a large number of historic monuments. It is impossible to do full justice to all of them, but the most famous buildings and some of special interest have been included below.

Isfahan (altitude 1,585m; population 1.5 million) – the name comes from *sipahi:* soldier – has been an important trading centre since Parthian times, and possibly both the **Pol-i Sharestan** bridge and the **Ateshgah** (fire temple) just on the outskirts are early Sasanid in construction, built when the city already had separate Jewish and Christian quarters. It fell to the Arab Muslims in 643 and quickly gained a reputation for its textiles, becoming the capital of the Seljuk sultan Tughril Beg (d1063). Bitter quarrels broke out among local Shi'is and Sunnis, so its prosperity suffered and then plummeted as the Mongols invaded. Then it was the onslaught of Timur Leng's army, which slew at least 70,000 (and possibly 200,000) Isfahanis. The rivalry between the Aq Qoyunlu and Qara Qoyunlu tribal confederations in the 15th century prevented any sustained revival, but with the Safavid court's move from battle-threatened Tabriz and Qazvin to Isfahan in 1598, the city's fortunes changed.

Town planning began in earnest immediately with the Chahar Bagh gardens, and then the main square with its royal buildings was constructed. According to the French jeweller, Jean Chardin, by the 1660s Isfahan had 162 mosques, 1,802 *caravanserais*, 48 colleges and 273 public baths to serve a population the size of London, then about 600,000. The sheer scale and the beauty of its buildings amazed most foreign visitors who marvelled at the turquoise domes and the dramatic minarets. But the Safavid regime was beginning to crack at the seams and in 1722 the capital was besieged for six months by Afghan rebels. Plague outbreaks and famine followed. Nadir Khan (later crowned as shah) ousted the Afghans but transferred the

THE ZUR-KHANEH

The sport of wrestling has always been popular in Iran. Wealthy merchants and court officials traditionally sponsored wrestling teams and patronised the gymnasia (zur-khanehs) where the athletes practised calisthenic exercises. Traditionally, a young man has to be at least 16 years old, with a beard growth thick enough to support a comb, before being accepted for training. There are some 50 holds to learn and two tests to pass before being recognised as a junior athlete, and progress is shown in the ways the wrap is worn around the hips. Only a select few were ever acknowledged as pahlavan or champion (one reason why Reza Khan chose this title as his dynastic name in 1925).

The exercise and wrestling place is one and the same: a sunken area, often octagonal in shape, large enough to hold 12 to 18 men during their exercising. One English visitor in 1833 described it with 'seats for the spectators... the roof, which was plastered, was painted all over with fierce figures of pehlewans performing their various feats of strength'. Today the zur-khaneh walls are usually decorated with photographs of past and present wrestlers, and objects strongly identified with sufi and dervish fraternities, like begging bowls, axes, a sheepskin mat and posters of Imam Ali, the shrines of Kerbela and Mashhad. This association with Ali and his descendants is stressed as the morshid (leader) beats out the rhythm for each exercise while shouting out Shiʿi sayings. Each calisthenic exercise builds up the muscles: a wooden board to strengthen the shield arm, 'Indian' clubs weighing anything from 4 to 40kg substituting for heavy warclubs, and an iron bow to exercise shoulder muscles. The gymnasts' strength is publicly recognised every year when they are asked to carry the heavy ʿalam standards in the Moharram parades, but in the 1960–70s many zur-khanehs were closed down as the late shah grew nervous about their loyalty to the crown.

There is at least one UK establishment, Zur-khaneh Pouri-e Vale, meeting weekly and organised by an experienced pahlavan, Hoseyn Bahmani, at (West) Kensington Sports Centre, London.

administration to Mashhad (see page 248). By 1800 the population of Isfahan was probably only 120,000.

Warning In recent years, several tourists in Isfahan have had cameras snatched by a motorcycle team, so carry cameras and shoulder bags on the side away from the kerb edge.

Getting there

There are daily flights from the major cities (and even a weekly flight from Kuwait in the summer), and numerous intercity buses. Once in the city, the major Safavid buildings are located within walking distance of the Maydan-i

Imam, but for the Armenian churches, the *Masjid-i Jami* and other interesting but less-frequented monuments, it is best to hire a taxi especially for Pir-i Bakran and Ashtarjan (see pages 131–3), or Varzaneh, Barsiyan, Ziar and Gar. For half a day in Isfahan, something around US$8 for the taxi (taking a maximum of four passengers), and US$12–15 outside the city is suggested; for further afield (eg: Na'in, Kashan), negotiate. Three days in Isfahan are barely sufficient to see the main historic buildings.

For precise directions to the fine pigeon house near Pir-i Bakran (see page 132), you are strongly advised to contact English-speaking guide Hoseyn Nassr of Donyayeparvaz Tour & Travel in Isfahan (tel: 0311 6673101-5; fax: 0311 6673106; email: Donyayeparvaz@aol.com), whose family comes from the area. He could organise a car (but it is preferable that he accompanies you to 'open doors'). Take a torch if you have one. He or his colleague, Iraj Jahanbakhsh, another English-speaking guide, can also organise the permission required to visit certain 18th-century Armenian houses, the Armenian cemetery, and the Malek house (see page 127). Also, in order to visit the Armenian churches in Shiraz, a letter of introduction will be needed from the Vank or All Saviours Cathedral Museum here in Isfahan.

Accommodation

The following price details are inclusive of taxes and breakfast.

Most foreign visitors wish to stay in the five-star **Hotel Abbasi** (formerly Shah Abbasi; tel: 0311 2226012–16; fax: 0311 2226008; email: info@ abbasihotel.com; 245 rooms; US$140 double, US$90 single) with its picturesque courtyard and richly decorated restaurants, but the high room charge reflects these photogenic qualities and tourist demand, rather than a reputation for good food and attentive staff. A small shopping mall opposite always has a good supply of film, books and postcards.

A few minutes' walk away is the four-star, but less exhorbitant, **Hotel Ali Qapu** (Bonyad) in Chahar Bagh (tel: 0311 2227929; email Aliqapu_hotel@yahoo.com; 96 rooms, US$92 double, US$64 single). The five-star **Hotel Kowsar International** (formerly Sheraton, Bonyad) on Boulevard Mellat (tel: 0311 6240230–39; fax: 0311 6249975; email: info@hotelkowsar.com; US$110, US$75 single) is located across the river, by the Se-o Se Pol bridge, a 15-minute drive from the main Safavid monuments. It has 138 rooms, and serves a much better breakfast, and a good dinner menu, especially the grilled quails. Next door is the three-star **Hotel Suite** (Bonyad) (tel: 0311 6616071; fax: 0311 6613872; US$53 double/single) but half the rooms have Iranian toilets, erratic air conditioning, and there's no laundry service. An adequate three-star hotel is **Hotel Azadi** off Masjid-i Sayyed Avenue, Takhti crossroads (tel: 0311 2204011; US$54 double, US$36 single), while the two-star **Hotel Arya** (tel: 0311 2227224; fax: 0311 2221983; 14 rooms; US$20 double, US$15 single) is in the same street as the Abbasi Hotel. A newly opened three-star hotel is the recommended **Melal Hotel** (tel/fax: 0311 224532–4; US$53 double, US$35 single) in Kamel Ismaili Street, four minutes' walk from Se-o-Se Bridge; half the rooms have a river view.

Restaurants

Apart from the numerous Iranian 'snack-bars' in Chahar Bagh, there is the good **Restaurant Shahrzad**, just down from the Hotel Ali Qapu towards the river and first right. Known for its good food (the lamb shank *mahicheh* is highly recommended) and attentive staff, it is open for lunch and dinner. Another restaurant used to foreign visitors is the **Se-o-se**, on the first floor of the (northeast) corner shopping mall near the bridge of that name.

Things to see and do

The hotel and your guide should be able to find out when one or other *zurkhaneh* (wrestling gymnasium) is meeting, so that you can attend. The **Zurkhaneh Kamal** is located off Maydan Qiyam near the Masjid-i Jami. There is no explanation in English of the high-volume series of responses and comments, so persuade an Iranian friend or guide to come along to explain the proceedings (see page 116).

Driving into Isfahan from the west, 7km from the centre, visitors see a rocky outcrop with the remains of a 13th-century citadel and so-called Sasanid **Ateshgah** fire temple on top. About 1km further on (on the same side), is a garden with a small building, the **Manar-i Junban** ('the Shaking Minarets'). Unless you have time to kill, both can be ignored particularly because neither is on a direct bus route from the city centre. However, as both are often promoted as tourist highspots, a few details are included here. The energetic can climb up the *Ateshgah* hill for a panoramic view, smog permitting, but take care as there is no defined path. Leaving aside the huge concrete cistern, the other visible remains probably date no earlier than the 13th–14th century, when it was a signal tower in the city defences. As for the Shaking Minarets, (entry 3,000 rials), this small building over a tomb takes its name from its two small towers; if one climbs up to the roof, clasps one or other tower in a firm embrace and rocks back and forth, it and the other will move. For onlookers at ground level, it is quite dramatic as deep cracks in the towers and walls visibly open. Lord Curzon wryly reported in 1892 that many travellers 'have exhausted their ingenuity' trying to explain this phenomenon: an underground chain linking the two minarets; an inner vertical beam in each tower resting in a socle; or a horizontal beam within the arch brickwork on which the minarets are 'balanced'. I prefer the theory that it is the Sufi Shaikh Amu Abdallah in his 1317 grave beneath the building, shaking with fury at being disturbed yet again.

Believe me, a **pigeon tower** (*borj-i kaftar*) is far, far more interesting and spectacular. About 12km east of Isfahan (Na'in direction) there is a good example just off the roadside (exiting Isfahan), and another near Isfahan Airport, about 18km before the city centre (but much further coming from the centre, as a continuous central barrier prevents turning on the carriageway). The best example I know is near Pir-i Bakran (see pages 131–2) so you could combine visits to this, Pir-i Bakran itself and also Ashtarjan by hiring a taxi for half a day.

Isfahan's Maydan Imam

As for Isfahan itself, a minimum of four hours is needed in and around the Maydan Imam (formerly Maydan Shah), laid out by the Safavid shah Abbas I (d1628), and an evening walk around is recommended as the square with the monuments are often floodlit. Said to be three times the size of St Mark's Square, Venice, this immense open space of 500x160m now has lawns and fountains but was once the royal parade ground, where the shahs watched military equestrian exercises, wrestling bouts and polo matches (stone goal posts are still visible at the south end). At the north end is the main entry into the bazaar, facing the *Masjid-i Imam*, with the coffee-coloured dome of *Masjid-i Shaikh Lutfallah* to the east, and opposite the *Ali Qapu*, the 17th-century ceremonial entrance into the royal palace compound; each are described below.

Shah Abbas I ordered the building of **Masjid-i Imam**, formerly Masjid-i Shah (entry 2,500 rials; *closes sunset, Fri till 15.00*) in memory of his ancestor Shah Tahmasp (d1576). Work was begun 1612 and totally finished in 1638, ten years after his death. Growing impatient at the length of building time, so we are told, Abbas demanded that the labour-intensive technique of 'mosaic' tilework as used for the main entrance was abandoned for time-saving underglazed painted tile squares elsewhere in the mosque. The best tilework, with a purity of glaze, colour and motif design, is indeed present on the majestically tall entrance portal flanked by soaring minarets, facing on to the Maydan. Incidentally, it has been suggested that the two peacock motifs below the central grille window were a Safavid dynastic device as they also feature at the Ardabil and Mashhad shrines. Through the great silver doors of 1636, you'll see the courtyard is set at a 45° angle necessary for the correct direction toward Mecca, so clearly Shah Abbas was primarily concerned that the Maydan had a north–south orientation. The call to prayer was never made from the mosque's tall minarets because, according to Lord Curzon writing in the 1890s, the shahs were fearful that the *muezzins* would have a clear uncensored view into the royal gardens. Instead the call was made from the little roof-pavilion over the ivan to the right of the central courtyard.

Walking slowly around the mosque allows the visitor to see the vistas as they open out, and the astonishing range in the tile colouring and patterns on the walls, vaults and side domes become apparent. Either side of the main prayer hall, set back in a small courtyard, is a small *madrasa* where students were taught until the late 19th century. But before entering the main prayer hall, do look at the bulbous shape and decoration of its exterior dome (54m high) because inside the dome has a different shape. This is a splendid example of a double dome, the inner one absorbing and distributing the structural load so allowing the outer dome to have a more eye-catching outline. At the apex there is a 14m gap between the two, the outer shell being supported on huge spars embedded into the inner dome. To the far right of the sanctuary hall you can see an immense curved section of a plaster former from the 1930s repair programme, used to prepare the tiled segments for this outer dome. Peace and calm rarely prevail in this hall as visitors stand on a central floor slab and clap to hear the resounding echo. Perhaps Bradt travellers could establish a quieter tradition – just as effective – of tearing a piece of paper. If your camera has a slow shutter release and a non-automatic flash, switch the latter off, alter the shutter speed to ½ or 1 second (check the light meter), and place the camera on the floor and you should take a good shot.

The Masjid-i Imam's angled entrance is best photographed from the small tea house balcony adjoining the Qaisariyeh bazaar (see below) or the **Ali Qapu**, constructed around 1600. Described disparagingly as a brick boot-box by Robert Byron (and even Della Valle in the 17th century called it 'pretty rather than magnificent'), the Ali Qapu is often called the Safavid palace, but it was actually the High Door (*qapu*: door) into the royal compound, from where the shah and his court viewed parades and celebrations in the Maydan. The staircase with steep steps rising to the four floors is to the left of the small ticket office (entry 2,500 rials; *closes sunset, Fri till 15.00*) up to this viewing area, or *talar*, added around 1644. As you ascend, explore the small rooms on each floor, looking out for blind niches covered with canvas as these conceal paintings now deemed too risqué for public viewing. Here and there is evidence of early revolutionary zeal as some painted faces have been damaged since the late 1970s, but more than enough of the beautiful decoration remains, including delicately carved, pink plaster friezes, although their original gilded top-layer has been largely lost over the centuries.

After enjoying both the breeze and view from the *talar,* continue up to the so-called music rooms. The floors of these rooms appear uneven but this is a result of inserting H-girders during the extensive repair programme; similarly the *talar* columns now have metal cores. The intricate plaster ceilings were devised to assist acoustics for court musicans, or to display *objets d'art* as in the Ardabil shrine (see page 153) and certain Moghal palaces in Northern India. Use the other staircase to descend.

Across the Maydan demurely stands the portal of the **Masjid-i Shaykh Lotfallah**, named after a famous preacher (entry 2,500 rials; *closes sunset, Fri till 15.00*). Rather than being a 'public' mosque, it possibly functioned as the mosque for the ladies of the royal harem; the portal dedication certainly emphasises the explicit Shi'i role of the shah as 'reviver of the virtues of his pure ancestors, and propagator of the doctrine of the pure Imams'. It also records that the decoration was started in 1603 but finished about 15 years later, the extra time needed to complete the amazing ceramic tilework throughout the building. A narrow corridor, angled to obtain the correct orientation, leads into the prayer hall, where the simple square groundplan is forgotten as the impact of the decoration kicks in. The surface patterns of ceramic shapes, sometimes set into unglazed brick, disguise massively thick walls which support the single shell dome (diameter 13m) while giant turquoise barley-twist cables outlining the full-length squinches lead the eye into the dome. I always wonder how the pattern designer calculated for the diminishing size of the motifs on the dome's concave surface. No wonder geometry, algebra and mathematics developed in the Islamic world. By employing the same technique as suggested with the Masjid-i Imam above, very successful photographs of the dome pattern can be taken, but to see the winter prayer hall below, with its *mihrab* of 1602, you must enter by the staircase near the main entrance.

The bazaar

Perhaps it's time to explore the bazaar. Since 1998 many more shops, including one or two selling the famous Isfahani *gaz* nougat, have reopened in the covered arcade running all around the square. Just to the left of the 17th-century door leading into the **Qaisariyeh Bazaar** is a steep, narrow staircase leading to a small tea house, with a beautiful view over the entire Maydan and an eclectic collection of ornaments. The 'Mario Lanza' lookalike poster depicts a famous Pahlavan wrestler of the mid-1960s, Ghulam Reza Takhti, assassinated (or so it's rumoured) by the SAVAK. And why not look into the government **Iranian Handicrafts Organisation** shop on the Maydan just to the right of of the Qaisariyeh, if only to get some idea of its (fixed) prices. Before walking through the main door of the bazaar, look up and if the scaffolding has finally been removed you'll see a Sagittarius figure, and Shah Abbas victorious over the Uzbek enemy, as described by Jean Chardin in the late 17th century. Above, there was a gallery where musicans banged and trumpeted every sunset, causing foreign merchants to suffer violent headaches, and a Portuguese bronze bell marking the Safavid conquest of Hormuz (see page 218). Just inside the door, immediately on the right, a narrow alley leads into a small courtyard of cotton **block-printing workshops**. One on the upper level produces cloths with Armenian inscriptions, and up here also is the elderly gentleman who carves the actual pear-wood blocks, working from a small cubbyhole. There is an endless variety of printed cottons; prices depend on size, quality of the fabric and the colour complexity of the design.

The bazaar runs northwards and eastwards intermittently. The main **carpet** quarter is situated to the far left (west) away from the main avenue; a short walk through here will raise serious doubts in your mind whether there are enough homes worldwide to house all these carpets.

West of the bazaar

From the carpet quarter, or walking down the tarmac road (west) parallel to the main bazaar avenue, keep an eye out for the **Jurjir** portal in a little side road, or ask for **Mosque of al-Hakim**. Discovered during 1955 repair work, this patterned (K3:16–18) doorway is all that remains of the late-10th-century Mosque of Sahib al-Kufa, a vizier (d995) known for his writings on theology, history and poetry. Everything else, which included a dervish centre, library, colleges, accommodation and assembly rooms and a tall minaret, was destroyed to make way for this Safavid Mosque of al-Hakim (built 1660–63), named after Shah Safi's physican Da'ud. After leaving the Isfahani court under a cloud, Da'ud made his fortune in India attending the Mughal emperor, Auranganzeb (d1707). Perhaps it is no coincidence that some of the Koranic verses used in the Taj Mahal are also included here on the 1660 *mihrab*. The prayer ivan has a calligraphic frieze (K2:256) suggesting Da'ud was a (Jewish?)

convert to Islam, while another quotation (K62:9) around the base of the dome tells people (perhaps like today's carpet dealers?) to forget business and attend the Friday prayer. In the neighbourhood, set inside railings, a large white building with a tall vaulted entrance originates from the 15th century, but was converted into an officers' club in Pahlavi times. It now functions as the local **Natural History Museum** (*open daily*) which explains the rather incongruous dinosaur and aged lion sculptures on the front steps.

Chehel Sutun

West of Ali Qapu, set within a garden, is the most important surviving Safavid pavilion, the **Chehel Sutun** (40 or 'many' columns), taking its name from the reflection of its 20 columns in the algae-rich pond in front of the main *talar* (entry 2,500; *closed sunset, Fri am*; no flash). As suggested by the wall paintings all around the outside of the pavilion, this was where the Safavid rulers received foreign envoys and where Shah Soleyman was invested in 1668, some twenty years after its construction. The 16m-high columns, once painted and gilded, used to be hung with curtains sprayed with rosewater to perfume the air, and the *talar* walls still retain some mirror work, originally imported from Venice at great expense.

The rooms either side of the *talar* have small, minimally labelled displays of Safavid (and later) ceramics, metalwork and textiles, but most visitors go straight into the main hall. On entry, immediately facing you, is a huge 19th-century painting of Shah Ismail I attacking the Ottoman Janissaries (note the different headgear and dress details) during the famous 1514 battle of Chaldiran, eastern Turkey; actually this battle was a resounding defeat for the Safavid army, although here Ismail looks victorious. Either side are 17th-century paintings: on the left, the royal reception held c1543 by Shah Tahmasp for the exiled Moghal ruler Humayun, and on the right, Shah Abbas I (d1628) entertaining the ruler of Bukhara, Vali Mohammed Khan; both guests seem ill at ease with their surroundings. Over the main door another 19th-century picture portrays Nadir Shah, the Afghan general who seized control in 1735, in typical battle mode, this time in India. To the left there's a Safavid painting of Shah Abbas II receiving another Central Asian ruler, and on the other side, Isma'il II on a hennaed horse fighting Uzbeks; the sense of perspective suggests a European artist at work.

The exit by the small door to the far right leads into a gallery reopened in 1998. Despite the depiction of a scantily clad female looking somewhat flirtatious among flames, the wall-painting on the right continues the theme of battles; it perhaps records the 1649 capture of Qandahar, Afghanistan, or more exactly the wife of the city commander, killed in action, about to commit *sati* on his funeral pyre. Before leaving the gardens, and to the right before the exit, there's a tiny *chay-khaneh* with toilets to the far side.

South to the river

Those lacking the strength or inclination to tackle the bazaar and carpet merchants could walk back to the **Abbasi Hotel** and sit in its main courtyard; its ice-creams are very good. This was an early 18th-century *caravanserai* built, along with a small bazaar behind, to finance the *madrasa* next door before being converted into a hotel in 1955. This was one of the late shah's favourite hotels and several tour groups in the 1970s returned after a day's sightseeing to find their luggage in reception, as the royal retinue had unexpectedly commandeered their rooms. Guests have the evening meal on the ground floor amid painted 'Safavid' beauties, while breakfast is always served in the upper restaurant section decorated in a 'Qajar' style with its marvellous view of the **Madrasa Chahar Bagh** (1706–14) next door. It is on the corner with the main avenue, formerly part of the **Chahar Bagh** ('four gardens') where centuries ago with 'Night drawing on, all the pride of Isfahan was met ... and the Grandees were airing themselves, prancing about with their numerous trains, striving to outvie each other in Pomp and Generosity' (Fryer, c1680). Before the revolution it was possible to enter the *madrasa* (formerly *Madrasa Madar-i Shah*). Built in honour of Shah Hoseyn's mother (as its original name suggests), its sun-yellow, patterned-tiled vaults, 160 rooms and a peaceful 'Persian' garden disguise a violent history, for Hoseyn was decapitated here in 1722 by the Afghan rebels. It is now a fully operational theological college once more so foreign visitors are allowed only on Thursdays from 08.00 to 20.00 (entry 4,000 rials).

On the far side of this *madrasa*, passing behind the hotel, is the single-avenue bazaar whose shop rents provided an endowment to the college to cover salaries, repairs, etc. In the early evening, after 16.00, it's a pleasantly cool stroll which can take you to a small public park and the intimate Safavid **Hasht Behest** ('Eight Paradises') pavilion, built 1669 and recently reopened (pavilion entry 2,000 rials; *closed sunset*). In 1667 an English traveller described how the court was entertained in its gardens by the re-enactment of naval battles in the water channels, while Jean Chardin a few years later waxed lyrical over the place 'expressly made for love... one's heart is melted ... one always leaves with a very ill grace'; many young couples today share the sentiment. The pavilion has 17th-century tiled panels decorating the external arches, a main domed ceiling set with mirror work, and remnants of wall paintings, the best preserved surfaces being in the small rooms in each corner.

A walk down the main avenue towards the river takes you to the **Allahverdi Khan Bridge**, built in 1603, so named after its patron (d1613), a famous king-maker, provincial governor and Georgian commander in the Safavid army; the bridge is also known as the **Se-o-se** (33) from its multiple arches. This walk is especially recommended in the evening, when it and the Khaju Bridge are also illuminated, but during the day it is a pleasure seeing young people enjoying themselves in pedaloes on the river. In times of severe drought (as in 2000–02) the river was dammed upstream to provide water for Yazd province, but now water is again flowing under the bridges. The Allahverdi Khan Bridge, on piers some 4m thick, with its two levels and high walls to protect camel trains from wind-buffeting, connected the Chahar Bagh with the Armenian Christian quarter across the river. Greatly admired in the 17th century – 'truly a very neat piece of architecture if I may say the neatest in all Persia' (Tavernier) – it is still a favourite place to walk and take

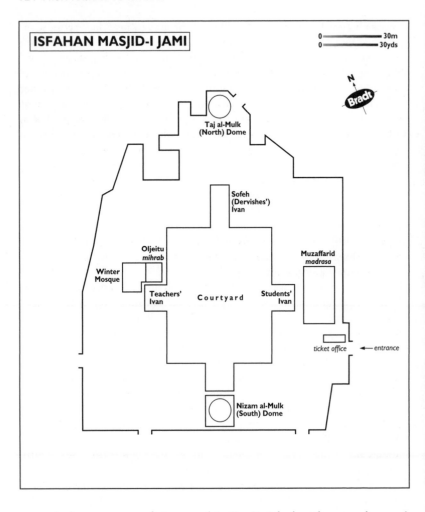

ISFAHAN MASJID-I JAMI

0 ———— 30m
0 ———— 30yds

N

Bradt

Taj al-Mulk
(North) Dome

Sofeh
(Dervishes')
Ivan

Oljeitu
mihrab

Muzaffarid
madrasa

Winter
Mosque

Teachers'
Ivan

Courtyard

Students'
Ivan

ticket office   ← entrance

Nizam al-Mulk
(South) Dome

tea, and why not get your fortune card (in Farsi) picked out by a caged canary? Further down is the **Khaju Bridge**, built in the 1660s by Shah Abbas II to join up with the old Shiraz road, with 24 arches and a central, two-storeyed, octagonal kiosk. Described by Kaempfer as 'more superb [when] compared with other buildings', it probably functioned as a toll bridge and also provided a spectacular water cascade when its channels were blocked by angled wooden boards. On the south side, 36m away, a stone lion stands looking at the river. The carved symbols on its chest and side show it was a gravestone or tomb marker of a local champion wrestler, as the same types of exercise equipment are still used in today's *zur-khanehs* (see page 116).

To see the third historic bridge in Isfahan will entail a taxi ride to **Shahrestan Bridge**, which dates from the Sasanid period or even earlier. Rebuilt by the Seljuks, and with a toll station added in the 17th century, it too acted as a weir, but the river has long been diverted.

Masjid-i Jami

No visit to Isfahan would be complete without a visit to the Masjid-i Jami, an architectural treasure in its own right. By comparison, the Masjid-i Imam may seem almost garish and over-decorated. Just beyond the ticket office (entry 2,500; *closed 11.00–14.00, sunset*) is a small room displaying a scale model of the complex, and photographs of the 1970s Italian archaeological findings. The rather dusty, insignificant-looking pillars with decorated brick-plugs to one side date back to the 10th century when a small 'Arab'-style mosque was built here on the remains of a fire temple. Then, between 1072 and 1092, work began in earnest: two huge domed chambers were constructed, one inside the complex, the other just outside. After a serious attack by the Assassins (see page 90) in 1122, as recorded on the northeast door, the mosque was re-organised according to a four-ivan plan, and then two centuries later extensively redecorated and repaired by the Mongol Il-Khanids. Some 50 years later the local Muzaffarid rulers extended the mosque, bringing the second Seljuk domed chamber into the enclosure. Thereafter, work in the mosque was more or less confined to replacing tile- and plaster-work.

Until January 2000, visitors were free to walk as and where they wished but 'student misbehaviour' (marijuana smoking) resulted in numerous metal fences and gates being installed. If these are locked, visitors will be accompanied by a patient guardian, who unobtrusively opens and locks gates; since October 2000, however, the gates are usually unlocked. From the main entrance, rather than continuing down to the central courtyard, cross over and walk through the arcades in a clockwise direction and you'll soon realise how beautiful (and subtly coloured) brickwork can be, and how quickly your film is disappearing. A yellow tile panel, far left, describes repair work after Iraqi bomb damage in the 1980s. This is the way to the first of two magnificent, 11th-century 'true' domes, covering the south chamber, constructed on the order of the Seljuk vizier and scholar Nizam al-Mulk (d1092) around 1087, judging from the titles used in the dome inscription. Let your eyes become accustomed to the darkness; what remains of the 10th-century plasterwork was probably once richly painted like the interior of Southwark Cathedral, London. Huge brick pillars support this glorious dome (diameter c17m), the four massive trilobed squinches and the 16-sided zone of transition. Ideally, the thickness of the 'perfect dome' at its apex should be 1/45th of the diameter; here it is 1/42nd. To meet the lateral thrust of the dome, the inclination should be 5 to 1; here it is 4.5 to 1. Compare this with St Paul's Cathedral, London, which is some 600 years later and its dome is conical. As one architectural historian wrote: 'The Seljuqs ... solved the difficulties which [Sir Christopher] Wren avoided.'

If you want to see yet more brick-patterned vaults, continue walking through, skirting the courtyard. At the far end is a small 'shrine', until recently boarded up by the authorities as 'un-Islamic'; the thick soot betrays years of candle burning. Moving into the courtyard, you pass the second large 'teachers' ivan decorated on the order of Shah Hoseyn, later murdered in the *madrasa* near to the Abbasi Hotel. The small door to its right takes you into a mid-15th-century chamber containing the famous 1310 carved plaster *mihrab*, constructed in honour of the Il-Khanid ruler, Oljeitu (see pages 164–6). Its long inscription surprisingly contains no Koranic verses, but eulogises Oljeitu alongside references to Ali, the first Imam – so it clearly dates from before Oljeitu's conversion to Sunni Islam. From this room another door leads down to the Safavid winter mosque with transverse vaulting springing from floor level. You will have to ask the guardian to unlock it and, more importantly, switch on lights.

In the courtyard again, walk down to the next (north) ivan, known as the *Sofeh* ('meeting or sitting area') of the Dervishes. Its elegant plaster cartouches and lozenge-shaped decorations were part of the 1682 repairs undertaken during the reign of Safavid shah Soleyman. A new door to the right takes you to the other dome chamber (c22m high, diameter c11m), built by Taj al-Malik, Nizam al-Mulk's bitter political rival, and perhaps designed by the famous poet-mathematician, Omar Khayyam. Built in 1089 then *outside* the mosque, it perhaps functioned as a robing, meditation or judicial chamber for the Seljuk ruler. Its proportions are so pleasing to the Western eye, relating as they do to the Golden Mean used by architects of Renaissance Europe. The dome inscription (K7:52,54), describing the creation of the world in six days' ends with 'Is it not His to create and govern' before immediately giving the Seljuk sultan's Persian titles and date; the implication is undeniable. The 32 blind niches in the zone of transition have short inscriptions, each specifying a name or quality of the Almighty, while those across the large niche panels are Koranic (17:79–81).

After taking photographs of the courtyard, most visitors leave, but if time allows, look at the small *madrasa* behind the 'students' ivan' with its fine mid-14th-century mosaic tile decoration. Because the Muzaffarid ruler who paid for the work was Sunni, the star motifs in the vault include references to the first three caliphs (after the death of the Prophet) recognised by the Sunnis but not Shi'is. Returning to the courtyard ivan, on the far back wall, a grille protects other Sunni formulae. As you leave the complex, a little before the ticket office, tucked back on the right in deep shadow, is another elaborate plaster *mihrab*, presumably dating from the early 14th century.

A word about the mosque gates. The present main (southeast) entrance was repaired in 1804 according to its inscription, while the southwest one is dated 1591. The north gate, usually locked, carries a lengthy Koranic inscription (K76:1–27) describing the delights and rewards in Paradise, while that (K2:114) on the northeastern entrance clearly refers to repairs after the Assassins' attack in 1121: 'Who is more wicked than the men who seek to destroy the mosques of Allah...'

From the Masjid-i Jami

Leaving by the main entrance, the main roundabout to your right offers two opportunities. The road to the right (west), the Jamal al-Din Abdul Razzaq, goes past (1km) a lovely but delapidated **19th-century house** which lost its garden in the road-widening scheme. It was purchased by the government and now serves as a 'clubhouse' for Isfahani calligraphers. It is not open to the public, but it is sometimes possible to see inside another lovely house of this period, the **Beit al-Malek**, in Malek Street off the main roundabout. However, as it is the venue for international Koranic reading competitions, access cannot be guaranteed (see page 117) and the elderly female guardian is very particular about ladies' hair escaping from under scarves. The garden has recently been ripped up to install new pools and paving, but the original entrance doorway and four porch columns have escaped unscathed. Leaving shoes in the passage, you enter the first room, with its Bohemian chandeliers and Qajar sash windows opening on to the garden, while a screened upper gallery allowed the ladies of the household to view visitors in secret. This room leads into a chamber, now rapidly disappearing under new highly veneered wood panelling. At its far end is a small room decorated with early 20th-century plasterwork and mirrored glass, which contains the grave of Mohammed Ibrahim Malek (d1922), the former owner. Theological permission for interment within the home is rarely given, but this Isfahani merchant was so renowned for his good works, feeding the poor and finding work for the unemployed, that an exception was made.

A short walk down the minor road (southwest) off the roundabout past the carpet-loom shops brings you to the shrine **Harun-i Vilayet**, built in 1513 and restored in 1656. Before the revolution, a stone lion thought to possess powers to cure sterility stood in the courtyard; today he has been banished to the exterior and a birth-control clinic operates in his place. A small door leads into the public part of the shrine; leave shoes at the door. Inside, 17th-century or later wall paintings of Ali, Fatima, and their two sons, Hassan and Hoseyn, introduce the main tomb chamber honouring Harun, whose life and attributes are cloaked in mystery; perhaps he was a son of one of the Twelve Imams. Outside, the two enormous paintings of modern-day theologians allude to contemporary suffering and martyrdom. Ayatollah Khameini is portrayed, and Dr Biheshti, formerly of Isfahan, who was the head of the judiciary who lost his life in 1981 in the bomb attack on the Tehran headquarters of the Islamic Revolutionary Party. In all about 100 were killed but here a clear reference is made to the 72 people who died with Hoseyn at Kerbela. As you leave the shrine courtyard, turn right and you'll soon find the lion looking into the shrine and also visual proof that the tiled plaster *muqarna*s decorating the semi-dome were literally suspended from the main brick structure.

In the distance can be seen the tall **Manar-i Ali**, now about 48m high but probably originally 2m taller. Built around 1200 (or perhaps 1235), the minaret has three main bands of brick decoration with blue glazed elements, although only two can be seen from street level, with inscriptions declaring that there is no God but Allah and that all power belongs to Him, along with a Koranic verse (3:16). The mosque was repaired extensively in the Safavid period according to the inscriptions, and its portal was constructed around 1522.

Another cluster of interesting monuments is in the vicinity of the Amin Hospital for Leukaemia (*Saratan-i Khoon*), off the Maydan Shohada, but you will need a patient taxi driver. Incidentally the crowds around the hospital gate are waiting to collect their blood-test results, legally required for marriage ceremonies. Most people around here know where the **Darb-i Imam** (also referred to as the *Dar(b)-i Islam*) is, but there are no road-signs. Much of this building, including the two domes, was restored in the 17th and 18th centuries, but the ivan portal, with its fine mosaic tile decoration guarded by a stone lion, the vestibule and mausoleum dates from 1453, the year when Constantinople fell to the Ottoman Turks. Constructed on the order of Jahan Shah of the Black Sheep confederation two years after taking Isfahan, the building houses his mother, but was dedicated to two Imams, Ibraham Tabataba'i (or Batha) and Zayn al-Abidin, the 4th Imam; in time so many were buried here that the original door was closed by a grille. Lines of Sufi poetry frame the portal telling the visitor:

> From the roof of this house of the world [ie: heaven] seek not the
> image of faithfulness
> At its coming be not glad, nor grieve at its going
> See with the eye of understanding, how that building whose ivan
> Passed above the seventh heaven [Saturn] fell to earth.

An inscription to the far left records that the man in charge of its construction suddenly disappeared, never to return. A large second courtyard gives access to the shrine itself, a series of rooms, some evidently restored, and a storeroom for some magnificent *alam* standards used in the *Moharram* parades.

A short drive away is the **Manar-i Saraban** (or Menar-i Saraban: camel-driver's minaret), a fine minaret, possibly mid 12th-century, amid small houses, whose front doors often have two knockers, each with distinctive sounds, so those inside know if a male or female visitor is calling. Its mosque has long gone, but the doorway (through which you can see the spiral staircase) some 5m up probably marked the connection with the mosque roof. Standing about 30m high, it still possesses after seven centuries good brick patterns and glazed inserts, although its balcony has gone. From here you can see the **Manar-i Chehel Doktaran** which has also lost its mosque, but the staircase doorway remains. There are no coloured glazed inserts, but just look at the richness of the brickwork. Up the cylindrical shaft (24m high) there are more than seven pattern zones of rhomboids, lozenges, octagons and six-pointed stars, picked out in recessed and relief brick. Near its base, a six-line Kufic inscription panel gives the construction date (1108), making this one of the earliest minarets to survive in Iran.

Just off the Maydan Ibn Sina nearby is the 1880 tiled tent-roof of the small, rather neglected **tomb of Baba Qasem**, built by a certain Soleyman Abu'l Hasan Tahit al-Damghani in 1341 'with the intention of honouring the theologian who has departed for Paradise'. The key is held by the gentleman in the shop next door to a very new shrine which itself lies in a former shop. This visit brings home how just twenty-odd years can affect a building which previously survived over six centuries with comparatively little damage. There is now no sign of its tiled portal inscription, noted in the mid-1970s, recording that Baba Qasem of Isfahan had been a devout Sunni. The original door has recently been blocked up and now entry is directly into the second chamber. In here there should be a *mihrab* decorated with Koranic verses (K9:18–22) which emphasised the difference between devout Muslims and those who pay lip-service to Islam, and indeed local tradition had it that liars and perjurers met horrid deaths at this shrine. The *mihrab* has gone, and the mosaic tilework (K17:1–6) embellishing the dome base has too; however, two cenotaphs, one commemorating a local hero-wrestler (d1577), remain, but are shoved against the walls. Nearby was Baba Qasim's four-portal *madrasa*, built in 1325.

Further afield
The first taxi drive
Mosques in Iran can be empty places except on Fridays. One Isfahani shrine, however, is always crowded, but its smallness makes it totally unsuitable for tour groups. It will mean a taxi drive to the eastern part of the city, off the Hasht Behest Avenue; take a camera in (the unlikely) case it is deserted, but don't attempt to use it otherwise. Isfahanis call it the **Imamzadeh Shah Zayd**, but happily admit the actual name is Zayn al-Din. A small courtyard precedes the entry portal (ladies enter to the right; men to the left). Its tiled frieze records repairs to the shrine in 1686, so perhaps this was when the paintings inside, depicting the harrowing tale of Hoseyn's last moments at Kerbela, were executed, but they are probably later, dating from the late 19th century. Protected by (grubby) glass screens, the scenes are arranged in an approximate sequence, showing Abbas bringing life-restoring water to the Imam, his family and supporters (he lost both hands in the process); the womenfolk are clearly depicted, including Rukayya, whose popular tomb-shrine is in Cairo. Look for a horse wounded by so many arrows that it looks like a pin cushion; this is Hoseyn's steed and he is shown veiled with a halo. The lion underneath recalls the miracle of a certain Sultan Qays who, attacked by a lion in India, invoked the help of Hoseyn just as the Imam was fighting for his own life in Iraq. Miraculously, Hoseyn was momentarily transported to India, causing the lion to cower in submission, while the Imam reappeared at Kerbela only to be slain himself.

The second taxi drive
If time allows, the Armenian section of Isfahan, known as **(New) Julfa**, should be visited. The best day is of course Sunday when most churches are open, but tour groups often come to All Saviours' (or Vank) Cathedral on Friday mornings, so avoiding mosque visits (entry, including museum, 30,000 rials; *closed Fri pm*). Authorisation to visit the Shiraz churches, and the Armenian cemetery outside Isfahan, is obtained here.

Around 1603 the Safavid shah ordered the resettlement of some 10,000 Armenian families from the Caucasus into this quarter and nearby villages, probably to ensure their skills in silk trading remained in Safavid hands, and to thwart any Armenian schemes of siding with the Ottomans to get autonomy.

The community was allowed freedom of worship, and Abbas I himself, we are told, attended Epiphany celebrations and commanded important Christian relics – such as the arm of St Gregory the Illuminator, who converted Armenia in 301CE – to be brought here; it was returned to Echtmiadin, Armenia, in 1637. By 1701 this quarter boasted about 30 churches but now only about 13 survive, and the community has shrunk considerably from 100,000 in the mid-1960s to approximately 7,000 in 1995. Several of the 18th-century **merchants' houses** with interesting painted decoration were open in the 1970s but as many now function as government offices, official permission is required (see page 117). The Jani house close to All Saviours Cathedral, for example, is now the art college.

Construction on **All Saviours' Cathedral** began in 1606 but it was largely rebuilt during 1650–63, with the belltower added in 1764. The decorative plaster and paintings covering the interior date from 1660–70, the gift of an Armenian merchant, Avandich, but the tiles are somewhat later. In the east dome, the story of the Creation, the Expulsion and the Killing of Abel are depicted, but elsewhere the painted decoration is arranged to show episodes from the Old Testament, with related New Testament themes below. So Abraham and the angels is paired with the Annunciation, Hagar and Ismail with the Nativity, and almost opposite the entrance, Moses and the Tablets above the Transfiguration. Over the door itself a huge Last Judgement fills the space; a small newly cleaned square high on the left reveals the original vibrant colouring, now darkened by centuries of candle-soot and incense. It is not known whether the artists were Isfahani Armenians or Europeans attached to the various East India Companies resident in this quarter, but clearly they had seen contemporary Van Sichem engravings. At shoulder level, small panels gruesomely retell the tortures faced by the early Armenian Christians, the costume and textile details proving these too are 17th century. One near the main door depicts St Gregory the Illuminator curing the Armenian king transformed into a pig as punishment for lusting after and torturing Christian maidens (or nuns), and then shows the conversion of the king and the people in 301CE, and the honouring of the saint.

Behind the west wall in the courtyard lie a few gravestones of British missionaries, their families and soldiers who died in the Isfahani and Yazdikast areas. Underneath the canopy another 19th-century grave is decorated with the famous bathing episode of Shirin, the Armenian princess, watched by Shah Khosrau who bites the 'finger of astonishment' (see page 97). Directly opposite is a striking monument, erected in 1975, marking early-20th-century Ottoman atrocities. Further down is the museum building with displays (labelling in English) on two floors of rich liturgical vestments and objects, illuminated and illustrated manuscripts, oil paintings, the first (1636) printing press in Iran, historic documents, etc. The small museum shop at the main entrance usually has pamphlets, cassettes and books including American publications difficult to obtain outside the USA.

If All Saviours' Cathedral is crowded, a short walk takes you to **Bethlehem Church**, lying immediately to the northeast behind the cathedral. The guardians, an elderly couple, are delighted to see visitors. The decorative scheme is very similar to All Saviours, but perhaps some 30 years earlier in date and in a strange sequence. The donor's picture is on the north wall, and horrific scenes on the west wall illustrate the tortures inflicted on St Gregory the Illuminator, St Sergius, St Mercurius and St Theodore. There are 11 other 17th-century churches in this quarter, such as the Church of the Holy Mother of God (**Surb Astuatsatsin**) built c1613 which has fine 17th-century tiles, and some paintings, including the Beheading of John the Baptist, with a figure of the donor in the bottom left. Another church of the same period with good tiling is **St Stephen**, while the Church of **St Minas**, completed in 1662, has 19th-century tiling, and wall paintings.

The main **Armenian cemetery** is located off the Sepahan Road near to al-Zahra Hospital (Shiraz direction), but visiting permission is needed from the cathedral authorities (see pages 117 and 129). Here are the graves of Rodolph Stadler (d1637), the Swiss watchmaker to Shah Safi I, and Claudius James Rich, the British Resident (Consul) in the early 19th century, among many others. There have been reports that this cemetery, as with some other non-Muslim burial places, has been vandalised.

The third taxi drive

At the beginning of this section (page 118) I strongly suggested a visit to a pigeon tower (with a torch), alongside other interesting buildings in the area of Pir-i Bakran. Most taxi drivers will know Pir-i Bakran but for the exact location of the pigeon tower, contact Hoseyn Nassr (see page 117). A taxi from Isfahan to Pir-i Bakran and back should cost approximately 100,000 rials, but extending the drive to include the other visits as described below will require further negotiation.

Pir-i Bakran is about 30km south of Isfahan, off the Sohan (Steel Factory) Highway in an area once strongly associated with the Jewish community and, in early medieval times, overshadowed by several Assassin castles from where attacks on Isfahan (see page 90) were conducted. Around here the famous small-grained Linjan rice, with its distinctive flavour, is grown. There is no direct access from the main road to the early 14th-century building which gives the township its name, so walk past with the enclosing wall on the left and then double back along the alley below. Many of the houses along here have two doorknockers, one for women, the other for male visitors. The children are helpful and will fetch the guardian to unlock the gate. Walk straight through, into the small tomb chamber at the back, pushing away a grimy curtain into a small domed chamber with faint depictions of cypresses or minarets on the walls. This was probably the actual teaching room of the famous Sufi shaikh (*pir*) 'revealer of the secrets of the Truth, venerated Master of the Way', as the inscriptions here repeatedly describe him. Shortly after his death in 1304, the small tomb chamber with its massive cenotaph was constructed and decorated in turquoise and cobalt blue tilework, but sticky fingers since World War II have removed most of the tiles. A steep slope behind the teaching room precluded any further building at that end, so in 1312 a lofty prayer hall was constructed in front of the tomb. It too was once covered in early 14th-century moulded tiles in two shades of blue and a few dusty ones remain, too high to be stolen. But fortunately most of the marvellously carved plasterwork is intact, whether calligraphic Kufic 'seal-squares' resembling Chinese seal-marks, 'baroque' leaf forms carved through several levels, once all highly coloured, or the beautifully patterned brick-end plugs. The *mihrab* is splendid. It is possible to climb up to the next floor and roof by the small doorway to the right of the tomb chamber. For those less energetic, look for the rock jutting out from floor level; this is where the horse of the prophet Elijah set down his hoof before riding into the heavens. This ivan extension of 1312 meant a new entry passage which didn't interfere with the *qibla* orientation and *mihrab* had to be constructed; as you leave, take time to look at its decoration, somewhat damaged but still fine.

In the township itself there is an old Jewish synagogue and cemetery. Only on Jewish holy days is there any sign that the place is loved and cared for; the cemetery also bears scars of vandalism. All the same, foreigners should visit, if only to show that such places are meaningful and important to others. The synagogue complex has rooms for pilgrims, but it is doubtful whether these are now much used. The main room, a domed chamber with the *torah* stand, is at ground level, while above there are small prayer rooms with stone panels carved with Hebrew. In a small garden behind is a freestanding domed chamber where Esther (or Sarah has also been mentioned) disappeared into the walls. The blackened walls and candle debris prove pilgrims still come here, but the guardian is monosyllabic and unhelpful. As yet, Jewish colleagues in the UK can find no information about the complex, known locally as Esther Khatun (Lady Esther).

About 5km away in agricultural land are two fine **pigeon towers**. There are no signposts (which is why you need Hoseyn Nassr) but aim for the main irrigation canal and the rail track, near Abnil. At a desolate crossroads, pass the police checkpoint near the railway lines on your left and head under the rail track, bearing right (east) before the zinc factory gates on to a gravel road, so the railway is on your immediate right. Continue and then take a right over the irrigation canal and keep it on your left. Just as the towers come into view, turn down a narrow road to the right, and then left, which takes you up to the larger tower. Hover and hopefully a key will materialise to allow you in, but even if it doesn't it is a splendid building even when viewed from the outside.

You will be just as awestruck with these immense edifices as the 17th-century traveller Jean Chardin was, amazed that they were 'six times as big as the biggest we have: they are built with Brick overlaid with Plaister and Lime'. Looking like giant chess pieces, they provide multi-storeyed nesting boxes inside for pigeons, not for breeding and eating (the birds have traditional sacred connotations) but for the guano used to fertilise the local melon fields; a cynic would argue that the pigeons destroyed more crops with their voracious appetites than assisting with the growth. To prevent snakes from getting in, there are no windows and only one door opened once a year to

Above left Qanat repair, near Bam (PB)

Above right Children in southern Iran (HB)

Left Carpet loom, Pir-i Bakran (PB)

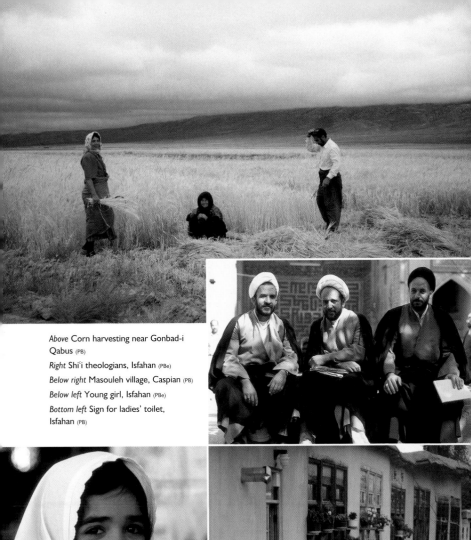

Above Corn harvesting near Gonbad-i Qabus (PB)

Right Shi'i theologians, Isfahan (PBe)

Below right Masouleh village, Caspian (PB)

Below left Young girl, Isfahan (PBe)

Bottom left Sign for ladies' toilet, Isfahan (PB)

collect the guano. Nothing prepares you for the size of these towers, and the simple grandeur of their interiors. Even without a torch, the impact is sensational, almost as good as any Gothic cathedral. Stairs go up to the roof but some of the steps are damaged.

Returning back towards Pir-i Bakran, you could complete this half-day with **Ashtarjan** (signposted as Oshtarjan), 35km southwest of Isfahan, for the little Masjid-i Jami, gifted by a local man in 1305, and there is the *Imamzadeh of Rabia Khatun* close by, dated 1308. While waiting for the mosque guardian, as perhaps the famous Arab geographer Ibn Battuta did during his visit in 1327, have a look at the exterior doorways. This small two-ivan mosque is quiet and serene, with exquisite decoration with numerous chinoiserie motifs. It has seen better days, but remains of painting show the detailed plasterwork and the dome interior were once brilliantly coloured, complementing the plain brick and coloured tilework (the work of Hajji Mohammed of Tabriz) and a lovely *mihrab*. The *qibla* ivan is dominated with a large lozenge motif giving the names of the 12 Imams, edged with Kufic inscription (K36:1–9) on one side, and on the other wall another containing the 99 names of God, edged with more calligraphy (K59:23–4). Around the dome inside, more Koranic verses (K48:1–6) ask for forgiveness of past faults, and the reward of Paradise in richly plaited Kufic, while the *mihrab* records the date of completion as 1316. A carved stone panel on one of the courtyard piers states: 'In the time of the caliphate of his majesty, the Emperor of Islam, the greatest Sultan, Lord over the necks of the peoples... Uzun Hasan [of the Aq Qoyunlu 1453–78]... the repair of this masjid-i jami' was undertaken by a local Sufi master 'at his own personal expense'.

The road from Isfahan to Shiraz or to Yazd via Abadeh and Abarku runs through interesting scenery scattered with remains of walled villages and *caravanserais*. Some 80km south of Isfahan is **Shahreza** with its *imamzadeh*, built in Safavid times and then greatly reworked in the 19th century; there are clean toilets here, just below the paved terrace area. Just before **Yazdikast** (also spelt Izad Khast) 60km further on, there is a dirt spur road to the right (notionally west) which leads directly to the old fortress which controlled the main caravan route to the southeast. Possibly built on Sasanid foundations, judging from the substructure, this fort is splendid despite its ruined appearance; even the remains of the old drawbridge are still visible. Walk down the alley directly opposite and this will lead to a vantage place for a superb view across the old river valley and the Safavid *caravanserai* on the other side. Below are the ruins of houses. In the 19th century the regional governor ordered the killing of all the menfolk (by throwing them down into the valley) as punishment for non-payment of taxes, and it was here that two young army officers buried in the All Saviours courtyard, Isfahan, lost their lives. Yazdikast traditionally had another claim to fame as a 17th-century French traveller recorded: 'That to live happy, a man must have a wife of Yazd, eat the bread of Yazdikast, and drink the wine of Shiraz.'

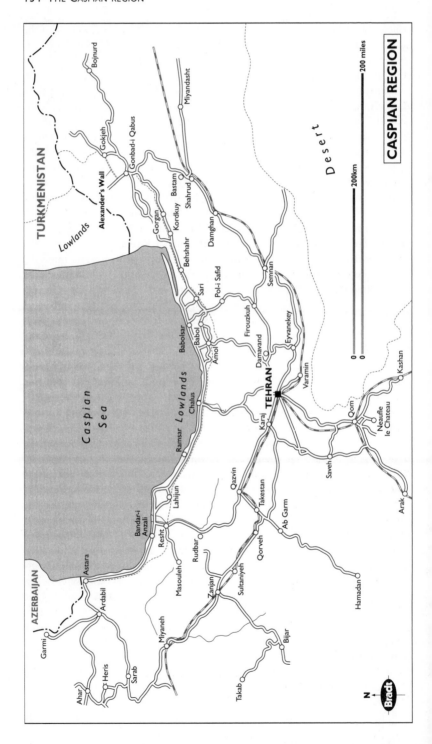

CASPIAN REGION

The Caspian Region

The road from Tehran to the shores of the Caspian is surely one of the most beautiful in Iran with the lush greenery, tree-covered mountains and valleys. The Caspian region has always been a favourite royal hunting ground over the centuries, while from the 15th century onward foreign visitors knew it for the cultivation of silk-worms, with all the associated processing. This was the source of the silk eagerly snapped up by Western and Russian merchant adventurers until the mid-19th century when pebrine, a disease of silkworms, struck. Attempts to revive the industry were made but by 1870 the Suez Canal was bringing cheaper Japanese, Chinese and Indian silk to the West. Another Caspian luxury product has since fared badly: caviar. And again the fault did not lie at Iran's door, but this time with inadequate Soviet and post-Soviet control of water pollution and poaching, which has largely killed off the sturgeon.

Getting there

Apart from daily flights to Resht from Tehran, there are 'express' rail services from Tehran via Shahrud, especially to Mashhad. Road transport, however, offers the greatest opportunity to enjoy the scenery and some of the sites. Daily intercity buses run especially to Resht, Chalus and Bandar-i Anzali from Tehran. Comparatively few non-Iranians come this way, as historic monuments are few and far between, but do go to this region before its distinctive village character is completely swamped in holiday apartment complexes which are taking over this shore-line. The roads are good and well engineered, but the hundreds of Tehrani families travelling to and from the region to these holiday homes mean the driving can be as mindless and dangerous as in the capital itself.

If there is no time to explore the whole of this region, there are two choices from Tehran northwards to Chalus (or alternatively Karaj and Qazvin, best for Alamut; see page 89): either west to Gilan and Azerbaijan provinces, or east to Mazandaran and Gorgan provinces and eventually to Mashhad.

Hotels

The severe earthquake of 1991, which killed some 40,000 in the Caspian region, and the comparatively few foreign visitors to this area have meant development priorities have lain elsewhere, building holiday apartments and villas for Tehranis eager to escape the capital. Finding accommodation, especially during *Nou Rouz* holiday, can therefore be a problem. For details, look under the relevant towns below.

TOWARDS GILAN

The tree-lined hillsides and the distinctive high-gabled roofs of Gilan houses begin after the town of **Rudbar** lying to the northwest. The whole area is associated with the marvellous finds from the Marlik royal necropolis, locally known as Cheragh Ali Tepe, excavated during 1961–6 by the Iranian authorities and already overgrown by the mid-1970s. Although most of the 53 stone-slab tombs excavated had been looted by graverobbers (probably a major source of the so-called 'Amlash' artefacts sold in the West in the 1950s) enough survives to show that this site continued to be used for burials over two or three centuries from about the 1st millennium BCE. The grave goods, some on display at Tehran's Reza Abbasi Museum, fell into three groupings: bronze weapons and ornament, belonging to 'warrior kings', jewellery and figurines associated with their ladies, and more domestic artefacts, which the archaeologists associated with their servants. For those interested in the transmission of beliefs about the afterlife, it is fascinating to note that tombs with horse skeletons were also uncovered which immediately recalls burial traditions found across Asia from northern Cyprus to China and Southern Siberia. Noting similarities in the finds with those from the Sialkh, Ziwiyeh and Hasanlu excavations and the striking parallels with Assyrian motifs, the Iranian archaeologists suggest that the population for some reason moved from Marlik to resettle at Sialkh (level VI) around 900BCE. A number of other archaeological settlements similarly dated have been identified in the region, for example Rostamabad, some 15km north of Rudbar. In this region were the valley strongholds associated with the medieval Assassins, the scourge of Crusader and Muslim leaders alike, but it is best to approach the so-called Valley of the Assassins from Qazvin, and also overnight there (see page 89).

The regional capital is **Resht** (also spelt Rasht), which in the 19th century was renowned for its high-quality patchwork (*resht* work) used for wall hangings, saddle cloths, floor coverings and for the gloriously coloured tents used in court circles when hunting. Like Ottoman tents currently displayed in the Military Museum, Istanbul, these Qajar tents bore no resemblance to canvas tents of early-20th-century Europe but were glorious architectural statements in rainbow colours with eye-catching designs composed of inlay appliqué, sewn in place by tambour stitch. Today, Resht is known only for its reputation as perhaps the wettest place in Iran, its good food (one well-known restaurant is *Moharram*, close to the new *Masjid-i Jami*), and a more relaxed attitude to separation of the genders. It boasts no historic buildings, as Russian forces ran amok in 1668 slaughtering the population. Further occupation during World War I caused more damage, with the total destruction of the bazaar by the Bolsheviks in 1920. The 1991 earthquake brought down anything that had survived, including the former Masjid-i Jami, now being rebuilt to a new design, an unhappy mixture of 'classical Safavid' and Gilani vernacular styles.

Visitors generally travel some 30km further northwest to Bandar-i Anzali to stay there but there are two hotels in Resht: the four-star Kadus Hotel (tel: 0131 3223075-9, 99 rooms, US$65 double, US$50 single), south of Azadi Boulevard, and Hotel Ordibehesht in Maydan Shahrdari (30 rooms).

In this region is the attractive hill village of **Masouleh**, 56km west of Resht via Fuman, which is always cut off by snow during the winter months. Stay clear on Fridays and holidays as crowds come from Tehran for a day out, picnicking near the river and in a small amusement area on the opposite hillside. Presently, the village is just managing to retain its character, but every other shop is filled with tourist tat. Cars and buses are stopped on the approach road and given a parking 'permit', so be prepared for some walking up steep narrow paths between the houses.

The road to **Bandar-i Anzali**, the main commercial port of the Iranian Caspian, goes through more green hills spotted with sharply angled thatched farm buildings. Development began as early as the 15th century, but major improvements were made during the 1920–30s to the port facilities celebrated in its former name, Bandar-i Pahlavi. By all reports the Saturday market is very good. The town itself is divided by the inlet: the easterly section is the commercial port area, while the west is less developed. A good and large three-star **hotel**, Sepid Kenar, 10km along the Anzali–Astara road (tel: 0181 4228032; fax: 0181 4383009; US$71 double/single) and popular with Tehranis during the holiday season, is in this western area. The hotel pool presently serves only as a breeding ground for mosquitoes, so for bathing, leave the hotel grounds (to the left, facing the hotel entrance); ladies and family groups occupy the section nearest to the hotel, while male swimmers should walk further on. The water is clean, warm and with a long shallow shelf making it perfect for young children. Iranian ladies go into the water fully dressed; foreign women can wear costumes but should cover themselves until they reach the water's edge.

From Anzali it is an attractive drive among conifers, beeches and rice fields along a good road westwards following the coastline. Some 15km on, and again 7km before **Talesh**, there are roadside displays of colourful kelims made in the hill villages, adding yet more colour to the vibrant greens of the rice fields. Keep an eye open for the low, long thatched silkworm sheds set within mulberry plantations, and the steeply dipping storage-roofs supported by chunky stone pillars. This road leads to **Astara**, the frontier with the Republic of Azerbaijan, and a new four-star Hotel Astara International (tel/fax: 0182 522 7050; US$110 double, US$69 single) has just opened on the southern outskirts of the border town. A kilometre or so further on, a turn-off west into the mountains leads to the famous shrine of Ardabil (see pages 152–3) strongly linked with the Safavid dynasty.

The road eastwards similarly follows the coastline but from here the beautiful views, trees and fields are rapidly disappearing under waves of building construction to provide holiday homes for Tehranis, eager to escape

SILKWORMS AND THE CASPIAN

Chinese histories record how Central Asia finally managed to learn the secrets of silkworm rearing and to acquire the eggs. About 1,600 years ago a Central Asian ruler was cunning enough to warn his bride-to-be, a Chinese princess, that as silkworms were unknown in his country, she could never have new silk robes to wear unless she brought her own supply. Knowing that imperial customs officials would search her luggage but never her person, she smuggled silk-eggs in her headdress out of the country to her wedding. By the early 9th century the shores of the Caspian were already famous for the quantity and quality of their raw silk, and plantations of mulberries were being harvested to feed the silkworms. There are no medieval descriptions of the 'nursery' huts but very probably they were essentially the same as today: long, low-lying huts with thatched roofs to maintain a shaded, warm but humid atmosphere so that the eggs hatched in large flat trays. The worms feed greedily and very noisily on white mulberry leaves, growing noticeably in size over the course of six weeks before beginning their cocoon-spinning over the next ten days. Some are kept aside to complete the full cycle, turning into the moth and producing eggs, but for most of the cocoons the end comes quickly. They are subjected to full sunlight or hot water, which kills off the pupa before it breaks out of its silk protection (so damaging the length of silk filament to be harvested). The natural gumminess of the cocoon is water soluble so a stick or fingers are used to gather up the fine filament, which is then reeled off, each up to a kilometre long.

the capital's smog and pollution. They are not the first to enjoy this retreat. Many of the Qajar kings and princes built retreats here as bases for hunting expeditions but, with the exception of Lahijun, one needs to travel further east if historic monuments are of interest. **Lahijun** was where the young Ismail (r1501–24) of the Safavid family was brought up secretly for five years, to protect him from further imprisonment and possible assassination by the Aq Qoyunlu. Today it is known for tea-growing and processing. In its thriving western bazaar area, just off the Maydan bearing the same local name, is the Masjid-i Chahar Padishah ('Four Kings'), more correctly called *Chahar Oleyeh* and better described as a mausoleum. Despite the name, only three cenotaphs of the family Sadat-i Keyeh are housed here in two main rooms under a low gabled roof. It has been suggested that the mausoleum dates from the early Mongol times but nothing about the building suggests that. The exterior wall paintings, depicting Abu'l Fazl Abbas riding off to find water for Hoseyn's supporters and their families at Kerbela, are late 19th century, as are the colourful dado tiles; both schemes bear 1920–30s repair dates. The beautiful wooden doors which once graced its main entrance from the bazaar have been removed to the new Islamic section of the Tehran Archaeological Museum. In the opposite (east) direction, about 3km outside the town, set up on the hillside from the main coast road, is the **Boghiyeh Shaykh Zahid Gilani**, a square mausoleum honouring the spiritual adviser to Shaikh Safi, founder of the Safavid dynasty. A carved inscription gives a construction date of 1419 but there is nothing 15th century about the present building and its unusual tiered, pyramidic tent-roof tiled in turquoise and yellow.

Further east by the coast is **Langerud**, famous for is late 19th–early 20th-century wall paintings decorating the Mahalla shrine of Aqa Sayyid Hoseyn and Ibrahim, largely rebuilt in the 18th century. Some 60km on, continuing eastwards is **Ramsar**, formerly a favourite haunt of the two Pahlavi rulers. The four-star Bozorg-i Ramsar Hotel (Bonyad; tel: 01942 235925; 160 rooms), built by the late shah, is a barn of a place with good-humoured staff with underworked barmen clearly longing to concoct (alcohol-free, of course) cocktails, perhaps a Gilan-sling or Caspian Sunrise. Next door is the smaller but stylish hotel, the original Ramsar Grand, commissioned by Reza Shah in the 1930s with only 30 rooms, echoing the furnishings of Istanbul's Khedive Palace on the Bosphorus. It was closed to guests in late 2001 because of problems with sewage disposal but it should re-open shortly. Ramsar itself is thriving thanks to the Tehran holiday trade, with many shops now catering for their custom; market day is Saturday. Look for the felt rugs sold in town but produced in the hill-villages.

AMOL

With the fast road linking Tehran with Chalus, passing through pleasant mountain scenery, new holiday complexes have largely taken over the shoreline, but a number of large national parks and woods still offer refuge. From Chalus, the more southerly road leads to Amol, once the capital of medieval Tabaristan Province and famous for a certain kind of 13th-century pottery that was, perhaps, produced here. The settlement was destroyed by Mongol forces, so its monuments post-date their ravages. The easiest to find was the **Imamzadeh Ibrahim** set within a cemetery enclosure on the northern outskirts. Locals understand this 'Ibrahim' to be the son of Imam Musa, but the 1519 wooden cenotaph – now totally cloth-covered – suggests another (unidentified) Ibrahim was interred here along with his brother Yahya and their mother. A large modern ambulatory has been constructed around the square tomb tower (c1426), but modern repairs and decoration have cheerfully ignored the historic architecture. Inside the actual tomb tower a riot of rainbow gloss paint overshadows remnants of 15th-century wall painting, while flat mirror-glass and highly varnished wooden pillars confidently detract any merit from the new construction. In the same cemetery is another 15th-century mausoleum, built to honour **Hajji Namdar**, who reportedly travelled from eastern Iran to repair his friend Ibrahim's tomb but died before completion. Judging from the exterior, more remains of the original building, but as it now serves as the local HQ for the revolutionary guard, access is totally restricted.

In the bazaar, off Mostafa Khomeini Street and Bahanor, is a modern complex, **Mashhad Mir Bozorg**, which includes a 17th-century building, possibly a *khanaqeh*, with some external tiling in place. No-one knew the whereabouts of its door key when I visited and unless you're into checklists of monuments you may decide to save your energy. Having read about the early-15th-century **Imamzadeh Qasem** 'located behind the main bazaar … adjoining a modern mosque', whose octagonal exterior was described as having rich plasterwork, we tried to find it. Finally we were directed 3km west outside the town, to a clump of trees shielding a sad cemetery with many unmarked graves, the final resting place of local Mujahedins killed during the early years of the revolution. Only recently have relatives been allowed to place some gravestones, but dried rose-petals and burnt candles show they are remembered as family rather than for any political activity. As for the *imamzadeh*, nothing about the small building there accorded with the published description. A case of mistaken identity? Or is the 'original' Qasem now known by a different name? Three more 15th-century **tomb towers** survive in Amol, all near to each other: that of **Nasir al-Haqq** (also known as Gonbad-i Sayyid Sadaf) has a square plan inside and out with an eight-sided tent-dome, as does the **Gonbad-i Gabri** (or Shams-i Rasul), but the **Imamzadeh Seh Tan** (three bodies) is octagonal in plan.

About 30km further east is **Babol**, which in the last 70 or so years has lost many of its architectural treasures and now just two 15th-century **imamzadehs** remain. One is set just back on the main Amol–Sari road, built to honour the dervish, Fakhr al Din, in 1430. Its basic circular form and tent-roof, separated by two rows of blind niches with light and dark blue tiles in the drum, is reminiscent of the Galata Tower, Istanbul, though of course it is much smaller. The other tomb tower stands some 4km to the north of Amol. It was built in 1471 to commemorate **Sultan Mohammed Tahir ibn Musa Qasem** by his two sons, using the architect Shams al-Din ibn Nasrullah Motarhhari according to the cenotaph inscription. One set of doors records another date twenty years after, which perhaps was the completion date.

A quick glance at the map and one could confuse Babol with the town of **Babolsar**, some 30km north, by the Caspian coast. This too has a couple of 15th-century octagonal **tomb towers** which have seen better years. One was built to honour Ibrahim Abu Javeh – or rather his head, which is all that is buried here; he was a son of Imam Musa and the brother of Imam Reza (see page 251), and some 300m away is another *imamzadeh* marking the burial place of Bibi Sakineh, a sister of Imam Reza.

You may prefer staying there rather than Babol or **Sari**, the next large city, some 40km inland from the coast.

SARI

Despite its size, and even though there are three flights a week from Tehran, friendly Sari lacks a decent central hotel, the best available being located 10km east on the Gorgan road: **Badeleh Hotel** (tel: 0151 2222174, 2223128; fax: 0151 2222548; US$60 double, US$48 single). If that doesn't put you off, market day in Sari is Saturday with money and people coming from the many rice and tea plantations in the locale. It was one of the last important Iranian towns to fall to the Muslim Arabs in the 7th century CE, and a strong

Zoroastrian community lasted here until the 19th century. Like many towns in this area, Sari suffered badly in both the Mongol and then Timurid campaigns sweeping through the eastern provinces. So, although the small local **museum** houses some Sasanid gold and silver artefacts found locally, its three historic buildings date from the Timurid period and once again they are tomb towers. The **Imamzadeh Yahya**, situated in the bazaar southwest of the Maydan Saat (Clock Square), is a great favourite with local women so foreign females will be subjected to much friendly fussing. The shrine has at its hub a cylindrical tower with a 12-sided tent-roof, built in 1442–6 to house the remains of a descendant of Imam Musa, but is now faced by a modern brick portico and its beautiful pair of doors has been removed for safe-keeping to Tehran. Just behind it is a slightly later square tower with an eight-sided tent-dome, the **Imamzadeh Sultan Zayn Abidayn** (though Jamal and Kamal are also named in the tile inscription); in some publications the monument is given as Sayyid Mohammed Reza. Originally constructed in 1448–50, the tomb retains some of its 15th-century *cuerda seca* tiling inside, and on the exterior some turquoise brick inserts survive in the zone of transition.

Some 3km from the centre, off Imam Reza Boulevard, stands the **Imamzadeh Abbas** in a small garden. Its beautifully carved cenotaph dates the octagonal tomb tower with its eight-sided tent-roof to 1492, stating that it was constructed after Imam Abbas, a son of Imam Musa, appeared here in a vision in 1424; an inverted Safavid blue and white bowl marks the apex of the inner hemispherical dome. A low-lying brick building has recently been added to the front while a young guardian who takes great pride in keeping the place immaculate sprinkles rose water on the paving and rugs.

If time allows, it is worth making a detour from Sari, dropping south via Qaem Shahr, formerly Shahi (or alternatively, a longer drive north from Semnan via Firouzkuh) to **Zir Ab** for the tomb tower at **Lajim**, 29km further east, and another at **Resget**, near Pol-i Sefid. Locally known as the **Imamzadeh Abdullah**, the Lajim tower was probably erected in 1023 and – although Iran had then been under Muslim rule for almost four centuries – the patron had the brick inscription for her beloved son, Shahriyar ibn al-Abbas ibn Shahriyar, written in pre-Islamic Pahlavi script as well as Arabic. So it's interesting on two counts: firstly, the Pahlavi script and, secondly, this is the earliest known building commissioned by a female patron in this part of Iran; she was possibly related through marriage to the famous tomb tower builder Qabus ibn Wushmgir (see page 143). To see the tomb tower at **Resget,** it is probably best to backtrack and continue to the village of Duab, just before Pol-i Sefid, although some prefer to walk the 2km or more cross-country. It is now thought the Resget tomb tower dates from c1106, during the first years of rule by the Seljuk sultan, Sanjar (r1097–1157), and once again Pahlavi occurs even at this late date, this time in the names of the two brothers interred here, Hormuzd and Hdyer. Yet at the same time there is the *shahada* ('There is no God...') recorded in the plaster door-plaque, and Koranic floriated Kufic inscriptions relating to death (K1:36) running around the cylindrical exterior, below the dome and the elaborate decoration.

From Sari, the road continues through woodlands, orange groves and rice fields towards **Behshahr**. Archaeological investigation carried out in the 1950s by a Pennsylvanian team in the limestone cliff-caves to the south, at **Turujan Tepe**, between Gelin and Fars Abad, proved the place had been settled around 9500BCE. Besides pottery shards and evidence of seal-fishing, the Neolithic skeleton of a teenage girl was found, whose bones had been ritually painted red after removal of the flesh. Signs of even earlier settlements were found in other caves, just south of Behshahr itself, by Cambridge (UK) archaeologists in 1964, pushing the date back another millennium. Behshahr, earlier known as Ashraf, does have a royal pavilion and gardens, established in Safavid times, which were heavily restored in the 1930s by Reza Shah, high in the hills overlooking the town. Its use since then as an important metrological station, and now as garrison quarters, means access is well-nigh impossible.

Some 40km further east, past Gaz, is **Kharabshahr** ('ruined city'), the 9th-century city of Tammisha, excavated in the mid-1960s by a London University team. In the Sasanid period, probably around the 550s, thick defence walls were constructed to protect the townspeople from tribal raids launched from the Central Asia steppes. It became the administrative centre for a local warlord with a Friday mosque and citadel, until destroyed by the first Mongol wave in 1220. From here, stretching eastwards along the minor road to Gokjeh and passing **Haji Qushan** (on some maps, Hajehlar) are the remains of the huge brick walls – originally over 170km long with some 33 fortresses – known locally as **Alexander the Great's Wall** (*Sadd-i Iskandar*), although it probably dates from Parthian times, ie: late 2nd century BCE. Thirteenth-century Iranian chroniclers and artists understood that it had been built to hold back those great enemies of civilization, Gog and Magog. Stretching east from Gumishan to Mount Pishkamer and perhaps continuing into present-day Turkmenistan, it consisted of a wide ditch, some 3m wide, before the wall, defended by towers and forts. On the Iranian side, field cultivation came up to the wall-line so the contrast between the wild steppe and settled agriculture would have been obvious.

Fifteen kilometres south of Kordkuy near the village of **Radkan** is an 11th-century cylindrical tomb tower 35m high, referred to as 'Radkan West' in academic publications. The two inscriptions, one above the door and the other just below the dome, in Arabic, plaited Kufic and also in Pahlavi, identify that a certain Abu Ja'far Mohammed ibn Wandarin was a local warlord whose Bawanid family had controlled the Eastern Caspian region from around 665 until fragmenting in 1349, having converted to Islam in 854. He ordered its construction in 1016, to house his remains after death.

Rushanabad is located 18km west of Gorgan, and within its main cemetery is the *imamzadeh* of Abdullah and Fazlullah, constructed in 1460 according to the doors, although some scholars have suggested 1420. A long prayer hall introduces the tomb tower, which is described as possessing an 'extraordinary use of glazed tiles' and 'unique painting' on the interior depicting buildings, perhaps symbolising the Ardabil shrine, Mecca or Medina.

The main road continues to **Gorgan**, where the occasional Turkoman woman still wears her distinctive colourful shawl with a floral dress. The medieval town was famous for its amazing lustre-decorated pottery vessels, and excavation work in 1970–77, some 4km west of the modern city, found superb examples. Today most visitors come to visit the tomb tower **Gonbad-i Qabus**, located some 80km away on the outskirts of Gunbad town. But Gorgan itself is worth a couple of hours' exploration, if only to look out for late 19th-century shops and houses which retain their traditional brick, wood and terracotta tiling, despite a severe earthquake in 1928 when over 50% of the population were Turkoman. Buried in the vegetable and fruit section of the bazaar, near to Maydan Wahdat, there is the two-ivan **Masjid-i Jami**, with the remains of a Seljuk minaret over the main entrance, but the courtyard tilework dates from the 20th century. The helpful guardian will unlock the ivan to the far left of the main entrance which contains some exuberant Qajar plasterwork as well as the original mosque doors, moved here ten years ago for their preservation. The lower carving has been worn away by the worshippers kissing and stroking the panels, but in the upper section the exquisite 15th-century work is clearly visible despite the thick modern varnish. Also here is a walnut *minbar*, gloriously unvarnished and decorated with the names of the 12 Imams; across the front section is a date corresponding to 1609. A five-minute walk behind this mosque and straight through the bazaar, passing some lovely traditional houses with deep overhanging eaves, leads to the **Imamzadeh Nur** (or **Ishaq ibn Musa ibn Ja'far**). Although this 12-sided tomb tower has lost its orginal roof, its brick patterning is still attractive, and inside a little of the original, deeply carved plaster decoration remains, especially in the *mihrab*. Although the original wooden doors have now vanished, one had a date corresponding to 1453 carved into it.

GONBAD-I QABUS

This monument is always mentioned in books on Iranian Islamic architecture. Its staggering size and strength of form look very out-of-place in the fragile, pretty garden now surrounding it (entry 2,000 rials). Two weary *kibitka*s or domed trellis-tents stand by its side. We know something of the man who had it built in 1006 as a suitable family mausoleum. This was before he was deposed in 1012 and deliberately left to freeze to death in the Gorgan winter snows. He was the military commander, Amir Qabus ibn Wushmgir, a famous calligrapher, known scholar (the famous medieval polymath al-Biruni dedicated his multi-volumed *Chronology of Ancient Nations* to him), patron of the arts and renowned, blood-thirsty warlord. An artificial mound conceals the formidable foundations (late 19th-century Russian archaeologists gave up digging down after 10m) for this 51m-high tower of coffee-colour brick. The basic circular plan, 17m in diameter, is quickly broken by ten soaring angular flanges and one small door. Two brick inscriptions run around the shaft in between the angled buttresses, one low down and the other high up, under the superbly 'tailored' conical dome which was once in grey-green brick though what you see now is a modern replacement; both refer to the promise of paradise awaiting the true believer. There is just one small window in the roof, positioned to catch the rising sun which would illuminate, according to local legend, a suspended rock-crystal coffin holding the body of Qabus (not quite the cheap wooden coffin recommended in Islamic law).

South of here, Cambridge archaeologists excavating caves found evidence that people had inhabited the region from at least 40,000BCE and possibly much earlier (65,000BCE), hunting, flint-working and living off bears, rhinoceros and also horses. This last point is interesting. The Caspian and Turkoman regions were once known for two special types of horse (see below).

Just as intriguing, but very different, is a cemetery about 70km northeast of Gonbad-i Qabus, named after a tomb to a certain **Halat (Khaled) Nabi**, near to the mountain called Gokjeh Dagh. No-one knows who Halat Nabi was, let alone if he was Muslim, but the real mystery is the 600 odd standing stones. Some are cylindrical and anything from 1m to 5m high, while others are rectangular with two upper lobes. There are no dating inscriptions, but a conservative guess is that these date from the 17th or 18th century, marking a traditional Turkoman tribal burial site.

From Gorgan, most travellers continue towards Mashhad, or indeed to the Irano-Turkmenistan frontier (see page 254), but if you have to return to Tehran there is no need to backtrack – go by the 'southern' road via Shahrud and Semnan, as detailed below.

CASPIAN AND TURKOMAN HORSES

The Caspian horse is similar but far from identical to the stocky Turkoman horse, the sturdy mount of the 12th-century Seljuk Turks and later Turkoman tribesmen. The Caspian stands about 11 or 13 hands high, but is narrower in width across the back, with a pronounced forehead and small ears, a distinctive oval hoof which needs infrequent shoeing, and a unique haemoglobin structure. A small stud was established in 1965 near Shiraz, and later in Tehran, and immediately after the Islamic Revolution this section of the then-Royal stables came under the Ministry of Jihad, but it is not known whether that stud still exists. The breed continues in the USA, Australia and also in the UK, as a mare and stallion were presented to Philip, Duke of Edinburgh, in 1971.

The Turkoman horse continues today in the modern breed known as Akhal Teke, often pale gold or possibly grey or bay in colour. It stands taller than the Caspian, at about 15 hands with a narrow chest, flat ribs and long back. The tail is comparatively short and the mane even more so. Its well-known stamina and ability to go without water for over 300km in desert conditions are put down to a distinct diet, low in bulk and high in protein, often made with animal fat and eggs mixed with barley.

Shahrud is on the main road from Mashhad, and if you want to visit the Masjid-i Jami and famous shrine at Bastam (also spelt Bistam), 12km to the north, perhaps this is the best place to overnight. Alternatively, the Tourist Inn at Semnan (tel: 0231 41433-5; 32 rooms; US$43 double/single) is perfectly adequate.

BASTAM

Like many other pilgrims, Oljeitu, the future Il-Khanid ruler of Iran (d1317) but then the local governor, came to pay homage to the grave of the famous sufi and charismatic mystic, Shaykh Bayazid al-Bastami (d874), and was initiated as a sufi here in 1300. He then undertook a massive programme of rebuilding, enlarging the **shrine complex**. Today one enters into a large court and to the immediate right (north) is a **tomb tower**, often referred to as that of Shaykh Bayazid, although his actual grave is in the courtyard immediately in front of the main shrine building alongside a later one of Azam Khan Afghani; it now functions as an office. Rather than walking ahead, bear left and walk through an east-facing portal, beautifully embellished with turquoise-blue strapwork and moulded brick-plugs, leading into a long hall. Constructed in 1313 as perhaps the main entrance, it now has an almost central position in the extended enclosure. High on the inside walls is a lengthy, elegant plaster inscription, the work of a Damghani master craftsman, naming Oljeitu and his brother, Ghazan Khan 'Sultan of the land of the East and China, king of the servants of the horizons' (r1295–1304) as patrons. At the end, not only Bayazid's tower comes into view but also another lofty ivan for teaching, also decorated with turquoise-blue tile inserts but largely hidden by scaffolding (my usual complaint). On the left, a small locked door – peek through the side window – gives entry into one of two small 'hermitages' which served as a *chehel-khaneh*, both richly decorated with soot-blackened, early-14th-century plasterwork.

In the main building, there is an *imamzadeh* shrine immediately to the right with a grilled cenotaph commemorating Mohammed ibn Ja'far; women have to don a *chador*. The hexagonal, tiled dado is much earlier in date than the painted decoration of the walls and dome, restored in 1894. Viewed from the outside, this shrine is underneath a tiled tent-roof with a 1120 brick-patterned minaret, its lower section incorporated into the hall further into the building. This vaulted hall was constructed after the decorative brick wall of the little mosque, with two intricately carved 14th-century doors now behind glass. In the late 15th century the roof of this mosque fell in and a wooden roof was installed but the carved plaster *mihrab*, dated 1314 and the work of Mohammed ibn Hoseyn Abi Talib al-Mohandis, was saved. Some beautiful plasterwork also remains in the winter prayer hall next door but its *mihrab* has been removed.

To get to the **Masjid-i Jami**, leave the complex by the main gate and walk southwest, keeping the shrine on the left. The mosque is down a side road nearby. At its back is a large 13.6m circular tomb tower of 1313, again the work of Mohammed al-Damghani, with some 26 vertical flanges and remains of glazed inserts in the two inscription bands under the roof. Inside, it is 12-sided (to symbolise the 12 Imams?) with blind niches in three zones accentuating the height. Its door, firmly locked, is located within the mosque at the end of a small vestibule decorated with 14th-century carved plaster and well hidden behind a curtain. Very little of the original *masjid-i jami* remains but do wait for the guardian to let you into the *mihrab* area as it still retains some wonderful plasterwork, exquisitely carved in 1306 with unusually shaped arch profiles, akin to upturned pagoda-eaves. This decoration was clearly applied on to an earlier structure, and above the *mihrab* the Qajar ruler Fath Ali Shah recorded his own 1809 repairs to the building.

About 55km west from Shahrud is **Mihmandust**, where a Safavid general, later famous as Nadir Shah Afshari, finally defeated the Afghan rebels in 1729. In a cemetery on the southern outskirts stands another lovely tomb tower, popularly known as Imamzadeh Qasem, a son of the 7th Imam, despite the fact that its Kufic inscription above the bird-like frieze clearly stated it was made for a commander, Abu Jafar Mohammed, 'the hospitable *mihmandust*' (thus the name of the township), before modern restoration messed up the reading. Built in 1097, the tower (external diameter around 10m) was about 21m high but its original conical roof has not survived. The number of flanges, twelve in all, was probably deliberate symbolism (12 Imams) as the verse (K41:31) in the inscription has strong Shiʻi connotations.

Nearer **Damghan** (altitude 1,120m) Mount Gird-kuh comes into view. Known for its Ismaili connections as early as the 10th century, this is where the Assassins (see page 90) constructed a fortress so well-defended that Hulagu, the grandson of Genghis Khan, laid siege for many months before finally taking it in 1256. By all reports, sections of the enclosing walls, the gatehouse and cisterns remain; as yet no archaeological survey has been undertaken. Access is through the village of Gird-kuh, and may still be difficult.

DAMGHAN

It is thought Damghan was originally known as Deh-i Magi (village of the magi/Zoroastrian priests), and in the past some scholars wondered if it was the city Hekatompylos of Alexander the Great. However, finds from the **Shahr-i Qumis** excavation in the 1970s have settled that debate for the time being: Hekatompylos was there (see page 148). Damghan was a prosperous walled city in Sasanid times as confirmed by American archaeological excavations in the early 1930s (Philadelphia Museum of Art, PA, has decorative plaster from the Sasanid palace at **Tepe Hissar**, southeast of the present town) and possibly its importance then was linked to certain Zoroastrian sacred fires in the region, although there had been occupation from at least 2,000 years before. The earthquake of 856CE destroyed the Sasanid defensive walls, killing about 45,000 people by some reports, so there was massive rebuilding in the 920s. As local warlords and governors battled for control, real authority rested in the Assassins' fortress above and Hassan al-Sabbah (see page 90) felt safe enough to enter the city itself. With the Mongol conquest, the power struggle continued with the rulers of Khwarizm (present-day Turkmenistan) also intervening. The city was taken by Timur Leng in 1381 but raids and massacres continued for the next 50 years. In 1528 the Safavid regime brought a measure of stability to the region, ended by Afghan incursions in the 1720s. By the time Nadir Shah finished bombarding the town in 1729, its population had shrunk to 3,000. Prosperity slowly returned with the Qajar dynasty (Fath Ali Shah was born here in 1772) but the town was torn apart in 1911 when pro-Constitutionalist activists met their opponents head on; hundreds were left dead. In 1929 the town had a population of 5,000 and today it is over 50,000.

Despite such a turbulent history, the city boasts some important historic buildings. About 500m southeast of the main square, Maydan Imam, is the **Masjid-i Tarik Khaneh** (also known as Masjid-i Chehel Sutun) thought to be the second oldest mosque surviving in Iran (entry 2,000 rials). Even if you don't want to enter, check out the small but good bookshop in the front garden, run by the helpful guardian, who also holds the key to Pir-i Alamdar (see below; entry 1,000 rials) and can direct you to Tepe Hissar. This is a 'majestically simple' mosque, retaining something of its 8th-century 'Arab' plan, a design which quickly fell out of favour with Iranian patrons. The arrangement of arches running parallel to the enclosing walls and some of the fat, stumpy brick piers are from the original 760 construction, but the remains of the brick and plaster patterning are from an 11th-century Seljuk restoration. Its **minaret**, just outside the mosque, 25m high, was erected in 1028, making it the earliest Iranian minaret still standing. Its inscription among the six bands of brick set in relief and recess records that the mason was the man who built the Semnan minaret (see page 149) while the costs were met by the governor who before his appontment also paid for the Pir-i Alamdar tomb tower nearby.

It takes about eight minutes to walk to the **Masjid-i Jami** (also called Masjid-i Imam Hoseyn), crossing the main road and going northeast. You've come here just for the Seljuk **minaret**, constructed sometime between 1031–5, which has ten lovely brick-pattern zones still retaining some glazed inserts, including the Koranic verse (24:35) which talks of the message of Islam burning brightly in a glass lamp, very apposite for Imam Hoseyn, often represented by a lighted candle. Presently it is about 27m high but the upper section was destroyed in 1933. About 100m away is the 16m-high **tomb tower of Pir-i Alamdar** of 1027; it no longer has its original exterior tent roof, but the brickwork with the main inscription below the dome is still lovely, recording that it was built for the then governor of Damghan, Abu Jafar Mohammed ibn Ibrahim, by his son who was also responsible for the Tarik Khaneh minaret just described. But the best work is inside: a splendidly ornate plaited Kufic band running around the interior (K39:53–4) in blue, outlined in red and justly described as 'a tour de force', speaks of God's forgiveness.

Also near the Maydan Imam Khomeini are yet more monuments, in the complex of **Khanaqeh of Shah Rukh**. The first building is a much-restored tomb, but the Sufi meeting place, which gives the complex its name, is a small square building with a 15th-century Timurid tile-panel high over the door, recording that Shah Rukh, Timur Leng's son (page 247), paid for extensive repairs. Today in its crypt it houses another Shah Rukh, a relative of Nadir Shah Afshar killed by the first Qajar ruler in 1796. Adjoining it is a large *imamzadeh*, still retaining its Seljuk inner dome, probably the reason for establishing a *khanaqeh* here. It commemorates Ja'far ibn Ali (d901), a descendant of the 3rd Imam. Just behind is a cylindrical tomb tower standing 14.8m high, called the **Chehel Dokhtaran** ('40 Maidens') but, as its two inscriptions used to record before modern restoration, it was built in 1055, by and for the military commander Abu Shuja' Asfar Beg 'preparing for his sleep a tomb for himself and his sons...'. Resembling the Pir-i Alamdar above, it is the second earliest dated tomb tower surviving in Iran.

Just 5km southeast of Damghan, close to the railway line, archaeological work at **Tepe Hissar** uncovered not only the remains of a 6th-century Sasanid palace, but also evidence of settlement from at least the early second millennium BCE with charred remains of skeletons and weapons. The main excavations were undertaken during the two World Wars when splendid conical bowls bearing fine black-painted motifs (see *Tehran: Archaeological Museum*, pages 74–6) were uncovered alongside finely modelled rams' heads in gold foil for textile decoration. Road widening in 1995 has presumably put paid to further discoveries. Again south of the main road from Damghan to Semnan (Qouseh or Ghouseh) another interesting archaeological site was found, **Shahr-i Qumis**. Excavation work here in 1967 revealed rich Parthian finds from mud-brick vaulted tombs (c70BCE), and evidence of a Parthian fortified encampment. Part of the site was then inhabited into Seljuk times, before its destruction by the Mongols in the early 13th century. But, importantly, the archaeologists left the excavation convinced that indeed they had found Hekatompylos or 'The City of a Hundred Gates' where Alexander the Great broke the news to his soldiers that they were not returning home, but carrying on into India.

Semnan is the next major city on the road back towards Tehran, with a very adequate Tourist Inn (tel: 0231 41433–5; 32 rooms; US$43 double/single). Centuries ago its wealth came from the trade caravans passing to and from Central Asia and Afghanistan via Mashhad going west, but now it is a centre for light industy and the provincial capital (population 450,000) on the main railway from Tehran to Mashhad. Famous for its pistachios, it also has a couple of interesting buildings as well as the remains of the mud-brick **citadel** which once defended the city. Its **Masjid-i Jami**, on the western outskirts off the Maydan Motahheri, was established in the 8th century but the only visual evidence of this are the restored fat brick pillars and a *mihrab* presently boarded up in the arcade opposite the excessively tall prayer ivan. That main ivan is part of the major Timurid rebuilding programme undertaken by Shah Rukh around 1424, and the large underground winter prayer hall may also date from this period or later, though locals think it is Seljuk work. What is clearly Seljuk is the prayer chamber itself. At first sight its proportions – height of walls to dome, squinches and zone of transition etc – seem illogical and the only explanation is that for some reason the later

Timurid repairs involved raising the original ground level of this chamber considerably. The **minaret**, standing over 28m high, is also Seljuk, constructed in 1031-5 by the same man responsible for the minaret at Tarik Khaneh, Damghan. It has at least eight pattern zones, including two bands of inscription (inc K41:33) and an attractive wooden balcony. Within easy walking distance through the bazaar, about 200m northeast, is the 19th-century **Masjid-i Imam Khomeini** (formerly Masjid-i Shah), proof of the city's prosperity in the Qajar period. Somewhat understated for Qajar religious buildings, the exuberant tiling and colouring dating from the reign of Fath Ali Shah (d1834) are delicious. Another Qajar monument, the **Arg-i Darwazir** dated 1884, once marked an entrance gate into the town but is now transformed into a busy roundabout. Its tile panels feature armed soldiers and a cannon.

From Semnan, there are two routes to Tehran: one heads off via Firouzkuh while the more southerly route goes through Garmsar. Both pass close to the town of **Damavand**, named after the mountain standing 5,678m high to the north. The area is dotted with ruins of numerous fortresses, strongholds of the Assassins in the late medieval period. Close to Damavand's Masjid-i Jami is a tomb tower known locally as the tomb of Shaikh Shibli, a Sunni mystic and former local deputy governor before his death in Baghdad in 945. His actual tomb still survives there, though it was probably built for someone completely different as its style suggests the late 11th century. It has an octagonal exterior with a rounded buttress at each corner, decorated in brick patterns with octagons, lozenges, eight-pointed stars and an octagonal flanged tent-roof.

The road from **Eyvanekey**, 25km west of Garmsar, into Tehran goes through marvellous scenery with spectacularly coloured rocks. But this route, known locally as 'Alexander's [the Great] Gate', has numerous sharp hair-pin bends which Tehrani drivers acknowledge only at the last moment.

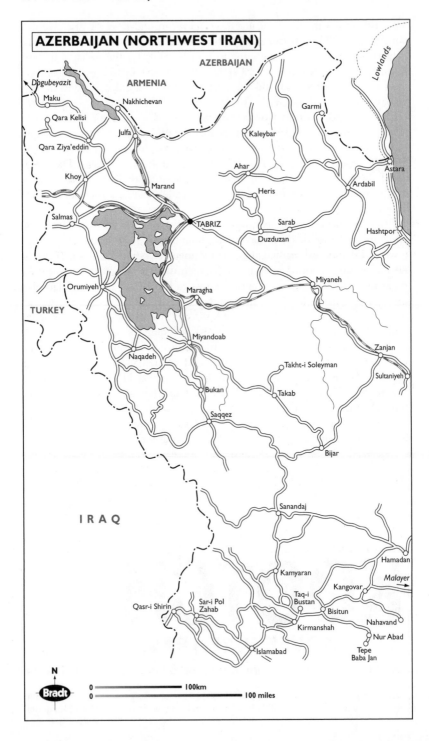

AZERBAIJAN (NORTHWEST IRAN)

AZERBAIJAN

Lowlands

ARMENIA

Dogubeyazit

Maku

Nakhichevan

Garmi

Qara Kelisi

Julfa

Kaleybar

Qara Ziya'eddin

Ahar

Astara

Khoy

Marand

Heris

Ardabil

Salmas

TABRIZ

Sarab

Hashtpor

Duzduzan

Orumiyeh

Maragha

Miyaneh

TURKEY

Miyandoab

Zanjan

Naqadeh

Takht-i Soleyman

Sultaniyeh

Bukan

Takab

Saqqez

Bijar

Sanandaj

IRAQ

Hamadan

Kamyaran

Malayer

Kangovar

Qasr-i Shirin

Sar-i Pol Zahab

Taq-i Bustan

Bisitun

Nahavand

Kirmanshah

Nur Abad

Islamabad

Tepe Baba Jan

N

Bradt

0   100km

0   100 miles

Into Iranian Azerbaijan

For centuries this region formed a major gateway into both Europe and Asia, with merchants and armies travelling the trade routes along the foothills of the Caucasus separating modern-day Turkey and Iran from the modern republics of Georgia, Armenia and Azerbaijan, and through the Zagros Mountains dividing Iraq and Iran. Today's political frontiers are less than a century old, so understandably excavations in this region of Iran frequently reveal archaeological proof of strong cultural links with ancient civilisations associated with Anatolia, Mesopotamia and across the Caucasus. Because of its location, surrounded on two sides by mountains and with the Caspian Sea to the east, the region was a battle arena in more recent times: some 400 centuries of conflict against the Ottoman armies and then Russian (and Bolshevik/Soviet) campaigns in the 19th and 20th centuries.

The region was always known for its Christian communities, which before World War I made up over 30% of the total local population. This was where Western missionaries came in the 19th and early 20th centuries, establishing medical centres and schools, and fired with the wish to 'convert' the Nestorians and Armenian Gregorians to join various Protestant denominations. Although tolerated by the central administration as long as there was no evidence of Muslim conversions, such activity caused problems to all layers of Iranian society and fuelled xenophobic anxieties.

Getting there

The main highway from the capital to Tabriz is good but not exactly spectacularly scenic, taking about 12 hours by express bus. If you wish to visit Sultaniyeh and Zanjan etc, the slower 'old' road will have to be used in part. To avoid returning on the same route, why not travel from Tehran to Bandar-i Anzali, staying there the night and then continuing up the western shores of the Caspian to visit Ardabil. There are regular bus services from there to Tabriz, the provincial capital (270km away). After visiting various sites to the north, one could then make one's way back to Tehran.

Do note that the winters in this region are very long and harsh. Snowfalls are heavy and the temperature plummets, so visits are best made from mid-April to mid-October.

Hotel accommodation for foreign visitors is limited really to Tabriz and also Orumiyeh (see pages 154–7 and 161).

ARDABIL

With the establishment of the Safavid regime (1501–c1735), Ardabil (altitude 1,300m) became increasingly important. Five centuries earlier it had been a walled town, but in such a ruinous, filthy state that the Arab geographer al-Muqaddasi (fl 967–85) described it as 'one of the latrines of the world'. Local campaigns against the Georgian princes in 1208, which resulted in the sacking of Ani (eastern Turkey) and the deaths of 12,000 Christians, led to swift and violent retribution in 1209 when over 12,000 Ardabil citizens were slain. Later, the conflict between the two great tribal confederations – the Qara and Aq Qoyunlu – had repercussions on the local economy. But once the Safavid leader Ismail took control in 1501, the town's future became more secure, for this was the burial-place of the Sufi teacher considered to be the founder of the dynastic family, Shaikh Safi al-Din (1251–1334). It also benefitted from its proximity to the new Safavid capital, Tabriz, until the court moved south to Qazvin and later Isfahan. Time and money were lavished on Ardabil, especially on the tomb of Safi al-Din, as the shahs sought to emphasise their lineage and championship of the *Ithna ʿAshari* branch of Shiʿi Islam. By 1656 the shrine and town were crown domain, endowed with superb costly carpets like the Ardabil carpet (Victoria and Albert Museum, London) and its twin in the Los Angeles County Museum of Art, USA, and a magnificent collection of Chinese porcelain and celadon (as in the Ardabil Shrine, and the Islamic section of the Archaeological Museum, Tehran). It also had a vast library, but this was ransacked by Russian troops during the occupation of Ardabil during the Irano-Russian wars of 1826–8, and anything valuable was taken back to St Petersburg.

Things to see and do

It was Shaikh Safi himself who established a *khanaqeh* in the 13th century, perhaps on the site of the present *Chini-khaneh* (Porcelain Room). After his death, his followers built a tomb to honour him and thereafter over the centuries buildings were added, torn down or converted. The main entrance into the shrine complex dates from 1926 when the four or so shops either side were built, their rents going towards the upkeep of the shrine. This leads directly into a garden laid out in c1834, which today is a favourite meeting place for elderly gentlemen. At the other end a porch of 1629 (currently being heavily restored), leads into a courtyard with 'very fair and spacious vault[s] arched above, paved without with green and blue [tile] stones', as seen by one European traveller in 1637. The domed structure immediately on the left, hidden by a large wooden grille, was originally constructed on the orders of Shah Tahmasp around 1540, perhaps as another *khanaqeh,* and it is possible that the two Ardabil carpets (if they were ever here) were made for this octagonal building. By 1843 it was in a sorry state, having lost its dome, and it was perhaps at this point it was turned into a mosque, the *Jannat Sura*; major repairs were undertaken from 1935 onwards to this building and in fact to all the tiled façades in this courtyard. A small door takes the visitor into the main building and a long prayer hall known as *Qandil khaneh* ('Lantern Hall') as the endowments paid for teams of Koran readers to sit and intone before the tombs. The portal inscription stresses the importance of reading the Holy Book, and it has long been assumed the door and hall was part of Tahmasp's building programme. However, recent research suggests perhaps both were constructed two centuries earlier. It currently houses a huge vertical loom, as some years ago the authorities decided a copy of the Ardabil carpet should be made but, like many projects in the new republic, resources have been diverted elsewhere and progress is painfully slow. The massive silver doors were a royal gift in 1602–3, and then ten years later Shah Abbas ordered the hall to be painted and gilded, with silver grilles erected.

A doorway immediately on the left leads into the *Chini-khaneh*, a large octagonal room with plasterwork niches which once held some of the fine Chinese porcelain pieces from the Safavid court. In all, over 1,160 pieces of costly, rare Chinese blue and white porcelain and celadon vessels were given by the Safavid shahs, some probably taken as battle spoils from the defeated Uzun Hasan, leader of the Aq Qoyunlu (d1478). In the 1930s about half of these were moved to Tehran for safe keeping. A number of dishes is displayed alongside manuscripts and other historic artefacts. Most of the structure dates from Safavid rebuilding programme of 1607–11 but, as you will spot, the domed roof is new, dating from 1971.

Returning to the *Qandil khaneh*, you can explore the other small rooms off to the left housing numerous cenotaphs marking interments in the crypts below. Thick but fine-quality 'inlaid' patterned felts cover the floors, getting dirtier and more moth-eaten every year. Important members of the Safavid court, military generals and the royal ladies rest here, including Shah Ismail's mother and the shah himself with a magnificent cenotaph (see below), presented, so the locals say, by the Indian Moghal Emperor, Humayun, in about 1530, in gratitude for giving him refuge during his exile from India.

The *Haram khaneh* should, as the name suggests, contain the cenotaphs of the royal ladies but as one scholar has noted, at least one of the deceased was the eldest son of Shaikh Safi, who died in 1324 when the room was probably constructed and not, as first thought, the wife of Safi. The tomb-chamber nearest that of the shaikh himself contains Ismail's large cenotaph and little else, other than deep cobalt blue tiles with stencilled fired gold patterns and smoke-damaged wall decoration. Next door, at the end of the prayer hall, once decorated with costly rugs and gold lamps but ransacked over a century ago, is the circular tomb-chamber of Shaikh Safi himself, constructed in 1334 and extensively repaired (on the outside) in 1949. Before you leave the courtyard outside, don't forget to walk round to see the exteriors of these tomb chambers with their tile decoration.

From Ardabil it is about 215km to Tabriz (altitude 1,340m), the provincial capital, but there is an interesting mosque about 75km east, coming from Ardabil on either the Ahar (north) road or that going through Sarab. Near the village of Miraban (south of Heris, north of Duzduzan, west of Sarab) is

Asnak, whose **Masjid-i Jami** is of red stone; very unusual. It was built around 1333 on the so-called 'Arab' hypostyle plan with wooden columns inside and a flat wooden roof. Very unusual for this pre-Safavid date, the foundation inscription under the left window of the entrance portal is in Persian, written in the Arabic script, recording that 'Malikshah ... made all its decoration with the point of an adze, may his hand be steady and may Allah preserve him.' About 70km north of Ahar is Kaleybar, known for its well-preserved **Babak Castle** (also known as Qaleh-i Jomhur) at an altitude of 2,300m, some 3km from the town. This Sasanid castle, named after Babak the warlord, managed to resist the Arab armies until 839. In the ruins of the rooms and corridors pottery and coins dating from the 13th century have been found by Iranian archaeologists and restoration teams, working here since 1998. Access is difficult.

TABRIZ
Tabriz, said to have been founded by Khosrau Arshakid (Arsacid) of Armenia in c220, has been hit by earthquakes many times during its history, with those in 858 and 1042 wiping out any structure from the pre-Islamic period. By the end of the 10th century it was such a prosperous trading centre that it was selected as the venue for the marriage celebrations of the Seljuk sultan Tughril Beg (d1063) and a daughter of the Baghdad caliph. It achieved the status of a 'royal' capital first with the Mongol Il-Khanid ruler Abaqa (r1265–81) and even then it had a reputation for business acumen as the city's traders rioted over the introduction of paper money to replace coinage. His descendant Ghazan Khan (r1295–1304) kept Tabriz as his capital and ordered the building of the city walls and defences, the bazaars and an enormous tomb mausoleum, spending a vast amount, but nothing of this has remained. Moreover, Ghazan's conversion to Islam was marked with persecution of all non-Muslims in the region and within Tabriz itself all churches, synagogues and fire temples were razed to the ground.

From the mid-14th century, the city and the surrounding area came under the control of various warlocals, until the Qara Qoyunlu tribal chiefs made Tabriz their capital from 1436–67, after which it came into the Aq Qoyunlu domain. For the early years of the Safavid regime it again had capital status, until hostilities with the Ottoman Empire became too close for comfort. (Tabriz was first occupied by Ottoman forces in 1514 and again in 1585.) A year after the 1721 earthquake, Russian forces invaded the region and attacked Tabriz, occupying the city 1826–8 until, under the terms of the 1828 Peace of Turkomanchay and the payment of a crippling war indemnity, it was returned to Qajar control, before returning again during 1909–14. No wonder a distinct Russian influence still lingers in the city's architecture. In 1916 the Russian Tbilisi–Julfa–Tabriz Railway was completed, but any idea of retaking Tabriz was postponed with the advent of the Bolshevik Revolution. As the Russians moved out, so Ottoman forces moved in until the frontiers with Turkey were finally settled. The city was reoccupied by Soviet forces in 1941, after Reza Shah was forced to abdicate by the Allies, and four years later the short-lived autonomous regime of the Democratic Party in Azerbaijan was set up by the

Bolsheviks. In December 1946 the army of Mohammed Reza Shah, assisted by American personnel, took the city and all Bolshevik and Communist elements were purged.

Getting there
There is a frequent 'express' train service from Tehran to Tabriz costing approximately 60,000 rials (US$7), and about four daily flights between these two important commercial and manufacturing cities. Tabrizi businessmen and manufacturers are known throughout Iran for their business acumen, and the city is mainly (light) industrial, specialising in food production.

Accommodation and eating out
The best hotel is the four-star **Tabriz (International)**, Imam Khomeini Avenue (tel: 0411 3341082–9; fax: 0411 3341080; 134 rooms; US$77 double, US$53 single), where most visiting businessmen stay. The staff are helpful, but the restaurant closes early. Its location is not central but it is situated on a shopping avenue so early evening strolls are pleasant (if you don't mind traffic noise), especially if you wish to buy good-quality dried fruit and nuts at Tavazo. Otherwise there is the four-star **Hotel Gosstaresh** on the intersection of Abressan/Imam Khomeini Avenue (tel: 0411 3345021–4; US$64 double, US$50 single, including breakfast) or, close to the railway station, the two-star **Hotel Darya** on Rahahan Street (tel: 0411 4459501–9; fax: 0411 4459510; 106 rooms; US$49 double, US$34 single, including breakfast). A variety of restaurants and cafés is located on Imam Khomeini Avenue; the local speciality is *abgoosht* (also known as *dizi* – see page 49).

Things to see and do
Shopaholics will be delighted with the extensive bazaar, parts of which date from the 15th century, arranged very compactly across two main roads; but otherwise Tabriz has a few historic monuments. Arguably, the most famous monument in town is the **Arg** (Citadel) as it is locally known. In fact, only the massive walls remain of the enormous four-ivan **Masjid-i Shah** (or *Masjid-i Ali Shah*), which were once smothered with tile panels. This structure of 1312–22 was the brainchild of a 14th-century vizier serving in Oljeitu's court (see pages 164–6) who obviously wanted to build bigger and better than anyone else. Judging from the surviving height (26m) and thickness (10.5m) of the walls, it is thought the ivan leading to the prayer chamber was about 66m high, with the vault springing starting around 24.5m, across a staggering span of almost 31m (wider than anything attempted in 14th-century Europe). Chronicles described the mosque as having a huge 285x228m marble-paved courtyard, surrounded by an alabaster-columned arcade and with an ablution pool so large that, two centuries later, Shah Ismail would sail across it in a beautiful barge. Its minarets, probably soaring over 60m high, were said to have so impressed envoys from the Mamluk Court of Cairo that they influenced the design of those built at the Mosque of Amir Qusun, Cairo (1330). By the 17th century the mosque was in ruins, although there was enough cover for the Friday prayer to be still conducted

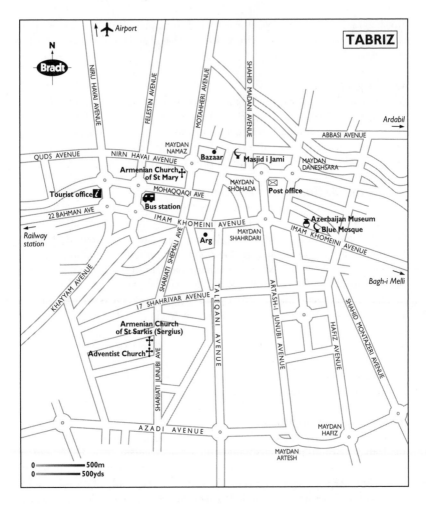

there. In 1809 the Qajar governor took over the building, turning it into a citadel (an earlier Arg built elsewhere under Ottoman occupation had been destroyed in 1603), with a defensive ditch. Even so, some original mosque tilework was seen in situ by the English envoy, Ker Porter, ten years later but shortly afterwards Tabriz fell to the Russians. The Arg's defences were finally dismantled in the late 19th century and by then not one tile panel remained.

Well worth the effort of a taxi drive and a short walk from the main road is the so-called **Blue Mosque** (*Masjid-i Kabud*, or *Masjid-i Muzaffariyeh*), known in Iran for centuries as the 'Turquoise of Islam' because of its tilework (entry 2,000 rials). This mosque was built on the orders of Saliha Khanum, the daughter of Sultan Jahanshah, chief of the Qara Qoyunlu, or of his wife, Khatun Jan. It was finished in 1465, two years before Jahanshah was killed in an Aq Qoyunlu ambush in 1467. A severe earthquake in 1776 caused some of the building to collapse, but an extensive and sympathetic rebuilding programme between 1950 and 1966 allows today's visitors to gain an accurate idea of the original layout, scale and proportions, and also to inspect the incredible 'mosaic' tilework inside and out. The main entrance portal still stands with its rich cable moulding and tiling, but otherwise much of the exterior façade has been rebuilt. This leads into a five-domed 'corridor' which in turn leads to two domed side aisles and a large central domed chamber (diameter 16m) supported by eight piers, which had internal staircases that led to an upper gallery. Essentially it is a fine example of the 'covered mosque' plan of nine domes, including the main central one, which is more usually found in early Ottoman architecture, for instance in Bursa, Turkey. But there's something else: behind the *qibla* wall and down a few steps there is another domed chamber, so the actual ground plan is similar to the so-called 'T-shaped' mosques of 15th-century Bursa (eg: 1414–20 Yeşil Cami), but function, emphasis and proportions are different. Only a fraction of the mid-15th-century tilework remains, but the impact is sensational, with the jewel-like intensity and depth of colour modern glazes rarely match. The second domed chamber behind was also at some point covered in cobalt-blue tiles embellished with a gilded pattern, but only a few remain. The impact must have been dramatic, but perhaps lightened by the calm grey of the marble panelling with its elegantly carved inscriptions (K26, 36, 48), some still in situ. The selection of the Koranic chapters is interesting: aside from describing the joys of Paradise (suggesting, perhaps, that it was intended to be a tomb chamber), there is a clear allusion to the then large Christian community in the region.

The **Azerbaijan Museum** is located nearby with an ethnographic collection and archival material from the Constitutional period, for Tabriz was in the forefront of the movement. The **Constitutional House**, dating from 1868, built by a local architect and used by so many of the activists, is on Motahhari Avenue near the bazaar. Of interest to lovers of Persian poetry is the Poets' Mausoleum (also known as **Sho'ara**) where a number of famous poets are buried. The central bazaar area is interesting to walk around because, apart from the shops, some sections are 18th and 19th century and even much earlier. There are some six churches still in the locale, the oldest being the Armenian **Church of St Mary** (1785), and **St Sergius** (Sarkis), extensively renovated in 1845. Do take a walk in this central part of town, for there are innumerable early 20th-century houses and businesses with patterned brickwork decoration around the windows and doors, especially around Maydan Shahrbari, Tarbiat and Mahabeh Streets. Not on a par with the Kharraqan tomb towers (see page 91) or the brick vaults of the Masjid-i Jami, Isfahan (see pages 125–6), maybe, but still worth a look.

In fine weather many Tabrizi families will spend the day in the **Golestan Gardens** National Park, established in the 1930s, which incorporates over 53,000m², or they'll go 4km south of the city to the slightly larger Bagh-i Melli Park (known locally as **el-Goli**) with its artificial lake, perhaps first constructed in the 15th century but definitely extended in the Safavid period.

NORTH OF TABRIZ

Travelling north takes one into the region once heavily populated by Armenian Christians. It was from here that Shah Abbas took tens of thousands of Armenians to 17th-century Isfahan to exploit their expertise in silk-trading with European and Russian merchants, and it was to here that many 19th-century European and American missionaries came hoping to introduce such Monophysite Christians into the Baptist, Methodist or other Protestant churches. In 1946–47 most of the Armenians were 'repatriated' into Soviet Armenia.

Things to see and do

There are still some beautiful but austere Armenian churches surviving in this mountainous area, the most famous being **St Stephanos**, Julfa, close to the Azerbaijan frontier, and the **Qara Kelisi** ('Black Church'), near Maku and the Turkish border.

The road to Julfa goes through **Marand**, 70km from Tabriz, whose Masjid-i Jami was established in Seljuk times and then rebuilt in the 14th century; it has a splendid plaster *mihrab*. Some 10km further north is a *caravanserai* built around 1330 but badly damaged in the mid-19th century. It is another 55km or so to Julfa and then a further 50km west to **St Stephanos** (locally known as **Kelisi Darri Sham**). A few years ago foreign visitors needed to obtain a letter from the Armenian Cathedral authorities in Isfahan, or a gendarmerie permit from Shah Abbasi, west of Julfa, but this authorisation is no longer required. The monastery-church is said to have been founded by St Bartholomew around 62CE, with the late 9th-century king of Armenia, Ashot, ordering its construction, but most of the present structure dates from the 16th century. The large church faces east with a long cloister along the north side, but surprisingly it does not possess the usual large *gavit* (where the congregation stood) seen in most medieval churches in the Armenian Republic; the monastery complex is to the south. Instead, the layout bears a closer resemblance to 10th-century Armenian churches in present-day Turkey (eg: Ani and Aktimar) of a single-nave form, with a tall belfry in the south wall. The exterior 'prismatic' tent-dome (and the interior hemispherical one) in red and white stone, along with the *muqarnas* portal, date from the 16th century and the numerous stone carvings of saints and patriachs, especially on the drum, remind one of churches at Aktimar, which were decorated some 600 years earlier.

A visit to **St Thaddeus** (**Qara Kelisi**), 45km from Maku, deep in the hills, definitely needs no letter of authorisation, but take some refreshments with you as there is no tea house (or toilets) here. You could overnight at **Maku**, but the hotels are one-star, the best available being Hotel Alvand on the western approach to town (tel: 0462 3223491; 17 rooms); or the Tourist Inn on Imam Khomeini Avenue (tel: 0462 3223185; 32 rooms; US$30 double, US$20 single). However, most visitors make a day-trip from Tabriz.

Nothing seems to have survived from the first church built to fulfil the dream of St Gregory the Illuminator (see page 130) to commemorate the martyrdom of St Thaddeus, whose death c68 was ordered by King Abgar of Edessa on revoking his brief conversion to Christianity. Part of the 10th-century church remains specifically in the area around the altar, to the right of which the saint is said to be interred, and the dome. The rest was destroyed by earthquakes in 1329 and in 1689, so most of the fortified church seen today dates from the rebuilding, with the exterior decoration added about two centuries later. Very few visitors come here except in the summer to celebrate the movable Feast of St Thaddeus (usually July) when pilgrims come and camp out. The guardian grudgingly allows people to explore the buildings (formerly refectory, kitchens, floor mill, stores and dormitories) around the huge courtyard, and to climb up to roof level to take photographs of the church façade. Why it is called the Black Church is a mystery. It is indeed very gloomy inside, with the austere walls covered in soot from the thousands of candles lit over the centuries, and the 10th-century eastern section is clad in dark tuff, but the exterior church walls are a wonderful creamy-yellow limestone, decorated with a lively narrow frieze running around the building, depicting scenes from the *Shah-nameh* (see page 253) among musket-bearing hunters taking pot-shots at wild animals. There is a similarity to the highly carved exterior of the 10th-century church of Aktimar on Lake Van (Turkey), perhaps because of early close links to that bishopric, and to the deeply worked decoration of the Ishak Pasha palace, Dogubayazit, eastern Turkey, which throughout the 18th century controlled the trade routes west to east. The Aktimar architectural details resemble Georgian church decoration, but the sombre interior of St Thaddeus is totally in the manner of the massive stone churches across the Caucasus in the Armenian Republic.

There are three other little churches nearby, all probably dating to the same period. The villages around here are mainly Kurdish, so the women dress in brightly coloured clothes rather than wearing dark *chadors*, or *manteaux*.

In this region close to the frontiers with Turkey and the Caucasian republics, archaeologists have identified over 50 Urartian settlements, such as the 8th century BCE citadel of **Sangar**, northwest of Maku, with its rock-cut chambers and steps cut from the bedrock. Perhaps you have visited Cavustepe, east of Lake Van; the stoneworking in that palace-citadel site and the presence of bichrome, recessed 'blind' windows have prompted more than one archaeologist to suggest an Urartian influence at Pasargarda and Naqsh-i Rustam (see pages 197 and 194).

The main road south from Maku passes many other Urartian sites, including the important **Bastam**, near Qara Ziya'eddin. This excavation site, 70km southeast from Maku and not far from Qara Kelisi on the old road, should *not* be confused with Bistam/Bastam to the east of the Caspian (see pages 145–6). This was the Urartian 'town' of Ruzu-Urutur, associated in the histories with the famous king, Rusa II (685–645BCE). The German archaeological team which worked here from 1968 until the late 1970s found the site extended over 850x400m, and something of the huge stone walls, once topped by mud-brick galleries and ramparts, may still be seen. A citadel was constructed by the north gate from the 8th century BCE but then, possibly due to political instability after Rusa's death in 645BCE, it was dismantled in preference for a new defensive structure near the south gate, with stables, barracks and storerooms. Above was the palace area with the remains of a 14m^2

URARTU

Today, Mount Ararat forms the frontier between Turkey and the Republic of Armenia, but the kingdom of Urartu, or Ararat, is mentioned in Assyrian texts dating from 1275BCE and also in the Bible (Jeremiah 51:27; II Kings xix). European scholars became very interested in this civilisation after the decipherment of a lengthy cuneiform inscription from the Van citadel, Turkey, in the 1840s, but it was almost a century later before serious archaeological investigations started in (then) Soviet Armenia, followed by British work around Van in the 1950s and in northwest Iran by German scholars in the late 1960s.

Urartian power grew during the reign of Sarduri (also spelt Sardusi) II, c760–735BCE, whose successful military expeditions were recorded in the Van text; from just one campaign his armies captured over 21,000 people, 1,600 horses, 16,500 head of cattle and nearly 40,000 sheep. Urartian merchants came to control the major trade routes across Anatolia and the Caucasus into the Mediterranean, as shown by finds of huge Urartian bronze cauldrons in excavations in France, Greece and Italy. Although increasingly threatened by the Assyrian Empire to the south, Rusa I (735–714BCE) undertook such major irrigation schemes that even Sargon II of Assyria grudgingly admitted he 'changed the entire surface of its unproductive region into meadowland and the fresh green grass of spring'. Much time and effort went into the construction of palace-citadels, carving down into the bedrock, and working ashlar stone blocks so accurately that a sheet of paper cannot be inserted between the blocks. Attention was given to temple buildings to honour the Urartian pantheon of some 50 gods, dominated by three deities with their consorts, each requiring a daily sacrifice of at least six bulls and sheep: Khaldi the warrior 'father' god often depicted as standing on a bull, the rain god Tesheba, and Shivini of the sun, always shown holding a winged disc.

After fending off Assyrian attacks, Urartu negotiated peace in 650BCE, which should have guaranteed its survival, but the 605 Battle of Carcemish marked the end of the great Assyrian Empire. Without this ally, the days of the Urartian kingdom were numbered. A Scythian attack from the north c590BCE and the rise of the Medians in the south dealt the final blows.

tower-temple (somewhat like those at Pasargarda and Naqsh-i Rustam) dedicated to the god Khaldi, and a large audience hall with 14 column bases. Banqueting was obviously important in court life and one chamber served as a meat store judging from the cuneiform tablets listing the stock found there. The site continued to be occupied in Median and Achaemenid times until the 13th century when, recognising its strategic importance on the trade routes, an

Armenian warlord built a fortress here. The Mongol invasion put paid to his activities and the site was abandoned to the nasty local black spiders.

Khoy is probably the best place for restaurants if you are continuing your journey southwest towards Orumiyeh. A Safavid gateway and an unusual Armenian church are the only reminder of Khoy's turbulent past, when it was a walled town belonging to local warlords. On the southern outskirts of Salmas (also given as Shahpur), a Manchester University (UK) archaeological team undertook excavations from 1968–78 at Butan Tepe, near **Haftavan**. Apart from signs of settlement since the 4th BCE and buildings and artefacts from around 2000BCE, remains of an Urartian citadel were found. Occupation continued during Median and Achaemenid periods, continuing up to Sasanid times when the settlement was walled. Some 30km south on the main road, those with sharp eyesight might see a **Sasanid relief** of Ardashir and his son, later Shapur I, recording his victories in this region. Above are the remains of the Urartian fort of **Qaleh-i Vaseriyeh.**

Orumiyeh (formerly Rezaiyeh; altitude 1330; pop 400,000) was, in the 19th century, a city of Christians, mainly Nestorian and Armenian Monophysite Orthodox along with Western missionaries. Hotel accommodation is limited as so few foreign visitors stay here – apart from Turkish truck-drivers overnighting – and so advance reservation is strongly advised. The best available is the four-star Sahel Hotel on Valfajreh Yek Street opposite the TV station (tel: 0441 3369972; fax: 0441 3363261; US$48

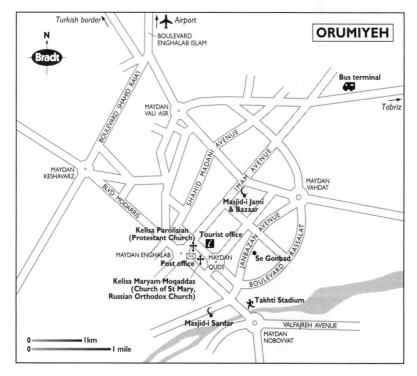

double/single, including breakfast), or the two-star Hotel Darya on Tarzi Street and Imam Avenue (tel: 0441 2229945, 2229564; US$34 double, US$22 single, including breakfast). The Masjid-i Jami, perhaps built in the Seljuk period with a domed prayer chamber over the remains of a Zoroastrian fire temple, has a beautiful plaster *mihrab* dated to 1277, one of the earliest post-Mongol architectural remains. On the southwestern outskirts is the Seh Gonbad tomb tower, standing 9m high; built in 1184, it has some fine plasterwork and *muqarnas* details. In the centre, a modern church (1960s) of St Mary (Kelisi Maryam Moqaddas), replacing a much older shrine, marks, according to local belief, the burial place of one of the Three Wise Men.

The road continues south, passing several important archaeological sites such as **Hasanlu** (probably Manaai in the Assyrian texts) about 5km north of Naqadeh. The main excavations carried out during 1956–74 by Pennsylvania University and then the Metropolitan Museum of Art showed that Hasanlu was settled from the 6th millennium BCE. Carbon-14 tests in the 1980s suggested that the main period of occupation was c1350–1150BCE. Around 1000BCE an impressive citadel, some 200m in diameter with defence walls, towers and gates, was built, along with multistorey housing decorated with Assyrian-tiled decorated interiors. At this point the earlier (outer) settlement became the city cemetery. A fierce attack (level III) caused the collapse of the eastern citadel gate, causing the death of some 40 people, mainly women, and at least another 30 met a violent end on the roof of a porticoed building to the north, one skeleton still holding a beautifully worked gold vessel. The walls were rebuilt on the charred remains of the citadel with Cyclopean stonework, and bronze horse trappings, helmets and mace heads alongside delicate ivory carvings were found. Soviet archaeologists argued that the Assyrian attack in 714BCE, as recorded in cuneiform texts, caused the Urartian occupants to flee. However, using data from further carbon-14 tests, the American archaeological team have since offered another sequence: the attack and fire occurred earlier (c850–800BCE) by Urartian forces, who then took over the citadel, rebuilding the defence walls using their distinctive masonry skills. This occupation continued and survived the Assyrian attack of 714BCE, when the then-famous temple mentioned in the Kul-i Shin stele (southwest of Ushnuyeh/Oshnaviyeh) was destroyed. This stele and also the six-line Urartian cuneiform inscription found at Qalatgeh (just before the archaeological site of Dinkh Tepe), west of Hasanlu, also supports the theory of Urartian campaigning in this area around 800BCE.

South of Nagadeh and 40km before Saqqez is the famous archaeological site of **Ziwiyeh** (also spelt Zawiyeh), where in 1947 a treasure of gold, silver and ivory was found by a shepherd boy; today these finds are divided between Tehran, New York (MMA) and Cincinnati. Archaeological investigation revealed that the main period of occupation was during 800-600BCE when, as indicated by finds of Scythian arrow-heads, the occupants fled their citadel. Illicit digging has since destroyed much of the site, but an Iranian archaeological team restarted work in 1994.

Much more is visible at **Takht-i Soleyman**, which can be approached from Miyanoab by travelling southeast to Takab, then north – but take some food and drink with you. A visit will take about 90 minutess. Its location is dramatic, up in the mountains at over 2,600m with a large volcanic lake in the centre. The asphalt road leads right up to the north entrance. The enclosing walls, built in early Sasanid (or possibly Parthian) times to honour this place, which is home to one of the four important sacred fires of Zoroastrianism, the *Adur Gushnasp* or Royal Warrior Fire (see page 165). Its reputation may even date from the Achaemenid period, as there is evidence of occupation around the small dead volcano immediately northwest of the walled site. It is thought that the Sasanid shahs always came here after their investiture at Ctesiphon, Iraq, to pay their respects to this fire, and there are the remains of at least two fire temples along the processional way from the north gate to the lakeshore: the Hasht Taq with its eight arches of fine stonework to the east, and the main temple marked by four huge brick piers facing the lake. A small shrine lies behind a columned hall, 'Khosrau's Palace', immediately to the west of the main temple.

The German archaeologists working here 1959–77 discovered that, during the last quarter of the 13th century, the largely abandoned site measuring some 550m by 400m was reoccupied as a summer palace by the Il-Khanid ruler, Abaqa, when the main temple building was used for a royal reception hall and the columned hall for private rooms. Certain alterations (eg: blind niche forms) were made at this time to the structure of the large west ivan. A south gate was also constructed and arcading erected all around the lake. A 12-sided hall, perhaps inspired by the nomadic felt-domed tent, is located just south of the two western octagonal buildings on the north-west corner of the arcading. This, it is suggested, possibly functioned as a storehouse where the wife of Abaqa kept the royal treasures for her grandson, the later Ghazan Khan. Numerous splendid examples of 13th-century tiles (which must have decorated the walls), remains of marble flooring and – an important find for Islamic architectural history – a carved stone slab detailing a *muqarnas* pattern composition were all found. Here finally was proof of how medieval masons calculated and devised the intricate arrangements of various three-dimensional architectural elements. Remains of kilns and a pottery workshop were found behind the main north palace hall, to the northeast.

If time allows, a short diversion to the southeastern corner of Lake Orumiyeh should be made. This is where you'll find **Maragha**, famous in the late medieval histories for its 'state-of-the-art' astronomical observatory, constructed on the order of Hulagu (r1256–65), grandson of Genghis Khan, the scourge of all Asia. Nothing remains of this Star House, as it was called, but it was from here that the scientist Nasir al-Din Tusi (d1274) solved the seeming incompatibility between Ptolemy's planetary model and Aristotelian theory about planetary movement, which was then taken up and developed by Copernicus. The city still possesses three fine tomb towers. The Gonbad-i Surkh (also known as Gonbad-i Qermez), built in 1148 for a local prince, a certain Abd al-Aziz, has been described by one scholar as 'the most beautiful example of brickwork known'; I am not convinced. The square brick mausoleum tomb rises from a stone base and then the brick patterns begin, 'contained' within two blind niche frames on three of the four external sides, including the foliated Kufic inscription over the door and over the blind niche frames. Twelve sizes of interlocking brick units were used, with some glazed strips inserted for highlights. The original, eight-sided tent-roof has gone, but the octagonal drum and the inner dome remain, though much restored.

Slightly to the north is the 12-sided blue Gonbad-i Kabud of 1197. Standing 14.5m high, it has long been associated with Hulagu as local people thought the tomb was built to honour either his mother or his daughter, though there is nothing to prove this assumption. It has lost its original roof but retains much of its very ornate exterior decoration of intersecting turquoise blue 'strap' brickwork of hexagons and six-pointed stars. Just under the exterior cornice is an inscription band (K2:255) while inside around the dome is another (K67:1): 'Blessed be He to whom all sovereignty belongs; He has power over all things', while downstairs in the crypt there is another inscription (K55:26–7) alluding to death and Paradise. Nearby is an anonymous tomb tower, circular in plan, built around 1330 and known locally as Koyburj, looking more like a defence tower than a mausoleum. Also in the northern outskirts is a 14th-century tomb tower known as the Gonbad-i Ghaffariyeh, which in its decorative scheme includes a heraldic device of two polo sticks, indicating the bearer was Master of the Royal Polo; he was Amir Qara Sunghur, who worked for both the Egyptian Mamluk regime and then the Il-Khanids, as a local governor at a time when Maragha was known as 'Little Damascus'.

It is known that Hulagu built a palace (or at least reception rooms) on the largest island in **Lake Orumiyeh**, *Jazir-i Kabudi* (formerly Shah's island) and indeed he and his successor are said to have been buried here. Like the water of Takht-i Soleyman, this lake, over 120km long and 25km wide, has a high mineral content which, although good for rheumatism, means fish and other wildlife are limited. The whole region was made a conservation area before the Islamic Revolution in order to protect the thousands of migratory birds, such as pelicans, flamingoes and wild duck, but the Department of Environment, responsible for such matters, is publicly acknowledged to be one of the most underfunded government sections.

It is admittedly a long drive, approximately 140km, from Takht-i Soleyman to Zanjan, but from there it is possible to visit Sultaniyeh and, unless one stays in Zanjan or Qazvin further east (see pages 85–90), such a visit would entail either a long detour en route to Hamadan, or add even more time to the 12-hour drive from/to Tehran and Tabriz. **Zanjan** itself is known for its distinctive, colourful, animal-covered *sumak* (warp-wrapped) rugs and a thriving bazaar, and there is an adequate two-star hotel: Hotel Sepid on Maydan Enghelab (tel: 0241 3226882-3; fax: 0241 3226944; 32 rooms, approximately US$35). Admittedly not a town known for historic monuments, it still has the richly tiled Khanum Mosque built in 1905 on the order of Jamileh Khanum, the daughter of a local tribal chief.

THE SACRED FIRE

The idea that Zoroastrians are 'fire-worshippers' is technically incorrect but traditionally great reverence has always been shown to this, surely the most important 'gift' to humanity. Prayer, for instance, is always made towards a fire or other light source such as a lamp, the sun or the moon. To devout Zoroastrians even domestic fires should be treated with care, their embers taken to the temple every third day for cleansing of any accidental pollution by adding cold embers from the temple fires. Every ninth day fires of blacksmiths had to be cleansed nine times before those embers could be taken to the temple for such renewal.

It is held that there were four great sacred fires, each later associated with a social class. The *Adur Gushnasp* originated near or in Lake Orumiyeh in the lands of the Medes. In around 400CE it was transported to Takht-i Soleyman where it became firmly associated with the royalty and warriors. The second, the *Adur Barzea* of the agricultural class, was known to exist in the 3rd century CE in Parthian lands, perhaps in a major temple complex between Shahrud and Sabzevar or further east on Mount Revand, near Borzinan. The Zoroastrian priests understood the *Adur Farnbag* to be their special fire, which had been brought into southwest Iran from Central Asia. To protect its survival during the Arab Muslim conquests, this fire was divided into two, one being kept in Fasa and the other transported to Sharifabad, north of Yazd. The fourth fire, *Adur Karkuy*, is associated with Kuh-i Khvaja, near Lake Hamun in Sistan, where the oldest known fire temple in Iran stands.

The Zoroastrian priest is the only person to attend the temple fire, during which he wears a white cotton robe and mouth-mask to prevent his breath polluting the sacred flames, which are fed five times a day. In ancient times a *barsom* bundle of pomegranate twigs was offered to the flame but today a bunch of brass or silver wire replace this. However, fires at shrines (eg: at Chak Chak, see page 225) are tended by laymen because they are used only in a minor role, such as cooking the special *dron* – unleaven cakes, used for certain Zoroastrian services.

Sultaniyeh

If there is an opportunity to visit the 14th-century **Mausoleum of Oljeitu**, descendant of Genghis Khan, in Sultaniyeh, take it (and a torch) even though you'll be met by a wall of scaffolding, inside and out. Constructed in a mere 11 years (1306–17), this huge mausoleum proudly stands on a fertile plain on the old road to Zanjan with a backdrop of purple-blue mountains. Nothing else remains of the 14th-century walled town although recent excavations have revealed foundations of a mosque, *madrasas*, *khanaqeh,* palace pavilions and other buildings, all part of Oljeitu's plan to make this small town his capital.

History records that Oljeitu (r1304–17), after sending architect-engineers to survey and measure the vast palace audience hall of the Sasanid shahs at Ctesiphon, Iraq, employed 10,000 men to lay the foundations of this tomb and the surrounding structures, as well as 500 carpenters and 5,000 marble-masons, . His idea, it was said, was not to build a funerary monument for himself, but rather to bring the remains of Hoseyn, the 3rd Imam, from Kerbela to this place; he had already procured a lock of the Prophet's hair. Oljeitu had been slow to accept Islam, preferring at first Buddhism and then Christianity, the faith of his mother, before adopting Shi'i Islam, and then deciding on Sunni Islam around 1313. It was at this point, so some argue, that he announced that the brick mausoleum was to be his own memorial.

Its size and scale are immense. The huge egg-shaped dome (interior diameter 26m) rests on eight internal piers but their massive size is disguised by their soaring, tapering height, high arches and a rhythmic arrangement of connecting galleries; pretend that the abandoned forest of scaffolding (which largely creates the gloom) is just a figment of your imagination. From the floor to the apex of the dome is a staggering 52m. And viewing from the outside, forget the untidy brick infills and imagine continuous open galleries all around. When completed, this once turquoise-tiled dome, framed with eight slender 'minarets' around the roof, must have appeared to be magically balanced on a graceful network of arches and vaults. Indeed, certain Italian scholars are sure it influenced the work of Brunellesci, the Renaissance architect, and in particular his St Maria della Mori in Florence. Inside, two different layers of decoration are apparent here and there: glazed brick strapwork and also patterned plasterwork, perhaps visual evidence of Oljeitu's change of faith from Shi'i to Sunni Islam. Access to the crypt, housing three tombs, lies to the south.

An internal staircase near the entrance leads up to the galleries, where the 'openness' and inner proportions of the building become much more apparent. In places, the intricate decoration of these galleries still survives, but for the best work another narrow and steep staircase to the exterior galleries has to be tackled. Here you'll find the richest, most exquisitely carved and painted plasterwork on the vaulted ceilings – quite mouth-wateringly superb. There are also wonderful views over the countryside, despite the higgledy-piggledy housing at ground level.

The curse of scaffolding continues all around outside. It's as if officialdom feels its work is done once scaffolding is erected. Funding then dries up, the labour force is removed and rusting iron is left as today's contribution to Iran's architectural heritage. But a short walk around the building means you can see some of the original tilework, along with some scattered 14th-century ceramic shards found during excavating work.

From Sultaniyeh, it is about 100km to Qazvin to the southeast.

Shiraz and Around

SHIRAZ

Shiraz (altitude 1,600m, 895km south of Tehran) is my favourite Iranian city. Despite its size, a population of about 1.5 million and an appalling traffic problem, it has retained the relaxed atmosphere of a provincial town, with a university which still retains its reputation. Many foreign visitors are surprised that the city itself has so few surviving historical monuments when there are such archaeological treasures in the neighbouring countryside, but earthquakes over the centuries have taken a heavy toll.

A settlement from Achaemanid times, it really prospered from the early Islamic era, quickly developing into a walled city. Local disputes between warlords during the 11–12th centuries caused problems, but Shiraz largely escaped severe damage by the Mongol armies, and its tactical surrender to Timur Leng in 1395 was rewarded by great prosperity under his grandson's governorship. The good fortune was not to last. In 1668 severe flooding (difficult to comprehend when glimpsing the meagre – and now dry – River Khoshk running through the centre) brought death and outbreaks of plague. The citizens had barely recovered when the Afghan rebels, destroying the remnants of Safavid authority, set about massacring the population in 1725. However under the rule of Karim Khan Zand (d1779), still remembered with great affection today, and his descendants, Shiraz regained its former prosperity as the Zand capital for some 20 years in the second half of the 18th century. Those days of tolerance were short-lived; 15% of the population were Jewish in the early 19th century, but few remain today. Shiraz was also the home of Bahaism, but the pogrom of 1852 and events since have altered that situation too.

Today it is the place to smell the beautiful Shiraz roses and to buy the perfume and rose-water. But, unfortunately, it's no longer possible to taste the world-famous Shirazi grape except as fruit. Shiraz is also a place to walk in the gardens and, close to the Hotel Homa, see the Azadi Park Ferris Wheel and roundabouts occasionally crowded with excited school-girls, their *chadors* flying in the breeze, or to inspect the carpets in the bazaar. Both there and in the major shrine, Shah Cheragh, you might glimpse the darker complexions of men and women from various tribal clans such as the Qashqai, the Qash Kuli and the Khamseh, visiting the city. The older men often wear a beige,

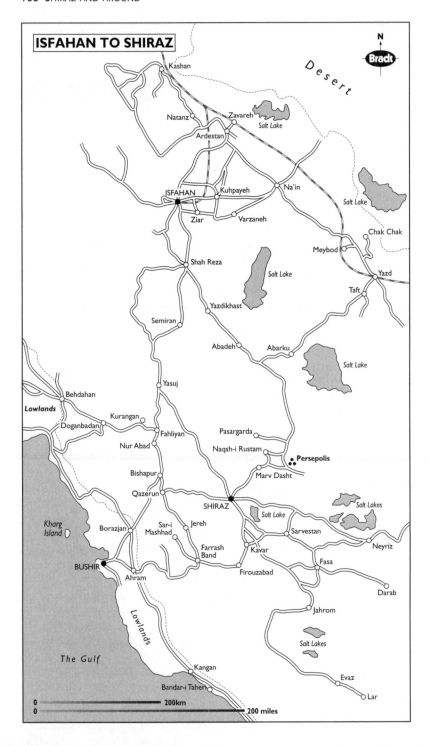

ISFAHAN TO SHIRAZ

N

Bradt

Desert

Kashan

Natanz   Zavareh
                         Salt Lake
          Ardestan

ISFAHAN   Kuhpayeh   Na'in   Salt Lake

       Ziar   Varzaneh   Chak Chak

                                          Meybod   Yazd

                              Shah Reza   Taft
                                        Salt Lake

                              Yazdikhast

          Semiran   Abadeh   Abarku

                                                    Salt Lake
             Yasuj

Behdahan
Lowlands   Kurangan
       Doganbadan   Fahliyan   Pasargarda
              Nur Abad   Naqsh-i Rustam   • Persepolis
          Bishapur   Marv Dasht
       Qazerun
                         SHIRAZ   Salt Lake   Salt Lakes
Kharg   Sar-i   Jereh
Island   Borazjan Mashhad   Sarvestan
                         Farrash Kavar   Neyriz
                         Band   Fasa
BUSHIR   Firouzabad
       Ahram   Darab
                                   Jahrom
                    Lowlands
                                   Salt Lakes
    The Gulf
                    Kangan   Evaz
0   200km   Lar
       Bandar-i Taheri
0   200 miles

hemispherical felt cap with a tall upturned rim, while the women cover their immense skirts and glittering lurex tabards with black *chadors*; both caps and skirts are made in the bazaar. A number of these families still retain a migratory lifestyle, travelling with goats and sheep from Hamadan to Shiraz and the south in late autumn, returning in the spring, but most are now settled in villages nearby. If you want to see the rugs and carpets associated with such clans, Shiraz is the place to look, but prices are no longer cheap and quality is variable since such work was highly acclaimed in the West during the 1976 *World of Islam* exhibitions in the UK.

Getting here and around
There are regular flights from Tehran, Isfahan, Bandar-i Abbas, Kirman and Mashhad etc, and also international flights from/to Abu Dhabi, Bahrain, Kuwait and Dubai, as well as numerous intercity bus links. If time allows, do spend four or five nights here, as one day is needed for Persepolis and Naqsh-i Rustam, another to explore around Firouzabad, a third for Bishapur and another for the sites around Bishapur. And you will want to see something of Shiraz itself. Travel to and from the major historic sites outside Shiraz, especially Persepolis, is difficult and time-consuming by public transport so consider hiring a taxi. A guide in Shiraz, who could organise a car, or a helicopter trip (see below) is Aria Gojerati, mobile: (098) 0917 3135938; email: ariagojerati@yahoo.com.

It is possible to arrange a helicopter trip, costing around €2,000, through Aseman Airlines, which will organise the necessary official permission; contact Aria Gojerati (see above). Also for those interested in trekking, camping, and nomadic migrations, contact Gasht Tour in Souratgar Av, Shiraz (tel: 0711 2339198/2301900); with prior notice the office can organise English-speaking wildlife or birdwatching specialists.

Accommodation
Presently the best available five-star (notionally) hotel is the **Hotel Homa** (IranAir) Meshkinfam St, near Azadi Park (tel: 0711 2288000-12; fax: 0711 2288021, 2288014; email: shiraz@homahotels.com; www.homahotels.com; over 200 rooms; US$125 double, US$85 single, including breakfast) with good-humoured staff, coffee area, shops, sauna, tennis courts and barber, situated near to the Bagh-i Eram and the university campus. The vestibule's striking gilt inscription calling for the destruction of the USA was 'lost' during recent building work on the new extension. In warm weather, dinner is taken in the extensive grounds; be sure to try the fish dishes as fresh supplies are flown in daily from the Gulf. Also a speciality here is the local 'burnt' flavoured yoghurt sometimes served at breakfast but, following 'complaints' from many foreigners, it is now rarely served.

Slightly cheaper and nearer to the centre is the four-star **Pars Hotel** in Zand Avenue (tel: 0711 2332255; fax: 0711 2336380; email: shirazparshotel@ yahoo.com; www.parsinternationalhotel.com; US$112 double, US$80 single, including breakfast). On the same street is **Hotel Eram**, three-star, (tel/fax:

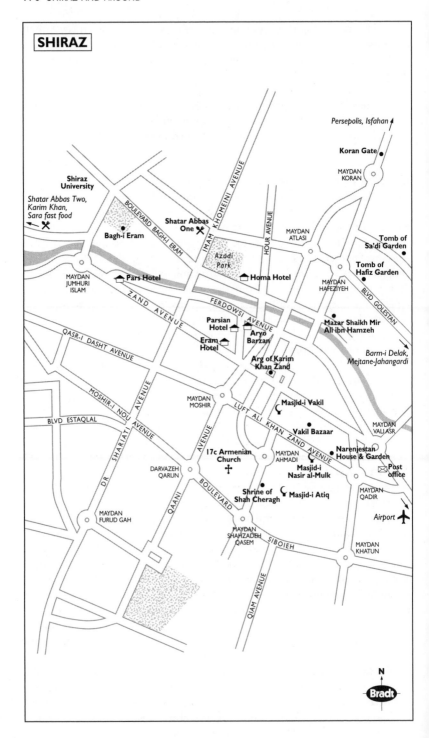

SHIRAZ

Persepolis, Isfahan →

Koran Gate

MAYDAN KORAN

Shiraz University

Shatar Abbas Two, Karim Khan, Sara fast food ←✗

BOULEVARD BAGH-I ERAM

Shatar Abbas One ✗

Bagh-i Eram

Azadi Park

IMAM KHOMEINI AVENUE

HOUR AVENUE

MAYDAN ATLASI

Tomb of Sa'di Garden

Tomb of Hafiz Garden

MAYDAN JUMHURI ISLAM

Pars Hotel

ZAND AVENUE

FERDOWSI AVENUE

Homa Hotel

MAYDAN HAFEZIYEH

BLVD GOLESTAN

Mazar Shaikh Mir Ali ibn Hamzeh

QASR-I DASHT AVENUE

Parsian Hotel

Aryo Barzan

Eram Hotel

Barm-i Delak, Mejtane-Jahangardi

MOSHIR-I NOU AVENUE

Arg of Karim Khan Zand

MAYDAN MOSHIR

LUFT ALI KHAN ZAND AVENUE

Masjid-i Vakil

BLVD ESTAQLAL

AVENUE

Vakil Bazaar

MAYDAN VALI ASR

DR SHARIATI AVENUE

17c Armenian Church ✝

MAYDAN AHMADI

Narenjestan House & Garden

Post office ✉

DARVAZEH QARUN

BOULEVARD QAANI

Masjid-i Nasir al-Mulk

MAYDAN QADIR

MAYDAN FURUD GAH

Shrine of Shah Cheragh

Masjid-i Atiq

Airport ✈

MAYDAN SHAHZADEH QASEM

SIBOIEH

MAYDAN KHATUN

QIAM AVENUE

N

Bradt

0711 2335292, 2337301; email: addshirazeramhotel@payamava.com; www.eramhotel.com; US$40 double, US$30 single, including breakfast). A comparatively new privately owned three-star hotel, originally designed for Arab and Gulf visitors, is **Parsian** (tel: 0711 2331000, 2330000, 2304965–6; fax: 0711 2337512; email: parsian@parsian-hotel.com; www.parsian-hotel.com; US$56 double/single, excluding breakfast); it is on Roudaki Street so again nearer the centre, as is three-star **Hotel Aryo Barzan** (tel: 0711 2247182–4; fax: 0711 2228959; email: info@Aryohotel.com; www.Aryohotel.com; US$50 double, US$37 single, including breakfast).

The nearest equivalent to a *mehmansaray* at present is the two-star **Mejtane-Jahangardi** (Tourist Complex) on Riasati Avenue (tel: 0711 7301023, 7322411; fax: 0711 7307503; email: shiraz@ittic.com; www.ittic.com; US$36 double, US$24 single, excluding breakfast). There are other hotels in Shiraz, with double rooms all in the range of US$30–77 but presently these do not have email nor web facilities.

Dining

There are very reasonably priced *chello-kebab* places in the area around the Arg-i Karim Khan Zand, but the **Sufi One** (Boulevard Afifabad; tel: 0711 6263877, 6275881) and **Sufi Two** (Boulevard Zargari/Boulevard Motahari; tel: 0711 6261573, nearer to the Homa Hotel and the university campus) are judged two of the best restaurants in town. Also highly recommended but open only for lunches and tea is the **Hamam-i Vakil** restaurant (tel: 0711 2226467), recently converted from the original 18th-century bathhouse whose rents once supported the upkeep of the Vakil mosque next door; it is located on the corner of the main road and the narrow street leading to the mosque. The *ab-goosht* (see page 49) is very good and comes de-boned. Also worth trying are the **Shatar Abbas One** on Khahshenasi Avenue (tel: 0711 2271612, 2270914) and another branch **Shatar Abbas Two** on Boulevard Chamran (tel: 0711 6244500); on the same road is **Karim Khan** (tel: 0711 6281911), and the fast-food **Sara** (tel: 0711 6289492–3).

Recently the authorities have given permission for more coffee shops to be opened where unmarried young people of both genders can meet, but be aware that if there is any crack-down (as happened after the 2000 landslide elections), these places will be the first to be 'visited' by the authorities.

Things to see and do

A number of tourist sights in Shiraz are not administered by the central government, so the July 2004 official ruling reducing entry charges for foreign visitors does not yet apply to these sites.

Entering Shiraz from the north, the first visible monument is the **Koran Gate**, originally built in the 10th century in the city walls. It was Karim Khan Zand who ordered a Koran to be placed in the gatehouse so that all travellers would be blessed as they left for the open road. In the 1950s increasing motor traffic dictated a new road and the demolition of the gate, whereupon a Shirazi citizen paid for its rebuilding in its present state. Halfway up the hillside, above the gate, is the tomb of one of Shirazi's famous poets, Khvaju Kirmani (d1352), and one of the eight known **Qajar rock-reliefs**, c1824, showing Fath Ali Shah (d1834) on a throne-dais supported by two angels, with two of his numerous sons in attendance. Recently, these hillsides have been landscaped with terraces, water cascades and the odd kiosk, and a tea house, the Khajou. While they offer unparalleled views of the city lights at night, the traffic noise and pollution are overpowering. Nearby, down from the 18th-century bridge, is situated the **Mazar Ali ibn Hamzeh**, constructed perhaps in pre-Seljuk times to honour a relative of the 4th Imam. Its two minarets, exterior dome, entrance vestibule and courtyard rooms, however, date from the late 18th and 19th centuries. If for some reason a visit to Shah Cheragh shrine (see page 177) is not possible during your stay, this shrine possesses similar extensive Qajar mirrorwork on its interior walls and vaults. There is one entrance into the shrine sanctuary (ladies are asked to don a *chador*) and as the *qibla* wall is immediately right on entry, one should move quickly to one or other side to minimise disruption to anyone praying.

Away from traffic is the beautiful **Bagh-i Eram**, a garden named after one of the four gardens of Paradise described in the Koran (entry 30,000 rials; *closed sunset*). It was created by a chief of the Qashqai clan around 1823, with a house later rebuilt by Hajji Mohammed Hasan Mi'mar with reception rooms, an orangery, stables and pavilion. Both garden and buildings were confiscated in 1953 and given to the late shah for his private use; this was when the original mud-brick enclosing walls were torn down and replaced by fencing. Later, the university was permitted to establish a botanical garden. After the fall of the Pahlavi regime it was returned to the Qashqai family, but then given back to the university, and today it houses the Law Faculty. Sections of the lower garden are out of bounds, and water rarely runs in the irrigation channels, but it is still a lovely place. Most plants and trees are labelled in Farsi, Latin and common English names. If you are keen on roses, they are in the formal gardens behind the main building.

Entry into the building itself is not permitted, but the exterior is photogenic enough with its late-**19th-century tiling** under the roof. The main panel shows the legendary Sasanid king, Khosrau, coming across the Armenian princess Shirin bathing (see page 97) while to the right is the Koranic/biblical story describing how the beauty of the prophet Yusuf (Joseph) caused the ladies in Pharaoh's court to cut their fingers while peeling fruit. Above, the meeting of King Soleyman (Solomon) and the Queen of Sheba, Bilqis, is portrayed.

There are three other major gardens in Shiraz but two are 20th-century constructions, owing little to the classic Persian garden layout but pleasant enough now the price for foreigners has been lowered (2,000 rials). One garden surrounds the **Tomb of Hafiz**, the great Shirazi poet (1326–c1390) who wrote lyrical poems about love and the beloved, which are understood to be imbued with deep Sufi mystical meaning; his epithet 'Hafiz' alludes to his memorising of the Koran by heart. Because of this association, one or two dervishes still come here on Wednesdays and Thursdays, while families enjoy the small garden and pleasant late 18th-century *chay-khaneh* to the far left.

THE PERSIAN GARDEN

From Achaemenid and Sasanid times, rulers and princes established formal gardens with stone watercourses feeding pools, shaded terraces and pavilions. This was the essential plan which spread across the Muslim world to Spain and North Africa and eastwards to North India, for this is the image of the heavenly Paradise as described in the Koran (K55:45ff). In the 'classical' Persian garden, mud-brick walls kept the desert out while providing support for climbing plants and shade from the fierce midday sun. The English visitor, Thomas Herbert, in 1628 described the Shirazi gardens as 'safeguarded with walls fourteen feet high and four feet thick; and which from their spaciousness and plenty of trees resemble groves or wildernesses... they abound in lofty pyramidic cypresses, broad-spreading chenars, tough elm, straight ash, knotty pines, fragrant mastics, kingly oaks, sweet myrtles, useful maples ... also flowers rare to the eye, sweet to the smell, and useful in physic'.

To Persian poets the cypress was like a young Muslim man, evergreen and enduring in his faith, while the *chenar* tree with its open five-fingered leaves was the prayer leader for all plants in the garden. Around the wall were planted climbing roses, whose very fragrance came from a bead of perspiration falling from the Prophet Mohammed's brow, jasmine and pomegranates. Fruit trees such as cherries (whose scented blossom was as short-lived as a woman's beauty), oranges, limes, apples and quinces were also placed by the walls or in raised beds divided by straight water channels in which fish, ducks and swans swam. Or the beds were planted with sweet-smelling herbs, or spring bulbs such as hyacinths, whose heavy scent reminded the poets of the beloved's hair, narcissi ('red-eyed' like a weeping lover) and red tulips (willingly shedding blood for the beloved). All would lower their heads in worship on hearing the nightingale's song (Koranic verses) on the evening breeze.

Karim Khan Zand ordered a suitable tomb to be built in 1773 to honour this famous son of Shiraz but that was torn down in 1938 to erect the present octagonal kiosk. Further embellishments were made for the 1971 Pahlavi extravaganza. Enough said. The bookshop here at the left end of the first porticoed terrace often has a good selection of history and art books in English, as well as maps and postcards, but the English translations of Hafiz on sale render the poetry incomprehensible. Before leaving, why not have your fortune told? For a small sum, a copy of Hafiz's best-known anthology, the *Divan*, will be opened randomly at a page, or a canary plucks out a card with couplets; the verses offer a portent to the future.

In an easterly direction, some 10km further on, is **Barm-i Delak**, where there are two battered Sasanid rock reliefs 6m above ground level. The larger one depicts a shah offering a flower to a lady, perhaps the goddess Anahita, though some scholars think this shows Shah Narseh (d301) making a peace offering to the consort of either Bahram II or III. The other panel definitely portrays Bahram II raising his hand with possibly the influential high priest Kartir to one side.

The **Tomb of Sa'di** is set in similar grounds near to the Hafiz garden, and has a similar entry charge. Born around 1185 or 1208 (or possibly 1215) and dying around 1292, Sa'di fled the Mongol invasions, going to Baghdad and then Syria where he was imprisoned by the Crusaders. Ransomed by an Aleppan man, he felt duty-bound to marry the man's daughter, an unhappy decision he commemorated by a couplet:

> A bad wife comes with a good man to dwell
> She soon converts his earthly heaven to hell.

His two major poetic works are the *Golestan*, a series of anecdotes composed in 1257, and the *Bustan* (1258) in which he wittily and humorously expounded his thoughts on justice and government. One of his most famous sayings has prompted comparisons with the 17th-century English poet, John Donne:

> The sons of man are limbs of one another,
> Created of the same stuff, and none other.
> One limb by turn of time and fate distressed,
> The others feel its pain and cannot rest.
> Who unperturbed another's grief can scan
> Is no more worthy of the name of man.

A version of this adorns the United Nations building in New York.

Again, the tomb itself is a product of the early 1950s, replacing a Zand structure. If a group has collected in one section beyond the tomb, the probable reason is the underground irrigation channel (*qanat*) running through the garden, whose water is said to be good for skin problems.

I also suggest the **Bagh-i Dalgousheh** (Garden of Heart's Ease) nearby, where currently there is no entry charge. The extensive grounds broadly retain their 1820 layout (actually originally set out in 1790) although the water channels have been re-lined with tacky turquoise tiles and the original mud-brick walls were destroyed in 2000 for new fencing. In the centre stands a pavilion from late Zand or early Qajar times, currently under restoration, in this dramatic setting with the surrounding hills and tall cypresses. Together with the Bagh-i Eram, this garden and a small one within the newly opened Arg of Karim Khan Zand (see below) are the best examples of the 'classical' Persian garden outside Mahan (see page 237) and Kashan (see page 110).

The city centre

The citadel **Arg-i Karim Khan Zand** was built around 1767 and is perhaps the best preserved 18th-century example in Iran. Its use from the 1930s as a police station and prison has long prevented access, but in autumn 1999 part of it was open to visitors (entry 1,000 rials). Four 15m round towers with good brick patterning mark the corners of the enclosure joined by 12m high walls which, in Zand times, surrounded an audience hall, barracks, bathhouse, and garden with two pools. When a Qajar prince used the Arg as his official governor's residence, further building and decoration were undertaken. Over the main entrance is a huge tiled panel depicting an episode from the *Shah-nameh* in which the famous Persian warrior, Rostam, fights the white Div (demon).

The entry vestibule leads into the main Zand court and I suggest a visit to the *hamam* (extreme left) is postponed until the end. A notice in charming, broken English quickly dispels any tiredness and it's pleasant walking around the central, four-garden layout, noting the original stone water channels in the paving. Restoration work is still uncompleted but it takes little effort to imagine colourful 18th-century public audiences held under the painted *talar* verandas, with waterpipes and tea prepared with hot coals from the numerous fireplaces. The local offices of the Cultural Heritage Organisation occupy the rooms on the far right (so letters criticising the modern canopy at Persepolis – see page 189 – could be personally delivered). The real surprise is the small *hamam* near the courtyard entrance; this has been recently turned into a tea house. An insignificant doorway leads into the *frigidarium* where bathers relaxed after the session (see box page 234). It still retains its splendid vault rib-network and at least three layers of decorated plasterwork. From here, the bathers would have walked through to the *tepidarium* for a shampoo and massage and then into the *caldarium* (steam room), where the vaulting is again still largely intact. There are no plunge pools – just pipes, fountains and basins, and a view into the boiler room.

Outside, across the street is the small octagonal reception pavilion of Karim Khan Zand, **Bagh-i Nazar** (entry 2,000 rials). Set in a small garden gloriously smothered in bougainvillaea, it offers another peaceful haven away from Shiraz's traffic and crowds. It used to house the small local museum but the items have been transferred to a new museum, close to the Naranjestan (see page 177). Most of its original interior is intact and the tiled panels outside are mainly contemporary with the building. Karim Khan (d1779) must have loved this place as it was chosen as his mausoleum, but he was not allowed to rest in peace. Agha Mohammad Qajar (not known for his generous nature) ordered his remains to be exhumed and sent to Tehran, where they were reburied in the Golestan Palace, so that every time the Qajar shah and his ministers crossed the threshold they trod on Karim Khan. At least Reza Shah Pahlavi stopped this practice in 1925, allowing the Zand family to reinter his remains.

Bazaar-i Vakil

The main bazaar area is within walking distance of the Arg. As the name suggests, its construction formed part of the extensive building programme of Karim Khan, so-called *vakil* (regent) to the last Safavids. Rents from the bazaar and its *hamam* endowed the **Masjid-i Vakil**, constructed around 1773, which until spring 2000 was out-of-bounds to foreign tourists; entry: 15,000 rials. It retains a sense of intimacy despite its large size and is organised on the two-ivan plan. Forty-eight stumpy stone columns, each carved in a barley-sugar spiral, mark the sanctuary area. The original *mihrab* of 1634, which suggested an earlier mosque had been demolished, is no longer in place, but the 18th-century, 14-stepped *minbar* is cut from one huge block of marble. Some idea of the tile decoration inside can be imagined from the exterior panels. Purists may raise eyebrows at the flamboyant flower motifs and the colourful pastel palette but my spirits soar at such cheerful ornateness. Not all the tiles are original, as some restoration was carried out in 1828 and later years.

Next door towards the main road is the bathhouse, converted in 2001 into a tea house and restaurant (lunches only), well worth a visit if only to watch the young couples acting so decorously. Backtracking past the mosque takes you into the carpet section of the bazaar.

The **Bazaar-i Vakil** maintains much of its late 18th-century character with a northeast to southwest orientation (the direction of Mecca) laid out about a century earlier. Originally, it was one long avenue with four large *caravanserais* to accommodate merchants, but in the 20th century a main road was constructed across the avenue and two of the four *caravanserais* were demolished in a rewidening scheme.

Exiting the bazaar by the carpet quarter, turning right and then right again, leads to a charming mosque, the **Masjid-i Nasir al-Mulk**, rarely visited by tour groups; entry fee 15,000 rials. It is also a two-ivan mosque built 1876–87 by Mohammed Hassan, with a covered arcade on the left (facing the sanctuary) and the winter mosque on the right. The entry vestibule is smothered in painted tiles (not *cuerda-seca* as sometimes described) of floral ornaments framing small pictures of landscapes clearly inspired by Russian sketches. The winter prayer-hall is interesting for it has stone cable-spiral columns very similar to those of the Vakil Mosque, and most of the vividly coloured window glass is 19th century.

On leaving, if there are workmen still restoring the large **walled house** on the right before reaching the main avenue, ask to see inside, for this was Nasir al-Mulk's house. The mirrorwork on the ground floor reception rooms is pure 19th century, as are the painted ceilings upstairs decorated with an assortment of coyly smiling ladies. Deliciously over the top.

Back to the main road, nearby on the other side and set back a little is the **Madrasa Khan Khvaja** (also known as Madrasa Hoja Tibnel Hassan Asgari). The four-ivan theological college is still a teaching institute, training young men, many from the Shi'i regions of Afghanistan, to become imams and jurists. The building was originally a warehouse, as the name suggests, built in 1615, although most of its extensive tiling scheme dates from the 1833 restoration.

If you enjoyed the excesses of the Nasir al-Mulk house (or if it was closed), return to the main avenue and continue down (to the left, if coming from the *madrasa*, or right from the house) away from the main bazaar. On the *madrasa* side of the avenue, there are two large 19th-century houses behind massive brick walls. The first is not open to the public but the second, a little further down, is. This is the **Naranjestan** (Orangery), home of the famous Asia

Institute in the 1960–70s, and still part of Shiraz University; entry 30,000 rials. It was built in the late 1870s by Mohammed Riza and Ibrahim Qavam al-Mulk, former mayor and tax agent of Shiraz, as public reception rooms, connected by a tunnel to the closed house next door, which functioned as the *anderun* or private quarters. A vestibule (where a pack of postcards relating to this house is on sale) leads into a small walled garden, essentially 19th-century in character, with tiled panels of attendants bearing platters of fruits. The house itself is barely furnished but the mirrors and floor tiles, the latter decorated to look like ikat fabrics, especially on the ground floor and *talar* (veranda), are decoration enough, with crude but amusing imitations of Persepolis reliefs decorating the lower exterior wall. A small museum has been opened in the basement. Nearby is the newly opened **Fars History Museum** (entry 2,000 rials), within the Zinat al-Mulk house, Lutf Ali Khan Zand Av, which houses the items formerly displayed in the Bagh-i Nazar pavilion (see page 175).

Most strangers to the city, whatever their nationality, visit the **Mausoleum of Shah Cheragh** ('King of the Lamp'); that said, from early October 2002 non-Muslims were not allowed entry even into the courtyard. However, in case the situation alters, it is worth noting ladies must wear a *chador*, for hire from the booth immediately left before the main entrance. The most popular shrine is the large one to the right after entering the courtyard, which commemorates the brother of the 8th Imam Reza, Sayyid Amir Ahmad, while the tomb of another brother, Sayyid Mir Mohammed, is situated further down on the left. Sayyid Amir Ahmad came to Shiraz in 808 and died here in 835. Only a *mihrab* remains from the mausoleum and *madrasa* built to honour him in the 1340s by the mother of the then local ruler, as the shrine was largely rebuilt in 1506, then extensively repaired after an earthquake in 1588. Its local reputation was such that Nadir Shah Afshar, despite being a Sunni Muslim, ordered further repair work in 1729, and Karim Khan Zand added further repairs in 1765. What is seen today is essentially 19th century, especially the mirrorwork smothering the interior, the silver doors and tilework, but the exterior dome is a 1959 fantasy, and the minaret dates from around 1970. Men enter the shrine from the far left while women access on the right.

Across the courtyard to the left is the mausoleum to Shah Cheragh's brother which has retained more of its 16th-century building programme, but the decoration is again predominately Qajar in date. For some undefined reason, this tomb always has fewer vistors, as does the mausoleum of a third brother, Sayyid Ala al-Din, situated in the southwest of the city. This is also a 16th-century structure on an earlier 14th-century building, but extensively repaired and covered with mirrorwork in the 19th century.

Nearby are two mosques, much repaired after the 1852 earthquake. The **Masjid-i Nau** is also known as the Atabak Mosque after its patron, the military governor (*atabeg*) of Shiraz, Sa'd ibn Zangi. To mark his sick child's miraculous recovery, he had this mosque, possibly with the largest courtyard (220x100m) in Iran, built on the site of his palace in 1201. The mosque was extensively repaired in Safavid times and then practically reconstructed after

1852. It now acts as the Friday mosque, so entry on Fridays will be curtailed.

Some 300m southeast is the **Masjid-i Atiq** which functioned as the *Masjid-i Jami* until the Islamic Revolution. Nothing remains of the original structure of 894, and recently the little free-standing building in the courtyard, thought to date from 1351, has been reassessed. This is the *Beit al-Mashaf* (or the *Khodah khaneh* ('God's house') echoing the shape of the Ka'ba in Mecca, and which once housed the mosque's Korans and other manuscripts. Its tiled portico inscription gives the 1351 foundation date, but recent conservation work has revealed that its present appearance is largely a result of an extensive post-1935 repair programme. Originally the complex had a *madrasa*, two hostels for visiting scholars, a reading room and hospital, but its dilapidated state persuaded Shah Abbas I in 1567 to rebuild in this present four-ivan layout, with large sections of the west and north sides reconstructed 50 years later. This was also when the main avenue of the bazaar was constructed along the procession way used by the Safavid and then Zand rulers riding from their residences for the Friday prayer. Such occasions offered one of the few regular times when the public were certain of seeing the ruler, and Islamic history is dotted by assassination attempts during the Friday procession: two 20th-century victims were King Feisal of Iraq and King Abdullah I of Jordan.

In the Shah-i Cheragh area, a very new private museum has opened, called the **Meshkinfam Museum of Art** (entry 25,000 rials); consult the website for details: www.meshkinfamartmuseum.com

There are still Christians, Jews and Zoroastrians living in Shiraz but community numbers have shrunk over the last three decades. Unfortunately, access to the **Armenian church**, built and decorated in the reign of the Safavid shah, Abbas II (d1666), in Darvazeh Qazerun (Sang-i Siah quarter) is permitted only with prior authorisation from the Vank Cathedral, Isfahan, but the new Church of Simon the Zealot, (**Kelisa-i Moghaddas-i Shamun-i Qaur**) in Nou Baher Lane, off Zand Avenue, is open on Sundays; according to local tradition, Simon was martyred in Iran. Close by is one of the several **synagogues** in the city, and Shiraz also has a **fire temple**. Few will admit to knowing the whereabouts of the original house of the Bab, the founder of the **Bahai movement** (see pages 25–6), but Canadian sources say it is located near Beit al-Mahdi, Shahid Dastgheyb Street, 100m from Shah Cheragh Shrine. Exercise great diplomacy in your enquiries.

OUTSIDE SHIRAZ

Most visitors stay in Shiraz in order to visit Sasanid Bishapur and Firouzabad, and most importantly the Achaemenid palace complex of Persepolis – situated in the west, south and northeast respectively, some way from the city. To visit all three will entail a minimum three-night stay, and even then this leaves little time for exploring Shiraz itself. A new development is **trekking and bird-watching** trips with Gasht Tour, which has connections with the European 'adventure' company, Echo Tours. The guides received their training in Tehran so their local knowledge may be weak, although their enthusiasm will probably be unquestionable. Note that the migratory bird population fell dramatically during the three-year long drought, but it is reviving.

It is also possible to take a **helicopter** trip but it is expensive, costing some €2,000, and official permission has to be obtained (see page 169).

A good-quality taxi or car (eg: Peugeot GLX 405) to go to either Bishapur or Firouzabad and return to Shiraz will cost about US$45, slightly more in the 'tourist' season; if the driver has been very helpful, tip him around US$5–10.

A separate section after this chapter deals with Persepolis and other neighbouring sites (see *Chapter 9*).

Bishapur

Bishapur (125km west of Shiraz) lies off the Qazerun road, which passes through some dramatic scenery, climbing up to and then through 'The Old Woman' Gorge. Other than Qazerun there is no place to buy lunch in this area, so take a picnic with you, and a torch for the palace ruins at Bishapur. With a very early start it should be possible to incorporate a short visit to Lake Parisan (formerly Famur), a bird sanctuary, but recent severe droughts have taken a heavy toll. The road is asphalted but there is little shade. That diversion takes you past a small bridge, Pol-i Abgineh, and a Qajar rock-relief of 1829, depicting the prince-governor conquering a lion. This commemorated the re-opening of the road in 1824, after a severe earthquake. The prince, a grandson of Shah Fath Ali Shah, had to flee to England in 1834 after his father's unsuccessful attempt to seize the throne on the shah's death. Also in this area is a Safavid *caravanserai* of Mian Kotal, for many years a police post.

Bishapur was a **palace-town complex**, built in 266CE according to certain column-inscriptions, to a Hellenistic-Roman grid system instead of the circular plan favoured by the Parthians and early Sasanids; it was the brainchild of Shapur I, using Roman prisoners of war. Rusting rail tracks and dumptrucks scattered over the site are legacies from a decade of archaeological work before World War II by the French, and then from 1968 by the Iranian Archaeological Service, but these excavations involved only 3% of a site which, it is calculated, housed over 50,000 townspeople. It is best to visit these ruins first (if only for the reasonable toilet facilities), not forgetting that torch. Then have a picnic by the river, looking at the low reliefs either side of the gorge.

On entering the site (entry 2,500 rials), there are the Sasanid walls surviving up to about 3m high with solid round towers, but at some point one in three were demolished, perhaps contributing to its capture by the Arab armies around 637. The place has a rather desolate air as it was stripped bare of all its sculptures, mosaics, decorative plaster and other treasures; most went to the Louvre, Paris, with a few pieces going to Tehran's Archaeological Museum. Before visiting the main buildings of the excavated site, head towards the guardian's house (and toilets behind, on the right) and you'll see in the distance, straight ahead, a votive column; this marks the centre of the original city. None of that vast area has been excavated.

Returning to the excavated area, the main building, some 20m² with its stepped cruciform plan and four huge ivans or portals, perhaps functioned as the **royal audience chamber**, although one scholar thinks it was a fire temple. Opinions are much divided as to whether it was covered by a huge dome or left open to the skies, but it must be said there is no evidence of springing high on the walls. Thick wallplaster remains in places, but you have to imagine the deeply carved, moulded and painted decoration. Behind here, close to the walls is stone-lined chamber below the ground level; several masons' marks are still visible on the ashlar blocks. This chamber was 'identified' by the French archaeologist as the prison of Valerian.

Retracing steps to the audience hall, west of this on the same ground level is another chamber entered through a triple-arched doorway. This was where most of the mosaic work was found, depicting entertainers and courtiers, and some small tesserae can be seen close by the doorways. The way the walls meet the ground level strongly suggest that radical alterations were made at some time. This is just one reason why modern archaeologists are now questioning the early excavation conclusions which were reached after digging in such a small sector of the whole site.

There is an intriguing building to the north with high-quality, honey-coloured ashlar stonework. The staircase down is restored but 15m of the original walls remain, forming four faces of a central courtyard, with a covered ambulatory behind. This was in fact a huge shallow pool, for inside the interior ambulatory (the reason for bringing a torch) there are narrow water-channels with occasional blocking or damming devices. This probably was a **temple to Anahita**, the Zoroastrian deity associated with battle, fertility and water, an identification further supported by the two (damaged) bull capitals found nearby and now incorporated high on the wall opposite the stairs, for bull sacrifices were regular offerings at various other Anahita shrines. As the Sasanid shahs traced their lineage back to a high priest at the Istakhr Temple of Anahita, near Persepolis (see page 196), what could be more logical than Shapur I, victorious over Rome, honouring this goddess by constructing a temple in his new city by the river.

A short walk away are the remains of a small **mosque** built, possibly, over a small fire temple, as a fire altar was found incorporated into the structure. The French archaeologists believed the entire site was abandoned in the 10th century, but with so little of the site excavated it is impossible to be sure.

Leaving the site, look up into the hills on the immediate right; all that rubble was originally **defence walls** and towers guarding Bishapur. The minor tarmac road on the right river bank brings you to the first of the **rock reliefs**. It is badly damaged but enough survives to identify the characters as the Zoroastrian Uncreated God, Ahura Mazda, on the left, investing Shah Shapur I (c240–272) on the right. Both are on horseback, but there is a prone figure under Shapur's mount, thought to depict the Roman Emperor, Gordianus III, killed by his men after their defeat on the Euphrates in 243. The kneeling Roman is thought to be Philip the Arab (r244-9) who paid 500,000 gold *dinarii* to secure peace terms a year later. His monumental buildings, still standing in his birthplace Philippopolis (today's Shahba) south of Damascus, reveal nothing of this ignominious submission. Further along this road, but set up

Above Persepolis detail (PB)

Right Persepolis doorway, showing Achaemenid shah and attendant (PB)

Below Overview of Persepolis (PB)

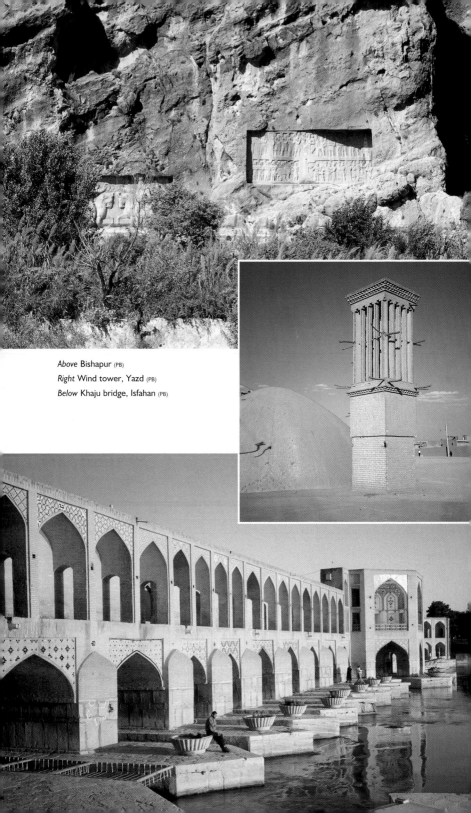

Above Bishapur (PB)
Right Wind tower, Yazd (PB)
Below Khaju bridge, Isfahan (PB)

high, is another panel in better condition, once plastered and painted. In billowing drapery, Shapur grips the wrist of a Roman emperor, probably Valerian (r253–60) who was captured by the Sasanid army in Edessa (Sanliurfa, southeast Turkey), an event which brought Queen Zenoubia of Palmyra into the conflict. Shapur's horse tramples on a fallen enemy, thought to represent Gordianus III again, while the kneeling figure is Philip the Arab; this panel therefore records royal victories over a 20-year span and was perhaps completed for Shapur's funeral. Behind the shah are courtiers and generals, while the figures behind Philip may represent the Roman governor of Syria and a court archivist witnessing the submission. To the right are two rows of figures, one set carrying the sacred *barsom* to feed the fire, and others, perhaps builders of Bishapur, carrying swords and spades.

From here, look up across the river to the far hills. Close to the top ridge you will spot a large cave, the **Mudan-i Shapur**, so named because a free-standing statue over 7m high of Shapur I was carved from the living rock, perhaps to mark his (as yet unlocated) tomb. The statue collapsed some years ago but has been re-erected. In order to visit, keep on this river road past the Qashqai village of Abdallah Khan and then walk for about an hour; in all, four hours there and back to the Bishapur archaeological site.

Returning to the main road, pay the entry charge (2,500 rials) to get into the picnic area on the other bank, generally crowded with welcoming family groups on Fridays. The first **low relief** again depicts Shapur I with his three sons victorious over the same three Roman emperors, with five rows of soldiers, elephants, lions and chariots, in all numbering over 200 figures. It probably dates from 260–273CE. This is followed by a panel showing Bahram II (r274–91) receiving the submission of the Arab tribesmen whose thumbs have been removed to prevent them drawing bows again; this could commemorate his victory at Mesene (in modern-day Iraq), around 282CE. Further on there's a low relief of Ahura Mazda, on the left, handing over the ring of authority to Bahram I (r271–4); Bahram's brother Narseh (r292–301), however, later had his own name inscribed in Pahlavi, top right, presumably still smarting that Bahram I selected his son and not him as successor. In removing the water conduit in 1975, a figure lying under the horse's hooves was revealed, possibly representing the troublesome Bahram (later III) or his adviser Wahnam, who persuaded him to seize power after his father's death (Bahram II); both caused Narseh several sleepless nights.

The last relief, with two rows of figures, looks very crude, but perhaps it was never finished. Who the centrally placed shah is, is unclear; eight 'possibles' have been suggested. Probably it is either Shapur I accepting the submission of Central Asian rebels or Shapur II (309–79), the grandson of Narseh, celebrating his victories in eastern Iran over certain Indian tribes. There are altogether over 200 figures, along with elephants, carved into the rocks, some carrying decapitated heads.

Some 10km north of Bishapur is Qandil (45km south of Nur Abad) which has another Sasanid relief panel known as **Sarab-i** (or Tang-i) **Qandil** measuring 2.75x2.10m high. Scholars cannot agree who is represented here:

Western archaeologists identify the king as Bahram II, being offered a lotus flower by his queen, with the crown prince, later Bahram III, holding the ring of authority, but Iranian specialists understand it to be Shapur I welcomed by Anahita with the powerful high priest, Kartir, in attendance. Also in this area, once on the Achaemenid royal road from Persepolis to Susa, is **Sarab Bahram**, 29km after the Qazerun junction on this Ahvaz-Shiraz road. A Sasanid rock panel, known locally as Naqsh-i Bahram, depicts Bahram II with two attendants either side; the one at the shah's right is clearly Kartir as his cap carries the distinctive 'scissor' motif.

Some 20km further on, the remains of a possible Achaemanid stone tower, resembling those at Naqsh-i Rustam and Pasargarda (pages 194 and 197) were found and about 10km further on (5km northwest of Fahliyan) Sir Aurel Stein, famous for his archaeological discoveries along the Silk Road, discovered column bases of an Achaemenian palace. North of Fahliyan, about 10km, there are the Elamite rock-reliefs of **Kurangun** located high up the hillside, close to Seh Talu and, to the east, **Tal-i Sepid**, an Elamite settlement from c1500–1000BCE. It was a local route across the mountains that took Alexander the Great behind Achaemenid defence lines to take Persepolis. The main Kurangun panel shows two divine – or perhaps regal – figures, one sitting on a serpent-coiled throne pouring a libation. Their date is disputed, some scholars arguing for c2400BCE, while others prefer 16–15th century BCE. Most agree, however, that the second section, depicting three rows of worshippers returning from the libation ceremony, was carved much later, probably in the 8th century BCE.

West of here is **Dai-i Dokhtar** ('Nurse of the Daughter') 3km from Kupan, between Fahliyan and Do Gonbadan. This is a rock-cut tomb thought now to date from the Seleucid or possibly early Parthian period because there are visual similarities in the carved columns 'supporting' a crenellated frieze to the rock tombs at Naqsh-i Rustam (but I am more reminded of Petra, Jordan), though it was identified as Achaemenid when it was first recorded in the late 1920s.

Do check, but there should be a dirt track southwest of Jereh (55km south of Qazerun) via Hasan Abad to **Sar-i Mashhad** (otherwise, from Firouzabad, turn northwest at Farrash Band). There, a rock-panel depicts the Sasanid Bahram II (r274–91) personally protecting his wife and son from a lion attack, with a lengthy Pahlavi inscription detailing Zoroastrian religious teachings and rituals; four figures, one of whom may represent Anahita, witness the episode. Some 12km further south is Bozpar, famous among archaeologists for one small building, the **Gur-i Doktar**, first noted by Western scholars just after World War II. A small limestone tomb with gabled roof stands on a three-tiered platform, bearing remarkable similarity to Cyrus the Great's tomb at Pasargada (pages 196–7), northeast of Shiraz. This is smaller, being 4.45m high, 5.10m long and 4.40m wide (Cyrus's tomb at Pasargada is 10.6x13.2x12.2m). It was first thought that this was the resting place of Cyrus' grandfather, but the metal clamps holding the stone blocks suggest not a 7th-century BCE date after all but a 5th-century one, so perhaps it was the final resting place of Cyrus the Younger (d401BCE) killed in battle nearby.

Firouzabad (about 110km south of Shiraz) itself is an enjoyable day trip in striking scenery, passing the large salt lake of Maharlu with its saltpans, some 20km after leaving Shiraz. Emerging from the second road-tunnel, about 15km before reaching Firouzabad, look for a well-preserved Sasanid fortress on the cliff-top on your left. This is the palace complex known as Qaleh-i Dokhtar ('Daughter's Castle'), from the local legend that a girl continually carried a young heifer from birth to maturity up to the castle and down to the river (the *Shah-nameh* contains a related story linked with the Sasanid shah Bahram V). Access is possible but entails about 40 minutes' hard walking, the path snaking upwards opposite (and just past) the small téléphérique on the bend of the road. A German archaeological survey of the late 1960s identified a three-terraced complex, with a large circular tower, visible from the road, and a central square chamber preceded by a barrel-vaulted hall and series of chambers, originally set within a garden. Given the neighbouring rock reliefs depicting Shah Ardashir (d240CE), it seems likely the palace was constructed for him, but Shapur I (d272) has also been suggested. There is a parking place just past the téléphérique, and a short walk down below the road allows you to see the remains of a Sasanid bridge, which presumably once connected a small fort on the other bank with the palace path. Continue walking to see an eroded Sasanid rock relief on the far bank, showing Ardashir standing before a fire-altar with three sons and a page, all facing Ahura Mazda on the left. About 1km further on, but very difficult to spot, is another relief (18x4m high), depicting Ardashir unseating the last Parthian ruler, Artabanus V, from his horse in 224, while his son Shapur tackles the Parthian vizier and a Sasanid courtier dispatches another opponent. Recent road building and dam construction make access extremely difficult.

From this road, the remains of a huge Sasanid palace (c105x55m) soon come into view on the right, but to visit it one has to drive down into Firouzabad and approach by a parallel road, so you can also visit the remains of the Sasanid city of Ardashir Khurreh ('The Glory of Ardashir'), usually called **Gur**. On the way turn right at the roundabout bearing a gas-flame through the modern town, taking the left fork at the cemetery. On the town outskirts, opposite a small cluster of light-industrial buildings is a dirt track leading through what remains of the massive circular defence walls of Gur, to the far right of the solitary ruined tower. Follow until it threatens to take you into a farmhouse, then swing on to the left (pot-holed) track which leads closer to the ruined tower. The last 1km or so must be walked. Despite the noisy, excited children, it is a marvellous site crying out to be properly surveyed and excavated. Even in its overgrown state you can make out the ruins of city walls, buildings, wells and water channels, and Sasanid pot shards litter the track. Archaeologists think this circular city, over 2km in diameter, was originally a Parthian settlement, but tradition says that Ardashir built it to mark his victory over the Parthian regime. A deep ditch and huge ramparts with four gates protected it. The centrally placed solitary tower, with traces of an external spiral staircase, was probably a huge fire-altar standing some 30m high and 10m square. To one side in the near distance a stone terrace 25m² is visible, on which stood a cruciform domed chamber with side rooms, perhaps functioning as the main temple compound.

Retrace the rough drive to get to the huge **Sasanid palace** seen earlier. Continue past the light-industrial building, keeping the tower of Gur on the right and eventually the road leads right up to the site (entry 2,000 rials). The present-day entrance is not the original one, so walk from the small car park to view the little lake and the huge ivan opening on to it, once the official palace entry. The thick stone walls, relieved by groups of three engaged columns, look unprepossessing without their top layer of plaster, once painted and decorated. Today's entrance leads immediately into a series of huge domed chambers with early examples of squinches; tall blind niches decorated with Pharaonic-looking cornices elegantly spaced along the walls accentuate the vast space. The doorways go either to the audience ivan, once possibly decorated like the royal 'coronation' ivan at the Sasanid capital of Ctesiphon (near Baghdad), Iraq, which had a huge jewelled crown suspended from the apex and a rich bejewelled, gold and silver floor carpet; or, in the opposite direction to a courtyard surrounded by rooms and passageways. A spiral staircase connects with the upper floor and roof, but yet again the blight of Iranian historic buildings, a jungle of scaffolding, blocks access, so instead young and energetic visitors scramble up over walls, risking life and limb and causing far more damage to the structure.

In modern Firouzabad, a well-known trading centre until the 11th century, there's a simple but clean **Tourist Inn** set in a small garden to one side of the gas-flame roundabout (on Imam Khomeini Avenue; tel: 0712 663699; fax: 0712 6222105; around US$30 double/single); it has basic accommodation but good food and is presently being refurbished.

From Shiraz, a main road leads southeast to **Sarvistan** (80km from Shiraz). The small town has a mausoleum, the Imamzadeh Pol (known also as *Mazar-i Shaikh Yusuf Sarvastani*), with a 1282 dating inscription that seems at odds with its form, which resembles a Zoroastrian fire temple. In the early 14th century a large complex was constructed behind it. But the real reason for stopping is the Sasanid palace complex just outside the town. A triple-arched portico formed the entrance, the two smaller arches leading into a series of halls with interesting vaulted systems, which connected to other smaller rooms. The central arch opens directly into the main brick-domed chamber, a large central courtyard and then other rooms, each architecturally different from the other. Perhaps built for Bahram V (r421–39), it could have functioned as a royal hunting lodge before being converted into a fire temple at some point. Surface pottery shards litter the ground everywhere. From here, it is approximately 140km due east to **Neyriz** (and eventually Sirjan) with its *Masjid-i Jami*, important for its single barrel-vault ivan, thought to be the oldest to survive in Iran. This section of the present building could well date from 951 when the mosque was constructed over the remains of a fire temple, or perhaps 20 years later as its Seljuk plaster *mihrab* refers to further work here begun in 972. The south ivan and side arcades were added in the Seljuk period.

Fasa is no longer the sleepy village seen by Sylvia Matheson in the late 1970s but a thriving township with the municipality busily landscaping its historic mounds into leisure areas. The road continues to **Darab** (275km from Shiraz) and neighbouring **Darabgerd**, 8km southwest, known for its Sasanid remains. Before being abandoned in the 12th or early 13th century, the circular fortress Qaleh-i Dahyeh measured 1,850m in diameter with a 55m-wide defensive ditch, and walls at least 12m high with four gates. On the hillside nearby is the rock-relief known locally as **Naqsh-i Rostam Darab**. It depicts a Sasanid shah on horseback, with rows of courtiers behind receiving the submission of two important men, while a third lies on the ground and rows of Roman captives line up to the right. Opinions are divided over who is depicted here: the shah's crown suggests it is Ardashir, once the regional governor here, recording his victory in 230 over the Romans Severus Alexander and Maximus Thrace before overthrowing the Parthians, but perhaps it is Shapur I with Valerian and Philip the Arab. About 5km further southeast is a rock-cut chamber. Although it has a *mihrab* dated 1254 and is known locally as **Masjid-i Sangi**, the presence of a narthex and a cruciform chamber has led some archaeologists to associate it with the 3rd-century Nestorian bishopric in the locale.

Persepolis and the Surrounding Area

PERSEPOLIS
Getting and staying there

There is presently no overnight accommodation available at Persepolis (locally known as *Takht-i Jamshid*) or at Pasargarda, another 120km further north, so a visit will entail overnighting in Shiraz. Transport is another problem. There is a scheduled bus service between Shiraz and Marv Dasht but not to and from Persepolis itself, so the easiest solution is to hire (and retain for the return trip) a taxi, if not from Shiraz (50km southwest) then from Marv Dasht. If possible, two visits should be made to the site: in early morning to explore when the light is much 'whiter', and about 90 minutes before sunset, when the stone takes on a softer, golden colour. Most of the stone now has a rough grey appearance, a result of wind-blown dust over the millennia, so do make a point of visiting the Tehran Archaeological Museum to see the 'waxed' reliefs and column ensemble from Persepolis. This rich, dark-brown stone set alongside a creamy limestone was the original colouring. If you are limited to one visit, it will take three hours or so to walk around and take photographs, especially if you plan to walk up to the royal Achaemenid tombs behind for a magnificent view over the site. Take a telephoto lens or binoculars for viewing these tombs; these will also be useful if you're going to Naqsh-i Rustam (usually included on the same day).

The site of Persepolis

Archaeological excavations began here in earnest in 1931 and have continued on and off ever since. The immense scale and grandeur of this site (over 13ha or 33 acres) has long been recognised. Locals thought it could only be the dais-throne (*takht*) of Jamshid, a legendary figure in the *Shah-nameh* (see page 253), while in the 14th century it was known as *Chehel Manar* (40 Minarets) from the standing columns seen from a distance. In the early 1980s hysterical reports in the Western media announced that revolutionary zeal had destroyed much of this pre-Islamic site. Nonsense. Admittedly few visitors appreciate the new 'protection measures' recently installed, but there has been no gratuitous damage.

It was Darius the Great who began construction around 515BCE, with his successors adding buildings, but it was still unfinished when, in early

330BCE, Alexander the Great razed it to the ground, seven years before his death. It took him, according to Plutarch, 10,000 mules and 5,000 camels to carry away the booty from this revenge-attack for the Achaemenid firing of Athens. The stone came from nearby quarries but the labourers came from all over the Achaemenid Empire including Greece, as the marks of the Greek toothed chisel testifies. Gold and silver foundation tablets (now in Tehran's Archaeological Museum) were found on the site but more fascinating, for their wealth of detailed information, were the 30,000-odd clay tablets which were uncovered. The complex consisted of military quarters, treasury stores, small private rooms and huge reception areas, but the exact function of the complex remains an intriguing mystery. Susa was the Achaemenid winter capital and Hamadan the summer residence, while Pasagarda was perhaps built to commemorate Cyrus the Great's victory over the Medians. But Persepolis? On the evidence of low-reliefs showing gift-bearing visitors, and lions attacking bulls (Leo ascendant over Taurus), many assume Persepolis was used once a year to celebrate *Nou Rouz*, the spring equinox (March 21), but such festivities are not mentioned in Achaemenid and later sources. There seem to have been only two occasions when the Achaemenid ruler received gifts: on the official imperial birthday, and the annual sacrifice to Mithra.

The only access to the site is at the end of the main avenue. A clutch of wooden 'chalets' (slightly larger than garden sheds) have been recently erected on the north side, some 150m short of the roundabout near the Achaemenid terrace wall. Cars, taxis, buses etc have to stop here and park behind this new development and visitors have to walk from here, having purchased the entry tickets (entry to site 3,000 rials, museum 2,500 rials; *closed sunset*) from one of these 'chalets'; the others will doubtless open as souvenir shops when foreign tourists come back to Iran. There are some toilets in this area, located at the back and to the east of this new complex, but it's a walk. The other toilets are on the site, to the right of the museum entrance.

Ticket in hand, walk down the avenue, round the roundabout and through an irritating glass-screened entrance, some ten years old. In full sunlight any information (in Farsi) printed on them is rendered totally illegible, and the ancient stonework immediately behind silently roasts. However, essential signs (location of toilets, cafeteria etc) are shown clearly in international symbols. If you're already feeling hot and bothered, just count your blessings as, before July 2004 you would have parted with 60,000 rials for the ticket, and it is such a wonderful site.

The great double staircase with low rises, perhaps to allow horses to be ridden up, leads up to the monumental **Gateway of All Lands**, constructed c475BCE on the order of Xerxes I, successor to Darius the Great. Here trumpeters would have sounded a welcome as visitors walked through enormous wooden doors flanked by giant sculptures of two quadrupeds, while two huge human-headed winged bulls in the Assyrian style face into the palace area. High over the sculptures is a 24-lined trilingual cuneiform inscription proclaiming: 'I am Xerxes, the great king, King of Kings, King of the lands of many people, King of this great earth far and wide…. By Ahura Mazda's favour I have had made this Gate of All Lands. Much that is beautiful has been built in this … [region] which I and my father have built. All that has been built and appears beautiful … we have built by the favour of Ahura Mazda.' It is one of the 110 inscriptions here, many of which reaffirm belief in the Zoroastrian creator-god. Please resist the temptation to add your name to all the graffiti, which includes Stanley (of Dr Livingstone fame).

Past the gate, on the left are examples of bird-headed 'push-me-pull-you' capitals designed to carry ceiling crossbeams of Lebanese cedars; this *homa* bird is used as the logo of IranAir. If the light is good, you may wish to go immediately towards the right to photograph the **Northern Apadana staircase.** The informality of the carved figures, the Medes in their rounded caps and knee-length tunics, and the Persians with distinctive 'Victoria sponge-fingers' caps and long pleated robes, is charming. They slowly ascend up the left side chatting, carrying lotus buds, touching arms, holding hands. The 19th-century Lord Curzon must have felt very jaded to comment wearily, 'It is all the same, and the same again, and yet again … there is no variation in their steady, ceremonious tramp.'

Most visitors, however, continue past the defunct Sound and Light seating to the second gate or doorway flanked by horse figures, once the formal entrance into the **Hall of 100 columns** (70m²), probably constructed c480–60BCE. Having borne the brunt of Alexander the Great's arson attack, the hall no longer possesses the thick brick walls, once colourfully decorated with painted plaster or glazed tiles (as displayed in the Tehran Archaeological Museum and the Louvre, Paris) between the stone window and door frames. The far door-jamb reliefs, showing the enthroned Achaemenid ruler protected by his Median and Persian guards, suggest this was where the envoys presented their gifts, which were then stored in the Treasury beyond. Above, as on reliefs here and elsewhere (eg: Bisitun, Naqsh-i Rustam) a winged composition hovers over the royal canopy; it represents Ahura Mazda, the One Uncreated God according to Zoroastrian scriptures, and/or the spirit of the royal ancestors holding out the *farshang* (ring of authority). The door jambs of the hall's side chambers are carved with a giant male figure, perhaps the emperor as the Perfect Hero, slaying evil spirits. Similar images are repeated on the doorways of the **Palace of Xerxes** near the museum.

To the far right is the famous main **Eastern Apadana staircase** which can be glimpsed through rusting supports of an enormous canopy. Erected at the same time as the glass entrance, the canopy's purpose is likewise totally unclear. It is a badly designed, corroding eyesore, casting slanting shadows so infuriating for photographers. Furthermore, as of early 2000, the reliefs are roped off, preventing close examination of the fine sculpted detail. (Now you understand the reference to hand-delivering any letters of complaint to the local Shiraz offices of Iranian Cultural Heritage Organisation on page 175.)

This staircase was uncovered in 1932, so it has the best preserved reliefs. The right-hand section has lines of Medes and Persians representing the

PERSEPOLIS

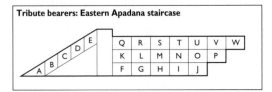

Tribute bearers: Eastern Apadana staircase

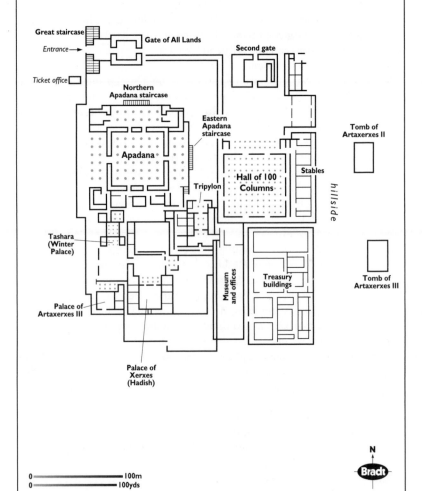

KEY

First rise upwards

(A) Ethiopians or Nubians bringing a giraffe or okapi
(B) 'People of the Punt', probably Libyans, with an antelope and chariot
(C) People of the eastern regions, possibly the so-called Carians with a bull
(D) Arabs leading a dromedary camel
(E) Unidentified, but possibly Greeks, wearing pointed caps and offering a horse

Panels at ground level, left to right

(F) Indians from Sind wearing skirt wraps, bringing an ass
(G) Parthians leading a Bactrian camel and carrying metal objects
(H) Ionians holding cloth and honeycombs or balls of yarn
(I) Cappadocians carrying garments and leading horses
(J) Lydians with a chariot

Middle row, left to right

(K) Soghdians (today's Samarkand region) with gifts of a horse and metalwork
(L) People of Gandhara (Pakistan) with a humped bull
(M) Scythians with a distinctive pointed cap, bearing clothing
(N) Assyrians with sheep
(O) Babylonians with a fringed cloth and a humped bull
(P) Armenians, bringing a horse and double-handled ewer

Top row, left to right

(Q) Median peoples? or Sagartians? with a horse and textiles
(R) Bactrians with a Bactrian camel
(S) Egyptians (very fragmentary)
(T) Drangianans (north of Afghanistan) bringing a Bactrian camel
(U) Arians (Baluchistan) with a Bactrian camel and a lion skin
(V) Elamite archers from Susa bringing a lioness – the only female form in Persepolis – and two cubs
(W) Medians with metal objects and clothing

famous 10,000 Immortals, the imperial bodyguards, and attendants leading small horses, Elamite chariots, or carrying intricately worked furniture and textiles etc. To the left side, the panels depict envoys from the 23 subject nations in fine detail, right down to finger-nail cuticles, bringing gifts. They are usually identified as in the key above.

Neither this nor the northern staircase still possesses its original centre panel of the enthroned ruler *in situ*. The central panel of the northern stairs is

DARIUS THE GREAT

When Cyrus the Great died in 529BCE, both north and south Iran had been brought together under Achaemenid rule and most of Libya, Sudan and Egypt were added by the military campaigns of his son, Cambyses II, before his death in Egypt in 522BCE. Having just quelled an uprising against Cambyses, a small group of courtiers including Darius, a close relative, agreed that Cambyses' successor should be chosen by supernatural forces: the owner of the first horse to neigh at dawn would be crowned. Darius's groom decided to assist the gods and Darius was selected, only to be immediately faced with an Elamite revolt in southern Iran and uprisings in the northern regions (see pages 7–8). Order was restored, and Darius then campaigned successfully in India, returning with cargo-loads of booty. Four years later the Achaemenid Empire was further extended by moving into Anatolia, crossing the Bosphorus and marching into the Balkans and along the River Danube, although a Greek revolt in 500BCE regained some ground. By the time of his death in 486BCE, he had consolidated the foundations of an empire of 23 peoples that was to last for another 200 years, using an efficient administration with standardised weights and measures run from at least three major centres, Ekbatana, Susa and Persepolis. His legal code, only fragments of which have survived, was praised by Plato, while merchants and others travelled safely along the patrolled Royal Road from Sardis, in modern-day Turkey, to Susa, and sailors navigated through the ancient Suez Canal, started and abandoned by the Egyptian Pharoah Nekho but completed by Darius. As the Persepolis Apadana foundation tablet proudly recorded: 'This is the kingdom which I hold. From Saka beyond Soghdia to Ethiopia, from India to Sardis, which Ahura Mazda greatest of the gods presented me.' As his name suggested, he was 'the Holder of Good'.

now in Tehran's Archaeological Museum, but the one from this eastern staircase is here albeit in the Treasury building near the site museum (see below). But both staircases retain their dramatic depictions of a voracious lion sinking its teeth and claws into the neck of a bull, which cause some to think Persepolis was used in *Nou Rouz* festivities.

On reaching the **Apadana** level, look back at the low central section of the Eastern stairs, to see various stages of stone-carving in the row of shield-bearing guards. The vast platform was the floor of an enormous audience hall capable of holding 10,000 people, covered with a timber roof supported by 36 columns, each 20m high, surmounted with a capital shaft and a huge double-headed protone capital. Tall cedars from newly conquered Lebanon permitted Achaemenid masons to space out the column bases, unlike the close-sitting ones seen at Pasargarda (see page 197).

To the south, on a terrace some 2m higher, is the **Winter Palace of Darius** (*Tashara*, as given in trilingual cuneiform), built around 486BCE. It is entered by a western staircase ordered by Artaxerxes III, decorated with figures of servants carrying food, vessels and lambs. As with the Apadana's lotus-bell column bases, there are echoes of Egyptian architectural detail here with the curved mouldings over the doors. The intimate scale of this room, the polished stone, remains of a red plaster floor, the low reliefs showing royal attendants with parasol, fly whisk, towel and perfume box, have led some archaeologists to identify these rooms as royal private apartments with a bath. In the central area Darius, again as the Perfect Hero, is depicted slaying legendary animals trying to enter. The now empty spaces between window and door frames would have been filled with mud-brick walls decorated with painted plaster or glazed brick.

Across the courtyard, due south, lies the **Palace of Artaxerxes III**, c359–338BCE, entered from staircases carved with further figures of delegates and attendants. A keen eye will spot the siting marks on stones at ground level left by the Achaemenid masons for positioning columns and corner stones. To the left (east) is the *Hadish* or **Palace of Xerxes** ('Ruling over Heroes') with its 36 columns and five doorways with low-reliefs showing Xerxes himself. To its northeast is the small building known as the Tripylon because of its three doors. This is where the polished staircase, now in the Tehran Archaeological Museum, came from. On the eastern doorway, Xerxes is shown standing behind Darius who is seated on a throne, supported by representatives of the subject nations. Down in the hollow is the small **museum** (entry fee now included in main ticket) constructed in the Achaemenid style over the foundations of a building identified on very slim evidence as the **Harem** (Queen's apartments). It houses a number of the smaller treasures found on site, including an Achaemenid trumpet, and has a small book-cum-giftshop. To the far right of the entrance (exterior) are toilets, and facing the museum door a small cafeteria selling drinks.

In front of the hillside, low walls mark the **Treasury** buildings where tens of thousands of clay tablets were unearthed, recording the numbers, nationalities and wages of the palace labourers. Its main feature today is the central relief panel from the **Eastern Apadana staircase**, moved here in late Achaemenid times. This damaged panel shows an enthroned Achaemenid emperor, perhaps Darius or Xerxes, holding the royal staff and a lotus flower. Behind him is the crown prince, a court eunuch and an official, while in front a general pays homage.

If there's time (and especially if you aren't visiting nearby Naqsh-i Rustam; see below) walk up the hillside for a good panoramic view and a close-up of two of the four **royal tombs** cut into the rock. There are paths both behind the Treasury and to the side of the Sound & Light seating, the latter an easier path. This tomb above the Hall of 100 Columns is thought to have housed the bones of Artaxerxes II (d358BCE), the other further on behind the Treasury was perhaps constructed for Artaxerxes III (d338BCE) but the owners of the other two concealed from immediate view are not known. (The title Artaxerxes meant 'Ruling through Truth'.)

NAQSH-I RUSTAM

A 3km-drive northwards from Persepolis across the main Shiraz–Isfahan road brings you to Naqshi–i Rustam. Take your binoculars or telephoto lens. The words *naqsh* ('picture') and 'Rustam', a legendary Persian warrior (see Matthew Arnold's poem *Sohrab & Rostam*), were given to this place by locals seeing the Sasanid rock reliefs of jousting and investiture scenes, but the four **Achaemenid tombs** carved high into the rock face are more dramatic for today's visitors; entry 2,000 rials; *closed sunset*.

The first, on the left was probably the tomb for Darius II (d405BCE), the next for Artaxerxes I (d424BCE); the third and most imposing, when not hidden behind abandoned rusting scaffolding (now for over seven years), held the remains of Darius the Great (d486BCE), and the last, on the adjoining rock face, was carved for Xerxes I (d465BCE) or possibly Xerxes II (d423BCE). Why the rockface was worked in such a cruciform shape is unclear. Perhaps it symbolised the empire, covering the four quarters of the known world, the four cardinal points or perhaps an abstract stylisation of the Ahura Mazda figure (the head and torso, the protective wings etc). Or perhaps the surfaces were prepared for inscription panels, as at Bisitun, which were never added.

As with the Persepolis tombs, the Achaemenid ruler is depicted as if standing above a columned portico, making an offering to the fire-altar with the composite Ahura Mazda figure flying above. He stands on a platform (which, incidently, has the same proportions as Solomon's dais, as mentioned in Chronicles II) held up by representatives of subject nations. Their inclusion is deliberate, for the Darius tomb inscription states: 'If now you shall think: how many are the countries which King Darius held? Look at the sculptures...'

Before going over to the rock reliefs below the tombs, walk over to the half-submerged stone cube-building to appreciate the original ground level. Known locally as the **Kaba-i Zardust** ('Zoroastra's *Kaba*' or 'shrine'), it is a single-storeyed building with one entrance and no windows, standing 12.6m high. Perhaps inspired by earlier (Anatolian) Urartian architecture, it is clearly Achaemenid but its function is a mystery, although it is far better preserved than its Pasargarda cousin (see page 197). It could not have been a fire temple as there is no smoke vent. Perhaps it held royal archives or royal battle standards or served as a mortuary chamber. There is a long inscription along the bottom at the far right of the staircase, but this is Sasanid, added by the High Priest Kartir recording the victories of Shapur I, including his own name wherever possible, stating that he, Kartir, was responsible for establishing fire temples in Cappadocia, Syria, Armenia and Georgia.

Clearly the Sasanid shahs wanted to associate themselves, historically and visually, with the Achaemenid monuments in this place. Apart from this inscription there are seven **Sasanid panels**. Starting on the far left by the boundary fence, they are as follows:

(A)   Ardashir I on the left with a courtier behind is invested with the ring of authority by Ahura Mazda, holding the sacred *barsom* of twigs (fuel for the sacred fire), carved near the end of his reign in c240CE. Here, as on other

Sasanid reliefs, the shah sees himself as the equal, physically at least, of the Deity. His horse tramples on the last Parthian king, while Ahura Mazda's steed crushes Ahriman, the evil one.

(B)   The next relief on a convex surface shows Bahram II (d291) with his courtiers, each with a distinctive headgear. This was carved over a much earlier panel, c9th century BCE, of which the figure of an Elamite king is clearly visible on the far right, whereas to the far left the crowned head of his queen is less distinct.

(C)   Under the first tomb and opposite the stone building, is an unidentified Sasanid jousting scene.

(D)   Under the second tomb is another jousting scene, possibly showing Bahram V causing his opponent to fall dramatically from his horse.

(E)   Below Darius's tomb, slightly to the left, Shapur I on horseback holds captive the Roman Emperor Valerian, while a kneeling Philip the Arab sues for peace (see page 181). Behind is the bust of his vizier, the High Priest, Kartir, responsible for collating the remains of the Zoroastrian scriptures after Alexander the Great burnt the Achaemenid library, and who initiated official persecution of Christians and Jews in the Sasanid Empire.

(F)   Directly under the tomb are two Sasanid equestrian battles one over the other. The shah lancing the enemy's horse is probably Hormuzd II (r302-9) or perhaps Bahram II.

(G)   A relief showing Shah Narseh (d301) with two attendants, invested with the ring of authority by the Zoroastrian divinity, Anahita; between them the small figure is, perhaps, the crown prince. The depiction of Anahita, the goddess of fertility and also of war, indirectly supports the theory that the *Kaba-i Zardust* was a depository for battle flags. One of her main temples was located at Istakhr nearby (see below).

If you have a free hour, walk up the hill to view the two fire-altars still standing on the top. The path is situated behind the first Sasanid relief (A) but outside the perimeter fence.

Return to the main Shiraz–Isfahan road. Opposite the junction is a lay-by in front of **Naqsh-i Rajab** ('picture of Rajab') so-called after a former local café owner; since late 2001 a metal fence and a ticket booth have been erected. The entry fee is 1,000 rials but often the booth is unmanned and locked as is the gate. Exactly why these important Sasanid investiture reliefs are carved here is unclear. The first relief on the left, possibly worked in c250CE, shows Shapur I on horseback, with his distinctive crown and a bilingual inscription on his chest, while behind him are courtiers and perhaps the crown prince. On the panel almost opposite he is shown again, taking the ring of authority from Ahura Mazda on the left, so perhaps this relief commemorates Shapur's investiture in March 242. As at Naqsh-i Rustam, both god and shah are shown as equal in size. The last relief at the back depicts Shapur's father, Ardashir I, the first of the dynasty, with Ahura Mazda on the right handing him the *farshang* ring while holding a *barsom* for the sacred fire. The figure behind Ardashir is probably Shapur, then the crown prince, and behind him – and clearly added later – the *éminence grise*, Kartir, crooking his finger in respect.

Between Ardashir and his god are children, perhaps the shah's grandsons. Two female figures to the far right complete the panel: these are thought to represent the queen, or Ardashir's mother with an attendant, but it is a mystery why they are depicted leaving the scene.

You could ponder over this in the pleasant garden-restaurant (with spotless toilets), **Laneh-i Tavoos** (mobile tel: 0917 128 0058), identified by a white stone porch just set back from the main road, on the same side, very close by. It often caters for tour groups so service is efficient, with reliably good food. Opt for the main dish of the day with or without soup, yoghurt and salad; if there's *fasinjan* on the menu, just check the number of ducks in the pool before and after the meal. There is usually one English-speaking member of staff on duty.

The place perhaps most associated with the Sasanid dynasty is **Istakhr**, less than 3km on from Naqsh-i Rajab towards Isfahan. An ancestor served as high priest at the Temple of Anahita here and it is possible the shahs' investitures were celebrated in this place. But as only one column and a few corner blocks remain standing, the site requires a great deal of imagination. Preliminary excavation many years ago revealed a vast walled enclosure (1,400x650m), with stone blocks reused from Persepolis. It was taken by the Arabs in 643CE, and later totally sacked as punishment for a local rebellion, so that by the 11th century only a village of 100 inhabitants remained. The site is totally overgrown but lots of Sasanid shards of the distinctive turquoise-blue glazed earthenware still lie on the surface. Foreign visitors rarely stop here, so expect any passing police or army vehicle to drive over to check you out.

PASARGARDA

About 115km further on, past brick-kilns, towards Isfahan is the turn-off for Pasargarda, some 4km from the village and not regularly served by any intercity bus. A small tourist inn with toilets but no accommodation is located just off the main road well before the village, so why not picnic under the trees looking at Cyrus the Great's tomb. Go through the village, bearing left at the fork, until the road is barred; the ticket office (with toilets) is on the right (entry fee 2,500 rials; *closed sunset*).

Undoubtedly, Persepolis was a ceremonial centre fit for an emperor, but Pasargarda's buildings are on a more intimate, smaller scale, as if catering for a warlord about to emerge on the world stage – perhaps Cyrus himself commemorating his famous victory against the Medes. Excavation work started here in 1949–54 and continued with a British team in the 1960s, when the full extent of the site was realised. The first monument to be seen is the **Tomb of Cyrus the Great** (d529BCE) standing on its three-stepped platforms, the lowest one measuring 13.5x12.2m. As of October 2001, yet again the scourge of Iranian historic sites hit: scaffolding … and as of autumn 2004 it is still there. It surrounds the stepped platform and the chamber itself and in visits since I have seen only one workman on the site. Perhaps the authorities wish to conjure up memories of the sacred grove which once surrounded it and even the Achaemenid columns, reused for a 13th-century mosque here, were cleared away to construct helicopter pads so that royal guests attending the 1971 celebrations could pop in and pay their respects to the great man. Alexander the Great, on his pilgrimage here, relied on simpler transport. The tomb chamber has a simple almost square form (5.25m², 6m high) with a gabled roof. Its form has reminded scholars of Mesopotamian work, Turkish Phrygian or 7th-century BCE Urartian buildings (I always think of Cavustepe, by Lake Van in Eastern Turkey). A few of the lead/iron swallow-tail clamps remain in situ, but the small entry doors have long gone, as have all the precious treasures they protected. Nor can one see from ground level the simple rosette form carved on top of the roof gable; such multi-petalled motifs, perhaps symbolising fertility, prosperity or the wingless disc of Ahura Mazda, are repeated throughout Persepolis. And there is no sign either of the tomb inscription recorded by Strabo: 'O man, I am Cyrus who founded the empire of the Persians and was king of Asia. Grudge me not this monument.'

Follow the road into the site. In the hills immediately in front a huge retaining wall and terrace are still visible, known locally as *Takht-i Madar-i Soleyman* (Throne of Solomon's Mother), and similarly Cyrus' tomb was locally attributed to her. This was the main **citadel** area, occupied until its destruction by the Seleucids in 280BCE; across from it is a platform with two stone **fire-altars**. In the foreground at ground level, looking like a Hollywood film stage-prop supported by scaffolding (this time essential) is all that remains of a single-storey building, known locally as the **Zenjan-i Soleyman** (Solomon's Prison). It probably pre-dates its cousin at Naqsh-i Rustam (pages 194–5), as here there is no sign of Greek toothed chisel marks, but its function is just as enigmatic.

The road to the right leads eventually to ruins of a **Gate House**, a small chamber whose huge stone corner-blocks once supported mud-brick walls. The eight large column bases are set remarkably close together, suggesting construction predated the Achaemenid conquest of Lebanon and easy access to its famous cedars used for ceiling beams. The four doorways were once embellished by human-headed bull sculptures as in Persepolis, but their present whereabouts (since the late 1930s) are unknown. However, one low relief remains to fox the archaeologists. It features a standing, winged genie figure facing into the building; its headgear is Egyptian in form, its robe Elamite and its four-winged stance is Assyrian. Perhaps it symbolises the submission and offerings of these conquered peoples entering into the Achaemenid stronghold. Retracing one's steps on the road, there is the first of two **audience palaces** whose columns, except for one, were removed to build the mosque at Cyrus's tomb. Again, huge corner blocks once supported the walls, one with a trilingual cuneiform inscription recording 'I Cyrus, the king, the Achaemenid, built this'. Around the eight-columned central hall on all four sides were porticoes with stone doorways. Their carved decoration suggests to some visitors that this was a temple rather than an audience hall; only the feet and ankles have survived but one set appears to belong to a priest in a fish-like costume accompanied by standing bulls and huge bird forms. In Persepolis a similar combination, but much more confrontational, can be found (see page 193).

Further on to the right are the remains of a larger **audience hall** with some 30 central column bases and two porticoes, one originally stretching the length of the building. Its flooring is worth looking at, a veritable jigsaw of limestone slabs with small repairs to imperfections. Polished, it would have served Fred Astaire and Ginger Rogers splendidly. Facing into the building from this portico, the corner-block to the left carries another of the 24 trilingual inscriptions found on the site, which records 'Cyrus the Great King the Achaemenid...'; the omission of the personal pronoun leads some scholars to suggest that a successor, perhaps Darius, ordered the carving. At the far end a doorway relief, to the height of 1.5m, showing a standing figure in a pleated robe inscribed with cuneiform characters, again reading 'Cyrus, the Great King...' Again there are small drilled holes, perhaps to carry jewels or gold plaques as in Persepolis.

Walking back to the tarmac surface, look for signs of stone water-channels. In 1963 David Stronach found evidence of a garden with pavilion, and unearthed a jar containing jewellery, beads and charms, hidden in Achaemenid times perhaps to foil Alexander's men.

The South Coast

For centuries this mainly Arabic-speaking region was one of the most prosperous in all Iran, handling the cargoes and supplying the ships calling in for water, food and repairs on their voyages to and from Europe and Asia. (Continual trade with the Arab world has meant that many residents speak Arabic as their first language.) The 'discovery' of the sea-route around Africa by Vasco da Gama resulted in a certain loss of trade, and Shah Abbas battled endlessly to promote the advantages of shipping Persian silk and India chintzes from these Iranian ports on the south coast. He had limited success, possibly because European merchants and sailors found the high humidity and the extreme summer temperatures very difficult, and because once the cargoes were unloaded traders were still faced by tortuous journeys into the interior. The one wide river, Karun, was unnavigable until 19th-century British soldiers took matters into their own hands and blew obstructing rocks and boulders out of the water. Caravans and travellers also had to contend with raids by tribesmen; even in the 1920–30s foreign oil companies paid protection money to the tribes to prevent damage to the oil lines and installations.

The Iran–Iraqi War set back the oil, petroleum and natural gas industrial development in this region, but now a number of projects are back on line, and the number of foreign business people visiting this area is increasing.

AHVAZ

Ahvaz (population 2 million; altitude 27m; see *Geography and climate*) once witnessed Achaemenid ships unloading goods for transportation on the royal road to Susa and Persepolis, and later the fleets of Alexander the Great moored here on their return from the Indian campaign. The port and town centre were developed by the early Sasanid shahs and an extensive Christian community here had its own bishop by 410. Its fortunes declined in the 630s after the Arab conquests, and uprisings against the Abbasid regime in Baghdad in the 9th century brought further retribution. Matters did not improve, with the Mongol armies blamed for the destruction of the 9th-century bridge-cum-dam, and by the 14th century it had an unhealthy reputation for voracious mosquitoes and jaundice. The local economy revived a little in 1857 when Anglo-Indian troops were stationed there during the Anglo–Persian War, and

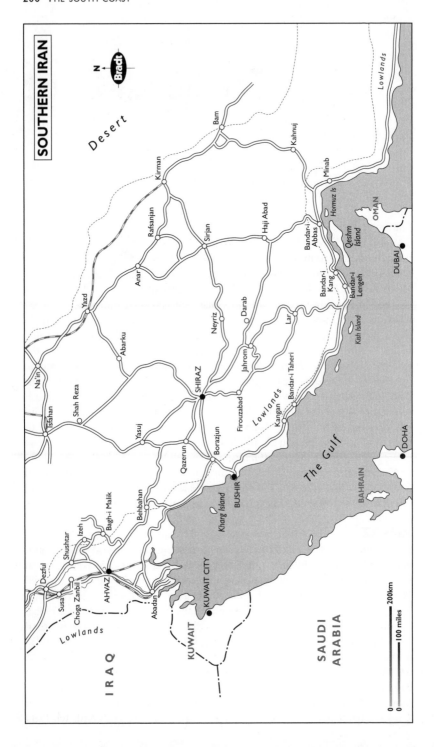

the opening up of the lower Karun River area in 1888 which facilitated water transport led to a new settlement, but still the population was estimated at a mere 700 people.

Then oil production started in the Masjid-i Soleyman area and Ahvaz was established as the provincial capital in 1926. With the disruption of the late 1970s, many of the 330,000 population left and did so again in the 1980s because of the Iran–Iraq conflict. However, Ahvaz was not extensively bombed (unlike Dezful) because, it was rumoured, Saddam Hussein's mother-in-law came from Ahvaz. The 1986 census (during the war) gave the population as 580,000. The city today is arranged on the grid plan with a torturous one-way system. Foreign visitors come to the city for business purposes, or to see the archaeological sites in the region; the city itself is very modern.

Getting there and around

The quickest and easiest way to Ahvaz is by air from Tehran (daily flight, taking about 70 minutes) or any other major Iranian city; there is also a Thursday flight from Dubai. There is a train service from Tehran but the journey takes over 15 hours. Ahvaz is also served by frequent intercity bus services from the major centres, but entails lengthy journey times. The main roads are good but the lorries and oil tankers plying between Ahvaz, Abadan or Bushir and the interior means congestion is inevitable. Once in the city, the best mode of transport to travel between the sites is by taxi, hiring it for the day to visit Shushtar, Susa and Choga Zanbil unless you have time to investigate and utilise the local bus connections. Another reason is there is a distinct famine of direction markers, both within the city and outside, at all major crossroads and roundabouts; everything seems to conspire to keep you wandering around in circles unless you have the help of a local driver. For such a trip, unless you are travelling February/early March and late October/November when temperatures are moderate, do leave very early in the morning. Remember Strabo's words 'Although Susa is fertile, it has a hot and scorching atmosphere' and there is little shade.

Unless you have business in Ahvaz, you will want to explore the surrounding area. From Shushtar, about one hour's drive away, one could continue to Susa (115km from Ahvaz; about 60km from Shushtar) and then visit Choga Zanbil (where there is a lovely picnic spot nearby). I would suggest this order of visits as you might well feel disappointed with the Susa excavation site, but note that access at Choga Zanbil is now *greatly* restricted. Not to pull any punches: it takes money, time and energy to travel down to this region, and archaeology has to be a passion to feel the effort has been worthwhile.

Accommodation

The nearest hotel to Ahvaz Airport, but at least 20 minutes' drive from the centre, is the two-star **Hotel Oxin** (formerly spelt Oksin; tel: 0611 4442133–4; 52 rooms; US$84 double, US$58 single, including breakfast). The best with regard to a central location and accommodation is the four-star **Fajr Grand Hotel (Astoria)** (Shaikh Abadi Street, 24 'M' Boulevard, tel: 0611

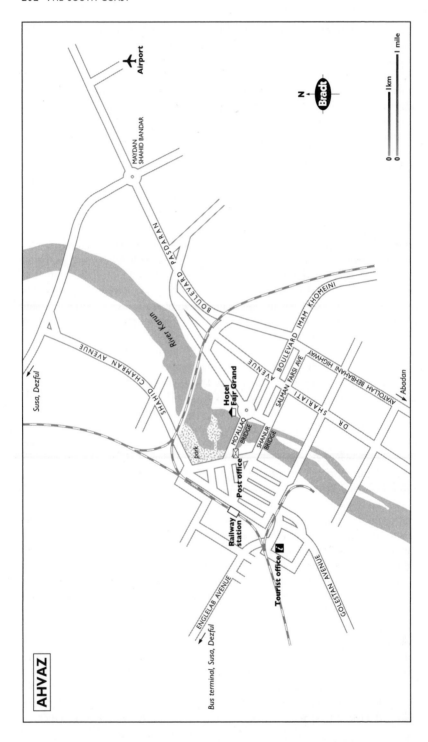

AHVAZ

220091–5; US$103 double, US$69 single, including breakfast) just north of the 'suspension' bridge, with reserved but helpful staff and 139 rooms, coffee lounge and breakfast salon, as well as a restaurant.

SHUSHTAR

Shushtar (approximately 80km north of Ahvaz) was once famous for its exquisite silks and other luxury textiles, one orator comparing the fabrics with 'every flowering plant in spring, the dewy freshness on the cheek of his mistress...' It was founded in Sasanid times and a few remains of the great dam-cum-bridges and canals, constructed by Roman POWs from the 3rd century, survive. One barrage of dressed stone and concrete (**Band-i Qaisar** or Valerian's Bridge) is seen when coming from Dezful. Also visible high up on an outcrop are the ruins of the upper citadel with 18th-century walls on Sasanid foundations, with 3rd-century, rock-cut tunnels to provide agricultural irrigation. Further along the road on an outcrop, with its white sugar-loaf dome and two minarets, is the **Shrine of Khadr-i Zindeh** (the Green Man), reputedly the anonymous friend of Prophet Moses described in the Koran (K18:59–81). Local tradition holds that Hajji Khadr took a boat to Abadan, telling the boatman to accompany him as he walked. The boatman refused but the boat followed, recognising his saintliness, and its anchor is kept as a relic in his shrine at Abadan (see pages 211–12). In Shushtar itself there is the mid-9th-century **Masjid-i Jami**, one of a dozen or so in Iran retaining something of its early 'Arab' plan, evident in the fat piers placed parallel to the enclosing walls. A major rebuilding scheme was completed c1125 when its *minbar* and *mihrab* were probably installed. The minaret with its glazed brick spelling out the word Allah was built in 1419.

The town has a pleasant welcoming atmosphere with young Baktiari men proudly wearing their distinctive 'piano keyboard' black and white jackets, black pillbox *kulah* caps and wide-legged black trousers. On the northern outskirts the road passes over a small modern dam, **Ab-shar**, built on Sasanid foundations. A narrow staircase to one side heads down to impressive archaeological remains of the mill races, drop towers, rock-cut steps and carved rock-channels to the left and right. In the 1930s there were some 40 mills here grinding silica (for glass making), sugar cane and cereals. Only a few mills remain in private hands, and the Sasanid bridge has been destroyed, but the area is being imaginatively landscaped for a park with *chay-khanehs*.

In this region (but its exact location is not locally known) is the site of **Gelalak**, excavated since 1986 by the Iran Cultural Heritage Organisation. Five splendid brick tombs, one with a pottery sarcophagus decorated with vines and garlands, have reportedly been found along with burial finds thought to date from the Parthian period (1st–2nd century CE).

SUSA

Shush, as it is known today, suffered during the Iran–Iraq War, the front line being a mere 4km away. Few scars are now visible and earlier requirements for official authorisation to visit Susa and Choga Zanbil have been dropped.

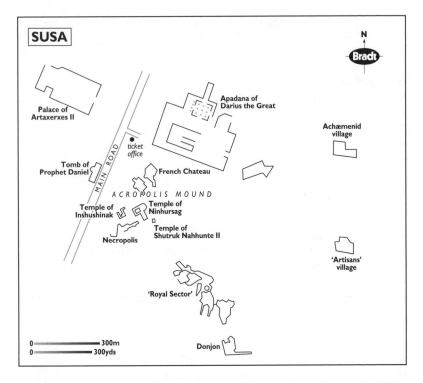

It was a British amateur archaeologist, William Loftus, who in the 1850s first identified Susa with the biblical Shushan and located some Achaemenid palace remains, but Sir Henry Rawlinson persuaded the British Museum that the site had little to offer. So French archaeological teams took over from 1885 and this is why such a wonderful range of artefacts from Susa is displayed in the Louvre Museum, Paris, instead of London. Archaeological work is still continuing. The earliest carbon-14 dating, c4300–3500BCE, was recorded from finds mainly discovered from the Acropolis sector. It was from here that a bronze and copper statue of Queen Napirasu, wife of Untash (r1359–1333BCE) known from Choga Zanbil, was uncovered in 1903 in the **Temple of the Goddess Ninhursag**. Weighing 1,750kg, it stands now headless 1.29m high, inscribed with a warning to anyone causing it damage that 'his name shall become extinct, that his offspring be barren...' Unlike Choga Zanbil, where construction ceased after Nebuchadnezzar's invasion, new buildings at Susa were erected, perhaps to mark the victories of the Susan ruler against the Babylonians, and to exploit a new ceramic technology in making glazed moulded bricks. Then the city declined into obscurity, only to be devastated by the Assyrian armies in c640BCE, in a sacking that continued for over 50 days.

About a century later it was rebuilt by the Achaemenid rulers as their winter capital, and it is this settlement that is associated with the story of Esther and her uncle Mordechai (see page 94), the biblical Shushan king 'Ahasuerus' being either Darius the Great's son and successor, Xerxes, or possibly Artaxerxes, his grandson. It was from Susa that Xerxes set out against Greece and Athens, an action which later provided Alexander the Great with a motive to destroy Persepolis (page 198). Alexander's generals continued to reside here after his death in 323BCE, as did the Parthians, but the final battle between Artanbanus V and the Sasanid leader, Ardashir, in 224CE resulted in great damage. Further destruction followed in c339, possibly linked to Shapur II's persecution of Christians in the town.

Soon after arriving on the site, you'll understand why virtually every photograph of Susa shows the **French chateau** constructed to house the archaeological teams. There is precious little else to see as all the excavation trenches which clearly revealed the foundations of buildings have collapsed, and once again signposting is virtually non-existant. But if archaeology is a passion, it will still be fascinating to try to identify the important locations. The little museum has not yet reopened (as of autumn 2004).

To the left (actually signposted!) is where the most important Achaemenid remains were found, including the huge **apadana** terrace of Darius the Great (d486BCE), measuring 109m^2 with remains of 36 column bases, column shafts and massive animal-headed protone-capitals which once supported the roof beams of Lebanese cedars. In 1970, under the pavement two foundation tablets were located on which Darius acknowledged divine help from Ahura Mazda and described how workers had come from all over the empire – Babylonian brick makers, Assyrian carpenters, Egyptians and others – as indeed did the treasures, such as gold from Anatolia and Afghanistan, lapis lazuli, turquoise and cornelian from Central Asia, silver from Egypt and ivory from Ethopia and India. Your imagination will have to go into overdrive to envisage the colour and ornateness of the original decoration of the ceiling and walls. Any surviving painted plaster and glazed brick panels of pacing animals and motionless military guards and attendants were all removed to Paris, with a few examples going to Tehran. Was it here or in the enormous Palace of Darius (246x155m) to the south where Esther revealed the duplicity of the minister Haman, plotting to kill all the Jews, and was it here where Alexander held the celebrations in 324BCE to mark the wedding of 10,000 of his soldiers to Persian women? Did either of these legendary figures enter through the monumental doorway (40x30m) where the fragmented granite statue of Darius, now in Tehran (page 76), was found in 1972, its quadrilingual inscription recording his victories in Egypt?

The mounds far behind the chateau mark the so-called **'Royal Sector'** where the French found evidence of at least 15 layers of occupation, reaching from 2700BCE up into the Islamic period. Remains of the streets and buildings uncovered dated from the Elamite period, c1900BCE, but this section, especially House A, proved to be rich in Seleucid figurines so this was probably where the Seleucid military garrison was stationed after the death of Alexander the Great. Various Seleucid inscriptions suggest that, as with Dura Europos in eastern Syria, a stadium, gymnasium, archive and law court were constructed along with at least three temples: to Apollo, to the Mesopotamian goddess Nanaya and to Ma, an Anatolian deity. Later this area was occupied in the Sasanid and early Islamic periods, up to the 10th century. To the east in the distance is the **'Artisans' village'** where clear evidence of Seleucid and Parthian workshops, and an early Islamic mosque were discovered. Immediately south of the chateau was the Acropolis where a mass burial place was found and the Elamite temples uncovered. It doesn't seem possible that from such a jumble of lumps and humps, such unique and fascinating artefacts were uncovered in such a marvellous state of preservation. Make a mental note to visit the Louvre in Paris.

Across from the Acropolis, the white sugar-loaf conical roof of the **Tomb of Prophet Daniel** is visible. Many pilgrims throughout the centuries came here, especially during times of drought to pray for rain. This association with water goes back at least to the 12th century when the Seljuk ruler decreed that Daniel's body be put into a (rock) crystal coffin and suspended from the bridge. The present shrine has been carefully restored following serious damage by Iraqi bombardment, and prior to that, as a result of floods in 1869. Visitors are welcome, ladies entering by the left door, men by the right, and currently the main courtyard is decorated with an interesting selection of contemporary wall paintings.

The remains of another Achaemenian palace came to light during ploughing in 1969, across the river to the northwest. Excavation uncovered an **apadana** of 64 columns, probably constructed on the order of Artaxerxes II (d359BCE) because cuneiform inscription on certain column bases on the earlier Apadana of Darius record Artaxerxes's rebuilding works after a fire there in his predecessor's reign.

TO THE NORTHWEST

From here the road northwest goes towards Kirmanshah, Khorramabad and Hamadan (see page 100). Just south of **Dezful**, itself almost obliterated during the Iran–Iraq War, there are two sites of textbook interest to the archaeologist and historian, but a very knowledgeable taxi driver/guide is needed to find both: Choga Mish (about 25km south) and 6km further on the Sasanid site of Jondi Shapur (sometimes spelt Gundeshapur). **Choga Mish** was first excavated in the early 1960s by the University of California. Besides Achaemenid and Parthian remains, the real interest lay in the early Elamite defence walls, platform and private houses, with a drainage system dating from the Proto-Elamite period (c3000BCE). Then the teams found evidence of earlier settlement, perhaps dating back to 7000BCE. Carbon deposits showed a serious fire caused damage around 4500BCE, and shortly afterwards about two-thirds of the site was abandoned, perhaps to be resettled at Choga Zanbil.

Jondi Shapur was a city (re)built to a grid plan to accommodate the many Roman captives taken by the Sasanid shah Shapur I (r240–72), and it was perhaps here that Emperor Valerian died (see pages 180–1), as did Mani in 276, the founder of Manichaeism (page 209). It was a Sasanid winter palace until the first half of the 4th century, but its real reputation came from Shapur's famous hospital, run on Hippocratic lines, which endured until 869 when

Baghdad became the centre for medical science. The city is mentioned in Syriac Christian documents, in the Talmud (as Beth Lapat etc) and by the Byzantine chronicler, Procopius. The numerous surface Islamic pot shards on the site, described in the 1970s as 'indistinct clusters of low mounds', show it had been a cultural centre of some standing, with a strong Nestorian Christian community housing the metropolitan bishop until 1318.

TO THE SOUTHEAST
Choga Zanbil

From Susa/Shush a short drive (30km) due south and then east will take you to Choga Zanbil, the Elamite city of Dur-Untash, dating from around 1340BCE (2km or so before the site is a lovely spot with trees, ideal for a picnic). The site was spotted from the air by oil survey engineers in 1935 and archaeologists were quickly sent in, but main excavation work was delayed until 1950, lasting 12 years and recommencing after 1965. The visitor is immediately struck by the huge brick stepped construction nearly 3,500 years old, surrounded by remains of a vast walled precinct (1,200x800m) originally with seven gates. This ziggurat (105m^2), originally with four, now three, terraces connected by external staircases, was surmounted by a temple dedicated to the god Inshushinak, 'Lord of Shush'; its total height was probably 53m. The similarity with ancient Mesopotamian ziggurats is striking but archaeological work has shown that this at Choga Zanbil has a different construction, erected from the centre outwards; in other words, the highest (now vanished) section was built first and then each of the 'steps' built around to a lower height. All around the lower terrace there are, in every eleventh row or so, bricks inscribed with Elamite cuneiform giving the king's name Untash Napirisha (r1359–1333BCE), who ordered its building. The numerous remains of glazed brick, glass and ivory suggest that the temple was richly decorated on its exterior about two centuries later, and at least one wall (northeast) had moulded glazed tiles in the figure of a huge winged bull, the symbol of Inshushak, guarding the main staircase at ground level. Here and there, especially on the eastern wall, the odd glazed brick is still visible. At ground level there are still signs of the original sacrificial tables and a pit, presumably to catch the blood of the slain animals. A 12th-century BCE bronze tableau found at Susa, now in the Louvre, depicts two naked priests or worshippers kneeling between such tables and trees, preparing a sacrificial offering, one pouring water on to his colleague's outstretched hands. Just next to the brick construction, identified as a sacrificial altar-plinth of Gal and Inshushinak, there is a footprint in the clay pavement, presumably that of an Elamite worker.

Iranian archaeological work from 1965 found yet more evidence that this was not the only temple within the precinct. In all, remains of some eleven sanctuaries were identified along with three palaces, an elaborate water system of a reservoir and channels, tombs and tunnels, but everything suggests that after the invasion of Nebuchadnezzar I (r1125–1104BCE) all building stopped. The final end for this 'holy city' came around 640BCE with Assurbanipal, the Assyrian ruler, devastating the region, proudly recording: 'I levelled the whole of Elam, I deprived its fields of the sound of human voices, the tread of cattle

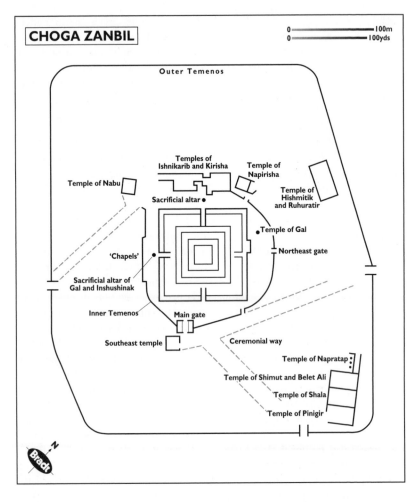

and sheep, the refrain of joyous harvest songs.' Visitors were once permitted to climb up between the terraces and also to see the eastern vaulted tomb chamber, but now all access is blocked with scaffolding.

Haft Tepe

On the way here and on the return to the main Shush–Ahvaz road, about 25km from Choga Zanbil, you will have passed the road to Haft Tepe, where the Iranianian Archaeological Service excavated during 1965–78. The police checkpoint is happy for you to make a detour to this site among the eucalyptus trees and the sugar-cane fields, but nothing remains among the flourishing kitchen gardens. A small museum on the 30ha site, opened in 1973, used to display some of the finds, and the two main 'royal' tombs were accessible, but during a recent visit no-one could be found who knew their exact location. Archaeological work revealed remains of ziggurats (much smaller than Choga

MANI AND MANICHAEISM

Think of St Augustine and one thinks of an early Church father, but he was a Manichaean for at least nine years before his conversion. Mani was born in 216CE in southwest Iran of princely parents. Inspired by revelations when he was 12 and 24 years old, he formulated a religious philosophy which appealed to many in Iran, Central Asia, China and west into Syria, North Africa, Italy and Roman Gaul. To him the essence of all religion was Truth, and that existence was a constant cosmic battle between Good and Evil, the former offering peaceful harmony and the latter constant agitation. The importance of such religious leaders as Buddha, Zoroaster and Jesus was acknowledged, but their roles defined according to Manichaen scriptures. Believers were divided into two groups, the elect and the hearers. The role of the hearers was to assist the elect by performing tasks which would, if carried out by the elect themselves, pollute them, in the manner of Hinayana Buddhism. Circumcision was practised, as was vegetarianism (though hearers could eat meat), and the Sabbath kept, while in devotions St Paul was abhorred.

On his return from India, Mani converted the brother of Shapur I in 242 and from then was greatly honoured at the Sasanid court. At this time Zoroastrianism, although influential, especially in the figure of Kartir the High Priest (see page 194), was not officially the state religion and Mani gained many converts in eastern and northwest Iran. On Shapur's death Mani was still allowed to preach but succeeding shahs, probably persuaded by Kartir, were increasingly hostile. In 276 Mani, accompanied by two disciples, was summoned before Bahram II and arrested, to die horribly in captivity. His followers were persecuted in Iran, and then across the Roman Empire by Diocletian, but pockets of Manichaens survived in Iran and Iraq until the mid-10th century, dying out in Europe some 50 years later but continuing until the 15th century in Central Asia and western China.

Zanbil), temples, palaces with water channels and little bridges and royal tombs. The first settlement appears to date back some 8,000 years and part of the enclosing walls were constructed before the early 3rd millenium BCE, with numerous finds produced c1500–1300BCE, from the Proto–Elamite period according to the archaeologists. The larger of the two **tombs**, measuring about 10x3m, contained 21 skeletons on a raised platform, while the other adjoining it held in all 23 bodies, with nine others bundled unceremoniously in the doorway. Their brick vaulting system caused much excitement in archaeological circles as it pre-dated that at Choga Zanbil, as well as the stone vaulted passages at Bögazköy, Central Turkey and at Ugarit, northern Syria, which were probably constructed a hundred or so years later.

EAST TO IZEH

If time allows, the region east in the direction of Izeh has interesting sites but there are no tourist hotels, so it means setting out very early and then continuing on to Isfahan via Shahr-i Kord on a new fast (but long) road, or returning to Ahvaz for the night. Some 35km out of Masjid-i Soleyman, the centre of the local oilfields, is the Seleucid–Elymaian–Parthian site of **Bard-i Nishandeh**. Its name ('Raised Stone') comes from the huge stone platform or terrace, about 54x91m, reached by staircases to the north (the best preserved), south and east. A cult-niche and crudely carved relief of a king offering a *barsom* of sacred twigs to the fire-altar were found, which supported the theory that a Parthian temple once stood on this terrace, but the numerous Seleucid/Elymaian figurines, pilgrim flasks and coins found under and around this platform strongly suggest it was constructed in pre-Parthian times. To the south of Masjid-i Soleyman, at **Sar-i Masjid**, were found fragments of a larger-than-life-size statue of Herakles (Hercules) with a Nemean lion on a platform surrounded by remains of a porticoed temple, probably Parthian in date, although the defence walls are thought to be older. Most of the finds, including this statue and other beautifully carved heads from the first site (often clearly deliberately smashed, perhaps in post-Sasanid times), were moved in the 1960s to Susa Museum for safe keeping. Also in this region, a new discovery of a Parthian rock carving was made in 1990 at **Shirinau Movri**. Only a few details have been released; it measures about 2x1.45m high and features an enthroned figure with attendants.

Further south lies **Izeh**, with its important Elamite remains, and to its north (via Peyan and Mehrenanis) is **Shami**, where the superb bronze Parthian king or warrior, now in Tehran Archaeological Museum, was found in 1934 by the famous archaeologist, Sir Aurel Stein, on an artificial terrace in a torched building. The scattered fragments of stone slab tombs below suggests it was a royal Elymaian cemetery. Further on in the same direction is Tang-i Butan, where rock reliefs depict four investiture scenes with both Zoroastrian and Heraclian imagery. More accessible (although comfortable, tough shoes are needed as the ground is very stony) is **Kuh-i Farah** (see page 211), 7km northeast of Izeh, which clearly was an open-air sanctuary of deep religious significance for local Elamite rulers.

Izeh

If coming from Bagh-i Malik, about 25km before Izeh, keep an eye out for a cemetery on the left which contains three or more standing **stone lions** thought to mark the graves of Bakhtiari tribal chiefs. Just on the southwest outskirts of Izeh itself is the grotto of **Ishkaft-i** (or **Shikaft-i**) **Salman**. The Izeh municipality has really made an effort here, planting trees, landscaping the hillside, and even installing toilets below the goldfish pond. Inside the shallow cave, two badly eroded **Elamite reliefs** commemorate a local 8th-century BCE ruler, Prince Hanni, and his consort. A large notice provides the full inscription in Farsi, giving Hanni's royal lineage, listing the villages and areas under his authority and dedicating the grotto to an Elamite goddess. High on the right-hand rockface is the carved figure of Hanni and his queen and another, showing, according to some scholars, his chief minister and family, facing the grotto. Purists will dislike the modern plaster animals scattered around but young children adore them.

Kuh-i Farah is straight across town from here. At the far end of the tarmac road is the village, in a hollow at the foot of the hills, now totally deserted after a new dam cut off its water supply. In a recent visit we could find only two series of Elamite rock reliefs out of the six published, but the megaron layout of the village houses, and the evident reuse of old stone columns to support roofs and floors, make the village itself interesting to explore. As one faces the village, the reliefs are to the far right (east). One cluster is high on the limestone rock, with attendants facing into a deep crack, while on the other face a larger regal figure, Prince Hanni again, mirrors the direction. Despite severe erosion, the multiplicity of figures is amazing and some of the figures retain a great amount of fine detail. On another surface the prince is shown seated witnessing animal sacrifices. From here, walk downwards and towards a dried-up stream. You're looking for a massive boulder carrying reliefs on all sides, carved probably in the 8th century BCE. One side depicts a religious procession featuring nearly 200 figures and 21 animals, with a (badly eroded) kingly figure welcoming a cult image carried by four priests. On another side the prince is attended by three rows of courtiers, priests with vessels and harpists. Their hands held at the waist presumably denote a posture of prayer or reverence. Another face of the boulder depicts the priests despatching the sacrificial animals. If the proposed dating for this and all the other carvings is accurate, this place held sacred connotations for the worship of the Elamite deities of Tepti, Tirutur, Napir and others for some 400 years.

Tang (or Hung)-**i Nouruzi** (some 6km north), among other villages in this area, has similar representations, but these are generally thought to have a much earlier date, c1950–1800BCE. Alongside it is a Parthian investiture scene, first attributed to Mithradites I (171–138BCE), but this is no longer accepted. Also in the locality of Izeh, some 30km east, a rock relief depicting four reclining figures was discovered in 1987, but there are no details of its exact location; it is thought to date from the Parthian or Sasanid period.

SOUTH OF AHVAZ
Abadan

Business affairs often take foreigners, but very few tourists, to Abadan (altitude a mere 3m), 150km south of Ahvaz. The heat here is fierce during the summer months (58°C has been recorded) and the humidity can be as high as 99%.

Since at least the 4th century CE its location at the junction of the rivers Tigris, Euphrates, Karun, and the Gulf gave Abadan a significant commercial importance, and in medieval times many came on pilgrimage to visit the **Shrine of Khadr** (the 'Green Man'; see page 203) with its relic of the anchor from a boat which faithfully followed him. The grid layout of the city dates from the early 20th century when the oil and petroleum refineries were constructed and urban expansion went hand in hand with increases in output; it has been described as the Surbiton of Iran. Needless to say it was a prime target for Iraqi bombing during the 1981–9 conflict but there has since been an extensive rebuilding programme.

Getting there
There are daily flights from Tehran to Abadan, two flights a week from/to Mashhad, and one a week from/to Shiraz.

Accommodation
Currently tourist accommodation is limited: the best is **Hotel Carvan-i Sahra** (tel: 0631 3334002–9; fax: 0631 3332107; US$80 double/single), or the **Azadi Hotel** (tel: 0631 330060–9; fax: 0631 3330068).

EASTWARDS ALONG THE COAST
A slight detour along the coast road from Abadan, or on the eastern route from Ahvaz to Bushir via Behbedan, will take you to **Tang-i Sarvak** (54km northwest of Behbehan) where boulders are carved with Elymaian or Parthian reliefs dating from c200BCE onwards. Registers of standing figures attend a figure reclining on a couch, while another rock face depicts a ruler and his family. Elsewhere the representation of a priest standing by a fire-altar is carved alongside depictions of hunting activities.

About 10km northeast of Behbahan is **Arjun**, where a 9th–8th century BCE stone burial chamber was found during construction work for a dam in 1982. Inside was a U-shaped coffin and the remains of a body with grave goods including ornate gold jewellery, a bronze lamp stand among other pieces, and daggers. A magnificent decoratively patterned bronze platter, over 43cm in diameter, is engraved with over a hundred human figures, 66 animals of 33 kinds, trees and rock formations in scenes of banqueting, hunting and harvesting, processions and musical performances. The deceased, according to an inscription on a beautifully worked bracelet in the grave, was the Elamite ruler Hutran, son of Korlash. All these treasures are now in the Tehran Archaeological Museum, but unfortunately not on public display.

Kharg Island
About 31 nautical miles northwest of Bushir is Kharg Island (*Jazir-i Khark*) whose oil-pumping facilities suffered such serious bomb damage during the 1981–9 war that French engineers said the Kharg Fire Brigade was the most experienced in the world. It has a population of some 15,000, mostly employed in the oil industry as 90% of Iran's oil exports pass through these facilities. In the 1950s archaeological finds of bricks with cuneiform inscriptions proved the island was under Elamite authority during the 3rd millennium BCE, but the **two megalithic tombs** found probably date back only to c1000BCE. Thirty years later, a marble figurine, probably of Sumerian manufacture, was uncovered suggesting the importance of the island to maritime trade. Strabo, writing in the 1st century BCE, was probably referring to this island when he reported the remains of a large temple to Apollo with an oracle, and two centuries later Pliny recorded that Kharg was 'sacred to Neptune'; the ruins of

a **Roman temple** may relate to this. On top of this complex a **Sasanid fire temple,** dated by a coin find to the early 4th century, was built, and then a mosque was later constructed. Today there stands a **mosque and shrine** of Mir Mohammed, both surmounted with a 'sugar-loaf' dome, characteristic of the region. Nearby more than 80 rock-cut **tombs** were found, probably carved in Sasanid times for Zoroastrian use, though Christian crosses have been carved on some doorways. Two hypogea for multiple interment were located, which the French archaeologists thought suggested Palmyran merchant occupation. To the west, extensive remains of a **Nestorian monastery** and a **basilica church** were uncovered. The 60 cells, each containing three stone-and-plaster bed-couches, suggest a community of over 150 monks.

The island's strategic position between India and Arabia resulted in occupation by the Portuguese and then the Dutch East India Company after it closed down its Basra operations in 1752. The French then moved in with the blessing of Karim Khan Zand (see page 13) but the island was returned to the Qajar dynasty in 1809, and again in 1857 after a brief British occupation.

Bushir

It is stiflingly hot and humid here in the summer months. Bushir (also spelt Bandar-i Bushehr) first became important as a port when Nadir Shah Afshari made it the principal naval station in 1734. Some 25 years later the English East India Company set up its 'factory' (headquarters) here after losing its Bandar-i Abbas base. Control then passed to an Arab family until 1857 when it came under Qajar authority. Its current importance as a military establishment means personal exploration is somewhat restricted, and so much was destroyed in the severe 1806 earthquake. However, the old quarter still has good examples of traditional architecture with wooden doors and overhanging balconies with lattice windows that allow the ladies of the household to view the streets below without being seen. There is a beach, and swimming facilities for men.

Getting there
As Bushir is fast becoming the main centre for the North Pass oil development project (on- and offshore), there is a daily flight from Tehran and bus services from the major cities.

Accommodation
There is a limited choice of hotels, but construction is under way. Currently the best is **Hotel Delva**, on Raesali Delvari Avenue (tel: 0771 252627; approximately US$55 double/single); the centrally located two-star **Hotel Reza** (tel: 0771 27171; 40 rooms) on Imam Khomeini Avenue; reservations may be made through the Homa Hotel in Shiraz (see page 169); also the **Sadra Tourism Hotel**, two-star, on Vali-e Asr Avenue (tel: 0771 252346).

Things to see and do
The Anglican Church (*Kelisa-i Engelisi*), founded in 1819, is now in the hands of the local Armenian community. The British Cemetery, located 7km south

of the city at Bahmani, has apparently been badly damaged and desecrated since the Islamic Revolution, but no doubt the local authorities are planning to rectify matters. A few kilometres further on are the remains of the original port of **Rishahr**, which got its name either from the Elamite word meaning 'great' (*rishair*) or from a Sasanid fortress here, Rev-Ardashir – named after the first Sasanid ruler – which was later built over by the Portuguese and Safavid occupiers. Elamite remains have been found: there are foundations of a town near to the original port and about 14km away (4km from **Sabzabad**) the site of an Elamite temple has been identified. French archaeologists concluded the main period of settlement was c2500–1200BCE, and possibly a millennium earlier.

Driving from Bushir towards Shiraz via Qazerun gives the opportunity of seeing a series of rock-cut caves on the old medieval road which have intrigued several archaeologists, who have suggested they functioned as Christian or possibly Buddhist monastic dwellings. **Chehelkhaneh** with, as its name suggests, some 40 caves (*chehel:* forty), is situated some 17km northwest of Borazjan (itself 70km from Bushir). South is **Qalat-i Haydari**, where there is another cluster of caves with intersecting passages, and rectangular and 'domed' chambers on two levels. In the early 1970s, some 5km before Chehelkhaneh, the remains of an Achaemenid palace (Sang-i Siah) was found. Its layout (the closeness of the column bases) and the use of black and white limestone suggested it was constructed during the reign of Cyrus the Great c529BCE, but abandoned after his death. Nearby on the large Tepe Mor (also known as Tal-i Mor) traces of an Elamite fortress were located.

FURTHER ALONG THE COAST ROAD

Almost due south from Shiraz (though there is no direct road) is **Bandar-i Taheri** (220km southeast of Bushir) where British archaeologists excavated the medieval port of Siraf for over nine years from 1966. The fishing port of **Kangan** is 45km to the northwest.

According to the histories, **Siraf** was an important port trading with India and China, and by 950 its population approximated that of Shiraz. However, a severe earthquake in 977 caused many to leave, and by 1200 most of the trade had been tranferred to the eastern port of Qais. The final report describing the excavations on this enormous 250ha (620 acres) site and its finds is still in preparation, but the quantities of Chinese ceramic shards uncovered in the first season of work proved the accuracy of the medieval historians. It was discovered that the large ruined mosque noted in 1930 had been built on top of a large Sasanid fort constructed shortly after 804, and which was then altered some five times before the site was abandoned c1263. Nearby, a six-roomed *hamam* with hypocaust system had been in operation, along with the workshops and warehouses of a bazaar, some clearly involved in metalworking. Remains of some 30 pottery kilns were found with their shelf-support systems still largely intact. Streets with residential buildings, often incorporating a well for drinking water, were also identified, and a large cemetery with 9th and 10th-century tombs was located.

Kish

From Bandar-i Taheri there is a good road eastwards along the coast to the island of Kish (*Jazir-i Kish*). In the past, like Hormuz (see pages 218–20), it had a lively trading community over ten times as large as now, and was known for its pearls and beautiful women. The late shah had a large villa with an airstrip, and desalination plants (for drinking water) constructed here, and this infrastructure remains the basis of the recent development of this Free Trade Zone. The Kish Free Zone Organisation (KFZO, formerly KIDO) which answers only to the president, is currently targeting foreign companies for investment, promoting the island as an offshore banking centre, and a number of the official regulations (eg: partnership with an Iranian representative) were removed in spring 2000. Many Iranians come here to shop, as, reputedly, the prices are lower than in Dubai, or to play in the newly opened aquapark.

A visa waiver system operates for foreigners wishing to visit Kish (see page 33), but this is not valid for further mainland travel.

Getting there

Flights are generally twice a week from Shiraz and more frequently from Tehran, but advance booking is essential. From May 2004, Air France was offering cheap return flights to Kish. There are daily or more frequent sailings (depending on weather) from Bushir, Bandar-i Abbas and Bandar-i Lingeh.

Accommodation

Until recently, hotel or villa accommodation for foreigners was excessively expensive (approximately US$250), eg: five-star **Ana Hotel** (tel: 0764 442410-4); five-star **Parsian Hotel** (tel: 0764 24991–50), but as of spring 2000, it was possible to find hotel rooms for US$50–60 a night, including the **Kish Grand Hotel**.

Things to see and do

Reporting Air France's cheap return flights to Kish, Simon Calder of *The Independent* (May 1, 2004; Travel section) noted that Kish's main attraction, as listed on the web (www.kfzo.com), was a stranded Greek steamship, beached since 1966; internet users are advised that 'Watching the sunset behind the Greek ship is an unforgettable and everlasting memory'. Who needs Persepolis, when Kish offers the visitor this?

The main attraction is of course the duty-free shopping; if you are going inland from Kish, check out the 'voucher' procedures for the (temporary) importation of goods. Otherwise, perhaps the turtle colony and scuba diving (men only) may be of interest. Although it is very cheap to dive here, diving equipment is not easy to find on the island; windsurfing, jetskis and waterskiing are also available. The facilities of the aquapark are likewise limited for women. There is, however, a designated beach where mixed bathing is allowed for foreigners.

In the northern corner of the island, between Saffeyn and the New Jetty, there are a few remains of the palace and fort complex built in the 11–12th century when, according to the chronicler Benjamin of Tuleda, Kish was an important and prosperous trading port with large Jewish and Indian communities. In 1135 the ruler of Kish felt strong enough to attack Aden, and 15 years later it is known that his navy consisted of 50 vessels, each capable of carrying 200 men. Its wealth attracted the attention of the ruler of Hormuz who seized the island in 1229, only to divert traffic away. There was a brief period of prosperity from 1292 when Kish became a major port for the Il-Khanid regime (see page 11) but again Hormuz acted to stop trade in 1330, and the island never recovered. An archaeological survey in 1974 recorded a number of cisterns and kilns, while surface finds of 13th–14th-century Chinese pottery shards revealed a busy trade with medieval China. In the early 1990s **archaeological excavations** in the Harireh sector uncovered evidence of workshops, a mosque and a bathhouse from the medieval (or later) period, and plotted the coastal location of numerous man-made loading bays, with rock-cut steps to serve the trading dhows in these waters.

Probably the fort and mosque at Bandar-i Langeh and the traditional *dhow* building yards at Bandar-i Kong, both on the south coastline, will prove far more interesting than Kish.

Qeshm Island

Some 150km further east along the coast, the large Island of Qeshm (1330km²), with a population of 55,000, comes into view, but the landing point is on the far eastern tip of the island, easily reached by ferry from Bandar-i Abbas less than an hour away. The vast resources of natural gas here has led the government to promote the island as an Industrial Free Zone since 1990, and again, unless one has business here, there is apparently little to attract foreign tourists. In the 1970s, preliminary archaeological surveys recorded an Achaemenid and Sasanid settlement and for centuries many cargo ships docked here for supplies and cargo, as recorded by Marco Polo. Although the tourist potential for watersports, diving and recreation on the island has remained largely undeveloped, there is excellent birdwatching to be had on the island, justifying a day trip here.

Bandar-i Abbas

As with the rest of the south coast of Iran, the best time to visit Bandar-i Abbas (population 500,000, altitude 3m) is in the winter months, November to April. Summer temperatures often soar over 45°C with the humidity of a Turkish bath; 18th-century English sailors used to moan that 'there was but an Inch-deal betwixt Gombroon [Bandar-i Abbas] and Hell'. The heat and humidity explains why a blind eye is turned to local women having bare feet. Bandar-i Abbas was the name given to the medieval port of Suru in 1615 by the Safavid shah Abbas I (d1629) after ejecting the Portuguese from their forts here and on Hormuz Island, ending both their occupation and their strategic and commercial control of the Straits of Hormuz. He saw the possibility of circumventing the Ottoman embargo on Persian silk passing through its empire by sending bales by sea, as well as the potential of pearl-fishing, and it was probably this commercial connection which led the English in particular to refer to Bandar-i Abbas as 'Gombroon' (Turkish for customs house), a name later given to the high-quality soft paste porcelainware from Iran so avidly collected in 19th-century Europe. A preliminary archaeological survey undertaken near Tiab, southeast of the present city, shows this trade had a long history; over 2,000 sherds of fine 13th–14th-century Chinese porcelain from the site are now at the Ashmolean Museum, Oxford.

Work on port facilities in 1964-7, and then the setting up of the Iranian naval headquarters in 1973 meant increased business, and an international deep-water port was constructed in 1976-86. Now Bandar-i Abbas is the main port of Iran with daily passenger sailings to Dubai. The traditional dhow boats can still be seen in the old port, plying their trade between India, Zanzibar and Dubai, carrying tyres, oil drums, children's bicycles, spices and bales of cloth.

Getting there

There are daily flights from Tehran and others from Isfahan, Yazd, Kirman; there are also international flight connections with Dubai and Sharjeh. Daily sailings link with Hormuz, Qeshm and Kish, and also Sharjeh. Intercity bus connections run between the major cities, such as Shiraz and Kirman, but allow at least eight hours' travel time. The road from Shiraz and the north (1,050km to Tehran) is good, but as it is the main route from the coast to the interior there is a constant stream of lorries and tankers from Gahkum and the coast, a reminder that Iran relies heavily on imported manufactured goods and raw materials.

Accommodation

The best available is the **Homa Hotel** (IranAir; tel: 0761 553080–9; fax: 0761 551732) on Imam Khomeini Boulevard in the western outskirts. Notionally five-star, it has 180 rooms (singles are broom-cupboards), a restaurant, breakfast salon and bank, all totally lacking sparkle and enthusiasm. The restaurant staff remind the visitor of ageing 'family retainers' but a sense of humour lurks below the surface. Many Iranian families come to Bandar-i Abbas in the winter months and over *Nou Rouz*, so prior booking is strongly recommended.

Things to see and do

It has to be said, there is not a multiplicity of tourist attractions in the city; even in 1622 one Portuguese diplomat described it as 'more of an emporium than a town', while his English counterparts remarked that the town's fame rested on its *panj* ('five') or punch, made of arak (date alcohol), lemon juice, sugar, nutmeg and water, which 'occasions a Guddiness in the Head, Feavers and Fluxes, and is so corrosive that some, who have drunk immoderately of it, died'. The much-vaunted **Hindu Temple** is a small stone and concrete building set back from the main boulevard, but as it is no longer a functioning place of worship, all the temple ornaments, statuary and images have been removed. It was built during the 19th century to serve a large Indian community working for the English East India Company. Its 'factors' or merchants had withdrawn from Bandar-i Abbas after the fall of the Safavid dynasty c1735, but they returned in 1793 to administer the port and Hormuz on behalf of the ruler of Oman who had seized control. And as for the little **Masjid-i Khadr** ('Green Mosque') in the grounds of the Homa Hotel, it has been heavily repaired inside and outside with a new glass and metal-frame extension.

However, the thriving, bustling bazaars of Bandar-i Abbas are fun, offering a very different range of goods imported mainly from the Far East; sun-specs are very good buys. On sale also are the distinctive red cloth or leather facemasks and heavily (machine-) embroidered tight-legged trousers worn by women in the region. Offering different but just as colourful and fantastic produce is the small fishmarket at the western end of the coastal promenade.

Hormuz Island (Jazir-i Hormoz)

It's an enjoyable half-day trip from Bandar-i Abbas is to Hormuz, about 18km from Bandar-i Abbas and 85km from Oman. Today it has a population of about 4,000 but, in times of political upheaval and military confrontation, ten times this number have sought temporary refuge on the island, despite the limited fresh-water supplies; today water is piped over. If you have a torch, take it with you, as local children amuse themselves by damaging the electrical wiring in the fortress. (Finding a toilet is very difficult.)

Getting there

By fibre-glass speedboat from the quay (**Iskel-i Qadim**), in the town centre by the bazaar, the death-defying trip taking approximately 20 minutes, though there is no operation during bad weather. A certain level of athleticism is required to clamber in and out of the boat, and don't bother looking for lifejackets. For groups, it should be possible, with prior notice, to hire a *dhow*, but the sailing time will be much longer. To gain access to the pier itself, entry tickets have to be purchased from the roadside kiosk and surrendered at the gate opposite. Then it's a matter of chaotic bargaining on the pier. Hiring a boat for the journey over to the island costs approximately 60,000 rials (absolute maximum 13 people); otherwise join the crowd and pay the boatman approximately 10,000 rials each (US$1); the return fee is generally higher. Back in Bandar-i Abbas, on landing there is a notional customs check, ladies exiting to the left, men to the right.

Things to see and do

The **Portuguese Sea Fort** is located on the north tip (far left) of Hormuz Island, about 15 minutes' walk away from the ferry landing. To gain access, keep the castle walls on your left and walk past the loading quays; if the main entry door is locked, retrace your steps to the metal gates immediately by the loading sheds to find the Iran Cultural Heritage Organisation representative, who will be delighted to show you round. The fortress was built from local pink, brown and green coral shortly after the island was taken by the

Portuguese military hero, Alfonzo Albuquerque, in 1515, quickly taking advantage of the severe Safavid military defeat at Chaldiran (see page 122) to maintain and extend Portuguese control of the sea-trading routes from India and the East Indies to Europe. Portuguese military history tells of an eight-hour battle by a few hundred soldiers against 30,000 islanders and defence troops, but Persian records state Albuquerque took the island by bribery and treachery. The Ottoman navy tried but failed to seize the island in 1550, but after Shah Abbas I took control of Suru and renamed it Bandar-i Abbas in 1615, it was only a matter of time before the Portuguese were pushed out of Hormuz in 1622, for in the 1580s only seven or eight soldiers defended the castle. As the English had assisted the shah in this action, the fort and all of the 40km²-odd island, along with 50% of the customs dues, were ceded to the East India Company, but the gradual collapse of Safavid authority, advancing rebel Afghan forces, and changes to the customs levies led 18th-century European merchants to move trading activities further west to Bushir. It was not until 1868 that the Qajar shah regained authority, but it was too late, for the newly opened Suez Canal was causing most shipping companies to reroute their vessels. By 1893, life on the island was described by the British consul as 'miserable', with just 200 residents. Matters improved from the mid-1960s, when Bandar-i Abbas received development funds, and it later became the naval headquarters.

Originally the fortress was completely surrounded by water, but now the sea laps around less than half of the walls. By the main entrance are the **prison dungeons** but you need the torch to explore. A walk across the main courtyard leads to the **underground church**, whose cross-groined vaults are supported on great columns; the altar must have stood where the entry now is. From here it is a short walk to the splendid **underground cistern,** built with an inner walkway around it. It's easy to imagine off-duty Portuguese soldiers sitting, talking, smoking and drinking here in the delicious cool. There is no springwater on the island to speak of, so rainwater would have filtered through the coral stone to collect in this and other cisterns throughout the fortress. Other than a remains of a tower (now one floor) with windows and cannons, there are just the ramparts left to explore.

From the loading quays, the walk along the sea walls passes a pink-stone building with a pseudo-Portuguese frontage. Now an **army post** (so no taking photographs inside the gate), it was built as a residence for Mohammed Reza Shah. The commanding officer gently and sadly showed me the paintings on the exterior wall, among which are portraits of his close relatives killed while undertaking the Hajj to Mecca in the 1980s. (If you wish to explore the interior of the island, ask – and take – his advice.) Further on are fishermen's houses with nets placed ready for the evening fishing, and children playing table tennis on rusting metal doors. Some archaeological excavation was undertaken in 1977 during which 14th- to 17th-century pottery kilns and also shards, including Chinese export ware, came to light. It is known that the famous 14th-century Arab geographer, Ibn Battuta, stayed in the *Ziyaret-i Khadr*, located in the main cemetery alongside the *Ziyaret-i Mollah*, but little remains. The whole island has a desolate air, having been neglected for many decades, but that said, the municipality is installing a new sewage system and constructing roads (for non-existent cars), so this investment should benefit the community.

The road north from Bandar-i Abbas leads directly to Kirman but, as mentioned above, this is a very busy road, especially the first 150km climbing up into the mountains, crowded with lorries and tankers. But this does take you past **Sirjan** (see page 236) where a British team found the remains of a Sasanid palace in the 1970s. Less tortuous, and with almost as dramatic scenery, is the road east towards Minab and then north via Kahnuj and Sabzvaran. The shelters for the Baluchi migratory families in this region are very distinctive, reminiscent of **reed huts** in the Iraqi delta area. Tall reeds are bent over to form a long barrow vault and covered with palm fronds, so making a shaded but well-ventilated shelter.

En Route to Yazd and Kirman

COMING TO YAZD FROM THE SOUTHWEST

From the crossroads at Surmaq, the road to the northeast goes through **Abarku** (also spelt Aburqeh, literally 'On the Mountain') 45km away. The town had been a famous textile and trading centre in medieval times, but it never recovered from being devastated by rebel Afghan troops in the early 18th century. In the centre of town is the Masjid-i Jami with a classic four-ivan groundplan, probably established in the 14th century when its 'baroque' plaster *mihrab* (1338) was installed, although the domed prayer chamber could be from 12th-century Seljuk times. The town still has a very run-down air, though 50 years ago architectural historians began clamouring that urgent repairs should be made to a number of once-beautiful 14th-century tombs here before it was too late to save them. In particular, archaeologists pointed to tombs such as the Mausoleum of Pir-i Hamza Sabz Push, with its lovely Il-Khanid *mihrab*, and the 1315 square tomb of al-Hasan ibn Kaikhusraw (also known as Gonbad-i Taws) with its decorated interior. One mausoleum, one of the earliest tomb towers surviving in Iran, is on the hillside just to the south as you leave Abarku for Yazd. Small, austere and (over-) restored, this octagonal Gonbad-i Ali was built for a local warlord, 'the illustrious, the pure, the happy … Amid al-Din Shams al-Dawla' and his wife, by their son in 1057, according to the brick inscription around the exterior. The area is often litter-strewn, but there is a superb view across the plateau from which the local ice houses can easily be spotted.

If you are keen on good vernacular architecture, do examine the layout and arrangement of an ice house *(yakhchal)*. There is a fine example here at the entrance of Abarku, coming from Isfahan or, if this is not convenient, a restored one near Azadi Square in Kirman. As with the cisterns and wind towers, these are made of fired brick and probably those that have survived are no earlier than the 19th century in date. The basic plan is that of a large brick dome-chamber set deep into the ground, with a single door for access. Outside, there should be the remains of a long high mud-brick wall facing south to keep the lower dome section in shade. Beneath, there may still be signs of shallow beds along the wall. In winter months, 15–25cm of water was let in to flood these beds and freeze overnight. The ice was then broken up

221

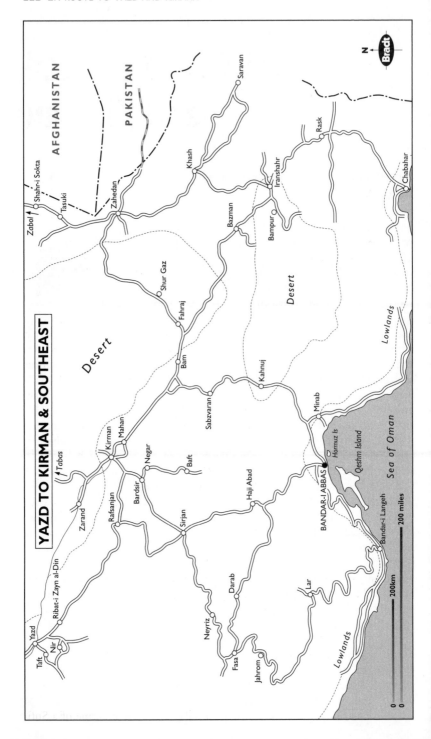

YAZD TO KIRMAN & SOUTHEAST

into blocks, for storage among straw in the chamber for the summer. Simple but very effective.

After the last roundabout on the very outskirts of Abarku (in the direction of Yazd) there is a huge brick complex set back to the right (notionally south). This was the family house of an MP who served in a pre-revolutionary parliament, and nearby there is a small fort with thick corner towers. The late 19th- and early 20th-century residence, known locally as Amidsalar, is ruined; the ground floor has a large high central room surrounded by small chambers, while a well-worn exterior staircase at the back gives access to the first floor. To get into the fort, known by the same name, it is possible to scramble around the walls but, as its entrance is on the other side, it's quicker and easier to return to the main road and continue to the next (tarmaced) turning, which takes one almost directly to the entry gate. It is well worth exploring; you'll find the latrines, stables, bread ovens and a mosque, as well as the corner watchtowers.

In the south of the town is Masjid-i Birun near the cemetery. It has a two-ivan plan with a domed sanctuary, which could be earlier in date than its (ruined) Timurid minaret and repair work. The prayer chamber area was heavily restored in the 18th century.

The road to Yazd goes through a 'desert' area with a salt lake lying to the south; there has been systematic planting of camel thorn and other desert shrubs here in an attempt to prevent the spread of the saline earth. Approaching Yazd, between the two chains of hills, (especially if you are flying in during daylight hours) you will see lines of holes, like ruined giant anthills coming from the hillside across the land. These are inspection holes marking *qanat*s or **underground channels** which brought water to irrigate the fields. The knowledge and skill needed to locate the right spot in the hills to tap into the water table, to angle and construct the tunnels to obtain the correct flow, beggar belief. Every year the *qanat*s were checked for repairs, removal of debris etc and although modern irrigation systems are fast taking over, just occasionally one still sees a windlass device resting on top of an inspection hole.

Taft lies about 26km southwest of Yazd and the drive there passes through wonderfully coloured rocks. Persian paintings of the 15th and 16th centuries often depicted landscapes with turquoise, green, pink, red, and purple rock formations which some scholars have argued were based purely on artistic fantasy, but seeing these colourings makes the observer wonder. Taft has an important Timurid building, the late 15th-century Mausoleum and Khanaqeh of Shah Khalilullah and the adjoining Masjid-i Shah Vali built by the sister of Safavid shah Tahmasp. The famous Sufi mystic, Ni'matollah Vali Kirmani (see pages 237–8) was responsible directly or indirectly in persuading the Timurid provincial governor to allocate four years of tax revenue to this complex, and since then it has always been important for Sufis of the Ni'matollah order. Later embellishments were paid for by the sister of Shah Tahmasp in the 16th century.

In the 14th century the Sufi movement evidently had a great following in this area as, some 30km from Nir at **Bidakhavid**, 57km southwest of Yazd, there are two shrines facing each other. One is the mosque-shrine of a Sufi

SUFISM

At the heart of Sufism is the belief that within everybody is a spark of the Divine, the Creator, and that through dedicated ritual and practice, this spark may be ignited so that the individual becomes at one with the Divine, perhaps for a mere split second, perhaps longer. (The word 'Sufi' is traditionally thought to come from the *suf* or woollen robe worn by devotees during their meetings.) Today there are still a number of Sufi orders or fraternities; arguably the most famous in the West is the Mevlani, known popularly as the Whirling Dervishes. Following the ideas of the 13th-century mystic, Jalal al-Din Rumi, buried in Konya, Turkey, the ritual practised by this Sunni Sufi order is characterised by devotees moving in a large circle around a room while spinning clockwise to music arranged in four musical movements, each representing the seasons of the year. There is also the Naqshbandi fraternity (which, incidently, has a keen following in Peckham, South London), again among the Sunni community, which has no esoteric ritual but dedicates all actions and deeds to the Divine. The ritual may be just the rhythmic voicing of the name of Allah, as it is with one order in Deptford, Kent. The aim is the same, the sublimation of the material self and ego, so freeing the spirit so that the divine spark may ignite.

Historically the government and the established clergy have often expressed hostility towards the Sufi orders because the fraternities were often organised as lodges separate and disassociated from the mosques, and their *pirs* (masters) were rarely reticent in pointing out any social injustices, worldliness and sham devotions of the *ulama*. Also, women were often given greater access within these 'unofficial' circles, which could include visiting dervishes who had given up their home and family life to show others the 'way'. One of the greatest mystics was Rabi'a of Basra (d801) who caused an outcry among the *ulama* when she announced: 'I have ceased to exist and have passed out of self. I exist in God and am altogether His.'

shaikh, Taj al-Din Binyaman, identified and dated (1379) by his elaborately carved tombstone and consisting of three elements: a courtyard, a mosque and the tomb. As the shrine is a little larger than the mosque, it seems likely that this was originally built as a *khanaqeh* or meeting place for his disciples, and then became his tomb after his death. The other complex is the Masjid-i Jami which possesses the unusual upper gallery arrangement in the square-domed prayer hall, as seen in Yazd (see pages 227–8). Its stone *mihrab* is decorated with Koranic verses (3:38–40) and dated 1437, perhaps marking the completion of the building works.

Another half-day trip from Yazd is to **Meybod**, about 50km northwest, which still has remains of its mud-brick fort that once protected the old caravan route and the town itself. As the name suggests, this used to be a strong

Zoroastrian centre (*moybed*: priest), but today Meybod's chief claim to fame is as a production centre for domestic pottery incorporating 'traditional' patterns and colouring. It also possesses a 15th-century Masjid-i Jami (in the mid-1970s, the mosque owned an historic double-cloth *zilu* floor-covering with a woven date corresponding to 1405). The building itself lacks decoration but the plain white plaster allows the pleasing proportions to be seen, especially those in the winter prayer hall. In this region is also **Bundar Abad**, 35km northwest of Yazd, with its 14th-century complex honouring the Sufi Shaikh Taq al-Din Dada Mohammed (d1301) buried here in 1321. It has one of Iran's handful of tiled *minbars*, patterned with eight- and 12-star motifs, probably made and installed at the same time as a carved marble panel, in 1473.

This visit could be combined with one to **Chak Chak**, some 50km northeast of Yazd (turning at Hoseyn Abad), to visit the shrine of Banu Pars, dedicated to the goddess Anahita. Only during the very crowded five-day festival during June is there a bus service from Yazd; at other times you should take (and retain for return) a taxi from Yazd. Local and intercity buses do travel from Yazd to Tabas, an historic town devastated by a recent earthquake, but there is a 4km gravel track snaking from this main road between the hills towards Chak Chak, and from the parking area there are numerous flights of steps up before reaching the small grotto-shrine. This is no living village, rather a desolate collection of houses and communal kitchens to accommodate pilgrims. Only a few families look after the place, including a reticent shrine attendant who ensures men enter wearing a (provided) head covering, and all visitors remove their shoes. The shrine itself is understated, consisting of a grotto housing an ancient *chenar* (Oriental plane) tree. The doors and walls date only from the early 1960s but it is known that pilgrims have come here in June since 1626, if not earlier. According to Islamic chronicles, this was the place where a daughter of the last Sasanid shah, Yazdigird III (d651), pursued by the invading Arabs, begged for help. Desperately thirsty, she was offered a bowl of milk, only for it to be overturned by a cow before she could drink (Anahita was traditionally offered bull sacrifices). Terrified for her life, she prayed that the rock face would open up for her and she disappeared into it; similar stories are connected with the shrine near Rayy (see page 81) and further afield in Maaloula near Damascus, Syria, at the grotto of St Tikla.

YAZD

The town (altitude 1,215m, 677km from Tehran) has long been associated with Zoroastrianism and the production of textiles. It fell to the Arab invaders in 642 but the Zoroastrian community was strong here until the late 17th century. There were still plenty left in the 19th century, when official persecution caused many to flee to India or to Tehran, where the foreign diplomatic embassies offered more protection. Today, Zoroastrians form less than 10% of the town's population; in 1995 there were an estimated 12,000 or less in the city, mainly located in the Pusht-i Khan Ali quarter. When Marco Polo visited in 1272, noting its fine textiles and its strategic location on trade routes from India and Central Asia, this 'Good and Noble city' was walled, but undoubtedly today he

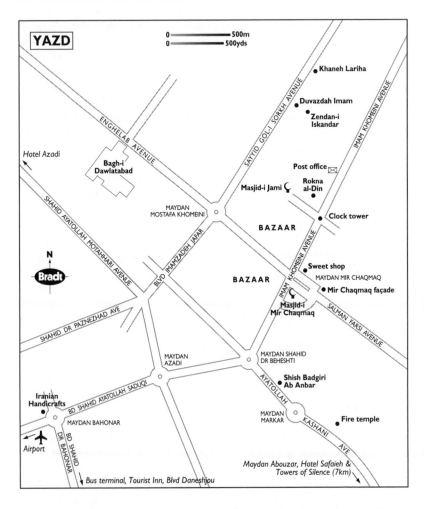

would get hopelessly lost in the confusion of ring roads and roundabouts. Today Yazd is slowly emerging from an economic depression affecting the whole province, an evident concern to President Khatami who was raised here.

Getting there

There are at least two flights daily to Yazd from Tehran (one-way: 186,000 rials or approximately US$22), and two a week from Mashhad. Yazd is also served by frequent intercity buses. The 'express' train from Tehran to Yazd entails a journey time of over 12½ hours, with an additional five hours or so from Yazd to Kirman.

Accommodation

The foremost hotels are the recently enlarged (in 2003, 90 rooms) four-star **Safaieh** (tel: 0351 8242812–5; fax: 0351 8242811; US$110 double (new rooms), US$90 single) on Timsar Fallahi Street, off Ayatollah Kashani Avenue. Arranged on a motel system with a luggage pick-up service for groups, the grounds are pleasant but the irrigation channels mean mosquitoes. The restaurant building situated to the right of the reception area is one of the best locally. The other smaller, notionally four-star hotel is **Azadi**, formerly Enghelab (Bonyad; tel: 0351 5254111, 5253111; fax: 0351 5256444; US$70 double, US$50 single) on Jomhuri Islami Boulevard (an extension of Shahid Ayatollah Motahheri Avenue). One wing of rooms has been totally refurbished with new bathrooms and room fitments, and work has begun on upgrading the few 'motel' units before moving to the other wing. The staff here are more visible and helpful. There is also the three-star **Tourist Inn** (tel: 0351 47221–2; fax: 0351 47222; 38 rooms; US$75 double & single) on Daneshjou Boulevard.

Things to see and do

Although it does not possess any royal monuments like those at Persepolis, Shiraz and Isfahan, Yazd is renowned for its **vernacular buildings**, including ice houses, water cisterns, domestic houses and spectacular wind towers (*badgirs*) constructed to channel breezes down into the building to cool the atmosphere in summertime. Such wind catchers were once common in cities and towns throughout the Middle East, but few now survive as new buildings are installed with expensive air conditioners. The idea is simple: a brick tower is built – anything from 30cm high upwards – with one or more openings at the top and directional vents to catch the prevailing wind. The air is channelled into the building, either at ground floor or at a lower level, and perhaps passed over a small pool and fountain to cool it further before travelling through other rooms.

Yazd boasts the tallest *badgir* in the world at 33m, gracing the (former) governor's pavilion in the **Bagh-i Dawlatabad**; entry is 2,000 rials. Although the garden is associated with a 1718 endowment which included the construction of a school, bath, *caravanserais* and *qanats* over 60km in length, the layout is one typically associated with a late 18th-century date. A long avenue of cypresses leads down to the main building (now private property), but the pavilion on the right after entering the garden is open to the public. This small, two-storeyed building has recently been carefully repaired. Both of the main chambers had fountains, each filling a large stone basin which fed others and also reflected the colourful window glass. If you walk through to the back room, you can look up the 'chimney' to see the wind-venting system.

The traditional water cistern (*ab-anbar*) also employed wind towers. One well-known Yazd example is the **Shish Badgir Ab Anbar** ('Six Wind-Towered Cistern') located on the north side of Shahid Dr Bihesti Avenue (the extension of Ayatollah Kashani Avenue) behind the shops. It is no longer used by the community, so to prevent rubbish being thrown in, a padlocked gate has been erected.

An interesting cluster of historic buildings lies further north around the **Masjid-i Jami,** which was founded by the local Seljuk commander in 1119 over a ruined Sasanid fire temple, and largely rebuilt during the 14th century.

Visitors to the mosque are immediately struck by the disproportionately high minarets over the entrance, which render the (double) dome almost insignificant. These are the first indication of 14th-century work, along with the 1324–8 entrance vestibule decorated with numerous plaques recording local decrees, taxes and endowments. Most of the splendid ceramic patterning in the main prayer hall beyond was put in place 40 or so years later. The work is worth looking at, whether for the geometric strapwork in turquoise against a brick surface with intricately cut and moulded plaster infills, or the 'mosaic' jigsaw panels of the magnificent 1375 *mihrab* – although each year it seems more replacement tile pieces have been inserted. The prayer hall has an unusual gallery arrangement (for women?) occasionally seen in other late-14th-century mosques, but here the heavy piers and vaulting system disperse the weight, allowing the side walls to be pierced by windows, bringing shafts of light into the chamber. On the right is a large winter prayer hall built in the 16th century by the Safavid architect Sa'd ibn Mohammed Kaduk. The bare whitewashed walls make the beautiful proportions and transverse vaulting fully apparent. In the courtyard (104x99m) there are steps on this side, leading down to an underground room with a disused *qanat*.

Leaving by the same entrance, take the second left in the parking area and nearby, on your immediate right, is the small entrance into the popular shrine **Imamzadeh Rokna al-Din**, dating to 1325. Little, but enough, remains of the original complex of school and library that was once renowned for its mechanical sciences. Its minarets were surmounted with automata such as a bird which turned to face the sun, and chroniclers described a huge circular wall calendar whose rings and sections constantly moved to show the passage of time. The exterior still retains some exquisite detail which is easily overlooked. Inside the gloomy, single-domed chamber housing the cenotaph is a mass of low-relief plasterwork carved and painted (and originally gilded) in strong 14th-century Central Asian style, akin to the Samarkand and Shahri Sabz architecture in Uzbekistan. The high walls are decorated with plaster moulding in blind niche forms of varying size in rows, and panels of plaited Kufic calligraphy. Huge teardrop medallions in plaster embellish the dome interior (diameter 12m) and underneath is the silver-gilt grille protecting the cenotaph. At certain (undefined) times, groups of women come to pay their respects, in which case male visitors are requested to view the interior from the doorway.

Continue along this alley, crossing the modern *Hoseyniye*h space (if in doubt bear left) and eventually you will reach **Zendan-i Iskandar** ('Alexander's Prison') tucked back in the same open space as the **Duvazdah Imam** ('12 Imams'). Safavid history tells that Alexander the Great built a castle in Yazd (then known as Kasah), but local tradition says he was actually imprisoned here in the extensive underground chamber beneath the courtyard. The present building is much later, finished in 1305, and is now used as a theological college. It was largely rebuilt in 1671, although the domed prayer hall to the right of the entrance retains some 14th-century decorative plaster. It is quite a trek to walk here and there is a charge for the *Zendan* but nearby

Previous page
Abandoned village, Yazdikhast (PB)

Right Maydan Mir Chaqmaq, Yazd (PB)

Below right Zoroastrian fire altar, Chak Chak, Yazd (PB)

Below left Masjid-i Jami, Kirman (PB)

there is also the little Duvazdah Imam which has recently re-opened after restoration. This latter building of 1038 is known for having fine-quality plasterwork in the *mihrab* and dome but, despite its name, none of the imams nor their relatives was interred here. It is thought the two Shi'i brothers who paid for the construction meant it to be purely a commemorative building, for the painted inscriptions (inc. K2: 158, 163, 255–6; 40:65, 67) stress belief in the Imamate, clearly a personal selection. You could walk north from here, asking directions to the **Khaneh Lariha**, a 19th-century merchant's house currently being repaired. It has a charming atmosphere with a large pool in the central courtyard over which sits a huge, gently disintegrating wooden *charpoy*.

In the central bazaar area around Maydan Mir Chaqmaq, you could visit the mosque of **Mir Chaqmaq**. It was constructed in 1437, along with a hostel, cistern and *qanat*, bath and *caravanserai*, built by a local prince and his wife, who was linked to the Central Asian family of Timur Leng (d1405); only the mosque and her tomb remain. The mosque layout, with its 16m² court, two ivans and the prayer chamber with an upper gallery like the *Masjid-i Jami* are original, as is the 'mosaic' tilework in the prayer chamber and on the *mihrab*. The eastern section, on the other hand, was extensively repaired in the 19th century.

But most visitors are attracted by the multi-storeyed building at the end of the *maydan*. Like the Palace of the Winds, Jaipur (North India), it is pure **façade**, constructed in the 19th century on early 15th-century foundations to provide a viewing stand for city parades and ceremonies, especially those of *Moharram*. A huge wooden *nakhl*, shaped like a giant (palm) leaf, stands on the right, waiting to be draped in black cloth and carried by 70 or so young men next year. The central gateway used to lead into another bazaar, now demolished; the few remaining shops include makers of sugar-cones, who are happy for visitors to take photographs (though the atmosphere will quickly catch the throat).

Turning away from the Mir Chaqmaq façade, walk ahead towards the main crossroads. The tin-box makers on the right are preparing containers for Yazd's famous **sweetmeat and biscuit shop**, Haj Khalife Ali Rabar, on the corner. Spoil yourself. Purchasing is quite a complicated procedure: queue up by the relevant counters (eg: biscuits far right) and specify size/weight of box required. (If you want a multi-selection, ready-packed white plastic 2kg boxes are on the extreme right of the main counter as you enter.) Take the filled box back to this main counter for weighing, and with the chit, pay at the separate cash desk (ladies to the right, men left) and return to the weighing counter to collect your purchase. Retain the receipt to give to the surly doorman who will unlock the exit. It is worth the effort.

After the crossroads on the other side of the road are some high-quality nut and dried-fruit shops. Walking down this side takes you past a marvellously understated pair of **wooden doors** dating from the Safavid period; the detail is superb. On the opposite side of the busy avenue are passageways into the fabric, furnishings and gold shops of the bazaar, but continue for another 400m or so and ask directions to **Maydan Khan**, the fruit and vegetable section. At the far end of this huge courtyard is a small *naqqash*'s office with his cartoons and drawings (for carpet making) ready for sale or hire. The narrow passage to its immediate right leads to the **Hamam Khan** of 1797, recently transformed into a pleasant *chay-khaneh* and restaurant (open late afternoon/evening). *Abgoosht* is usually on the menu. Visit, if only to take a photograph of the interior rooms and have a glass of tea.

Before leaving Yazd, make time for the central **Zoroastrian fire temple** (*closed Fri and some holidays, lunchtime*). Located in a side street off Ayatollah Kashani Street, it has the appearance of a family house set within a garden. Accommodation for pilgrims is located in the main section which, as with the actual temple area, is off limits to casual visitors. Nevertheless, the sight of the sacred fire burning in a huge steel vessel brings the philosophy and history of Zoroastrianism home. This fire, protected by a glass screen to prevent pollution from people's breath, has been burning since 470CE if not earlier (see page 165). In all there are some 18 fire temples operating in Yazd itself and the surrounding villages.

Two **dokhmas** (Zoroastrian 'towers of silence') are situated a little south of town, after the Hotel and Restaurant Safaieh. In accordance with Zoroastrian laws governing the sanctity of earth, fire, air and water, in Achaemenid times the dead were exposed and their bones later gathered to be placed in ossuaries or tombs in rock (see page 194). But in later centuries large circular stone walls were built on rock and the bodies of Zoroastrian men, women and children were placed on their designated, paved zone on the open stone platform inside. A small central pit, filled with sand, charcoal and phosphorus to prevent pollution of the earth, acted as the drain. These towers are no longer in use (Zoroastrians are now interred in the nearby cemetery within a concrete chamber to avoid pollution of the earth), so with time and energy visitors may climb up them – the smaller, lower one on the right entailing a marginally shorter, easier clamber with access high up. Access into the other *dokhma* is best made from the gentle rise on the extreme left rather than the track on the extreme right. These towers were constructed according to strict observance of prayer and ritual, so please treat them accordingly, even though others clearly have not. Below, there is a collection of buildings, a water cistern with two wind towers and rooms for mourners. There is also a mortuary reception area, where the body would be cleansed and dressed in a clean but old sacred shirt (*sudreh*), before being tied to a metal bier by the sacred girdle (*kusti*) for carrying to the platform. The local authorities have turned a blind eye to vandalism of these buildings, which only serves to fuel foreigners' negative perceptions of religious tolerance in modern Iran.

On the road to Kirman, the most visible monuments are *caravanserais*, the first standing to the west of the main road about 55km from Yazd, the other approximately 65km further on and almost straddling the modern highway. The first is known as the **Ribat Zayn al-Din**, built by a Safavid governor of Kirman. It consists of a circular enclosing wall with five towers and a monumental entrance. Inside, the accommodation and relaxation areas were arranged around a 12-sided court with a large hall opposite the main door. The whole building has been so extensively restored that the functions of the various rooms can no longer be distinguished, but in a *caravanserai* of this size there should have been a small mosque, kitchen area and perhaps *hamam*. About 100m away is the ruined, two-storeyed stable block with its mangers still intact. Heavily vitrified bricks in the broken dome of the small corner chamber, with two broken fire-boxes in the extreme right corner of the courtyard, suggest to me that this was the blacksmith's forge for making horseshoes and the like. The second *caravanserai* before Anar is thought to be earlier in date. The smaller section on one side of the building perhaps acted as the toll house, levying the dues from passing merchant trains, while the main building offered accommodation and stabling.

From here head on to Kirman via **Rafsanjan**, from where the former Iranian president takes his name. There are numerous groves of pistachio trees on either side of the main road. It is not a dramatic landscape but there is another large *caravanserai* complex about 10km the other side of Rafsanjan, and with all the *qanat* inspection holes dotted across the plain, you might spot local repair teams in action.

KIRMAN

Perhaps founded by the Sasanid shah Ardashir I in the early 3rd century (it was called *Beh-i Ardashir* until Safavid times), the town of Kirman (pronounced 'Kerman') quickly succumbed to the Arab armies in 642. Thereafter, all the major regimes in the region were eager to control this important town linking the old caravan routes from Afghanistan, India and the south coast into the Iranian heartlands. It came under Seljuk authority in 1041, but severe damage by Turkomen tribesmen in 1187 resulted in Zarand (87km northwest) becoming the provincial centre, and this opened the way for a Mongol general to establish a short-lived principality here. The town continued to pass from hand to hand – Muzaffarid authority to Timurid (until that empire fragmented) to the Qara Qoyunlu and then Aq Qoyonlu tribal confederations – until Iran was 'united' under the Safavid control. Kirman had always had a large Zoroastrian community, but in the last years of the 17th century the Safavid Shah Soleyman yielded to theological demands that the community be relocated to the north of the city. By the mid-19th century, perhaps only 150 Zoroastrian families remained in Kirman itself. From 1750 until 1792 the region, including Bam, was controlled by the Ismailis with the agreement of the Zand family. With the Qajar advance and takeover of Zand authority, the Ismaili community left for Tehran and then migrated to India.

Despite such a troubled political history, the region had a long-established reputation in textile production, especially carpet weaving, even before Safavid Shah Abbas I (d1629) established a royal carpet workshop here. Marco Polo mentioned its leather workers and silk embroiderers in 1271 and, even today, keep an eye open for the distinctive Kirman embroidery of chain-stitch and/or tambour on scarlet-red wool cloth (but reject cheaper man-made fabrics); again one pays for quality. Its rug production achieved such quality that Kirman carpets graced the imperial Mughal court of northern India as well as

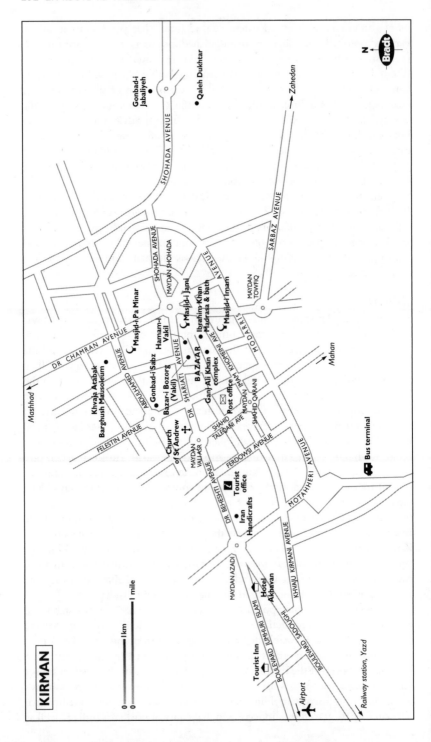

KIRMAN

Safavid palaces and pavilions. Such carpets were described by Engelbert Kaempfer (d1716), doctor and secretary to the Swedish envoy, as decorated with animal motifs, so possibly the famous 16th- and 17th-century 'Animal' and 'Hunting' carpets (such as those housed in the Victoria and Albert Museum, London and the Metropolitan Museum of Fine Art, New York) were actually woven here.

Getting there
There is a daily flight from Tehran, and two flights a week from Isfahan and Zahedan, plus a train service from Tehran and Yazd (see *Yazd* pages 225–31). Numerous intercity bus-services run along this route.

Accommodation
Good, clean accommodation for foreign visitors in Kirman has been a problem in the past, but in autumn 2003 a new five-star **Kirman Pars Hotel** opened (tel: 0341 2119301-3; fax: 0341 2119333; US$95 double, US$65 single, excluding service, breakfast; www.parshotel.com). The privately owned, three-star **Hotel Akhavan** (tel: 0341 2441411–3; fax: 0341 2449113; US$37 double, US$27 excluding service, breakfast) on Boulevard Sadoughi, has been investing in repairs and redecoration; the owners and staff are also friendly and helpful. On the opposite side of this dual carriageway, walking towards Maydan Azadi, is one of the best restaurants in town; look for the mirrored-glass frontage. A new three-star **Hotel Hezar** (tel: 0341 2260040, 2267099; fax: 0341 2269301; US$35 double/single) is on Khvaja Kirmani Avenue in the northwest outskirts of town; also in this direction is a fine (restored) ice house (see page 221). The **Tourist Inn** (tel: 0341 2445203-5; fax: 0341 2444087; US$54 double/single excluding service), also three-star, is on Boulevard Jumhuri Islami.

Things to see and do
Comparatively few foreign tourists make it to Kirman, and those that do have come to visit Bam, which necessitates a day trip. Yet Kirman itself has a relaxed atmosphere and its bazaars hold great attractions, and not only for buying. Inside the **Bazar Bozorg** (also called Bazar Vakil) is the Safavid **Ganj Ali Khan** complex, essentially 17th century in date, which includes a mint, a *caravanserai* and bathhouse (*hamam*). The latter is now an ethnographic museum displaying all the accoutrements one needed to visit the bathhouse in Safavid times; the exterior painted decoration is some two centuries later in date. There is an opportunity for men to go to an operating bath nearby, the 1817 **Hamam Ibrahimiyeh,** whose rents, with those of the neighbouring *khan* (warehouse), went to endow the *madrasa* next door, both built and colourfully decorated by a local governor (and son-in-law) of the Qajar shah, Fath Ali Shah. Much of the bazaar was constructed in Safavid times but as its other name, Bazar Vakil, suggests, many of the *khan*s off the main passages were part of extensive rebuilding by another energetic Qajar governor (*vakil*), Mohammed Ismail Khan, 1859–66. A *caravanserai* bearing the name Vakil is

still in use as offices for local merchants. The **Hamam Vakil** now operates as a tea house-cum-restaurant (afternoon/evening), but for a small entry charge the manager is happy for visitors to explore the complex (including the clean toilets). Further down the main avenue from here, on the other side, look out for a richly ornamented doorway in Qajar style. Its blue-tiled panel identifies it as the 19th-century office which dealt with locals wishing to make the Hajj pilgrimage to Mecca.

The **Masjid-i Jami** is located just off the main Maydan Shohada. The basic four-ivan plan dates from its construction in 1349 by Mubariz al-Din (r1314–58), the founder of the Muzaffarid regime (1314–93), but there have been extensive repairs since the 16th century. The modern additions (glazing in the courtyard, etc) are cheap and nasty, but some splendid tilework in both 'mosaic' and *cuerda seca* techniques remains in the prayer chamber. Visitors are usually riveted by the intriguing notices written in English, and the Farsi notices are just as confusing. Some 200m northwest is the **Masjid-i Pa**

THE HAMAM

The bather having undressed in the outer room, and retaining nothing about him but a piece of loose cloth around his waist, is conducted by the proper attendant into the hall of the bath; a large white sheet is then spread on the floor, on which the bather extends himself [and warm water is poured over him]... The attendant then takes his employer's head upon his knees, and rubs in with all his might, a sort of wet paste of henna plant, into the mustachios and beard... Again he has recourse to the small pail, and showers upon his quiescent patient another torrent of warm water. Then putting on a glove of soft hair, yet possessing some of the scrubbling brush qualities, he first takes the limbs, and then the body, rubbing them for three-quarters of an hour [after which, follows pumicing]... To this proceeds the shampooing, which is done by pinching, pulling, and rubbing, with so much force and pressure as to produce a violent glow over the whole frame. Some natives delight in having every joint in their bodies strained till they crack... that the very vertebrae of the back are made to ring a peal in rapid succession... This over, the shampooed body, reduced again to its prostrate state, is rubbed all over with a preparation of soap confined in a bag, till he is one mass of lather. The soap is then washed off with warm water, when a complete ablution succeeds by him being led off to the cistern and plunged in.

R Ker Porter
Travels in Georgia, Persia, Armenia...
vol I, 1821, page 232

Minar, now being heavily restored. Its 1390 entrance portal did have (note the past tense) splendid 14th-century tile decoration which were still in situ in the late 1970s; visit only to mourn the substitution of such bad-quality work.

But the **Masjid-i Imam** (formerly the Masjid-i Malik), with just a stub (7.5m) of its original Seljuk minaret standing, is worth some time. The main domed prayer chamber dates from the late 11th century, perhaps slightly post-dating the essential four-ivan plan, but the prayer ivan and portal, with its geometrical brick patterns and fragmentary inscription in deep relief, date from about a hundred years later. Even a cursory glance at the tilework reveals wide-ranging repairs in the Safavid period, and the essentially black and pink tiling with yellow inscription in the prayer hall can only be 19th-century Qajar work. Publications of the 1970s mention 12th-century stucco *mihrabs* in the prayer hall, but these have now been relocated to the roof. To see them, find the narrow staircase to the extreme left (facing the prayer ivan) and, emerging at roof level, look for a metal canopy to the left. The three carved *mihrabs* are there, damaged and dusty but lovely. Another interesting – and obviously early – *mihrab* is now kept behind locked doors downstairs, so you need to find the knowledgeable building supervisor, who clearly loves the place. He thinks this fourth *mihrab* is pre-Seljuk and describes how local tradition says it was visited by Hassan, Ali's son (the 2nd Imam).

In the first edition of this guide, I asked if anyone knew the location of the 12th-century Seljuk tomb tower of **Khvaja Atabeg Barghush**, and Robyn Lyons made contact in September 2003. It lies on recently cleared ground not far from Abdulhamed Avenue, behind the bazaar, and a renovation programme has started. After collapsing in a 1897 earthquake, the dome was rebuilt but then years of neglect has meant the octagonal exterior has been shorn of its decorative patterned brickwork highlighted with coloured ceramic tile elements. However, the square interior still retains some decoration including fine calligraphy, although the tiled *mihrab* has gone.

Kirman postcards often show a simple octagonal mausoleum, the **Gonbad-i Jabaliyeh** (also known as Gabri-i or Jabel-i Sang) located in a cemetery, east of the Maydan Arg on the outskirts of town. Some scholars consider it to be one of the earliest surviving tombs with a double dome in Iran, but it is debatable if anything of the original fabric now remains. But another reason for making this short journey is to see the extensive remains of the old Sasanid fortifications, the **Qaleh-i Dokhtar**, built by Ardashir I, situated on the other side of the road, behind the houses before the mausoleum.

In the 19th century Kirman was an important centre for Western Christian missionary work, so you may wish to find the Anglican **Church of St Andrew** (*Keliseh Moqaddasi*), well-hidden off Shari'ati Avenue. A recent earthquake destroyed the original building, but the small Christian community in the city has built a new church, usually open only on Sunday.

The road to the northwest of Kirman leads to **Zarand** (87km) which at the end of the 12th century superceded Kirman as the provincial centre, and was also famous for its textile manufacture. Its **Masjid-i Jami** was founded in the

10th century but, other than the remains of a minaret constructed some time before 1074, the present building is 18th century. Just a little backtracking on the main road, brings one on to a main highway to Mashhad.

To the southwest, past Kirman Airport on the road to Sirjan, is **Bardsir** with Tell-i Iblis (Devil's Mound); American-funded archaeological work here in the mid-1960s found evidence of continuous settlement from c4400BCE to 400BCE, and proof that both copper smelting and ceramic production were in operation. And in Bardsir itself there is a 13th-century tomb of **Sayyid Muhammad**, with later buildings around. It has a double dome, good plasterwork and fine *muqarnas* along with three historic cenotaphs.

Returning to the Sirjan road, continue for another 20km to **Nigar**, off a side road. Here there are the remains of a Seljuk citadel and a minaret probably 1216 in date with a brick inscription from the Koran (K.97); glazed infills provide colour to the patterning. Both the mosque and the old *hamam* nearby could be Seljuk in plan. This village is on the centuries-old migration route, so there is a possibility of seeing families and flocks on the move in the spring and autumn. About 23km east of here is **Ghubeyra**, an Islamic site probably destroyed by Timur Leng's armies in 1393. It was excavated in the early 1970s by a British team of archaeologists, whose final report was published in summer 2000.

Sirjan is another 100km on the main road. Some 5km before it and to the east, you should catch sight of **Qaleh-i Sang**, a huge medieval fortress which managed to resist Timur Leng for two years. The town itself was a regional capital from Sasanid times until the 10th century, and before the revolution the British Institute of Persian Studies undertook preliminary excavations that revealed an important medieval complex which, judging by the richness of its decorative plasterwork, could have housed the governor.

Continuing down this road towards Bandar-i Abbas, the road passes through Haji Abad (approximately 300km from Kirman) on the eastern road leading to Dawlatabad and, 30km further on, the site **Tepe Yahya**, first systematically excavated by the Peabody Museum of Harvard University in the late 1960s. Some seven distinct layers were identified, the earliest dating from c4500–3800BCE, when the inhabitants were evidently growing cereals and raising domesticated animals. By 3500BCE the settlement was prosperous enough to import turquoise, alabaster and ingots of copper. Occupation of the site continued without a break until the late Parthian or Sasanid period. The latest level and Period 2 (second level down) is clearly Achaemenid in date, leading scholars to believe this was Carmania, where Alexander the Great stationed his men returning from the India campaign. About another 100km further east is the gorge, **Tang-i Mordan**, again associated with the Macedonian warrior, with a 'fantastic number of cairn burials' according to Sylvia Matheson. A handful of similar cairn tombs at Sar-i Asiab, 40km north of Kirman, were excavated by the Peabody Museum. The finds ranged widely in date, even up to the 7th century CE, although it is generally considered the cairns, originally standing perhaps 2.5m high, were erected in prehistoric times.

MAHAN

From Kirman, most foreign visitors head southeast for **Bam**, stopping en route to see the shrine and gardens at **Mahan**. This takes a full day. Arguably Mahan, 40km from Kirman, is best visited in the evening, perhaps on a return journey from Bam, for during the summer this **Qajar garden** and pavilion are open and illuminated at night. Set back about 2km from the main road, the layout of this restored garden is one of the few in Iran that retains its original plan. A series of terraces descends down the hillside with main and side water channels. On occasions the fountains are switched on, to the enjoyment of both ducks and visitors. The 19th-century pavilion offers a splendid place to take tea and enjoy both a *nargileh* (hubble-bubble pipe – but see page 42) and the lovely view over the garden.

Mahan itself is known for the famous shrine complex of (Shah) **Ni'matullah Vali Kirmani** (d1430), the Sufi mystic poet-saint who spent his last 25 years here after residing in Mecca, Kerbela and Samarkand, where he had incurred the wrath of Timur Leng. Called the Iranian Nostradamus, he is said to have foretold the rise of the Safavid regime, the separation of Bangladesh from Pakistan and the Islamic Revolution in Iran. The main entrance has bright yellow and blue tiles from Qajar restoration work in 1871, as recorded on the floral tiles in the shrine doorway. Part of the large entry vestibule, to the right, has been converted into a *chay-khaneh* and, to the extreme right of the courtyard, a small museum has been recently opened. The original silver grilles of the cenotaph and an enormous gold inlaid steel *kash-kul* (dervish begging-bowl) presented to the shrine by a Safavid shah are now kept in here. Apart from a large gift and bookshop, all other rooms in this courtyard offer basic accommodation for pilgrims.

The actual shrine building itself is an engaging mixture of architectural and decorative styles. If it is uncrowded, do enlist the help of the kind and very knowledgeable guardian (Farsi-speaking only). The inner square chamber dates from 1436 and its inner walls are still decorated with high-quality Timurid 'mosaic' tilework, while a new steel and glass screen protects the Sufi's cenotaph. The doorway into this area opposite the main door has a 19th-century three-images-in-one glass picture on each wall, one with different verses of the Koran, and the other showing Hoseyn's head, his tent at Kerbela and his desecrated body. The carpets to the left are of Mahan production, incorporating the saint's poetry in the long cartouches. Walking anticlockwise – so the cenotaph chamber is on the left – look at the vaulting. The superbly proportioned fan of intersecting ribs was constructed in 1436 on the order of Ahmed I Vali Bahmani, ruler of the Indian Deccan and a devotee of this Sufi master. Halfway round, the Safavid alterations are visible to the right of the cenotaph chamber, where the Timurid tiling disappears under a later Safavid wall constructed to support the vaulting system. On the outer wall are double wooden doors, which the guardian will proudly open to allow you to inspect them and see fragments of Safavid velvet, and to see how the complex was enlarged in the 19th century to make it symmetrical. Returning to the central area, the room in the next corner is richly decorated with magnificent early 17th-century calligraphy arranged in a giant sunwhirl around the vault; this was the *chehel-khaneh* where, as the name suggests, Sufis spent 40 nights in spiritual devotions.

The next door leads outside the shrine complex to a photogenic view of the shrine's exterior. Back in the building, look for a wooden door further along. Small figures along the top depict Sufi shaikh Abu'l Hassan Kharaghani (d1033), known for his miraculous abilities to tame wild animals, riding a lion and using a snake as a whip. A simple, small chamber in this final section is the resting place of the master who died recently.

BAM

From Mahan it is about 170km to Bam (*vahma*: glorification, prayer), which was struck by a severe earthquake on December 26 2003. It is thought to be the city of Haftvad mentioned in the Iranian epic, *Shah-nameh*. The story goes that Haftvad's daughter was spinning cotton with friends when she spotted a worm in her apple. Refusing to kill it, she found her output magically increased as the worm munched and grew in size. As it brought great wealth to her family and town, a citadel was built to protect it, but this only aroused the interest of the Sasanid shah, Shapur. Eventually killing the giant worm by forcing hot metal down its throat, he took the city and its riches. This sounds purely the stuff of legend, but we know that, according to Iranian tradition, it was Shapur I (or perhaps Shapur II) who destroyed the Chinese silk monopoly, by actively promoting silkworm cultivation and silk production in Iran and promoting Bam as a trading station for eastern caravan routes. Furthermore in silk processing, to avoid the pupa damaging its silk cocoon, it *is* killed by heat (see page 138).

Aerial photographs taken shortly after the devastating earthquake have revealed the complexity of the medieval *qanat* system, and evidence that the site was occupied as early as 2600BCE. The town was an important frontier and commercial post, trading in dates, cotton and other textiles until it fell to rebel Afghan forces in 1719. Its economy never fully recovered. Then the citadel's defences were partially dismantled in the 19th century, following Agha Muhammad Qajar's capture of the Zand ruler, Lutf Ali Khan (see page 13) in 1794. More local trouble in 1838 caused the Qajar shah to take direct control, and many of the townspeople were moved to a new residential area to the south. By 1958 most families had left the old walled town, and the site was declared as an open-air museum. It was the new town that suffered most in the 2003 earthquake but the historic walled city also was damaged. Repair work is already underway.

Getting there and accommodation

The airport here is being repaired and currently there is no commercial flight connection, but inter-city buses continue to serve the town. The four-star **Hotel Azadi** (Bonyad; tel: 0344 90099; fax: 0344 90092; 63 rooms) was opened in autumn 1999.

Things to see and do

A walk in the **walled town** before the recent earthquake was unforgettable. Surrounding an area of approximately 3km diameter, the main defence wall was over 12m high, with ramparts 3m wide, four gates and an external moat. Enough remains for the visitor to see the main housing, shops, work units – including a bakery and police station – *caravanserai* and the main mosque, all located just inside this wall. Above, defended by a further wall, were the barracks, stabling and housing for the bureaucrats and soldiers, while a third enclosing wall protected the inner citadel and the governor's apartments. Right at the top were a **watchtower** and **pavilion** of the Four Seasons, both offering marvellous panoramic views over the plain, but it was these upper sections that were most severely damaged. Originally the tower was seven-storeyed but in the 1810 Qajar dismantling three floors were demolished. Below, on the second level, a massive repair and rebuilding programme had recently been completed before the earthquake and, perhaps because of this strengthening work, this area has suffered less. It contains the **officers' quarters**, a series of rooms around courtyards set behind the main street. On the way down to the next gate there are more **barracks** and also a huge water **cistern** (not in existence in 1994) to the right. The walkway led down to the second gate which now no longer exists. At ground level, the avenue to the left led to a small caravanserai, which had been converted into a restaurant, its two main chambers cooled by multi-vent *badgir*s. This area and beyond containing a *hoseyniyeh* – with a characteristic 'theatre' stage and 'boxes' for the audience – a school, and a large mosque perhaps founded in the 7th century were largely levelled in the 2003 earthquake. It is unclear whether a large domed building to the left, in the distance, still stands. This was a *zur-khaneh*, possibly the earliest surviving Iranian example, complete with its octagonal wrestling pit (see page 116).

ZAHEDAN
Getting there

From Bam, a road south leads to Minab and Bandar-i Abbas, but the main Kirman–Bam road continues to the Irano-Pakistani frontier after Zahedan (population 282,000); petrol stations are few and far between.

Aside from road transport from Bam, there are two daily flights from Tehran, and from Isfahan, Kirman, Mashhad and Chabahar (on the coast) at least twice a week. Zahedan and Quetta (across the border) used to be on the hippy trail in the early 1970s, but since then services have deteriorated badly, and by all reports any idea of a land crossing other than by the weekly train service from the Pakistani border should be abandoned. Some 60 km west of Zahedan is the Nosrat Abad checkpoint on the border with Afghanistan.

The whole region has a reputation for drug trafficking, so expect a stringent searching of vehicles and lengthy document checking, both in town and on the road. Also there is large-scale smuggling into Afghanistan and Pakistan of cheap Iranian petrol contained in secret compartments underneath the inter-city/frontier buses. One such 'travelling bomb' exploded in June 2004 at Nosrat Abad, and at least 90 people in the bus and other vehicles died in the inferno.

So few Westerners now come this way that their presence attracts much interest; it is important that you find out whether the official requirement to register personally with the authorities after hotel registration is still in force. Be careful, *very* careful. Think before travelling in this region.

Accommodation
The best hotel available is the four-star **Esteghlal Hotel** (tel: 0541 3238068-71; fax: 0541 3222239; US$99 double, US$70 single, excluding tax, breakfast). Otherwise the **Tourist Inn** (0541 3220113/3222330; fax: 0541 3224440; US$35 double/single excluding tax) is adequate.

Things to see and do
Zahedan has little to offer other than its bazaars, but the surrounding landscape is strewn with the crumbling remains of *caravanserais* and signal towers, the most important being at **Fahraj**, 100km from Bam. Its signal tower, **Mil-i Naderi**, standing 19m high with a diameter of 13m, was perhaps built on 10th-century foundations, but the brickwork patterning dates from the reign of Nadir Shah Afshar (d1747). Beacons would be lit for signalling communication to Kirman and beyond, and they served to guide the trade caravans making their way into and from central Iran; another lies some 15km away to the north near Shur Gaz.

To the north of Zahedan lies Tasuki, about 35km after the turn-off for Zabol. The ruins of **Qaleh-i Gird**, about 20km from the Gird-i Gahr police checkpoint, are visible with its well-preserved towers and walls. Further on there are some 14th-century buildings, but the proximity to the Afghan border means the authorities may wish foreigners to avoid the area. Northwards is the excavated tepe of **Rod-i Biyaban**, where the remains of some 50 large kilns were found, dating from the 3rd millennium BCE. About 25km further on (56km south of Zabol) is the similarly dated site of **Shahri Sokhta** ('Burnt City') which an Italian archaeological team excavated from the mid-1960s until 1978, and by the Iranian authorities since 1997. A series of rectangular buildings were uncovered, some with walls still 3m high, with doorways, window, staircases and roofing timber in a fine state of preservation, 'as if kept in a pot of pickles', covered in a thick layer of saline earth. It turned out that what were first identified as floor levels were in fact the roofs of buildings. Four main periods of settlement were identified: level I (c3100-2900BCE), then levels II and III, with pottery similar to that found at Bampur from c2500–1900BCE, and level IV, about 500 years later and characterised by pottery animal figurines. A huge burial site over 42ha, containing about 40,000 graves of nine types, was found with 'literally tens of thousands' of skeletons laid in a horizontal 'kneeling' position facing east, the largest known Bronze Age cemetery in the Middle East. The rich pottery (often decorated with stylised scorpion motifs), over 40,000 clay figurines, flint tools and beads point to a prosperous settlement dating back over 5,000 years, but the whole settlement seems to have been destroyed in an intense fire in c1250BCE, and abandoned after the river changed course. The finds again prove a strong trading connection both with the northern Indian subcontinent and with Oman.

Some 6km away from here is **Qaleh-i Rustam**, locally associated with the Persian warrior-hero in the *Shah-nameh* epic (*Sohrab & Rostam* of Matthew Arnold). Noted as an attractive town in its own right during the mid-1970s, Qaleh-i Rustam has clearly had a long history of settlement, as over eight prehistoric mounds have been identified and there are signs of an important Sasanid fort. The road leads onto **Zabol**, about 55km away, where for many years the Italian archaeological team of Shahri Sokhta had its headquarters. The proximity of the Afghan border means a heavy military and police presence in Zabol and the surrounding region.

The site of **Kuh-i Khvaja** is visible from a distance but reachable only by boat during the spring and autumn. This mound has been revered by both Zoroastrians and Muslims for centuries, and every *Nou Rouz* pilgrims still come to pay their respects. Nearby is the **Lake Hamun** (originally known as Kasaoya, and mentioned in the Avesta) in which Zoroastrians believe their Messiah, Saoshyants, will be conceived. On the site, a small fire temple complex could perhaps date from the Achaemenid period but many believe it to be later, pointing out similarities in layout with the *Adur Gushnasp* fire sanctuary at Takht-i Soleyman in the Zagros Mountains (see page 165). Extensive Parthian and Sasanid remains were uncovered, with plaster wall frescoes of a king and queen, attendants and a line of deities, which formerly decorated a Parthian palace compound. Unfortunately they are no longer in situ, but two pieces are in the Metropolitan Museum of Art, New York. Archaeological work has been carried out since the mid 1990s and remains of a citadel with a religious precinct including a fire temple have been found, probably dating from early Sasanid times, 3rd–4th century CE. **Bibi Dost** is situated about 35km from here, where again there are clear signs of historic occupation. Just to the southeast are the ruins of **Deh Zahidan**, perhaps once the old city of Zaranj, with a citadel, forts and mosque.

A series of old forts and *caravanserai* mark the landscape, but few have been securely identified or dated. One of the sites much further south, excavated in the mid-1960s, is **Bampur**, close to **Iranshahr**. The dig focused on a site west and northwest of the (post-) medieval citadel mound; six stratified levels were found, with interesting pottery and other finds proving that as early as c2500–1900BCE there were strong trade links with Afghanistan and Oman. Much of this region was destroyed during Timurid times in revenge attacks by Timur Leng and his son, and it has never recovered. We know that Alexander the Great passed through on his campaigns to India and, as the Persepolis reliefs suggest, earlier there had been close military co-operation between the people of Sistan (or Drangiana as it was then known) and the Achaemenian emperor. The region was considered strategically important during Parthian times, some saying that a local ruler Gondophernes (r20–48CE) was none other than Caspar, one of the Three Wise Men.

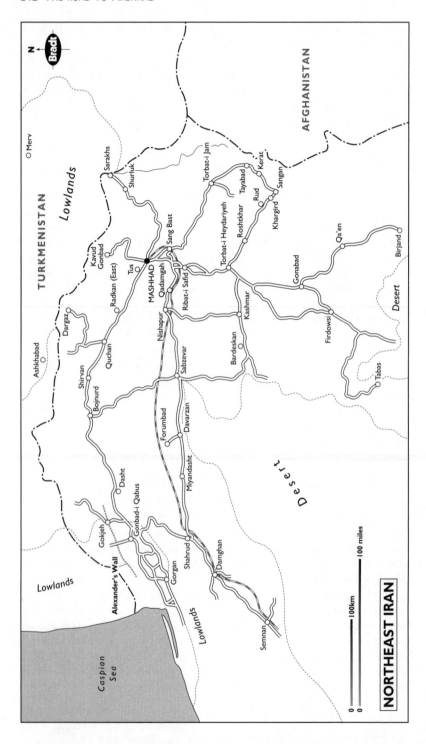

NORTHEAST IRAN

The Road to Mashhad

The city of Mashhad (also spelt Meshhed) is considered the holiest city in Iran, renowned as the burial place of the 8th Imam, Reza. Although most of the shrine complex is out of bounds for non-Muslims, there are interesting excursions, often entailing lengthy drives, which can be made from the city. This region of Iranian Khorasan once formed an enormous province encompassing sections of today's Turkmenistan, Uzbekistan and Afghanistan. This province was not always under Iranian authority, so its historic monuments record the patronage of such regimes as the Khwarizm shahs, the Mongol Il-Khanids and the Timurids as well as the Safavids, the short-lived Afsharid dynasty and the Qajars. This section looks at the region east of Gonbad-i Qabus and Shahrud (see pages 143–5), Mashhad and sites close to the Afghan border. The security situation near the Afghan border is presently good but the gendarmerie advises that road journeys should be completed before sunset, as there have been isolated incidents of cross-border robbery and kidnapping.

OVERVIEW
Getting there
Frequent flights and an overnight train service link Tehran to Mashhad (30,000 to 150,000 rials, depending on service and class), and of course there are numerous bus services to this popular pilgrimage centre. There are two main roads eastwards: a northern one skirting the Caspian Sea to Gorgan, Shirvan and Quchan to Mashhad; and the more southerly route following the old caravan trade road from Shahrud via Sabzevar and Nishapur (also spelled Nev Shabur).

The best time for travelling in Iran's eastern provinces is in the late spring and early autumn, as the winters in the Khorasan province are long and bitter, with heavy snowfalls – as one 11th-century ruler found to his cost (see page 143).

Accommodation
There is limited but adequate accommodation at Gorgan, and south of Mashhad at Tayabad and Sabzehvar (see below), but elsewhere the situation is much more difficult. However, Mashhad itself is awash with hotels, so it is best to stay in

Mashhad and make day visits by local taxi or bus from there. Such excursions make the long journey to Mashhad and Khorasan worth the time, expense and effort, especially as the shrine itself is largely off-limits to non-Muslims. It should be stressed that there is no up-to-date road map showing the mass (or do I mean 'mess'?) of complicated ring-road systems currently being built, and road signs, even to the shrine, are rarely written in the Roman alphabet.

THE NORTH ROAD TO MASHHAD

The road from Gorgan and Gonbad-i Qabus towards Mashhad quickly leaves rice fields and sloping farm roofs behind, winding up into wooded hills populated by wild boars and deer, passing the newly named Golestan National Park and then cutting through shrubby hillsides that are ideal trekking or riding territory. Close to the road are three known Timurid *caravanserai* dating from c1487, and probably many more still to be identified, as the then governor of Astarabad, Mir Ali Shir, is known to have built 49 altogether in his lifetime to serve this important trade and pilgrimage route. The **Ribat-i Qarah Pil** is situated 25km east of Dasht, behind the roadside gendarmerie. (If a ruined *caravanserai* isn't appealing, the numerous inquisitive *pika* 'gerbils' that inhabit the site are.) Its south entrance once led immediately into the stables along this façade and on both sides. Despite the *caravanserai*'s present state, even a casual inspection will reveal the different phases of construction, with certain chambers built in the late 16th century to provide more stabling. The vestibule led into a four-ivan courtyard, 16m², with living accommodation on all sides. This essential plan was followed in two other *caravanserai*, both a day's journey away in pre-motoring times: **Ribat-i ʿIshq**, 23km east off the main road at Chaman Bid, which also included a small mosque on site, and the **Ribat-i Qilli**, 30km southeast. From Ribat-i Qarah Pil or Ribat-i Ishq, **Jajarm** is about 55km due south. Its position on the former main caravan route from Nishapur to Bastam presumably accounted for the need for a protective fortress, whose remains are still visible. Its *Masjid-i Jami*, surprisingly small in size, probably dates from the late 15th century.

The good road skirts the mountainous barrier between Iran and today's Turkmenistan Republic through Bojnurd and Shirvan, passing petrochemical and cement works. Some 6km west from Shirvan (market day Monday) is **Ziyarat**, so-called after its Ziyarat-i Timur Leng located in a modern cemetery. It is not the main, centrally placed building with a brick-patterned dome, the interior of which is decorated with a beautiful star-burst ceiling of plaster *muqarnas*, that has interested scholars, but the octagonal tomb behind it. Some think this dates from the 1330s but others, looking at its kite-shaped squinches in the zone of transition and other architectural details, argue that, as its name suggests, it is Timurid, c1430. Local children will happily show you the internal staircase up to the roof. Hardly anything now remains of the painted internal drum inscription and medallions recorded in the mid-1970s.

Well worth a short detour for its early 13th-century tomb tower is the village of **Radkan**, known in certain publications as Radkan East (Radkan

West tower is south of Kordkuy; see page 142). Some 75km before Mashhad, after Quchan and the village of Seid Abad, there is a turn-off for Radkan. The village roundabout, boasting a modern replica of the tower, soon comes into view, but there is no signpost to the actual monument which is on a rough but serviceable road across agricultural land. The tower's octagonal brick base is quickly transformed into a 12-sided exterior, presumably symbolising belief in the 12 Imams, decorated with 36 semicircular engaged columns terminating in trilobed forms. Here and there are fragments of turquoise-glazed inserts, also used for the Kufic inscription. Only the exterior tent-roof survives but inside the octagonal chamber, the brick supports for the internal dome are still visible. Take care where you tread inside as local shepherds keep a few sheep and donkeys in the tower. Looking around, one sees the ruins of a huge four-towered *caravanserai*, also used for local flocks, and in the village there's an ice house.

North of Quchan and close to the Turkmenistan border, 3km northwest of Dar Gaz (also spelt Darreh Gaz), the Iranian Archaeological Service has recently been carrying out excavations at **Bondiyan** (also spelt Bandian), since 1994. From the brief reports published so far, a Sasanid columned hall with a corridor and room with remains of rich plaster decoration to a height of 70cm have been unearthed. These depict scenes of hunting, battle and feasting, resembling both in content and composition the (later) painted walls at Pjanzikent (Tajikistan), south of Samarkand in Central Asia. Fragmentary Pahlavi inscriptions carved into the plaster refer obliquely to two military commanders controlling this region, one of whom is recorded as serving under the Sasanid Shah Bahram V (r429–37). The work is lively but atypical and, according to the usual Sasanid scale of proportions, the figures have overlong arms. The archaeologists now think this was a Zoroastrian fire temple complex including a tower of silence.

Back on the main road, just before hitting the outskirts of Mashhad, is **Tus**, the birthplace of the famous medieval poet, Firdousi (d1020) but the confusing road directions indicate only Firdowsi, not Tus (although local bus companies still refer to 'Tus'; see page 254). Given the continuing construction of ring roads and the inadequate road signs on the Cento Highway, it is probably easier and quicker to continue into Mashhad and then come out by local taxi or bus.

MASHHAD

It was here, when the town was known as Sanabad, that the famous Abbasid caliph, Harun al-Rashid, died in 809CE; 19th-century Western literature always associated him with the anthology *Tales of 1001 Nights*, written centuries later. His son, al-Ma'mun, ordered a tomb for his father, and another to commemorate his son-in-law, Reza, in whose death in 817 he was strongly implicated. This is the Imam Reza, honoured in Shi'i Islam as the 8th in the line of 12 Imams and to whom today's huge shrine complex is dedicated. Almost two hundred years later this tomb to Imam Reza was destroyed by the local Sunni ruler, who forbade any rebuilding, but Sultan Mahmud of Ghazni

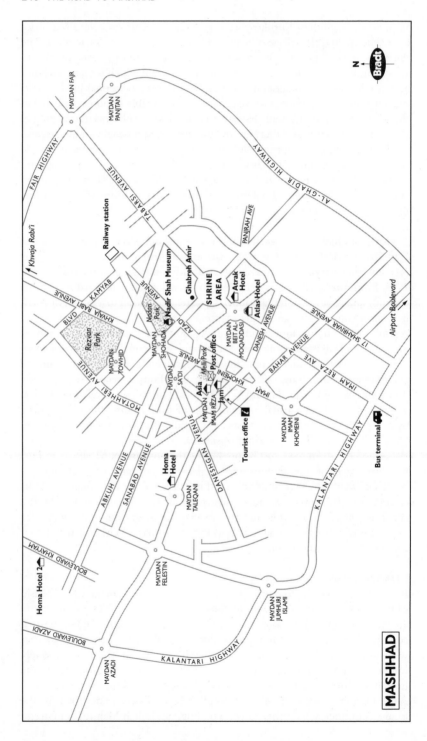

MASHHAD

SHAH RUKH

The fourth son of Timur Leng (Tamerlaine, as he is known in the West), Shah Rukh owed his name to the moment of his birth, which coincided with his father taking his opponent's castle (*rukh*) at chess. As Mongol tradition laid down that territorial possessions should be split between the ruler's sons, he was appointed governor of Mazandaran, Khorasan and Sistan in 1397 at the age of 22, but arguments between the brothers continued. He had two wives: Ghawhar Shad and, to keep the bloodline of Genghis Khan in the Timurid house, he married the young Malikat Agha, widow of one of his brothers. On Timur's death in 1405 he made no move to take the throne but bided his time until Timur's successor died two years later. Shah Rukh immediately went into action, installing his son, Ulugh Beg (who gave the mathematical world sine tables) as governor of Samarkand while he remained in Herat. Through his generals, he restored Timurid authority in the steppes of today's Turkmenistan, crushed local warlords and difficult nephews attempting to seize control of the Isfahan region in 1417, and then successfully moved against the Qara Qoyunlu in Azerbaijan.

A ruler who preferred to hunt around Sarakhs and to visit Mashhad than lead his troops on the battlefield, Shah Rukh ordered many gardens to be built in his capital of Herat, but he was also known for his piety, personally accompanying Muslim officials to remove the secret wine stores of his son and grandson. He was heartbroken when his favourite son died, and powerful factions centred around both queens broke out at court. The target of at least one assassination attempt, he was stabbed in the stomach when leaving the Friday prayer in 1427 but made a full recovery. The intrigue continued, especially when he fell seriously ill during 1444, and Ghawhar promoted her own candidate as the rightful heir apparent. Many court officials were banished from the Herat palace when Shah Rukh improved. He died in 1447 (Ghawhar survived for another ten years) and within 15 years, the house of Timur Leng had fallen and the empire was in fragments.

(r998–1030), inspired by a dream – or perhaps the need to win the loyalty of his Shi'i subjects – ordered its reconstruction in 1009. From then on, the town's fortunes were inextricably linked to the shrine.

But the city's vulnerable location offered rich pickings for any marauding force, such as the Turkomens in 1153, or the Mongols in 1221, and the shrine was always hit during such attacks. Piecemeal repairs were undertaken by local Sunni rulers, but major rebuilding was undertaken only by the son of Timur Leng, Shah Rukh (r1405–47; see above), from 1418 along with the construction of gardens and a royal pavilion to enhance the shrine. His queen, Ghawhar Shad, 'Jewel of Happiness', already an active architectural patron in their capital, Herat, was already having a new *madrasa* built. A century later it was the Shi'i Safavid regime which promoted the city as a major Iranian pilgrimage centre. The shrine's main dome and minarets were gilded and much of the Timurid eastern section was demolished to cater for the thousands of Iranian pilgrims flocking here, rather than undertaking the long, hazardous *hajj* to Mecca and Medina, then in Ottoman control. The city's royal association continued into the 18th century. Sweeping away the remnants of Safavid power, Nadir Shah Afshar (d1747), though a Sunni, had his son marry the daughter of Safavid Shah Tahmasp II here, established his capital in Mashhad, ordered costly and highly visible repairs to the shrine after his successfil Indian campaigns, and was buried here. Re-establishing the *Ithna Ashari* Shi'i faith as the state religion, the Qajar shahs then undertook a massive restoration programme in the shrine, extensively covering surfaces with tiles and mirrorwork and regilding the dome. Official pressure in the 19th and early 20th centuries caused many in the Jewish and Christian communities in Mashhad to move to Afghanistan or Central Asia, where their expertise in both manufacture and commerce were fully utilised; but at least one church still survives in Mashhad, close to the hotels Asia and Jam.

Although Qom is now acknowledged as Iran's leading theological training centre, this city (altitude 985m) has grown significantly since 1979, now having approximately two million residents. Numerous houses and bazaars have been demolished to improve access to the shrine area. Non-Muslims are welcome in Mashhad (its full title being *Mashhad-i Moqaddas*, 'Place of the Martyr') but are not allowed far into the shrine complex itself.

Getting around
The quickest and easiest way to sites in and around Mashhad is undoubtedly by local taxi: half a day (eg: 3½ hrs from the city) should cost about US$15 for the taxi which, if divided between three or four passengers, is very good value.

Accommodation
As the hotels cater for tens of thousands of pilgrims visiting during *Ramadan*, *Moharram* and the following Muslim month, accommodation is markedly easier to find outside these times. Some hotels are very close to the shrine (eg: Atlas and Atrak), but suffer from constant traffic noise, so consider hotels within walking distance but away from main roads, eg: Asia, Jam.

Best possible
Homa Hotel 2 Bd Khayyam; tel: 0511 7611001–9; fax: 0511 7688859/7610033; approximately US$100–120. In own grounds, far from the shrine. Constructed in mid 1990s. US$110 double, US$90 single.

Four-star
Atrak Hotel east side of Maydan Beit al-Moqaddas; tel: 0511 3642044; fax: 0511 3647279. US$52 double; US$ 40 single.

Homa Hotel 1 (IranAir) nr Maydan Taleqani; tel: 0511 8432001–9; fax: 0511 8437019. Under renovation.
Pardisan Hotel Close to Sedasima Park, Kalantari Expressway; tel: 0511 8791820–39; fax: 0511 8791830. Approx. US$40–60. A Bradt reader suggests this newly built hotel, near the Ferdowsi University campus in the south of the city, but a taxi into the centre will be needed.

Three-star
Hotel Asia Pasdaran Av; tel: 0511 2220071–4; fax: 0511 2258030. Under renovation, scheduled to re-open March 2005, with prices quoted US$50 double, US$40 single. Reception will lend *chador*s necessary for the shrine-visit.
Hotel Iran Khosravi Av; tel: 0511 228010; fax: 0511 2228583; 122 rooms; US$55 double/single.
Hotel Jam Pasdaran Av; tel: 0511 8590041–5; fax: 0511 8596044. 154 rooms; US$45 double, US$30 single. Close to Hotel Asia, with a good, helpful travel agent next door.

Two-star
Hotel Atlas South side of Maydan Beit al-Moqaddas; tel: 0511 8545061–3; fax: 0511 8543081; US$45 double/single.
Hotel Amir Azadi Av; tel/fax: 0511 2220442, 2221300; US$35 double/single.

One-star
Hotel Mashhad Imam Reza Av; tel: 0511 2222666; fax: 0511 2226767; 92 rooms, no room rate available autumn 2004; usually fully booked.

Restaurants
Opposite the entrance of the Hotel Homa 1 entrance is a basement restaurant **Ihsan**, and the hotel itself has a good-value à la carte menu. Other restaurants come and go, so ask your hotel reception for advice.

Shrine of Imam Reza
Since the establishment of the Islamic Republic, much more money has been spent on the shrine, including the gilding of the main dome and minarets using four times more gold than before, retiling, construction of new courtyards and so on. The main road, which formerly encircled the shrine, now runs underground; the London Barbican road network now has a twin. So the former walled complex of some 30 historic structures, the oldest dating to the 14th century, connected by four huge courtyards, has been transformed into an enormous building site. The result is bewildering and aesthetically unsatisfactory. Most buildings and courts have been renamed, yet signposting is almost non-existent and in Farsi only. Guides are allocated to non-Muslim visitors to ensure they don't wander into forbidden areas, but their knowledge of and interest in the remaining historic architecture are minimal.

Fluvius (see pages 40–1) has been fortunate in witnessing the blowing of long Alpine-like horns, some 2.5m in length, at the shrine's roof levels. This

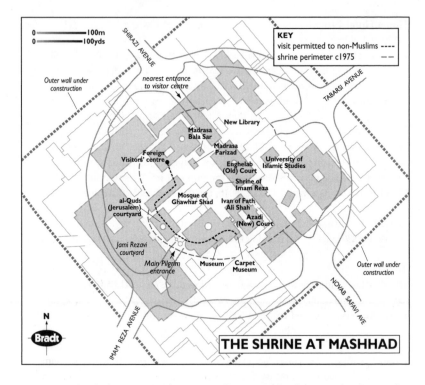

means a miracle has occurred to a supplicant within the complex but, as he warns, 'this cannot be organised to fit into a tourist schedule'.

Procedure

All women have to don the *chador* to enter the complex but none is available for hire at the shrine; ask your hotel reception or a friend if one may be borrowed. Following a bomb explosion here in the mid-1990s, all bags, cameras, etc must be surrendered with proof of identity (eg: passport) to the depositories (gender-separated) at each entry point. Then there is a security check/frisking, men one way, women another. Non-Muslims should not enter by the main pilgrims' entrance (*Maydan Beyt al-Moqaddas*) on Imam Reza Avenue but walk to the next entry to the left (Shirazi Avenue) as this is nearest to the Office for Foreign Visitors (*Daftar-i Ravabet-i Beynolm-i Laleh; open 08.00–14.00*); an entry guard will take you there. In the office (men in one entrance, women at the back, leaving shoes at the threshold) forms have to be completed and a guide is assigned. Pamphlets in six languages are theoretically available, as is a CD; we were informed a 20-minute video showing the 'forbidden' areas may be copied if visitors provide a blank tape (presumably entailing another visit to collect).

Non-Muslims are permitted in the new *al-Quds* (Jerusalem) courtyard, constructed in the 1980s, and to the two museums. The main **museum** displays on four floors some of the treasures of the shrine; some are outstanding, such as two 14th-century *mihrabs* of Kashan lustre tiles, while

IMAM REZA

The last years of Ali al-Reza, the 8th Imam in Iranian Shi'ism, encapsulates the tensions at the Baghdad court and throughout the Abbasid Empire in the early 9th century. Exploiting the Shi'i cause, the Abbasid family had overthrown the Umayyad regime in 749, but quickly proclaimed its allegiance to Sunni Islam. Before his death in 809 the Abbasid ruler, Harun al-Rashid, tried to ensure a smooth succession by securing the agreement of all concerned to his two named heirs: al-Amin, and his brother al-Ma'mun, then governor of Khorasan. But within two years al-Amin had reneged on the agreement, and al-Ma'mun in Merv (Turkmenistan) retaliated by proclaiming himself caliph. Al-Amin's action won few friends and he was killed in 813. Chaos ensued in the heartlands of Abbasid authority with Shi'i uprisings throughout Iraq, threatening the capital Baghdad. Court officials raced to Merv hoping to persuade al-Ma'mun to leave his stronghold and take charge; they also advised he join forces with the young Ali al-Reza (b765 probably), living in Medina near Mecca, who was recognised among *Ithna 'Ashari* Shi'is as the 8th Imam. Imam Reza (his title in his community) agreed to go to Merv in 816 and within a year al-Ma'mun named him as his heir, and marriages between the two families were arranged. Finally yielding to pressure, al-Ma'mun left Merv for Baghdad, but one of the court advisers who had stressed the importance of Imam Reza's support was assassinated. Imam Reza too died unexpectedly on the journey (September 818), supposedly after eating grapes sent by al-Ma'mun. Al-Ma'mun continued on to Baghdad and seized control, eventually dying in 833, knowing that the *Ithna 'Ashari* community held him directly responsible for Imam Reza's death.

others, like the extensive seashell display on the top floor, look decidedly out-of-place. Presently, no works from the extensive library collection of manuscripts, books and documents are included, but a number of 19th- and 20th-century paintings are shown, indirectly revealing which styles have 'official approval'. (A small collection of framed photographs on the ground floor record the totally ruinous state of the other Mashhad monuments before 1960; for this reason, no detailed description of the heavily reconstructed buildings has been included in these pages.) Labels are in Farsi and English, and the exhibits are well displayed. A little further on is the **Carpet Museum,** arranged on two floors (leave shoes at entry), a collection of mainly late 19th- and early 20th-century carpets, including some rare and decidedly beautiful Moghal Indian examples, two fine double-sided pile 'curtain' carpets as well as bucolic Qajar work. Labelling here is minimal and in Farsi only.

The rest of the complex is accessible only to pilgrims (unless prior official authorisation has been obtained and reconfirmed). Maps showing the current layout and new construction work are not available, but clearly much of the earlier floor plan has been altered and many of the historic structures so extensively changed that the published descriptions of the 1970–80s have little immediate relevance.

The most sacred place is the tomb chamber of Imam Reza, situated within the structures lying southwest of the Old Court. It was laid out in Safavid times along with the sanctuary of Allahverdi Khan, who ordered the construction of the famous Isfahan Bridge. Some 13th-century lustre ceramic tiles may still remain in situ within the shrine but the tall golden sanctuary portal and its two flanking minarets were constructed in the late 15th century. Restoration work was carried out in the mid-18th century on the order of Nadir Shah Afshari, and the mirrorwork added by the Qajar regime. To the west when walking to the al-Quds courtyard, you'll glimpse the dome of the **Mosque of Ghawhar Shad**, which the Timurid queen had constructed in 1416–8. A masterpiece by the Shirazi architect, Qavam al-Din, thought to have also designed the *madrasa* at Khargird (see page 259), it was built on the four-ivan plan with two minarets, with beautiful proportions and an emphatic rhythm of arcading and galleries. The mirrorwork was installed in the late 19th century. How much of the original extensive tilework, 'the most beautiful example of colour in architecture ever devised' (Byron) still survives is questionable as the north and south ivan were demolished in 1977 and then rebuilt; the southeastern façade is clearly new work. The high portal, taller than usual, necessitated a very tall drum and dome, the latter replaced by a concrete one in the 1960s.

Close to that mosque was built a four-ivan college, **Madrasa Parizad**, possibly paid for by Ghawhar Shad or one of her attendants. Both this and another, **Madrasa Bala Sar** to the east, were extensively repaired in 1680 and restored in the 1970s, as was the adjoining 1439 **Madrasa Do-Dar**, still used as a college until 1975. Then it was still possible to see wonderful 15th-century decorative plasterwork, 'more surviving than any other Timurid monument', in the barrel vault of the latter's mosque entrance. The college was donated by a governor of Qom, Yusuf Khvafa (d1443), interred in the southern dome chamber, where the drum inscription reminded visitors that the only access to Paradise is through love of the Prophet.

Many of the great and good have been laid to rest in the shrine and city: Allahverdi Khan, the Safavid kingmaker (see page 123) whose tomb was constructed with a soaring 21m high dome and superb tilework, and another important Safavid vizier commemorated in the Gonbad-i Khatemkhaneh 1609. Then, of course, Nadir Shah, whose tomb was rebuilt in the 1960s complete with a huge sculpture in the 'Soviet realism' style; now the tomb operates as a small museum.

Leaving the shrine by the same entrance (remembering to pick up any bag, camera and identity document), walk a short distance (east), keeping the shrine's new perimeter fence on your right, to see at comparatively close quarters a lovely 1451 building, the **Ghabreh Amir** (in the literature as *Masjid-i Shah*) repaired in 1708. To Professor Pope, doyen of Iranian architectural history, its Timurid dome was the perfect form, but his contemporary Robert Byron felt it had 'an uncouthness which has no parallel'

FIRDOUSI AND THE SHAH-NAMEH

As England's national poet is William Shakespeare, so Firdousi is seen to embody Iranian history and culture, saving from oblivion the Persian language, legends and history. He started work on composing the 60,000 couplets which were to form his *Shah-nameh* (Book of Kings) when he was 40 years old, c980, working from at least three versions. Despite being the son of a prosperous landowner in Tus, he soon needed to look for financial support and approached Mahmud of Ghazni (d1030), who, it is said, promised him a gold coin for every couplet written but paid only a silver pittance. Firdousi was practically destitute when his great work was completed.

The opening chapters concern the creation of the world and the first rulers who brought civilisation and culture to the people of Iran, whether it was the skill of weaving or the invention of fire. Firdousi then saw later developments as a series of cyclic events, in which just rule descended into periods of anarchy and despair redeemed only by the superhuman strength of spirit, courage and family loyalty of the individual. Progress was marked by a constant battle between good and evil, vividly portrayed throughout this epic poem, concluding with the reign of the last Sasanid king and the Arab invasion, c640. The couplets relate the court intrigue and sibling rivalry, military triumphs and disasters, and immense strength and heroism pitted against supernatural demons and wicked rulers. The imagery remains powerful even after a millennium; no-one in the late 1970s could fail to understand political posters depicting the late shah as Firdousi's despotic ruler Zahhak, whose evilness was manifested by two snakes growing from his shoulders; indeed, this same imagery, with the faces of Hitler, Himmler and Goebbels, was used in World War II British propaganda distributed in the Middle East.

in other similarly dated buildings in the region. It was built as a double dome, the exterior shell resting on eight internal brick buttresses. The tilework is still good on the exterior, especially the fine-quality 'mosaic' work by a Tabrizi tilecutter, with a green hexagonal tile dado, once embellished with gold stencilled decoration and a tiled inscription in the portal with a Hafiz couplet:

> ...written in gold on this emerald arcade
> Nothing will remain except the good of the generous.

Presently, the exterior, with its two corner minarets, retains most of its original tilework and its deep jewel-like colouring, despite a restoration programme completed in 1977.

The shops around here form one of Mashhad's many bazaars, selling tourist mementos such as posters and 'instant' prayer sets consisting of a rosary, *mohr* clay tablet and cloth, perfume etc, and green fabric swatches for touching the grilles in the holy sanctuaries. On their return home, pilgrims will cut it up and distribute the pieces among family and friends to share its *baraka* (blessings). Mashhad is also (perhaps justly) famous for its saffron, as well as for turquoise sold in great chunks (see page 261), set in 21-carat gold, and sheepskin waistcoats. There is a noticeable use of the Cyrillic on shop signs, as in the early 1990s President Rafsanjani worked at revitalising the historic Silk Road routes with the new republics of Tajikstan, Uzbekistan and Turkmenistan, even extending the railway to the Turkmenistan border. Today, according to Mashhad and Sarakhs taxi drivers, few Central Asian tourists cross the border.

OUTSIDE MASHHAD

Several half-day and day excursions may be made from Mashhad. One is to **Firdowsi** (also called Tus), the birthplace of the medieval Persian poet, Firdousi (d1020) author of the renowned epic poem, the *Shah-nameh*, narrating the exploits and adventures of the legendary kings of Iran. Once again, after some 20 years' silence, it is now sometimes possible to hear verses recited in *chay-khanah*s and restaurants. Tus was sacked in 1389 by Timur Leng and then largely abandoned a century later as Mashhad assumed growing importance, but remnants of its citadel walls are still visible from the modern gardens and tomb commemorating the poet, Firdousi (entry 2,000 rials plus 2,000 for the separate museum). His memorial is a ponderous stone structure (not at all like his poetry) with architectural details loosely based on Achaemenid work. Contemporary plaster panels depicting various characters or episodes linked to the *Shah-nameh* decorate the steps down into the cavernous basement, where a similar theme forms the decorative friezes. Opposite the garden is a large space being prepared as a memorial to military pilots from Khorasan killed in Asia.

About 1km before the Firdowsi gardens is a much earlier but heavily restored mausoleum, **Haruniyeh**, said to be that of the Abbasid caliph, Harun al-Rashid (d809). The mud-brick ruins in the fields behind the tomb are locally known as Harun's Palace, but most scholars think this mausoleum in fact marks the burial place of the Muslim philosopher, al-Ghazali (d1111). Is a taxi drive worth the expense? Yes, if you combine a visit to a spectacular tomb tower at Akhangan, nearby off the branch road to Sarakhs, or with the drive to Qalat-i Naderi (see below).

Mil-i Akhangan (also spelt Ahanjan) is an early 15th-century Timurid mausoleum in good condition with an unusual prismatic 'pleated' roof, now banded in turquoise and cobalt blue tiles. The cylindrical brick exterior is broken by eight rounded, engaged columns forming frames for (once-) tiled stars and crosses; those have long since gone but their imprint remains. With such detail it's easy to believe the local tradition that it was constructed to honour the sister of Queen Ghawhar Shad. It is located in agricultural land some 4km off the main road between Dorqi and Faimad on the road to Qalat-i Naderi.

Qalat-i Naderi

The 140km drive on the signposted Kalat and Kavud Gonbad roads will take a full day but the light industrial buildings on the Mashhad outskirts are quickly left behind for dramatic but gaunt scenery, with hairpin bends and long curves climbing up into the hills that mark the frontier with today's Turkmenistan Republic. Signposts are few and far between in this region; just a few distance markers. At the bridge over Qara Su ('Black Water'), the road tunnel, if completed, will take you directly into the village of Qalat-i Naderi, which occupies a long fertile east–west valley (altitude 765m) between two hill chains – a superb natural defence. As Lord Curzon wrote in the late 19th century: 'If in their war with Olympian Zeus the Titans had ever occasion to build for themselves an unassailable retreat, such might well have been the mountain fortress that they would have reared.' This was the place where Nadir Shah Afshari (d1747) returned after his victories in India, with so much booty that his army could stagger back at only four miles a day. He ordered the building of a large octagonal pavilion, the **Khorshidi Palace**, set in a garden, perhaps as his mausoleum (entry 2,000 rials), but early 20th-century writers said that the vault was never intended to be a crypt but a secure place for his treaures. Its rose-pink sandstone, the fluted drum-tower and the carved exterior panels depicted flowering plants all speak of Moghal Delhi, but the painted interior (behind rusting scaffolding) recalls Safavid Isfahan. Originally, marble slabs brought from Orumiyeh 1,900km away embellished the lower internal walls.

The garden kiosk has a good pack of postcards, and the manager will direct you to the 18th-century **mosque** at the far end of town and the **dam** (approximately 6km in same southeast direction) constructed by Nadir Shah to ensure a good water supply to the village. The mosque is built on the four-ivan plan with enough of the original tiling remaining to show the decorative scheme, but the actual chambers – including the large domed chamber – have been completely replastered and/or painted.

Sarakhs

Another day trip (or a long half-day if only Ribat-i Sharaf is visited) lies to the east of Mashhad, leaving by the Hemmat Highway, to Sarakhs some 175km away, one of the border crossings with Turkmenistan. Frontier formalities here crossing to/from Ashkhabad involve much time and patience, and Sarakhs has little else to offer than a 1356 **Mausoleum of Shaykh Baba Loqman**, a famous 10th-century storyteller, on its far western outskirts on agricultural land, or a bus terminal restaurant, whose manager enjoys using his English. Essentially it has a similar plan to the Haruniyeh near the Firdousi tomb, but both have been heavily restored. Something remains of a surprisingly shallow plaster inscription set with a tight arabesque scroll over the door, and of the blue glazed inserts in the ruined soffit arch of the entry portal. Inside, two internal staircases (now blocked) led up to the upper gallery running between the four deep *muqarnas* alcoves.

Some 58km from Sarakhs (or 125km from Mashhad) is the Seljuk *caravanserai*, **Ribat-i Sharaf**; take the minor road (southeast) at the road-side village of **Shurluk**, and then almost immediately the dirt track straight ahead for 7km. Don't despair: this *caravanserai* on what was the old Merv–Nishapur desert trade route is wonderful and, if you visit on Tuesday, Wednesday or

Thursday the enthusiastic architect in charge of current restoration, Mr Kandarhari, may agree to take you round; after years studying in Hamburg, his spoken German is very good. Probably constructed in 1115 with changes made to its layout some 40 years later, it is called a *caravanserai* but the patterned brickwork and plaster decoration have led scholars to wonder whether it sometime served as a royal lodge. The exterior looks like a fortress with one main entrance, but inside it is fit for a king. There are two main sections, both with courtyards displaying amazing brick patterns, dome supports, carved plaster, decorative brick end-plugs and intricately plaited kufic inscriptions. Inside the *caravanserai* there is the usual arrangement of stabling and rooms, with at least one small mosque, complete with plaster *mihrabs*, off both courts, and at the far end there are rooms with underground cisterns. As yet a kitchen area or 'refectory' has not been identified, nor is there a sign of a bathhouse, but a number of rooms and chambers were blocked off or altered during the mid-12th century. This work is recorded in the beautiful plaster and brick inscription of the portal leading into the second courtyard, giving the date 1154 and mentioning Sultan Sanjar (whose father is commemorated in Isfahan's *Masjid-i Jami*). As Sanjar was then a prisoner of the Turkomens in Merv, it is thought his wife ordered this work, possibly to repair damage inflicted by these marauding tribesmen after their sacking of Nishapur.

Khvaja Rabiᶜa

Returning to Mashhad from Ribat-i Sharaf or indeed from Firdowsi, look for roadsigns on the ring road for this shrine, now in the city confines. It commemorates Rabi'a ibn Khothaym, who led 4,000 men to help Ali, the son-in-law of the Prophet Mohammed, and as such was visited by the 8th Imam, Reza. However, the structure today dates from the first quarter of the 17th century, financed by Shah Abbas in 1618, and its design is said to have influenced the form of the world-famous Taj Mahal in Agra, India. Immediately to the right of the entrance, a small chamber has been made into a memorial to a local theologian, and his two sons killed in 1974. Much of the exterior tilework and painting has been recently restored and further messed up by air-conditioning units and scaffolding, but look for two small dragon heads worked in Safavid 'mosaic' tiles around to the far left of the entrance. Inside, a great deal of the Safavid gilded plaster ornament remains, but in dire need of cleaning.

SOUTH OF MASHHAD

The road south also offers some interesting sites, especially if you like Timurid buildings (some interiors are very dark so a torch is useful). Just as one leaves the city, after the bus terminal and following signs for Turbat-i Heydariyeh (see below), are two popular shrines. The first commemorates **Khvaja Abbasalt** (sic) **Haravi** (dc851) who, it was said, witnessed the death of Imam Reza, who died after eating poisoned grapes from his father-in-law, the Abbasid Caliph al-Ma'mun. In the 1970s the shrine still retained elements of its Safavid construction. Not today. Words fail me. Less than 5km further south along this main road – look for an avenue of trees from the roadside leading into the hillside – is **Khvaja Murad,** commemorating a famous orator (d832) of the Kerbela story. The gift of such narrators is difficult to communicate, but perhaps you too have stood entranced with other non-Farsi speakers listening as a storyteller speaks to Iranian Shi'i pilgrims in the Great Mosque of Damascus (see page 52). The shrine building itself is small and unremarkable but it is a pleasant family picnic spot with stalls, an airy cafeteria and even a small photographic studio offering the sitter a backdrop of the Mashhad shrine, Caliph al-Ma'mun handing Imam Reza the lethal grapes, or even Bruce Lee fighting a dragon.

There are richer treasures further south along this road in both the southeast and southwest directions. Branching off the Torbat-i Heydarieh road, southeast to Torbat-i Jam brings one quickly to the Sang Bast junction.

Sang Bast

A white building, formerly the *caravanserai* **Ribat-i Sangbast,** marks the turning leading to the 11th-century (?) tomb (locally known as Mil-i Ayaz) built for Arslan Jadhib, former governor of this region for the Ghaznavid dynasty of Afghanistan. The *caravanserai*'s internal location of stabling, staircases in the vestibule area, raised platforms etc, has suggested to scholars that it was built around 1400, with further stabling facilities added before its use in 1856 as barracks during the Qajar campaigns against Herat. It then served as a gendarmerie and is now a prison, so access is not permitted.

The **Mil-i Ayaz tomb,** important for architectural historians as the only surviving Ghaznavid monument this side of the border, stands now in a deserted area pock-marked with small craters, not the result of mortar shelling but of illicit digging for medieval ceramics and other artefacts. It was Arslan ('Lion') who advised Sultan Mahmud of Ghazni (d1030) to cut off the left thumb of every man taken captive in his military campaigns, thus preventing him using a bow in battle again. Sultan Mahmud may have concurred but it didn't stop his mercenary forces, the Seljuk tribesmen, from later controlling most of Iran and present-day Turkey. Essentially, this tomb follows the Sasanid fire temple plan of a cube broken by four arches (now blocked) surmounted by a dome. Very little of its decoration survives, but in the mid-1970s the external dome inscription consisted of Koranic verses (K21:35–6; and 12:101), while on the inside a painted band (K10:25–6) could be seen alongside a quadrain asking for heavenly rain and decorative brickwork. Close by is a 20m brick minaret, c1028, with a Kufic inscription (K41:33) naming the builder as coming from Sarakhs, but there is no sign of the mosque it once served.

Torbat-i Jam

If Timurid history or Persian poetry is a passion, you'll want to make a short detour to see a small building at **Langar,** 25km northwest before Torbat-i Jam, just off the asphalt road. This village was the birthplace of the Persian poet al-Jami', but the late-15th-century square building (restored in 1966) with two deep alcoves inside is not a memorial to him. It was dedicated to the mystical poet Qasem-i Anvar, who worked with the great Timurid ruler-scientist, Ulugh Beg (d1449) in Samarkand, and it probably functioned as a *khanaqeh* or hostel with a kitchen (or *langar*; thus the village name) to accommodate eager disciples. A short distance away is the water cistern with stepped dome, of the same date.

Torbat-i (Shaykh) Jam, 160km southeast from Mashhad, is known for its complex honouring the memory of the mystic, noted author and teacher, Shaikh Ahmad ibn Abdul Hasan (d1141). The guardians may ask for a permit, directing visitors to the large domed chamber opposite the main (north) gate and then to the local archaeological office just around the corner; the procedure is very quick and everyone is very helpful. We recently visited on the afternoon of the Prophet Mohammed's birthday; that is 'ladies' day' so no men were permitted entry and the main chambers were firmly padlocked. Hordes of bored, hyperactive children and masses of very inquisitive, friendly women meant decibels soared, a surge of bodies swept every which-way and we had to retire gracefully without seeing the central domed chamber of 1236, as well as the five-bay chamber to the east, with its rich plaster decoration, *muqarnas* vaulting and rib-network of the mid-14th century. The work in the west chamber of Gonbad-i Safid is similarly dated, but neither as elaborate nor exquisite. Nothing remains of a mosque built around 1320 behind the five-bayed hall, nor much from the so-called 'new' mosque erected in 1440–3; only a mass of new brickwork and white plaster is visible. The small high-domed 1441 building to the west was probably conceived as a *madrasa* and mauseolum for Amir Jalal al-Din Firouzshah, chief commander to Shah Rukh, but never finished before his fall from grace. His 35-year service and status should have ensured him burial in Herat, then the Timurid capital but, inadvisedly, when Shah Rukh (see page 247) was taken seriously ill, he openly supported the favourite son of Ghawhar Shad instead of the official heir apparent. Shah Rukh recovered and exacted revenge.

Tayabad

From Torbat-i Jam it is 60km to Tayabad (or Taybad), close to the Afghan border (225km southeast of Mashhad), passing villages with small barrel-vaulted houses topped with small windcatchers that resemble miniature periscopes. There is a small **Tourist Inn** in Tayabad which can offer accommodation (seven rooms) and a simple but adequate restaurant, so visitors could stay overnight, continue via Khargird to Torbat-i Heydariyeh and then return to Mashhad on the southwest route.

The reason for coming here is the 14th-century **Masjid-i Mawlana**, honouring an influential Sufi mystic Shaikh Zayn al-Din (d1389), whose grave lies in front of the main ivan portal. Timur Leng visited him in 1381 before attacking Herat, and was well pleased to hear that only the Angel of Death would prove his better. Built by a vizier for Shah Rukh, and completed in 1444–5, it is an intimate building although at first the portal looks disproportionately tall. The tile decoration here (including K18:1–11, story of the Seven Sleepers) is exquisitely elegant, especially the lyrically flowing calligraphy in clay set on a turquoise tiled ground, and scholars have linked both the building and decoration to Mashhad (Ghawhar Shad's *madrasa*), and Khargird (see below), suggesting it is the work of the same architect. The guardian will proudly open the actual prayer chamber and, despite continuing problems with dust and damp, the visual impact of the 'virtuoso complexity' of the *muqarnas* vaults and rib-network is stunningly beautiful. On the floor, double-sided blue and white *zilus* from Torbat-i Jam date from the late 1980s.

Having come all this way, don't turn back just yet but continue south. About 30km further on at **Kerat** there is a beautiful Seljuk minaret (c1106) by the side of the road. Its very location on a slope suggests it served more as a lighthouse (*nar*: fire) for travelling caravans than for a mosque. Here and there a few glazed inserts survive among the complex brick patterns.

Khargird

At Sangan, some 40km on, turn northwest for Khargird for the mid-15th-century Timurid **Madrasa Ghiyathiyeh** (also spelt Ghiassieh). Over 25 years of restoration work remains unfinished, but at least it hasn't been as heavy-handed as elsewhere. It has the typical four-ivan ground plan, with a very symmetical arrangement of arcades and galleries working to a strict set of proportions. For at least one scholar, the careful arrangement and proportions of windows, niches, and arches create a 'visual crescendo' where everything works in harmony. Just enough remains of the original tiling to show the various pattern schemes and, despite the grime, pigeon droppings and repairs, the *muqarnas* decoration of both chambers either side of the entry portal – the small mosque on the right, the main lecture hall on the left – is fine work. But virtually nothing now survives of the painted wall decoration, recorded in the mid-1970s. In the court, staircases in each corner lead to the upper accommodation. Each room comes with a niche for books and belongings, and a chimney. Behind the far ivan a *badgir* (windtower) has been constructed.

If you can't get here, you can see an example of the original superb workmanship by visiting the British Museum, the Victoria and Albert Museum or indeed New York's Metropolitan Museum of Art, which all managed to 'acquire' samples of the tilework, especially the star tiles. The inscriptions record that the patron of this beautiful college, far away from any centre, was not a member of the Timurid house but one of their long-serving viziers, Pir Ahmad Khvafi, born in the area and linked with the monument above. Whether it was an act of piety or as a guarantee against royal confiscation if he fell from power (by consigning his property and land as an endowment), is unclear.

Also in the village is a Seljuk **Madrasa Nizamiyeh,** c1154, named after its patron, another famous vizier, Nizam al-Mulk, linked with the superb domed chamber in the *Masjid-i Jami* in Isfahan. Hardly anything remains except fragments of its plaited, floriated Kufic inscription but it must have been a superb building. About 3km northwest is [Khvaf] **Rud** with a *Masjid-i Jami*. It was built about 1503, a date given on the seven-stepped *minbar* (a section now in the Mashhad Shrine Museum), but has been much repaired since. It is probable that the domed prayer chamber and its ivan are Timurid, if not earlier, but the two winter prayer rooms could well be a product of the extensive repair programme of 1971. **Roshtkhar** (or Rushkhvan) is about 55km from Torbat-i Heydarieh; in the mid-1970s its *Masjid-i Jami* was collapsing, but something of the Seljuk vaulting remained, with a domed prayer chamber and splendid herringbone brickwork. The painted inscription around the zone of transition consists of Koranic verses (48:1–14) with a date of 1455.

If you are returning to Mashhad from here via Torbat-i Heydariyeh, look out for the village of **Bazi-i Hur**, some 65 km before Mashhad. Its late 15th-century *caravanserai* **Ribat-i Safid** behind the road-side shops is unloved and rapidly collapsing (there are much better restored ones on the road to Mashhad) but it's worth stopping at the lime kilns just before the shops to take a photograph of the restored 3rd-century CE Zoroastrian fire temple set high before the hills.

TO KASHMAR

You could extend your journey west from Torbat-i Heydariyeh to Kashmar, which possesses two *imamzadehs*, one dedicated to Hamza and totally renovated recently, and the other at the end of a long avenue of trees, the **Imamzadeh Sayyid Murtadeh**, essentially a Safavid construction but restored in 1975. On the Friday of our visit there was a busy local fruit and vegetable market there, with families having picnics, a storyteller relating the tragedy of Hoseyn against a painted screen and, further away, a troupe of eight actors giving their dramatic rendition to an enthralled audience. The shrine isn't bad either. The road west goes through a lovely lanscape of vineyards behind mud walls, each with one or more drying sheds. About 10km before Bardeskan is a minor road north to **Aliabad Kishmar**, leading to the village *hamam* and then the magnificent **tomb tower**, standing among the houses. Its exterior is basically 12-sided, presumably to remind visitors of the 12 Imams, but with alternate flanged and rounded engaged columns with moulded turquoise tile inserts highlighting aspects of the brick decoration. It is a masterpiece of 13th-century architecture but very dark inside, so a torch is useful. Local children will readily fetch the guardian to unlock the door to the octagonal interior and then race up the internal staircases to the upper gallery, to the space between the inner and upper domes, to peer down on you.

South of Kashmar and Torbat-i Heydariyeh was once Assassin country in the 12th century. One of their strongholds, very effectively dismantled by the Mongols, is at **Qaleh Dokhtar**, about 30km south of Kashmar. Further south, Gonabad and Ferdows also lived in the shadow of Assassin castles, but earthquakes in 1968 and more recently, which destroyed most of Tabas, caused much damage.

NISHAPUR

According to the locals, the road to Nishapur (or Nev Shabur) from Kashmar is good but not first-class, and if you wish to visit Qadamgah, 20km east of Nishapur, you may wish to backtrack to Mashhad. **Qadamgah**, 'Place of the Foot', has a small 17th-century octagonal shrine erected by the Safavid Shah Soleyman in 1642 and restored by the Qajars, in honour of a large black stone bearing the imprint of two highly arched feet, it is believed, of Imam Reza. Presently a conservation team is working on the painted ceiling and vaults so scaffolding yet again mars viewing. Nearby is a well-preserved Safavid *caravanserai* called Fakhri-i Daíud, and another as you near Nishapur.

Just the name 'Nishapur' – like that of Tashkent – conjures up images of medieval buildings, busy bazaars, camel trains and dramatic landscape. Unfortunately, like today's Uzbek capital, virtually nothing historic is left in Nishapur despite its well-chronicled past. The original settlement was destroyed by an earthquake, so the Sasanid Shah Shapur II (r309–379) rebuilt the city, recorded in its new name *Niv Shapur* ('Shapur's good deed') and if it was true that one of the four sacred fires of Zoroastrianism, the *Adur Burzin Mihr* of the agricultural class, was located nearby, this would have had added importance to the Sasanid Court. Finally taken by the Arabs in 661, it became

TURQUOISE MINES OF NISHAPUR

... to my unpractised eye there was nothing different in that one hill from any of the others around. It was apparently composed of the same dark-rock so common throughout the country... The only implements used by the miners are short iron jumpers about eighteen inches in length, and a small hammer with which they drive holes into the rock, which is then blasted out with common country gun-powder...outside a lot of small boys break the rock into little pieces with small hammers and pick out any bits of green or blue they see...

Turquoises at the mines are divided into three kinds -1st, the Angushtari, or stone fit for rings; 2nd, the Barkhana, or stones fit for trappings, &c; and 3rd, the Arabi, or stones fit for Arabia. The first are all carefully cut and polished at Mashhad, and are always sold separately...The first two [grades of the second category].. are largely exported to Europe, while the third and fourth are sold in Persia for the ornamentation of the Kalian ['hubble-bubble'] pipe-heads, horses' trappings, and small-arms, &c. The third kind are as a rule bad and light-coloured stones, for which there is no sale in Persia. The name arose owing to some miners going on pilgrimage to Mecca... and found a good sale for them in Arabia, which is now the market for them and the origin of the name.

C E Yate *Khorasan & Sistan* 1900, pages 400, 406

the administrative centre of Khorasan Province (then including Afghanistan) and later of the Seljuk sultan, Tughril Beg (d1063), who established well-stocked libraries and two universities here. However, if Westerners recognise the city's name today, they associate it with either the splendidly decorated slip-painted earthenware ceramics, made in the region during the 10–11th centuries, or the poet and mathematician, Omar Khayyam (d1131). A catalogue of disasters: serious earthquakes in 1115 and 1145, followed by Turkoman incursions, then the Mongol conquests of the 1220s and Timur Leng's destructive campaigns c1390 has meant few historic buildings survived. In later centuries, Mashhad's growing importance as a pilgrimage centre and then as Nadir Shah Afshari's capital meant Nishapur received little investment.

The two-ivan **Masjid-i Jami** was largely rebuilt in 1494 by Ali Kurukhi, a local notable, whose tomb is left of the entrance through an office. The foundation inscription in the *qibla* ivan gives him the title of Pahlavan, which suggests he was a champion warrior or indeed wrestler (see page 116). His wish that '...this building remain as a memorial for the town of Nishapur' has been honoured, but only at the expense of extensive reconstruction. The *mihrab* records many early 18th-century repairs to the building, but because its Koranic verses (K 36:55; 89:27–30) relate more to a mausoleum than a mosque, there is some debate whether this *mihrab* was moved here as part of those repairs. An inscription on the entrance portal tiles speaks of further work undertaken in 1869, and in the courtyard there is much new tiling.

In the southeastern outskirts, across the railway line, are the gardens (no entry fee) including the modern **tomb** canopy to honour the mathematician and poet Omar Khayyam, and another poet-scientist Farid al-Din Attar is commemorated with a small garden about 1km further along the tarmac road (entry fee 2,000 rials, but take a photograph from the kiosk). Local tradition has it that Farid al-Din's tomb was built by a penitent Hulagu, grandson of Genghis Khan, who had ordered the execution of this renowned mystic in 1221, but as Farid al-Din died around 1194, this is unlikely. Today's double-domed tomb probably dates from the late Qajar period, as an earlier Safavid building was seen in ruins in 1909. A majestically tall pillar gravestone of 1486, now encased in filthy glass, recalls this saintly man:

> Who was such a fine perfumer (*attar*) that from his breath
> The world from one end to another was fragrant

Farid al-Din was the writer of *The Assembly of Birds*, a deeply mystical work. In the gardens under a modern tiled canopy is the grave of the famous Qajar painter Kamal al-Mulk. To the south in the fields beyond were the remains of old Nishapur, excavated in the 1930s by the Metropolitan Museum of Fine Art, New York, which yielded numerous finds of decorated plaster, glass and slip-painted ceramics, produced before Hulagu's devastation of the region in 1220.

The site is a flat plain, with turquoise mines in the mountains to the northeast. Here lies **Sabzevar**, some 115km further west from Nishapur, once a small town in the shadow of nearby prosperous **Khosraugird** less than 10km west. Both towns suffered severely from the Mongol invasions and then from the Timurid armies in 1381 but miraculously their **Seljuk minarets** survived. The one at Khosraugird was constructed in 1111 and today stands with glorious brick patterning about 18.5m high, whereas the Sabzevar minaret is not quite as tall. To see the latter, ask in Sabzevar for *Masjid-i Pa Menar* off Maydan 22 Behman, situated near the gendarmerie. A nasty group of thuggish teenagers roam the streets around the *masjid*, so take care of your bags, cameras etc.

Head some 75km further west to Darvazan, then north up into the hills to the village of **Forumbad** (also spelt Farumbad), charming in the 1970s and now rapidly being swamped with new buildings. Dating from Seljuk times, its two-ivan *Masjid-i Jami* was revamped around 1320 when the small town became important to the local Il-Khanid rulers, who built a good hospital and library. The building may have seen better days, but the interlaced terracotta square tiles, the plasterwork and glazed brick inserts are high quality and it is worth a short detour; the guardian lives nearby.

Returning to the main road, another 70km or so brings one to **Miyandasht**. Boasting no less than three *caravanserais* linked together, it gives some indication of the huge numbers of travellers and pilgrims along this road in the 19th century. The smallest, about 50m square, to the left of the main entrance, was constructed in the early 17th century and, following the typical Safavid plan, is octagonal in layout, with the main chambers located in the eight corners, with stabling behind protected by the outer wall. It was repaired in Qajar times when two large additions were made to cater for increased traffic: the *caravanserai* which is now the main central courtyard with accommodation and another one adjoining immediately to the right. The guardian is delighted to show the various staircases to the roof areas. Two *ab-anbar*, or water cisterns, are located in the central court and at least one other is outside. Another 110km brings you to Shahrud (see page 145).

Appendix 1

LANGUAGE
Useful phrases in Farsi

A surprising number of French words have found their way into Farsi. Pronunciation is fairly straightforward except for the letters 'kh', which have a guttural sound, similar to the 'ch' in the Scottish 'loch'.

Greetings

hello	*salaam*	سلام
goodbye	*khodaa-haafez*	خداحافظ
	(pronounced 'ho-da fiz')	
Good morning	*sobh-bekheyr*	صبح بخیر
Good evening	*shab-bekheyr*	شب بخیر
How are you?	*halae shomaa chetoreh?* (formal)	حال شما چطوره ؟
	khoobeed? (informal)	خوبید ؟
Fine, thank you	*khoobam, mersee/*	خوبم مرسی /
	khubam motshakeram	خوبم متشکرم

Useful words and phrases

please	*khaahesh meekonam*	خواهش میکنم
thank you	*mersee/motshakeram*	مرسی / متشکرم
yes	*baleh*	بله
no	*nakheyr/na*	نخیر / نه
excuse me	*ma'zerat meekhaaham*	معذرت میخواهم / ببخشید
(to get attention/apologise)		
help	*komak*	کومک
I am ill	*mareezam*	مریضم
open	*baaz*	باز
closed	*basteh*	بسته
I	*man*	من
you	*shomaa*	شما
I am English	*man engelisi hastam*	من انگلیسی هستم /
(American/Canadian)	*(amrikaa'i/kaanaadaa'i)*	آمریکائی / کانادائی
I don't speak Farsi	*man faarsee nemeedaanam*	من فارسی نمیدانم
I don't understand	*nemeefahmam*	نمیفهمم
How much is this/that?	*chand ast?*	چند است ؟

Please help me/us	khaahesh meekonam beman komak koneed	خواهش میکنم بمن کومک کنید
Where is...?	... kojaast?	...... کجاست ؟
	thus Toalet, kojaast?)	
Please show me the way to...	raah raa beman neshaan daheed...	راه را بمن نشان دهید
airport	foroodgaah	فرودگاه
bank	baank	بانك
bus station	eestgaah-e otobus	ایستگاه اتوبوس
church	keleesaa	کلیسا
embassy	sefaarat-khaaneh	سفارتخانه
hospital	beemaarestaan	بیمارستان
hotel	hotel/mehmankhaaneh/ mehmaan-saraa	هتل / مهمانخانه / مهمانسرا
mosque	masjid	مسجد
museum	mooseh	موزه
police station	kalaantaree/edaareh-ye polees	کلانتری / اداره پلیس
police	paasbaan/police	پاسبان / پلیس
post office	post khaneh	پستخانه
railway station	eestgaah-e raah aahan	ایستگاه راه آهن
restaurant	restooraan	رستوران
station	eestgaah	ایستگاه
toilet	tualet	توالت
tourist inn	mehmaan-khaaneh/mehmaan-saraa	مهمانخانه / مهمانسرا
I need a...	man ehtiyaj be ... daaram	من احتیاج به ... دارم
ticket/seat 1st (2nd/3rd) class for ...	beleet-e darejeh yek (dou/se) baraayeh ...	بلیط درجه یك / درجه دو / درجه سه / برای ..
doctor	doktor	دکتر
dentist	dandaan pezeshk	دندان پزشک
room for one/ two/three nights	otaaq baraayeh yek shab/ dou shab/se shab	اطاق برای یك شب / / دو شب / سه شب
taxi	taaksee	تاکسی

Numbers

1	۱	yek	یك
2	۲	dou	دو
3	۳	se	سه
4	٤	chahaar	چهار
5	٥	panj	پنج
6	٦	shesh	شش
7	٧	haft	هفت
8	٨	hasht	هشت
9	٩	noh	نه
10	۱۰	dah	ده
11	۱۱	yaazdah	یازده
12	۱۲	davaazdah	دوازده
100	۱۰۰	sad	صد

Days of the week

Saturday	shanbeh	شنبه
Sunday	yek shanbeh	یکشنبه
Monday	dou shanbeh	دوشنبه
Tuesday	se shanbeh	سه شنبه
Wednesday	chahaar shanbeh	چهارشنبه
Thursday	panj shanbeh	پنجشنبه
Friday	jom'eh	جمعه

Appendix

GLOSSARY

ayatollah   Literally 'sign of God' (K41:53); an honorific title for theologians used much more frequently since the 1950s; in the past was rarely bestowed by public acclaim on any notable, fully qualified Muslim jurist of superior learning.

bagh   The 'Persian' garden. The original Persian word *pairidaza* (later *firdaws*) passed into Greek, and later into Middle English as 'paradise'.

chador   A full-length fabric wrap, roughly semicircular in form and often black in colour, worn by Iranian women. As Ayatollah Khomeini announced that the (black) *chador* was the 'flag of the Islamic Revolution', it is required dress for women in government service.

cuerda seca   A ceramic glaze technique whereby different opaque coloured glazes (eg: on a tile) are kept separate from each other by manganese oxide. (Confusingly, several art historians use this specific technical term when referring to both under- and over-glaze painted decoration on clay.)

caravanserai   A pre-motor car 'motel', often built by rulers and governors to provide accommodation for travellers and their pack animals on the caravan routes, generally sited one day's journey (approximately 35 km) apart.

chehel khaneh   Room or building where *Sufis* pass 40 nights in devotions.

dervish   Literally 'door', 'path'. A mendicant *Sufi* who has removed himself from his family in search of the ultimate truth, largely dependant on the charity of others.

gonbad   Tomb tower constructed to commemorate a deceased individual.

hamam   'Turkish bath' developed in the Islamic world from the Roman bathhouse. There were three main chambers: the first room, *frigidarium*, was where one undressed and later relaxed with friends; the *tepidarium* and finally the hot room, *caldarium*. Like the 17th-century European coffee house, it was and is a place for gossip, business and meeting friends.

imamzadeh   Strictly speaking, a tomb or shrine honouring one of the 12 Imams of *Ithna-Ashari* Shi'ism in Iran, or their immediate relatives; over time, local shrines without such a proven family association have been given this title.

ivan   A tall, vaulted portal or doorway, fully developed in Seljuk architecture from the 11th century.

khan   The historic equivalent of a bonded warehouse for the storage and transit of a specific kind of goods from wholesalers to retailers.

khanaqeh	A meeting place/hostel for *sufis*.
kufic	An Islamic calligraphic script, characterised by a definite horizontal base line and vertical letter strokes, often with angular letter forms.
masjid-i jami	Often called a Friday Mosque. In past centuries only one mosque in any given town or city was 'licensed' to have the imam give a homily at the main prayer time on Fridays.
mihrab	A niche or panel, often very decorative, showing the correct direction to align oneself for prayer prostrations (see *qibla* below).
minbar	A stepped construction, often made of wood or stone, situated near the main *mihrab* within a mosque, from which the Friday homily was given.
muezzin	The mosque official who called the faithful to prayer three times a day in the Shi'i world (five times in the Sunni world).
muqarnas	Architectural detail usually found decorating vaults, domes and door lintels, formed of separate 3-D units composed into a 'honeycomb' layout.
pahlavi	The Persian script largely abandoned after the 7th-century Arab conquests; also the dynastic name adopted by Reza Khan (d1941).
pahlavan	A champion athlete, especially a wrestler.
qibla	The direction for prayer, ie: towards Mecca, usually marked in a Muslim religious building by a *mihrab* niche.
sufi	A Muslim, Shi'i or Sunni, seeking an individual spiritual path to achieve mystic union with the Divine, often through initiation and ritual practices. Traditionally associated with wearing a woollen garment (*suf* = wool).
talar	Veranda or terrace; in royal pavilions, often used for public audiences.
zur-khaneh	Gymnasium where wrestlers practise.

Other architectural terms

arch-soffit	The underside of an arch, often decorated.
'mosaic' tilework	Predetermined shapes cut from monochrome glazed tiles, and reassembled as a jigsaw, held in place on a plaster bed.
squinch	An architectural load-bearing structure essentially in the form of a hollow half of a hemisphere placed over a corner to support the weight of the dome.

Appendix 3

FURTHER INFORMATION

Following the Islamic Revolution in Iran and the broadly hostile media reaction in the West, few publishers could be persuaded to commission or publish any work on Iran unless it concerned contemporary political figures and issues. Therefore, many of the titles suggested below are now out of print, but a good library should be able to help, and of course searches in secondhand bookshops might bear fruit. Also most publications are weighty in more senses than one, written primarily for the specialist academic market and priced accordingly. As public demand grows, surely publishers will re-evaluate their lists.

In London, there are three 'specialist' **bookshops**, two known particularly for their selection of books on (Islamic) art, architecture and history, and the third for its travel selection:

Arthur Probsthain 41 Great Russell St, London WCIB 3PL; tel: 020 7636 1096
Al-Saqi Bookshop 26 Westbourne Terrace, London W2 5RH; tel: 020 7229 8543
Daunt (Travel) Books 83 Marylebone High St, London W1M 3DE; tel: 020 7224 2296

Do also investigate the British Museum bookshop, which stocks not only its own publications and those of the British Library, but also others in the same field.

Further reading

An invaluable publication for those new to Iran and travelling on business is Maria O'Shea's *Culture Shock – Iran: a Guide to Customs & Etiquette* (Kuperard, London 1999).

For those with access to a university or major library with a Middle Eastern collection, the ongoing publications forming the multi-volumed *Encyclopaedia of Islam*, and especially *Encyclopaedia Iranica*, are invaluable reference works.

Religion, history and literature

One of the foremost writers on Zoroastrianism is Mary Boyce; her paperback *Zoroastrians, Their Religious Beliefs & Practices* (RKP, London 1986) is clearly written, exploring the development of ritual and practice. Malise Ruthven's *Islam in the World* (Penguin, London 1991) discusses Islam in the modern world in an interesting and readable account, while N Keddie's *Iran: Religion, Politics & Society* (Cass, 1980) examines this in the context of Iran. For Safavid history, search out any publication by Roger Savory (Canada). *Persian Literature* edited by Ehsan Yarshater (Columbia University Press, 1988) is a useful academic survey of classical and contemporary literature. These should be obtainable through Inter-Library loan.

Travellers' accounts

No-one can argue that most contemporary travel accounts pale in comparison with those of 19th-century Western writers, who indefatigably asked all the right questions, checked the responses and recorded everything in detail. A particular favourite is Isabella L Bird, author of *Journeys in Persia & Kurdistan*, vols I & II (originally printed 1891; reprinted Virago Press, London 1989), and the abridged account of an earlier traveller, Sir John (Jean) Chardin, *Travels in Persia, 1673–77* (Dover, New York 1988) is still available and very, very entertaining; if you can't get hold of it, R W Ferrier produced a commentary of those travels: *A Journey to Persia ... Jean Chardin* (IB Tauris, 1996). Robert Byron's waspish wit comes through in his *The Road to Oxiana* (Picador, London, reprinted 2000); his comments on architecture force you to look again.

Archaeology

John Curtis of the British Museum has written an informative introduction to pre-Islamic archaeology in Iran, *Ancient Persia* (British Museum Press, London rep 2000), while D T Potts examines in detail the Elamite region and civilisation up to the 4th century CE in *The Archaeology of Elam* (Cambridge University Press, 1999). *Time-Life's* publication *The Persians: Masters of Empire* (Lost Civilizations series, 1995) is a clear, readable account aimed at the general reader with good maps and an interesting selection of images. It is both entertaining and intriguing to read Herodotus (490–80BCE) for his views on Achaemenid history, the court intrigues and the military campaigns (*The Histories*, Penguin Classics). Joseph Wiesehofer's book *Ancient Persia* (I B Tauris, London, reprinted 2004) has a strong academic flavour but does provide interesting information. For Dutch readers, the 1993 Brussels exhibition catalogue *Hofkunst van de Sassanieden* (KMvKG) has both an informative text and superb photographs of Sasanid pieces; available in the UK on Inter-Library loan.

Islamic art and architecture

One of the best introductions to Islamic art and architecture is Barbara Brend's *Islamic Art* (British Museum Press, London 1991), while my new book *Islam & the Religious Arts* (Continuum, 2004) approaches the subject from a different angle. The *Arts of Persia* (Yale University Press, 1989) under the editorship of R W Ferrier examines certain art forms in more detail. In the introduction to this guide, reference was made to Lisa Golombek and Donald Wilber's work and that of Bernard O'Kane on 14th–15th-century Timurid architecture, essential for any serious in-depth research, as are the studies of Sheila Blair on historic inscriptions. Any keen student of Islamic architecture should aim to acquire Robert Hillenbrand's *Islamic Architecture: Form and function* (Edinburgh University Press, 1994) which contains a wealth of material.

Sheila Canby's book *The Golden Age of Persian Art, 1501–1722* (British Museum Press, 1999), which gives a good overview of the arts in the Safavid period, is still available. On contemporary Iranian art with a strong political content, the paperback *Picturing Iran: Art, Society and Revolution* edited by Shiya Balaghi and Lynn Gumpert (I B Tauris, 2002) is highly recommended.

Islamic history

For those interested in the role of the Ismailis and the Assassins during the Crusades, Bernard Lewis's small book on *The Assassins: a radical sect of Islam* (Phoenix, reprinted 2004) has not yet been bettered.

A collection of articles examining various and varied aspects of Safavid history has recently been published under the editorship of Charles Melville, *Safavid Persia*, by I B Tauris, London.

Crafts

Although Hans E Wulff published his *Traditional Crafts of Persia* (MIT) in the 1960s, it has not been bettered. If you can find a copy, buy it. He traces the history and technology of the major crafts including agricultural implements and building skills, as well as ceramics and bread making. There are numerous publications about carpets, often not worth the paper they are printed on, but if you can find a copy of A C Edwards' *The Persian Carpet* (Duckworth, London 1953, reprinted 1983), it records the state of carpet weaving in Iran in the 1950s; his concept of a 'carpet aesthetic' and regional identification have, rightly or wrongly, proved to be very influential. As for Patricia L Baker's *Islamic Textiles* (British Museum Press, London 1995), all I can say is that I enjoyed writing it.

Biography

I simply could not put down Sattareh F Farmaran's *Daughter of Persia* (Bantam, London/New York, reprinted 2000), a critical but affectionate account of her family and Iranian society from the 1920s until the first years of the Revolution. A tender and often humorous book in strip cartoon format is Marjane Satrapi's *Persepolis – a story of a childhood* (Jonathan Cape, London 2003), first published in France; the title and format do not prepare the reader for its political content.

In the Rose Garden of the Martyrs by Christopher de Bellaigue (Harper Collins, summer 2004) compares and contrasts his memories of Iran in the late 1970s with today's actualities, and has been critically acclaimed.

Associations and institutes

The **British Institute of Persian Studies** annually publishes an academic journal, *Iran*, which contains recent research on the art, archaeology and history of pre-Islamic and Islamic Iran, and organises a number of public lectures; membership subscription. The Tehran office has recently re-opened after 30 years' closure. For details contact The Secretary, British Institute of Persian Studies, c/o British Academy, 20–21 Cornwall Terrace, London NW1 4QP.

The **Institute of Ismaili Studies**, London, publishes teaching materials and organises a graduate teaching programme; tel: 020 7881 6000; email: info@iis.ac.uk; www.iis.ac.uk.

The **Iran Society**, London, has a programme of lectures and meetings; membership subscription. For details contact The Secretary, 2 Belgrave Square, London SW1X 8PJ; tel: 020 7235 5122; email: iransoc@rsaa.org.uk; www.iransoc.dircon.co.uk.

The **Iran Heritage Foundation**, a non-governmental organisation, sponsors various activities in the UK, including exhibitions, occasional lectures, conferences, concerts, poetry readings, and film showings concerning the cultural heritage of Iran, past and present. For details: The Secretary, Iran Heritage Foundation, 5 Stanhope Gate, London W1K 1AH; email: info@iranheritage.org; www.iranheritage.org.

The **Islamic Centre England** (affiliated with the Institute of Islamic Studies), London, is a semi-official organisation which specialises in *Ithna 'Ashari* Islamic studies;

it organises an active programme of conferences and cultural events, also Persian language teaching; there is also a restaurant, Eram. For details, fax: 020 7604 4898; email: ice@icel.org; www.islamic-studies.org.

Zoroastrian House, presently at 88 Compayne Garden, London NW6 3RU; tel: 020 7328 6018, www@ztfe.com, is a friendly organisation running a series of classes and lectures examining the beliefs, civilisation and history of Iranian Zoroastrians and the Parsi communities. Part of the world organisation.

For information about the Bahai community, contact **Bahai Faith National Centre**, 27 Rutland Gate, London SW7; tel: 020 7584 2566.

Websites

There are over 500 websites on Iran: some are markedly partisan, others less so; some informative but most with out-dated telephone/fax regional codes and numbers for hotels, etc. Comparatively few Iranian companies involved in tourism operate websites as yet and these can vary greatly in quality, from the informative (such as **www.homahotelgroup.com** and **www.parshotels.com**) to 'useless', a description which has been used for the two large sites: **www.ittic.com** ITTO hotel website, and the **www.parsian-hotel.com** website; the general ITTO website (**www.itto.com**) clearly still uses some pre-2001/2 tel/fax regional codes, and other outdated information for many of the hotels listed. For Iranian embassy and visa information, however, use this site.

By contrast, the Iran Cultural Heritage Organization runs an attractive, useful service **www.iranmiras.ir**, and there is a good 'official' general information/news website available on **www.netiran.com**. If you wish to keep up with the news as published in Iran, two of the Tehran English-language papers are available on the net: *Iran Daily* on **www.iran-daily.com** and *Tehran Times* **www.tehrantimes.com**

If possible always use email or fax, especially for hotel bookings, as such messages are (almost) always dealt with promptly. See the details (where obtainable) under the relevant hotel sections.

Index

Page references in bold indicate major entries; those in italics indicate maps. For rulers (eg: the Achaemenid emperor, Darius) see under the relevant 'personal' name